THE MAKING OF THE
MODERN MIDDLE EAST

Also by Jeremy Bowen

War Stories

Six Days: How the 1967 War Shaped the Middle East

The Arab Uprisings: The People Want the Fall of the Regime

JEREMY BOWEN

THE MAKING OF THE MODERN MIDDLE EAST

A PERSONAL HISTORY

PICADOR

First published 2022 by Picador
an imprint of Pan Macmillan
The Smithson, 6 Briset Street, London EC1M 5NR
EU representative: Macmillan Publishers Ireland Ltd, 1st Floor,
The Liffey Trust Centre, 117–126 Sheriff Street Upper,
Dublin 1, D01 YC43
Associated companies throughout the world
www.panmacmillan.com

ISBN 978-1-5098-9089-7

Copyright © Jeremy Bowen 2022

The right of Jeremy Bowen to be identified as the
author of this work has been asserted by him accordance
with the Copyright, Designs and Patents Act 1988.

All rights reserved. No part of this publication may be reproduced,
stored in a retrieval system, or transmitted, in any form, or by any means
(electronic, mechanical, photocopying, recording or otherwise)
without the prior written permission of the publisher.

Pan Macmillan does not have any control over, or any responsibility for,
any author or third-party websites referred to in or on this book.

1 3 5 7 9 8 6 4 2

A CIP catalogue record for this book is available from the British Library.
Endpaper map artwork by ML Design

Typeset in Perpetua by Jouve (UK), Milton Keynes
Printed and bound by CPI Group (UK) Ltd, Croydon, CR0 4YY

This book is sold subject to the condition that it shall not, by way of
trade or otherwise, be lent, hired out, or otherwise circulated without
the publisher's prior consent in any form of binding or cover other than
that in which it is published and without a similar condition including
this condition being imposed on the subsequent purchaser.

Visit **www.picador.com** to read more about all our books
and to buy them. You will also find features, author interviews and
news of any author events, and you can sign up for e-newsletters
so that you're always first to hear about our new releases.

To my family, as always.

CONTENTS

List of Illustrations   ix

Prologue   1

1. Watch and Learn   5
2. Mission Impassable   17
3. All Flesh Is Grass   26
4. Jerusalem: God, Power, Possession and Loss   43
5. Guns and Olives   53
6. Tell Them He's Dead   66
7. Death on the Nile   76
8. Gaza   84
9. The Final Frontier   97
10. In the Name of God   108
11. Ground Zero   121
12. Mission Unaccomplished   132
13. One Thousand Saddams   141

Contents

14. The People Want the Fall of the Regime 151

15. The Road to Damascus 167

16. The Mosque on Makram Ebeid Street 181

17. The Pivot of War 197

18. The Road to Hell 211

19. The Russians Are Coming 226

20. Scorched Earth 239

21. The Taste of Fire and Smoke 251

22. Retreat to the Mountains 267

23. The Last Dance 279

24. Deal of the Century 291

25. Pawns on the Global Chessboard 308

Acknowledgements 329

Bibliography 331

Notes 337

LIST OF ILLUSTRATIONS

1. Operation Desert Shield, 22 November 1990. (Everett Collection Historical / Alamy Stock Photo)
2. American troops on Iraq's border with Kuwait in 1991. (Peter Turnley / Contributor)
3. Iraqi Kurds fight for food. More than one million of them fled to the mountains on the borders with Turkey and Iran as Saddam Hussein crushed their uprising in the spring of 1991. (Bhas Solanki)
4. Bill Clinton pointing to a peaceful future at the signing of the Oslo 2 accord at the White House on 28 September 1995. (Newscom / Alamy Stock Photo)
5. Reporting on the presidential referendum in Baghdad in October 1995. (Barry Iverson / Alamy Stock Photo)
6. Osama bin Laden declaring a holy war against the United States, August 1998. (CNN / Handout)
7. The power of religion in Jerusalem. A Christian believing she is in the presence of God during the Holy Fire ceremony in the Holy Sepulchre church. (By courtesy of the author)
8. The power of religion in Najaf, Iraq. Millions of Shia pilgrims come to pray at the shrine of Imam Ali, who they believe was the rightful heir of the prophet Muhammad. (By courtesy of the author)
9. The epicentre of Jerusalem. An ultra-Orthodox Jew reads psalms facing the Western Wall. (By courtesy of the author)

List of Illustrations

10. US Marines pulling down Saddam's statue in Firdos Square as they enter Baghdad on 9 April 2003. (Science History Images / Alamy Stock Photo)
11. Jewish settlers leaving the Gaza Strip in August 2005. (By courtesy of the author)
12. The people want the fall of the regime. Eighteen days of protests in Tahrir Square in Cairo at the start of 2011 ousted President Mubarak. (By courtesy of the author)
13. Children at a 'spontaneous' demonstration supporting Colonel Muammar al-Gaddafi in the months before he was overthrown, UN headquarters in Tripoli in April 2011. (By courtesy of the author)
14. President Bashar al-Assad of Syria in Damascus in 2010, about nine months before his forces opened fire on demonstrators. (Photo © Syrian Ministry of Information)
15. With rebels from the Free Syria Army in Saqba, a Damascus suburb, on 27 January 2012. (REUTERS / Alamy Stock Photo)
16. Morning coffee in Douma, one of the rebel-held satellite towns of Damascus in December 2012. (By courtesy of the author)
17. Bashar's boys. Young Alawites in Mezze 86 in Damascus in September 2013. (By courtesy of the author)
18. Christian militias joined the fighting on the regime's side in Maaloula in 2013, against the Nusra Front, a splinter group of al-Qaeda. (By courtesy of the author)
19. Supporters of the Muslim Brotherhood's President Mohamed Morsi took over parts of Cairo after he was deposed by the armed forces in July 2013. (By courtesy of the author)
20. Young Iraqi Shia recruits test their bravery in Najaf in June 2016. (By courtesy of the author)
21. Syrian children living as refugees in their own country in Aleppo in September 2016. (By courtesy of the author)
22. Sisters emerge in their best clothes in September 2016 from the rebel-held Damascus suburb of Daraya. (By courtesy of the author)
23. The rebel-held side of Aleppo after the Syrian regime and their Russian allies had finished with it. (By courtesy of the author)

24. Nael Abdallah, Christian warlord and supporter of the Assad regime in the town of Sqelbieh, on the front line in October 2018 as the Syrian war continued. (By courtesy of the author)
25. Iraqi government troops in March 2017 reloading with ammunition and tobacco in a pause in the long battle to drive Islamic State jihadists out of Mosul. (By courtesy of the author)
26. An Iraqi sniper waiting for a victim during months of street fighting to drive jihadists of Islamic State out of Mosul. (By courtesy of the author)
27. An Iraqi soldier resting during house-to-house fighting in Mosul in 2017. (By courtesy of the author)
28. Desperation and courage. A father saving his wounded son during the battle for Mosul in 2017. (By courtesy of the author)
29. Palestinians in Ramallah on the West Bank commemorate seventy years since Israeli independence, the event they call al-Nakba, the catastrophe. (By courtesy of the author)
30. Ultra-Orthodox Jews at an election rally in Jerusalem in September 2019. (By courtesy of the author)
31. Taliban in Lashkar Gar, in Helmand province, Afghanistan, just after their victory in 2021. The Taliban of the 1990s banned photography. New generation Taliban were deeply attached to their smartphones. (By courtesy of the author)
32. Afghan girls at a school in Helmand facing a frightening future after the Taliban's victory in 2021. (By courtesy of the author)
33. Aftermath of an Israeli air strike in Beit Hanoun in Gaza in May 2021. (By courtesy of the author)
34. British surgeons from the charity Action for Humanity operating on a victim of war in Marib in Yemen in 2021. (By courtesy of the author)
35. Yemen became the worst humanitarian disaster in the world in the years after 2015. Six-month-old Taqua Tarish was lucky enough to be treated in hospital in Marib for severe malnutrition. (By courtesy of the author)

PROLOGUE

On 15 February 1989, the last day of the Soviet occupation of Afghanistan, I peered through the wire at Kabul Airport, watching as the last Soviet soldiers and some wives and children, in quiet and well-behaved lines, walked up the steps of a small airliner that looked as if it had taken too many trips into the war. The aircraft climbed steeply, spiralling high to make it a harder target for the guerrilla fighters of the mujahedeen in the mountains that surround Kabul. The Soviets left behind an airport scattered with broken warplanes, a communist government that was fighting for its life, and their own equivalent of America's Vietnam disaster.

The last act of the occupation, carried live on state television, was the departure of a column of armoured personnel carriers, red banners flying, over the Friendship Bridge into Soviet Uzbekistan. Colonel-General Boris Gromov, commander of the Limited Contingent of Soviet Forces in Afghanistan, stopped his vehicle to walk over the last section of the bridge. His son was waiting on Soviet soil with a bunch of red carnations. Since the USSR invaded on 24 December 1979, nearly two million Afghans, mostly civilians, had been killed, along with around fifteen thousand Soviet soldiers. Gromov did not look back.[1]

As the Western world celebrated Christmas Day in 1991, the red flag with the hammer and sickle was lowered over the Kremlin for the last time. A few days earlier, state television in Moscow had announced that 'the USSR no longer exists'.[2] In Kabul, the communist government of President Mohammad Najibullah had outlasted the USSR. He was overthrown the following year, when the mujahedeen entered the city. Four years later, he would be taken from UN detention by the Taliban and tortured to death before his body was dragged through the streets.

I watched the final Soviet act in Afghanistan without being able to report on it, because I was being detained after failing to talk my way into the country without a visa. After a day or two in a small windowless room, the guards had worked out I was harmless and let me sit in the sun on a small patch of grass that was separated from the airstrip by a wire fence. I lost myself in the hubris of 1980s New York City in Tom Wolfe's *Bonfire of the Vanities*, feeling nothing like a master of the universe as I pondered how to extricate myself. The Afghans would not let me in, but they wouldn't let me leave either.

I had just celebrated my twenty-ninth birthday and getting assigned to a story in Kabul was a big step in my reporting career. It had been a gamble to send me there without a visa, so the potato curry the guards had shared in return for some of my whisky churned inside me with the gnawing feeling that a reporter with the right stuff might have found a way in. I had no idea that the events I saw would shape some of the biggest stories I was going to be reporting for the next thirty years or more.

The end of the USSR is a small part of a story about the Middle East. Its defeat in Afghanistan was less important than the way it happened and the seeds it sowed outside the Soviet Union. The Americans funded the Afghan mujahedeen's fight against the Soviets, a war that was enthusiastically joined by a generation of Islamist radicals, mostly Arabs, who travelled to Afghanistan to fight and went home as seasoned jihadists. Many embarked on a lifelong fight for the victory of their versions of Islam. Among them were a Saudi, Osama bin Laden, and an Egyptian, Ayman al-Zawahiri: the two top men in al-Qaeda when it attacked the United States on 11 September 2001.

In 1989 it became clear that the old planet we had grown up on, with the constant background hum of the Cold War, was turning into something else, fast. A few months after the Soviets left Afghanistan, I was in China as the state crushed a protest movement led by students in Tiananmen Square. The Communist Party of the Soviet

Union might have lost the stomach to liquidate threats to its power; its estranged brothers in the Chinese Communist Party had not.

The end of the Cold War removed the fear that any face-off between the superpowers could escalate into a catastrophic nuclear exchange, a nightmare coolly referred to as 'mutual assured destruction', or MAD. But it created a new set of dangers; it left the world safe for a hot war. Had the dictator of Iraq, President Saddam Hussein, been able to turn to Moscow, the cautious men in the Kremlin might have been able to talk him out of his great misadventure of invading Kuwait on 2 August 1990. It is equally possible that President George H. W. Bush in Washington, DC would not have responded by going to war if the Soviet Union had still been strong enough to oppose him.

The end of the Cold War, the last act of the world order that was created after 1945, had consequences that rolled around not just the Middle East, but the rest of the planet too. It opened the gates of the Middle East for a new period of foreign intervention and added rocket fuel to the revival of radical Islamism that had been gathering speed for more than a decade.

The Middle East had never been peaceful. Its place on the map, where Europe, Africa and Asia met, made it a corridor and a destination for invading armies. The governance of newly independent Arab countries in the twentieth century had been on a sliding scale of ineptitude that went from authoritarian to brutal. After 1990, the region was swept up in a storm of turbulence that still raged when the world changed again after Russia invaded Ukraine in February 2022. When that happened, the world's biggest nuclear-armed nations were caught up in the most dangerous crisis since the height of the Cold War. Arabs and Israelis tried to stay neutral. But to paraphrase a line attributed to the Russian revolutionary Leon Trotsky, they might not have been interested in the war, but the war, especially its economic consequences, was interested in them.

The invasion of Kuwait in 1990 and the war that followed was my first proper story in the Middle East, and I've spent much of my career since then trying to understand the new era it started. This book tries to explain what happened next, and why.

1.

Watch and Learn

The first time I drove through eastern Saudi Arabia to the Kuwaiti border, the Gulf was a dazzling turquoise mirror. I'd naively expected a ride in the desert to be more exotic, but we were travelling along a highway designed to carry everything from royal limousines to the heavy traffic needed by the world's biggest oil exporter. The flat, stony desert stretched to the horizon. When we stopped for a break, and a chance to see what a stroll felt like in fifty degrees of summer heat in the Saudi desert, I picked up a handful of small pebbles that had been polished like jewels by centuries of sun and wind. The real wealth was under my feet, great subterranean lagoons of oil and gas, and they were a big part of why I was there.

A couple of weeks earlier, on 2 August 1990, Iraq's president, Saddam Hussein, had invaded Kuwait, his small, rich neighbour. The long conflict between Israel and the Palestinians periodically blasted the Middle East into the headlines, but as the final decade of the twentieth century got going, the world had been looking elsewhere – at the collapse of the Soviet Union and its empire in Europe.

If it hadn't been for the death spiral of the USSR, I might not have been driving along the smooth black tarmac towards the Kuwaiti border. Saddam's decision to send eight divisions of his Republican Guard into Kuwait, around a thousand tanks and tens of thousands of men, would on its own have been a big event, but the invasion was elevated into a world crisis by the American response. Feeling new strength in the face of Soviet disintegration, the US plunged its armed forces into the region, and one way or another they have been there ever since. The rhetoric from the White House was about freeing Kuwait and deterring aggression – not a lie, but not the whole truth. America needed Saudi and Kuwaiti oil to stay in friendly hands.

A few days after the invasion of Kuwait, the CIA told President George Bush that the latest intelligence indicated the Iraqis were preparing to drive into Saudi Arabia. The president, according to one of his senior officials, asked when Iraq would be able to go onto the offensive. The director of Central Intelligence replied with a single word: 'Now.'

The same day, I watched on TV as Bush hinted that he was prepared to go to war. 'I will not discuss with you what my options are or might be. But they are wide open, I can assure you of that. Just wait. Watch and learn . . .'[1]

By the time I arrived in Saudi Arabia, America was moving in troops to deter Saddam from sending his men from Kuwait into Saudi's Eastern Province, but there were no Americans at the border. A few Saudi tanks shimmered in the distance, proof that the road from Kuwait was open and the heart of the Saudi oil industry was there for the taking.

We drove on to al-Khafji, a small town on the Saudi side of the border. It was almost empty. A worried hotelier looked glumly at his echoing lobby. His hotel's rooms opened onto a narrow, sandy Gulf beach, lapped by waves as warm as a bath. I thought about booking a beachside idyll as I waited for the war, not realizing that the fighting was still months away.

Saddam Hussein had been threatening Kuwait for months. His regime was in trouble and he believed his rich Arab neighbours owed him. In 1980 he had made the rash decision to invade Iran, hoping to take advantage of the chaos that followed the fall of the shah, the return of Ayatollah Khomeini and the Islamic Revolution. The conservative, rich Arab oil monarchies, happy for Iraq to be locked in combat with what they saw as the existential threat of Iranian revolutionary contagion, lent Saddam money for the fight. Iraq emerged from eight years of war with perhaps half a million dead and $80 billion of debts.

With careful management, a country with as much oil as Iraq should have been able to repay its debts, but Saddam was more interested in grand gestures. He wanted his Arab brothers to write off the money they had lent him to fight Iran, and help boost Iraq's income by pumping less oil to drive up its price. When they refused to help, Saddam scented betrayal and conspiracy. The small, militarily inconsequential and immensely wealthy Kuwaitis, it seemed, were shoving a 'poisoned dagger' into Iraq's back by pumping more oil than their quota, and stealing Iraq's oil by sinking wells that slanted laterally into its side of the Rumaila field.[2]

The Americans had also found it useful to have a strong and secular Arab leader taking on their new enemies in Tehran. Despite Saddam's unsavoury habits at home, their desires sometimes overlapped. They sold him weapons to fight Iran, which had been a close ally of the US until the Islamic revolution turned it into an enemy. The CIA was still sending intelligence to Iraq until the day Kuwait was invaded.[3] But as he made his plans, Saddam was also blaming his regime's problems on a Western conspiracy. He summoned the US ambassador, April Glaspie, to his palace overlooking the River Tigris in Baghdad to deliver a litany of complaints.

The ambassador's cable to the US State Department about her fateful meeting with Saddam described him as 'cordial, reasonable and even warm throughout the ensuing two hours'. He asked for a Marshall Plan to help Iraq recover from the long war with Iran, before laying into Kuwait and the United Arab Emirates for pushing down oil prices – an act of economic warfare. The Americans should not twist his arm, he said. He knew what they could do to Iraq, but he warned that President Bush should not force Iraq to the 'point of humiliation at which logic must be disregarded'.

The ambassador's cable seems to report a barely veiled warning. Saddam indicated that he would take desperate measures, and he talked of 'liberty or death'. This meeting became part of the indictment later assembled by those trying to work out why he had believed he would get away with invading Kuwait. In her cable, Glaspie reported that she had told him the United States took no position on border issues between Kuwait and Iraq – President Bush wanted friendship with Iraq and peace and stability in the Middle

East. She did not tell him to keep his hands off Kuwait (for which she became a scapegoat) but her position reflected US policy, which was to offer 'economic and political incentives for Iraq to moderate its behaviour'.[4] The Americans believed they were offering Iraq a mixture of sticks and carrots; however, their words were too soft, and only when it was too late did they show the Iraqis a modest-sized stick. The Pentagon moved a small flotilla of warships closer to Kuwait and sent two aerial fuel tankers and a transport plane to Abu Dhabi to reassure the Emiratis that their war-hardened neighbour would have to behave. As events proved, it was not nearly enough.

The Middle East was not high on Washington's agenda. At first, General Norman Schwarzkopf, in charge of US Central Command, which covered the Middle East, thought Saddam was bluffing. Then, as the intelligence piled up and Iraqi units deployed on the Kuwaiti border, he saw 'a battle plan taking shape'. The day before Saddam sent his forces into Kuwait, Schwarzkopf briefed US defense secretary Dick Cheney that an invasion was coming, but would be limited. He expected Saddam to seize the Kuwaiti half of the disputed Rumaila oil field and islands that controlled the sea lane to the Iraqi port of Umm Qasr. Saddam, he reckoned, was building up Iraq's navy and wanted better access to the Gulf than Iraq's existing toehold. The meeting, Schwarzkopf said, ended with 'no sense of urgency. In the hierarchy of world crises, this one was still a minor blip.'[5]

The Americans knew that Saddam Hussein was threatening to invade Kuwait and failed to deter him. If he had kept his objectives limited, he might have got away with it, or at least walked away with a deal, but he overreached in taking the whole of Kuwait. It was the biggest mistake he ever made – the consequences of the invasion changed everything for Iraq and set Saddam on a path that led to the American invasion in 2003, the destruction of his regime and his eventual execution. According to his CIA interrogator, only when he was asked about the invasion of Kuwait did he show any regret. 'His face took on an anguished look and he tried to change the subject . . . Saddam put both hands on his head and said, "Ugh, this gives me such a headache!"'[6]

Saddam's aggression catapulted the Middle East to the top of the world's agenda. The war with Iran had left him with a vast army, and an economy so damaged that it could not have provided enough jobs had a million men been demobilized. Saddam saw himself as heir to the great Muslim warrior Saladin, who captured Jerusalem in 1187, ending almost two centuries of Crusader control. Like his hero, he had been born in Tikrit, and he had built Baghdad into a capital fit for a modern Saladin, with a triumphal arch made of two gnarled, muscular forearms modelled on Saddam's own and forged by English craftsmen.

A fearless push into Kuwait, to fight Arab treachery and collect Iraq's reward for the bloodshed in the war with Iran, must have seemed an action worthy of his hero, but Iraq's latter-day Saladin was not well versed in world affairs. Saddam knew how to control Iraq's tribes and sects, but his experience of the outside world was mostly limited to his time in exile in Egypt after a failed attempt to assassinate Iraq's military ruler, Abdul Karim Qasim, in 1959. His miscalculation about the storm his invasion of Kuwait would cause suggests he missed the signs that the USSR, his main arms supplier throughout the war with Iran, was no longer a reliable patron with the will to defend its clients at the United Nations.

Since the Second World War made the United States a world power, it had always been fixated on its Soviet rival. The invasion of Kuwait was the first international crisis that fell under the new rules, which the Americans were realizing they now had a chance to rewrite.

In the long run, the Soviet defeat in Afghanistan had consequences that roared through the Middle East and the rest of the world. The war turbo-charged the ideology of violent, revolutionary, radical Islamist jihad. The Afghans had a long history of resisting invaders; the Soviet invasion was a catalyst for the radicalization of young Arabs who travelled to Afghanistan to join them in a holy war against atheistic invaders. Although no more than a few thousand flew to Peshawar in Pakistan and travelled through the Khyber Pass into Afghanistan, compared to at least 200,000 Afghans defending their homeland their influence was magnified many times over.

One of them was Osama bin Laden, a wealthy young Saudi whose father was a billionaire construction magnate. Osama started by donating cash and then travelled to Afghanistan to set up his own small militia. Most Muslims believe that the true meaning of jihad is a determination to live the way God intended, but for Bin Laden and his fellow travellers, the jihad in Afghanistan was about waging a holy war.

Western leaders relished the spectacle of disaster for their Soviet enemies and were prepared to help anyone who would pick up a gun to make matters worse for Moscow. The Americans brought in containers of cash, weapons and Stinger handheld anti-aircraft missiles. The Saudis also poured billions into the jihad against the USSR. Later they turned against the jihadist fighters when they became a threat to the Saudi regime, but at first they were seen as useful assets abroad.

When the Cold War ended with the Soviet collapse, it lifted a weight off all of us who had grown up with the threat of nuclear war. However, the threat of a man-made radioactive wilderness had actually put a dampener on crises. While the Soviets and the Americans fought each other through proxies, allies and clients, they imposed rules and limits to control the risks. But when Saddam Hussein ordered his troops into Kuwait in the summer of 1990, the paralysing weight of the Cold War had gone.

Under international law there are two legal justifications for war: self-defence and to uphold resolutions passed by the UN Security Council. The self-defence box was ticked when the Kuwaitis asked their allies to intervene. President Bush turned to the United Nations to make his plans legal, confident that he would not receive a Soviet veto. On the same day as the invasion, the UN Security Council in New York passed the first of a series of resolutions that turned into their most ambitious set of sanctions, condemning the invasion and then authorizing war.[7]

A war, legalized by the UN, was inevitable if Saddam Hussein did not pull out of Kuwait. None of that diplomatic helter-skelter would have been possible had the USSR not been failing and had it been led by someone like Nikita Khrushchev, who saw the UN as a place to take on the West, not to help it rescue its oil supplies. Instead, Mikhail Gorbachev was President and First Secretary of the Communist Party of the Soviet Union, desperately trying to reform his country to save it, and his attention was a long way from the Middle East.

A few years before the Gulf crisis of 1990, Gorbachev had written that the nations of the world were like climbers roped together on a mountain: 'They can climb together to the mountain peak or fall together into an abyss.'[8] The Kuwait crisis gave him the chance to put his views into action. He bought into the strategy laid out by the Western powers on the Security Council, which made him even more popular in Western countries that were already gripped by 'Gorbymania' but deepened resentment for him at home.

It was not simply that the Soviets did not use their veto; they also offered their backing. The Soviet foreign minister made it clear that the USSR would not oppose military action. Britain and France had already pledged to support the US-led coalition; China, the other permanent member of the Security Council, indicated it would 'look out of the window', as Britain's UN ambassador David Hannay put it, if it did not approve. President Bush worked hard to preserve the new atmosphere of cooperation, with Saddam's Arab enemies joining the coalition against him. The US was prepared to do a lot to keep its new allies onside. In October, after Israeli security forces killed twenty-one Palestinian demonstrators in clashes at the compound of the al-Aqsa Mosque in Jerusalem, the US supported a Security Council resolution condemning Israel that it would normally have vetoed. But most important in putting the coalition George Bush was building on the road to war with Iraq was the Soviet attitude to its Cold War adversaries, and to Iraq. The world really had changed.

At this point the UN also demanded the release of foreign hostages. Before the invasion, hundreds of thousands of foreigners had worked in Iraq. Tens of thousands of Asian migrant workers had left the country, but many from the countries in the anti-Saddam coalition were detained, with some of them sent to be human shields at possible targets like dams and factories. I was in Baghdad just before Christmas in 1990 when Saddam gave the order to let them leave after a personal intervention from Britain's former prime minister Edward Heath. Recently released British hostages tried to drink their hotel's bar dry. A grim-faced consular official from London muttered about Brits abroad as he tried to stop a few angry men punching hapless Iraqi waiters. The Brits were flown out of Baghdad in a Virgin Atlantic jetliner. Its owner Richard Branson was the other half in the Heath mission.

While that was happening, Western forces continued to gather in Saudi Arabia. The two holy cities of Mecca and Medina are on the Red Sea coast, the opposite side of the country from where troops were deploying, but distance didn't make Saudi hearts any more fond of their foreign visitors.

Conservative, pious Saudis were jolted by horror and anger. Most of the foreign soldiers were deep in the desert on the big bases like King Khalid military city, a long way from Saudi civilians; but the highways were full of long American convoys, with women who wore trousers and carried guns driving some of the trucks. Saudi women were not allowed to drive or wear trousers in public. When some took their cars out on an all-female protest drive through Riyadh, they were arrested, suspended from their jobs and verbally abused by the religious establishment.

In response, the Grand Mufti of Saudi Arabia, Abdul Aziz bin Baz, issued a fatwa against women driving. He was head of the Ulema, the council of Islamic scholars, and the embodiment of Saudi Arabia's austere interpretation of Islam. Blind since his teens, he was a legendary figure whose fatwas, often based on medieval precedents, had the force of law in Saudi Arabia's theocracy. He had a huge influence on social relations in Saudi Arabia and the final word on religion. Although Bin Baz condemned women drivers, he ensured that the Ulema approved King Fahd's decision to throw open the gates of Saudi Arabia to foreign armies that included Christians and Jews. The princes of the House of Saud often enjoyed highly un-Islamic pastimes. King Fahd had a reputation in his younger days as a playboy with a love of Western temptation, and he might have struggled to justify his actions had he not had the Bin Baz seal of approval.

For many Saudis, even Bin Baz could not make up for the sin of inviting infidel troops into the heart of Saudi Arabia. One was Osama bin Laden, home from the Afghan jihad, who condemned Bin Baz for his 'weakness and flexibility'.[9] He had his own plan, and thanks to his father's royal connections and his own cooperation with Saudi intelligence in Afghanistan, Bin Laden was able to pitch his ideas to the defence minister Prince Sultan bin Abdulaziz Al Saud, a younger brother of the king.[10] On no account, Bin Laden warned, should King Fahd accept help from the Americans and their allies; his decision to do just that caused a storm that had long-lasting consequences.

Direct military intervention in the holiest ground for Muslims, the land of Mecca and Medina, lit a fire in the minds of jihadists; in the attacks on the USA on 9/11, fifteen out of the nineteen hijackers were Saudis. Back in Afghanistan, Osama bin Laden had stopped his fighters criticizing the Saudi king, but now for him the Saudi regime was forever damned by its sinful decision to allow non-believers to violate the holy land of Islam.

Saudi Arabia was blanketed in the strict Wahhabi interpretation of Islam when I arrived there in August 1990, part of a wave of foreigners that would eventually amount to around 1,500 journalists and more than half a million troops. Life revolved around the five times during each day when devout Muslims turned towards Mecca to pray. The less devout did not have a choice, at least not out in public. Businesses closed when the loudspeakers crackled out the call to the faithful. Shopkeepers would shoo customers from their premises before following them to small street-corner mosques. Any soundtrack of Saudi Arabia in 1990 should always include the clatter and snap of metal gates being pulled shut when the time came to show faith and obedience to God. Any Muslim who did not would have to reckon with the Saudi Commission for the Promotion of Virtue and Prevention of Vice, also known as the Mutawa, the religious police.

Public entertainment did not exist in Saudi Arabia. On Thursday evenings, hundreds of workers from the Philippines, mainly women, headed to a mall in Dhahran, where they would sit for a coffee or take a stroll. It was their big night out. Hungry for foreign newspapers, I scoured hotel bookshops for weeks-old copies of *Time*, *Newsweek* or *The Economist*. Censors armed with scissors and marker pens removed or blotted out anything with a whiff of Western impurity. Photos of women in bathing suits or sports clothes were hacked out or covered with inky scribble, as were advertisements for alcoholic drinks. Many pages were so full of cuts that they fell apart in my hands.

My frustration as I leafed through the tattered magazines was a result of an alliance between the Al Saud family and an austere interpretation of Islam that began with Mohammed Ibn Abd al-Wahhab in the 1740s. A religious revivalist from Nejd, the central part of the Arabian peninsula, he warned Muslims of the dangers of embracing heresies that could be punished by death. It was an old idea, but one that is still manically enforced by extreme jihadists in the twenty-first century.

Ibn Abd al-Wahhab saw plenty of candidates for death, encouraging his followers to smash the tombs of saints and kill those who prayed at them. He was expelled from Mecca when he tried to stop men and women singing, dancing and smoking together. Back home in conservative Nejd, he was sheltered by Mohammed bin Saud, a local ruler and the founder of his dynasty. Their formal alliance, made in 1744, still provides the religious foundation for the modern Saudi state. The Al Sauds got their power while the clerics enforced purity. It was a good deal for both. They even occupied Mecca early in the 1800s, until they were driven out by Ottoman forces from Egypt.[11]

A century later, the First World War broke the Ottoman Empire and allowed one remarkable man, Ibn Saud, to revive his family's alliance with Wahhabi clerics and undo his rival Hussein bin Ali, the sharif of Mecca. By 1932 he controlled most of the peninsula and named the new state Saudi Arabia, after his own family. Wahhabi support was as important to Ibn Saud and his sons as oil, the black gold of the twentieth century. As American geologists mapped the new state's massive oil reserves, Abdulaziz strengthened his grip on it and secured the succession by fathering perhaps fifty sons by many wives. A century after he captured Mecca, Ibn Saud still had a son, King Salman, on the Saudi throne.

The House of Saud's lavish spending on yachts, mansions and Renaissance art would not have gone down well with Ibn Abdul Wahhab, but many Saudis accepted the way the royal family lived not just because oil revenue transformed their lives but because his religious successors told them to. The Wahhabi stamp of approval made it possible for King Fahd to allow changes after the invasion of Kuwait that only a few weeks earlier would have been scarcely conceivable.

Most of the Western troops in Saudi Arabia had no idea what was going on. I got to know a US Marine infantry unit who had been told by their commanders that they were on the Kuwaiti border when they were at least an hour's drive inside Saudi Arabia. The men wanted news, so I took them a couple of bin-bags of papers and magazines. When I reached them, they told me I'd had a lucky escape – they'd been locked and loaded and their anti-personnel mines were ready. They weren't apologetic – they had no way of knowing what was coming down the track.

The Marines spent much of the day sweltering in their tents, reading letters from home, smoking and talking. It was high summer, and so they trained at either end of the day when it was cooler. Years later, former Marine Anthony Swofford wrote about being caught up in the excitement: 'as a young man raised on the films of the Vietnam War, I want ammunition and alcohol and dope, I want to screw some whores and kill some Iraqi motherfuckers'.[12] But the Saudi desert in 1990 was not Saigon, and US Marine life there was comparatively monastic. So was mine. In a land of no alcohol and as a lifelong non-smoker, a French photographer persuaded me to smoke a cigarette over dinner. It was the closest thing to letting off some steam in a land without public entertainment.

The Americans were pouring soldiers and equipment into Saudi Arabia. The British were there too, though not as well equipped, having had to gut the British army in Germany in order to field two armoured brigades. I saw depots' worth of American military lorries being driven off ships at Jubail and other ports on the Arabian Gulf coast, along with armour and heavy weapons. They had not had to move so much, so quickly, since the Second World War. The retired American generals on the new twenty-four-hour news channels talked a great deal about the huge number of Iraqi tanks and battle-hardened troops; for the Vietnam generation, it was a chance to put right some old mistakes. The trucks and armoured vehicles coming off the ships were still the dark green of jungles and paddy fields – whoever sold the Americans the paint to turn them the colour of sand must have made a fortune. Someone reported seeing vehicles that still had improvised repairs made out of Vietnamese beer cans.

By the beginning of 1991, the Americans had half a million soldiers in the desert. Offshore, alongside six aircraft-carrier battle groups, were two mighty Second World War battleships, the *Missouri* and the *Wisconsin*, modernized to carry cruise missiles alongside their sixteen-inch naval guns. Watching it happen, I had the feeling that a great military giant was waking up to fight again.

Before the Kuwait crisis, the only permanent US military foothold in the Middle East was a naval base in Bahrain. But when US troops went to the region in 1990, they stayed. The Pentagon no longer needed to ransack its store cupboards; it moved plenty of them to the Middle East. In 1991 it began a habit of military intervention there that would have immense and deadly consequences.

When victory against Saddam came quickly, with almost all the casualties on the Iraqi side, it seemed in Washington, DC to be the promising first chapter of a new era. President Bush promised a new world order, more peaceful and secure than the old world of Cold War confrontation. The American political scientist Francis Fukuyama argued that victory for liberal democracy marked 'the end of history'. The flow of events wouldn't stop, but liberty and equality were irresistible.

They were wrong. Two diametrically opposed visions clashed after the ejection of Iraqi forces from Kuwait. One was the desire of Islamists — known as Salafists — to return the Muslim world to the way it was in the time of the prophet Muhammad; immersed in prayer and rejecting modern values, they saw Western impositions as godless. Not all Salafists were violent jihadists, but the ones who were believed they had to fight and kill to do God's will. The other vision came from the sense of power that surged around Washington, DC, as America exorcised the demons of defeat in Vietnam.

Most of my career has been spent watching what happened next, and it turned out that liberal democracy was not as irresistible as Fukuyama believed. George Bush's coalition was a tribute to his diplomatic skills and connections. While the Palestinians under Yasser Arafat, along with King Hussein of Jordan, came out for Saddam, Arab leaders who had decided that his time was up included the rulers of Kuwait, Bahrain, Oman and the United Arab Emirates. The Saudis bussed a couple of hundred journalists to Dhahran Airport, where a Boeing 747 was waiting to take us into the desert, to King Khalid military city. Egyptian troops were on parade and a token force of Syrians sheltered from the summer heat in carpeted, air-conditioned tents equipped with TVs, sofas and refrigerators. And on 16 January 1991, an air armada took off to bomb Iraq, as the American-led coalition went to war.

2.

Mission Impassable

On the drive north from Beirut up the coast of the Mediterranean, it is easy to miss the gorge of Nahr el-Kelb, which translates as 'Dog River'. Now you can whizz along the highway, through a tunnel cut through the mountains near Jounieh, and head north to Byblos or Batrun for lunch. It is a routine car journey these days; for millennia, passing the mouth of Dog River was so arduous that it was something to celebrate. The gorge is on a direct route from Europe to the Middle East, which meant that every invading army or beaten soldier retreating north had to pass it long before engineers bored tunnels through the rock. Foreign commanders reported approvingly of its tactical possibilities. In 1840, Commodore Charles Napier of HMS *Powerful* anchored his flotilla at Dog River to intervene in a war within the Ottoman Empire from 'an excellent position . . . protected by an impassable gorge'.[1] One reason why the Phoenicians, ancient ancestors of the modern Lebanese, became a sea power in the Mediterranean was that it was hard to navigate their home on dry land.

Getting past Dog River was a decisive moment in any campaign, and armies left memorials carved into slabs and pillars of rock to commemorate their achievement. The oldest is in Egyptian hieroglyphics, commissioned by the pharaoh Ramses II in the thirteenth century BCE. Later came Assyrians, Babylonians, Greeks, Romans, Phoenicians, Crusaders, Mamluks, Ottomans, and in modern times the French and the British and ANZAC troops in the two world wars. All of them left memorials. Another celebrates Israel's withdrawal from southern Lebanon in 2000; some Lebanese campaigned for a plaque to commemorate the moment that Syria's President Bashar al-Assad was forced to pull out his troops in 2005.

The Middle East attracts outsiders, and the desire to control it has led to suffering and slaughter. It possesses resources as well as sacred and strategic territory. Once the world entered the industrial era and craved carbon, the planet's biggest reserves of oil and gas were impossible to ignore. The region is the great crossroads of the globe: a thousand years ago, caravans of camels carrying incense from Yemen to Europe and East Asia wore tracks in the Arabian desert that are still visible from the air. Some old caravanserais still stand, just about. One is on the road south from Damascus, towards the Golan Heights, occupied by Israel since 1967.

The Middle East was the first place where humans grew crops and built settlements near their fields that became cities, civilizations and empires. More than five thousand years ago in what is now Iraq, thousands of people lived inside the walls of Uruk, most probably the world's first city. The peoples of the Middle East were, for a time, on the cutting edge of modernity and power; they could earn money through trade, or take the wealth of others while they spread their ideas. But that was a long time ago. The memorials at Nahr el-Kelb show that Western imperialists did not invent intervention, but they perfected it. Generations of outsiders have pushed their way into the region. In the twenty-first century, the decisions of these powerful outsiders have made lives in the Middle East dangerous, difficult and short.

For more than 600 years, the Ottomans dominated the Middle East and the Balkans. They started as tribesmen from Central Asia and in 1453 captured Constantinople, the city now known as Istanbul. On their way to becoming the greatest power of their age, they beat the Byzantines and the Mamluks, and in 1529 their sultan Suleiman the

Magnificent reached and besieged Vienna. Their path to decline was slow and painful. They lost territory to ambitious and rising European powers over two centuries, before the First World War finally broke their empire.[2]

The slow fall of the Ottomans presented hungry European Christian powers with an imperial buffet in the Middle East. They competed to appoint themselves protectors of Jerusalem. The Russians brought stone with them to build a cathedral and a complex of buildings outside the walls of the Old City, still known as the Russian Compound. Part of it became a British police station and later a notorious interrogation centre used by Israel's internal security service, Shin Bet.[3] France built a large centre for pilgrims across the road from the New Gate, the entrance to the Christian quarter, while Britain constructed an Anglican cathedral out of Jerusalem stone. In 1898 the German Kaiser Wilhelm II rode on a white charger through an opening in the walls near Jaffa Gate, escorted by a squadron of cavalry and wearing a helmet topped with an imperial eagle. Germany's attempts to get a foothold in Jerusalem before the First World War included the construction of a hospital that dominates the ridgeline leading to the Mount of Olives; it is still named the Augusta Victoria, after Kaiser Wilhelm's wife. German plans also included a railway from Berlin to Baghdad, and Istanbul still has a railway station shaped like a Rhineland castle. The Germans were hoping to outflank the British navy's control of the sea lanes to Asia; in the end, the spoils went to Britain and France, as Germany lost the First World War and Russia was swamped by revolution and civil war.

The carve-up of the Ottoman Empire, approved by the new League of Nations, created new empires for the overstretched British and French, but they did not last. Even before the Second World War they were struggling, with too much territory and too many people who were fed up with being told what to do by foreigners. Syria and Lebanon became independent of France, while Britain was forced out of Palestine. The imperialists stayed long enough to leave plenty of physical relics across the Middle East, from grand buildings, iron bridges and red post boxes to croissants for breakfast and road signs in French. But the legacy that matters most and still shapes events is visible in the borders they left on the map.

Two imperial grandees created the modern Middle East when they began the final dismembering of the Ottoman Empire during the First World War.[4] One was a British landowner and adventurer, Colonel Sir Tatton Benvenuto Mark Sykes, the young and energetic sixth baronet of his line. His contemporaries described him as a man of considerable charm who wrote books about his travels in the Ottoman Empire that got him noticed in Whitehall. Lord Kitchener, secretary of state for war, appointed Sykes as his Middle East advisor while he was still in his thirties.

The other grandee was a French diplomat, Charles François Georges-Picot, who in 1914 was French consul in Beirut, at that time an important city in the Ottoman Empire. Picot found himself on the enemy side as the Ottoman leadership gambled on a German victory and entered the war on the side of Berlin. He left in a hurry, leaving papers in his office that identified Arab nationalists who had asked for France's protection. When Ahmed Djemal Pasha, Ottoman governor of Syria, was shown the papers, he lived up to his bloodthirsty reputation and had the nationalists publicly executed. Some went to the gallows in Damascus while others were hanged in Beirut's biggest plaza, which was renamed Martyrs' Square in their honour in the 1930s. Half a century later, many others were killed there, when it was a front line in Lebanon's civil war.

Sykes and Picot were not natural allies. Sykes was a product of England's ruling class, the master of a large estate in Yorkshire; he was part of a Victorian generation that grew up expecting to rule the world. Picot, on the other hand, was an Anglophobic imperialist who campaigned for France to expand its empire at the expense of the British. However, in 1916 they were able to reach a secret deal – known as the Sykes–Picot Agreement – because they shared a strong interest in winning the peace as well as the war. Rather than drawing precise borders, the agreement defined zones of influence. It was also worked out and signed off by their ally, Tsarist Russia, only for the Bolsheviks to leak the details to C. P. Scott, editor of the *Manchester Guardian*, after the 1917 revolution; the revelation fed a mood of growing revulsion against private deals that affected millions being hatched behind closed doors.

Sykes's secret diplomacy was part of a series of British gambits to win the war in the Middle East and get their empire into the strongest position possible. In London, they spent months talking to Zionists who wanted a homeland for the Jews. The prime minister David Lloyd George, who like many of his contemporaries had an instinctive sympathy for Zionism, later mused, 'I was brought up in a school where I was taught far more history of the Jews than about my own land. I could tell you all the kings of Israel. But I doubt if I could have named half a dozen of the kings of England, and not more of the kings of Wales.'[5] It was about much more than nostalgia for Sunday school – the Jews were regarded as desirable allies. The leading Zionist in Britain, Chaim Weizmann, and the richest, the banker Lord Rothschild, found ways to play on deeply engrained prejudices about the world reach of the Jews among the British Christian elite.[6] Weizmann, professor of chemistry at Manchester University when he was not pressing for a Jewish homeland, had already impressed Lloyd George by inventing a new way to produce acetone, a vital ingredient for explosives. The prime minister believed Weizmann was the key to an alliance with a powerful global Jewish network that could keep Russia in the war and persuade the United States to join it. In his *War Memoirs*, Lloyd George did not hide his motives: 'We were anxious at the time to enlist Jewish support in neutral countries, notably in America.'[7] The British diplomat Ronald Storrs recorded hopes in London that an alliance with Zionists would not just impress American Jews, but might also sap the morale of Jews fighting for Germany, and would 'impart to the Russian Revolution, whose brains were assumed to be Jewish, a pro-British bias.'[8]

As they tried to tap into what they believed was the power of the Jews, the British were also looking for an ally to undermine the Ottomans. They found one in Hussein bin Ali, the sharif of Mecca and a direct descendant of the prophet Muhammad.[9] In the summer of 1915, the British High Commissioner in Egypt, Sir Henry McMahon, wrote to Hussein, starting a correspondence that seemed to offer an enticing deal. The British would make sure that the sharif would rule an independent Arab kingdom. Britain wanted present-day Iraq, and France wanted Lebanon and Syria. But the sharif's realm would include the Hijaz and most of the rest of the Arabian peninsula. McMahon used deliberately vague language, not least over the future of Palestine, but

Hussein believed him and kept his word. It is tempting to wonder what the Middle East would have looked like had the British kept theirs, but Hussein had to be betrayed for the security and prosperity of the British Empire. The Sykes–Picot Agreement rang alarm bells when it reached McMahon in Cairo, and he told the Foreign Office to keep it from the Arabs: 'I feel that divulgence of agreement at the present time might be detrimental to our good relations with all parties and possibly create a change of attitude in some of them.'[10]

Hussein did not get his kingdom. As a consolation prize – and to solve a problem for Britain – two of his sons were installed on the thrones of Iraq and Transjordan, new countries created by Britain under mandates from the League of Nations. Another son became king of the Hijaz, but father and son were exiled after the Wahhabis of the Al Saud family unified Saudi Arabia. A British official suggested that they named the new kingdom after themselves.

Historians argue about the degree of the deception perpetrated by the British during the First World War. The British-Palestinian scholar George Antonius would call Sykes–Picot 'not only the product of greed at its worst . . . a startling piece of double-dealing', but others warned that however imperfect it was, starting again with a new map and borders would cause even more chaos.[11]

A century later, the impact of the deal on the Middle East is still resented and debated. In 2014, a Chilean jihadist fighter with long hair, a bushy beard and the nom de guerre Abu Safiyya made a video called 'The End of Sykes–Picot' after Islamic State seized vast tracts of Iraq and Syria. Arabs and their supporters maintain that they were betrayed several times over by the British in the First World War: by Sykes–Picot, in the Hussein–McMahon correspondence, and then by Britain's support for a homeland for the Jews in Palestine. Sykes rushed out of a meeting of the War Cabinet in November 1917 to tell Chaim Weizmann the good news: 'It's a boy,' he gushed.[12]

The foreign secretary Arthur Balfour put the details in a letter to Lord Rothschild that became known as the Balfour Declaration, a promise that Britain would 'view with favour the establishment of a national home for the Jewish people'. Balfour added that 'nothing shall be done which may prejudice the civil and religious rights of existing non-Jewish communities in Palestine, or the rights and political status enjoyed by Jews in any other country'. The non-Jewish communities to which he referred were Palestinian Arabs, a big majority in the land between the River Jordan and the Mediterranean Sea. The Balfour Declaration was issued as British imperial troops were fighting the Ottoman Turks for Palestine, advancing from Gaza on the Mediterranean coast to Jerusalem in the mountains. Their commander General Sir Edmund Allenby's triumphal entry into Jerusalem was filmed for posterity – a crowd from Jerusalem's melting pot swirls around, with shoeshine men and tea-sellers looking for business as they wait for their new rulers. Allenby's arrival to take possession of the Old City, just before Christmas, was every bit as choreographed as Kaiser Wilhelm's had been in 1898. The Foreign Office in London recalled the Kaiser's entry on a white charger through the Jaffa Gate and resolved that Allenby should do the opposite. Unlike Wilhelm, who had been decked out in all the finery Prussia could offer, a khaki-clad Allenby walked in on foot.

The idea was to demonstrate that Allenby was the unassuming representative of enlightened British rule, a show of humility intended to make the Germans look arrogant. Several of Allenby's aides, fresh from battle, were armed with nothing more lethal than walking sticks. It was a classic example of British imperial hypocrisy – they were splitting the Middle East with France while making contradictory promises to Arabs and Jews, setting them up for generations of conflict. In case anyone doubted the global reach of Jerusalem's new overseers, Allenby's armed soldiers marched through the streets sporting an imperial range of pith helmets, turbans and tam o'shanters, while Jerusalemites stared back wearing homburgs and fezzes, keffiyehs and kippas. Identity still matches headgear in the Holy City. Jerusalem is a city of hats.[13]

Lloyd George gave thanks for a victory that he called a 'Christmas present' for the British people. At a time when tens of thousands of soldiers were being slaughtered in a bloody, muddy European stalemate, it was 'a patch of blue sky which lightened the gloom that hung over the battlefield as a whole'.[14] While Allenby's groom fed his horse, the general read a proclamation clearly stating the imperial view. 'I make it known to you', he told them, that every holy site would be 'maintained and protected according to the existing customs and beliefs of those to whose faiths they are sacred'. Allenby's proclamation drips with rich ironies, given the deep changes Britain was planning in the region. Sir Mark Sykes, fresh from his negotiation with Picot and his announcement to the expectant Zionists, had written Allenby's speech.

Sykes did not live to see the consequences of the promises that he and other British diplomats and envoys had made, especially the deadly contradiction built into the Balfour Declaration. Establishing a national home for the Jews while also upholding the rights of the (unnamed) Palestinians proved to be impossible. Sykes died in Paris in March 1919, one of as many as 40 million victims of the influenza pandemic. By the early 1920s, Arabs and Jews in Palestine were killing each other. They are responsible for what they did but it was the British who started the fire, making promises to both sides that they couldn't keep, and kept it stoked until in 1948 they left the Arabs and Jews to fight it out.

The dangers were obvious early on. The American newspaperman Vincent Sheean was in Jerusalem during the summer of 1929, when 'The Holy Land seemed as near an approximation of hell on earth as I have ever seen.' Anyone who knows Jerusalem now will recognize his account of the way the city radiated hatred with the summer heat. 'The temperature rose throughout the first fortnight of August – you could stick your hand out in the air and feel it rising.'[15] Trouble at the Wailing Wall between Palestinians and Zionist Jews exploded into a series of killings, including the massacre of sixty-seven religious Jews in Hebron.

Just over a decade after the Declaration, Sheean could see how conflict was built into Balfour's words, which 'seemed to promise the Jews everything and seemed to reserve everything for the Arabs, at one time and with one twist of the pen'.[16] He turned against the Zionists as well as the British, concluding that Palestine 'was the most flagrant example of the betrayal of Arab interests after the war . . . All the Arabs had been betrayed by the British, but the Arabs of Palestine were in worse case than any others.'[17] It was all done, Sheean said, to secure Britain's power in Palestine.

The Zionists were better strategists and better politicians than the Palestinian Arabs. In the end, it did not matter that they also believed the British had betrayed them – they emerged with their state and used the Balfour Declaration to give their national project legitimacy. When the Arabs rose against the tide of events in the 1930s, the British crushed the revolt so comprehensively that the Palestinian leadership had not recovered when the civil war to control Palestine began in 1947, as the British announced their departure and the UN voted to partition the territory. A century after Balfour signed his typewritten declaration to Lord Rothschild, Israel's prime minister Benjamin Netanyahu visited the Foreign Office in London. Balfour's successor, Boris Johnson, showed him around the foreign secretary's grand corner office overlooking St James's Park. He pointed to his desk and explained it was the place where the Balfour Declaration had been composed. 'Funny you should say that,' said Netanyahu with some satisfaction, as camera shutters clicked furiously. For Israelis, the Balfour Declaration had been a vital victory on the road to statehood; for Palestinians, it was a milestone that would lead to catastrophe.

3.

All Flesh Is Grass

The July sun flashed through the glass doors at the back of the auditorium Saddam Hussein had chosen for a public display of power and revenge. He had dressed well, as usual, in an elegantly cut dark suit and a shirt with a long pointed collar. His tie was knotted a little loosely, unlike the noose that would end his life on a high scaffold in Baghdad twenty-six years later, and his hair and moustache were freshly barbered for a special day. A few of the men packed into the raked rows of seats wore safari suits, but mostly they modelled their look on their leader. The right choice of outfit wasn't going to help anyone whose name was on the list on the table in front of the new president of Iraq.

Saddam had ordered Iraqi television to record the proceedings. The fear in the room seeps out of the video, monochrome with a tint of sepia. From his place on the stage, speaking quietly and taking puffs from a large cigar, Saddam radiates malice. Hundreds of people had already been tortured and shot in the few weeks since his assumption of the presidency in mid-July 1979.[1]

Many years later he would tell a CIA interrogator that his predecessor, Ahmad Hassan al-Bakr, had stepped down because he was old and ill, and that he, Saddam, had taken the job reluctantly at a time when he had been thinking of retiring to Tikrit to become a farmer.[2] Less far-fetched accounts have him sending tanks and troops to surround the presidential palace and despatch al-Bakr into retirement. Events moved fast: al-Bakr made it official by announcing in a final TV broadcast that he was retiring and that Saddam was the best man to follow him. This act confirmed what everyone knew already – Saddam was the most powerful man in Iraq. But now he had a presidency and a regime to strengthen, and that required decisive action.

Saddam used a classic tactic to clear out enemies (real and imagined), announcing that some of his lieutenants had been plotting against him with his rival, President Hafez al-Assad of Syria. Some of the lower-ranked conspirators had already been shot. The meeting in the auditorium on 28 July was to deal with the top men. The senior leadership of the ruling Baath Party was lined up in front of him. Saddam was suited and booted for a reckoning, and everyone there knew it. The only men in the room who could feel secure were his small coterie of close advisors in the front row, mostly members of his own family.

Saddam had just celebrated his forty-second birthday. He was setting the course for a presidency that would end in Iraq's destruction after three major wars and with the blood of maybe millions, and certainly hundreds of thousands, of people on his hands. The video he had ordered to immortalize the moment shows him asking a moustachioed, balding man about the events that transpired between President al-Bakr's decision to step down and Saddam's assumption of power. The balding man is Muhyi Abdel Hussein Mashhadi, and he appears to be holding it together well for a man who is trying desperately to save his own life. Until a few days before al-Bakr's removal, Mashadi had been secretary of the Revolutionary Command Council. He had fallen fast, and Saddam was toying with him. The footage shows him staring out into the audience, sometimes starting nervously when Saddam asks a question as he confesses his part in the alleged conspiracy. After the meeting, it was said his family would have been killed if he had not cooperated.

Saddam leaves the stage for a short time and sits with his cohorts in the front row. Puffing on his cigar, he offers Mashadi his place at the centre of the podium. 'Muhyi,' he says, 'you might be more comfortable to rest here for a while. Take the weight off your feet, my friend.'

It is the politeness of the torture chamber. The video ends with Saddam reading out his list of alleged conspirators, ordering any man who hears his name to leave. When one of them won't budge, party thugs drag him out. Another stands, desperately maintaining his innocence. From time to time loyalists stand up to shout their loyalty to the leader, clapping and chanting for his long life. Saddam allows them to speak, playing with his cigar and taking the occasional drag. His expression is cold as he enjoys the moment, watching the fear he has created.

A few days after this meeting came an announcement that twenty-two people had been executed for their part in the alleged conspiracy, including Muhyi Abdel Hussein Mashadi. Accounts of the killings vary, but they all agree that Saddam himself led the firing squad, which was made up of his trusted associates and some of the men he had spared. It was their chance to show loyalty as well as a warning to anyone who planned not to, and it implicated all of them in the new regime's bloody baptism. The men lined up to be killed included Adnan Hussein, deputy prime minister and Saddam's close friend for many years.

Was there a conspiracy? In many ways, it didn't really matter. Saddam, a president with vaulting ambition and without scruples, had points to make. His predecessor had talked to Syria's president Hafez al-Assad about unity between the two countries. Both were run by branches of the Baath Party, which had been founded in Syria to oppose the French occupation that lasted until 1946, before spreading to Iraq and beyond. The Baath ideology revolved around an Arab version of socialism built on pan-Arab unity and opposition to Israel and imperialism. As a new generation of Arab leaders emerged in the 1950s and 1960s, generally in military uniform, the Baath Party provided opportunities and a political voice for young, ambitious outsiders who were looking for a pathway to power: men like Saddam Hussein and Hafez al-Assad.

Pan-Arab unity was a favourite topic of nationalists in the second half of the twentieth century. Perhaps al-Bakr in Iraq and Assad in Syria were serious in 1979 – after all, it is easy to see why both men saw Saddam as a threat. He had been a leader of the coup that installed al-Bakr as president in 1968 and since then had become the regime's strongman, secret police chief and enforcer – a man with no limits in a country whose politics were suffused with violence. His videotaped purge of the Baathist leadership in 1979 was designed to be the clearest possible marker about the way he planned to do business as president of Iraq. At the time, foreign journalists based in Beirut reported that Saddam's real target was a group of potentially powerful dissidents including Muhyi Abdel Hussein Mashadi, who had protested about the brutality with which Saddam's men had crushed a protest by Iraqi Shias.[3]

Saddam Hussein's marker stood him in good stead for years. When I made my first trip to Iraq in 1990, Arabs were still talking about the purge, usually with a mixture of awe, horror, disgust and a weird kind of respect. After all, at least the man knew what he wanted. His image was everywhere. A huge oil painting of Saddam the huntsman, dressed in tweeds on a snowy mountainside, adorned the waiting room of the Iraqi embassy in Amman. In Baghdad there were posters of Saddam the builder, constructing the country; Saddam the jurist, surrounded by books and fair to all loyal citizens; Saddam the soldier, fearless and armed. In Basra, a line of statues of soldiers who looked like his long-lost twins pointed accusingly across the Shatt al-Arab waterway towards Iran.

Saddam's image, naturally, welcomed visitors at Baghdad Airport. Between Iraq's invasion of Kuwait in the summer of 1990, and the following year when the Western allies geared up to attack, it was possible to fly into Baghdad from Amman. But once President Bush announced that Operation Desert Shield had become Desert Storm, the only flights to Baghdad were the kind that dropped bombs. A couple of Iraqi airliners were left rusting on the tarmac at Amman Airport. By the time the Americans reopened Baghdad Airport in 2003, having overthrown Saddam, they were only fit for scrap. During the 1990s, Iraqi Airlines' inflight meal service repurposed itself as a catering company in Baghdad.

In 1991, with no air service, the only way back to report on the war was to drive across the desert from Jordan. A couple of nights before we left for the Iraqi border, I had a quiet dinner with colleagues to celebrate my thirty-first birthday and then wrote a few letters to be opened if I was killed, which I left in my hotel in Amman.

I didn't like the morbid thoughts I'd been having, but in the first week of February 1991 there were good reasons to be nervous about driving to Baghdad. The Americans were bombing the road and had destroyed petrol tankers, which Saddam was sending out to Jordan as a thank you for King Hussein's support. A BBC crew filmed us leaving Amman – ghoulishly, the cameraman said the pictures might be needed for our obituaries.

The Iraqi minders who had been waiting at the border insisted that we drive without lights because of the air raids. We had paid two young Jordanian entrepreneurs a lot of money to rent two vehicles; they sent Palestinian drivers, who took on all the danger with only a small cut of the fee. My BBC colleague Allan Little and I took turns at the wheel as our driver became more terrified and exhausted. Rory Peck, a brave and buccaneering cameraman, drove in the other pick-up, which was loaded with jerry cans containing all our spare fuel, a couple of hundred litres. His driver also became increasingly paralysed with fear as the sun went down, and I couldn't blame him. We sped through Fallujah, the first big town after the desert, as sirens screamed and people rushed to shelters, chivvied by air raid wardens on bicycles. It must have been terrifying for the citizens, but all I could think of was the air raid warden on *Dad's Army* telling Captain Mainwaring to 'put that light out!'

In Baghdad, foreign journalists were all billeted in the Al Rasheed Hotel, at huge expense. A sepia portrait of the young Saddam dominated the large concrete lobby. He may have been looking away from the lens, but his minions were watching us closely. CNN, for some reason allowed by the regime to operate with their own satellite dish and a big team of people, had occupied the bar at the end of the lobby as their newsroom. We assumed the hotel was wired for sound by Saddam's secret police. In muttered conversations, old hands warned that Saddam Hussein would not go easily if the war unseated him.

In Iraq, political turbulence often leads to deaths before deals. Sometimes there are no deals, just deaths. A culture of violence embedded itself after the British created modern Iraq in 1920, growing deeper every time force was used to change the men at the top. Britain joined together three Ottoman provinces – Basra, Baghdad and Mosul – to make Iraq, and while the new country looked coherent on the map, it was born with fractures. Britain imported a king, Faisal Ibn Hussein, from the family that had led the Arab revolt against the Ottomans in the Hijaz, and the country was declared nominally independent in 1932. It was equipped with institutions, including elections and a parliament, but they were a front for the fact that Britain took all the decisions that mattered.

Conflict was built into the system, with violence the currency of power. The British Empire was bloated after the First World War and they could not afford to garrison Iraq properly. In the 1920s, Britain was badly overextended and looking for ways to control its newly acquired possessions on the cheap. Winston Churchill was secretary of state for the colonies and seized on an idea of policing Iraq from the air. The Iraqi tribes were bombed if they rebelled and if they did not pay taxes, while economic violence was meted out to the poor in the cities and the countryside.

The end of the Cold War in 1990 made the invasion of Iraq possible, but the start of it had caused more bloodshed. Hard-pressed workers and peasants were easy recruits for communists in the late 1940s, and government forces clamped down hard – on a single day of demonstrations in 1947, between three and four hundred protestors were shot dead. Communist leaders were executed in public, their bodies left swinging on the scaffold as a message for early-morning commuters.[4] The monarchy tried to create a cult of personality but it was sustained by force, not popularity, until violence swept it away. In 1958 the Iraqi royal family, including twenty-three-year-old King Faisal II and his uncle, the one-time regent turned Crown Prince Abd al-Ilah, were lined up and shot during the coup that ended Britain's system of arm's-length domination. The regent's body was mutilated and dragged through the streets.

The victorious military junta modelled itself on the Free Officers who had ousted the Egyptian king in 1952, and even took their name to grab some reflected glory from the popular Egyptian leader Gamal Abdel Nasser. But Iraq's officers lacked a figure with the stature of Nasser, and attempts at political change descended into bloodshed. On 7 October 1959, Baathists ambushed the president, Abdul Karim Qasim, on Rashid Street, a colonnaded avenue in the centre of Baghdad. They killed the presidential chauffeur, but Qasim escaped with wounds. Among the would-be assassins who made off through the back alleys was Saddam Hussein, limping with a bullet in his leg. Communal and political tensions were high at the time of the failed assassination, and when they overflowed into the streets of Mosul and Kirkuk, hundreds of people were killed. The pattern of political action driven by force continued. When Qasim was finally overthrown in another coup in 1963, he was shot out of hand, with the Baathists who had taken power carrying out what one historian called 'some of the most terrible scenes of violence hitherto experienced in the post-war Middle East'.[5]

Saddam's tactics were no departure – he was simply more effective. The two Baathist dictators, Saddam in Iraq and Assad in Syria, imposed stability by taking ruthlessness to a new level. Internal dissidents were eliminated, either in exile, prison or the grave. It took the US Army to remove Saddam thirty-five years later; such was the strength of Assad's system that his death in 2000 delivered power to his son, Bashar. When Bashar's regime was threatened by a rebellion a decade later, he used his father's tactics to survive.

During the Gulf War of 1991, Baghdad was a city of empty streets, sirens and air raids. When we arrived, the BBC office at the Al Rasheed Hotel was like the *Mary Celeste*, with half-eaten meals abandoned by colleagues who had left in a hurry at the start of the war. We laboured long and hard, first to make the gear work and then to report the biggest story in the world. It was cold; the only electricity came from a generator. We had half an hour of running water a day, but we were lucky – most people in Baghdad had none. The Americans had bombed the power and water grids. When a gurgle in the cisterns announced its arrival in late afternoon, I would fill the bath in my room with water so I could flush the loo with the waste paper bin – I didn't have a bucket – and make myself take a freezing shower.

Baghdad was dark and deserted. Some days, smoke from fires started by the bombs blacked out the sun. A few kebab shops stayed open, but because there was no refrigeration they kept their sheep and cattle alive until they were needed, when a sharp cut across their throat caused lakes of blood to overflow the gutters. The days were chilly. I would sit at a table in the market eating kebabs and drinking sweet tea with Rory Peck, thinking about how we could get at the truth of what was happening. It wasn't easy. A man we interviewed came up and gave a stirring interview praising Saddam, but came back when the camera was switched off. 'That stuff I was telling you – it was all lies . . . We hate him.'

In the evenings, we would sit in our dark office drinking whisky and eating from mysterious self-heating cans and tins of foul Jordanian spam. We were exhausted by the fog of war and the struggle to cut through the censorship. Fuel was scarce, so we kept the generator off as much as possible and played Rory's three audio cassettes on a battery-powered tape player, with Brahms' *German Requiem* becoming the soundtrack to the air raids. One of the great themes of Brahms' masterpiece comes from a biblical quotation, 'Denn alles Fleisch, es ist wie Gras' – all flesh is grass. In a war, life does get scythed away like grass. The Americans even had a bomb called a grass-cutter, which mowed flat everything in its vicinity. When a bomb landed nearby, the whole hotel shook. When the Americans destroyed the conference centre opposite with a couple of cruise missiles, the noise of the explosion knocked me over. But our little team was all young and absorbed by the challenge of what we were doing, so we didn't feel too concerned about the danger.

Even though it was winter, we would leave the windows open to make it harder for a blast to shatter the glass. Gusts of hot wind from explosions blew into the office. Before each one, the bombers and missiles droned across the sky for a few seconds, a warning of what was coming. The Western allies were expecting heavy casualties when the land war began, but they were so much stronger than the Iraqis that the conflict was one-sided, with only hundreds of casualties on the allied side and maybe tens of thousands among Iraqis.

Before the ground war started, the Iraqis let Rory and me drive to Basra, around 350 miles away. In towns deep in the desert, thousands of men in scruffy uniforms ebbed and flowed. They looked cold and hungry, as if they wanted to be anywhere other than waiting to face the might of the most powerful armies on earth. Very few of them seemed to be carrying weapons. I assumed the self-preservation policy of the regime mandated that conscripts would only be given rifles when they were needed. In the distance, when it was dark, I saw a line of inverted cones of fire and the rolling thunder of carpet-bombing across the great plain of scrub and stones, B-52s hitting places and people that the Pentagon had decided to destroy.

Sometimes generals and politicians who wage modern war like to use words like 'clean' or 'precise' to describe the effects of weapons guided by lasers and satellites. In the Gulf War in 1991, the world found out just how accurate such guided weapons could be. It was also the first war that was covered by twenty-four-hour television news. The Pentagon released video footage of its air strikes that was replayed again and again. Sometimes senior officers offered a commentary. In a televised briefing, 'Stormin' Norman' Schwarzkopf, the American general commanding Desert Storm, commentated on a clip of a man crossing a bridge that was in the sights of an American aircraft. 'I'm now going to show you a picture of the luckiest man in Iraq on this particular day – right through the crosshairs.' The man made it across seconds before the Americans destroyed the bridge behind him. It looked like a video game. But it was war, so it wasn't playtime. High explosive kills, whether it is guided by laser or satellite or fired from a First World War howitzer.

I saw that for myself on 13 February 1991 when the Americans used highly accurate modern weapons to destroy a shelter in Amiriyah, a middle-class district of Baghdad. At around four in the morning, the first bomb or missile drilled a neat hole, the size of a garden pond, through a reinforced concrete roof that was at least a yard thick. A web of twisted steel rebar made a grotesque fringe around it, after which another missile followed the first and detonated inside the shelter, killing more than 400 civilians. The blast blew them to pieces or burst their internal organs, starting a fire that burnt the body parts that were left.

I arrived not long after the attack, as rescue workers were pulling out bodies and trying to damp down the fire. Many of the victims were tiny, the burnt fragments of children. Charred remains that looked like twisted pieces of charcoal were still being carried out by emergency crews on stretchers thirty-six hours later. Men who had taken their families to the shelter, leaving them where they thought they'd be safe, surrounded the small open lorries where the bodies were stacked. The crowd was silent, devastated by grief. As a journalist from one of the countries responsible for killing their families,

I half expected to be lynched; but they spoke politely to me, as much mystified as angry. One man said: 'I don't know why they hit children and that is why I lose my wife and my children. I can't say anything more.' Another man protested: 'This is a bomb shelter. You have murdered seven hundred families. This is a ghastly crime, killing the civilians. This proves that whatever was said about liberating Kuwait, it was absolute sham.' I couldn't blame him for his anger. I wondered how an Iraqi reporter would have fared at the hands of a British or American crowd if Saddam's men had killed 400 civilians in London or New York. The Iraqi minders who had tried to fabricate rage about casualties at other bomb sites, government buildings that had long since been evacuated, let reporters and camera crews into the remains of the shelter. Even thirty-six hours later, it was hot enough inside to make you sweat. I poked around the remains of a dormitory, blackened by fire and full of burnt, twisted bed frames.

The corpses were piling up too fast to be taken to the mortuary, which was full. Instead they were deposited at an anatomy lecture theatre. Bodies were left on examination tables, on the floors around them, and on staircases and the raked rows of benches where students once sat. There were so many bodies and blackened fragments that they piled up in the corridors, the entrance hall and the yard outside. A small lorry sat at the gate, full of more dead civilians, with no space to unload them. Men were going from corpse to corpse, trying to identify their wives and children. One man was carrying sooty, bloodstained rings. He had just found his wife's remains and had taken the rings from her fingers.

I reported what I saw, and was amazed when the Pentagon in Washington and the Ministry of Defence in London put out statements claiming that the shelter was a military command centre. Having spent hours exploring the site, I thought that they had made a mistake and were telling crude lies to cover up their error. Soldiers leave traces, ration tins, boots and discarded equipment, but I didn't find any. If the place had been a communications centre, as the Americans and British were insisting, there would have been radios and transmitters, and if they had been ripped out in a hurry there would still have been evidence of wiring and trunking. I was able to go to the lowest level, where the water pumped in by the fire brigade was knee-deep. A layer of fatty crud, which felt like something rendered from hundreds of corpses by fire, floated on the surface. Perhaps it was just the power of imagination, but whenever I laced up those boots afterwards I could smell burnt human fat.

My colleagues in London interrogated my reporting live on air, questioning whether it was possible that the shelter could have contained military communications equipment before being converted to civilian use, but I pointed out that at a time when Iraq was under such pressure, it was more likely that they would be converting civilian facilities to military use.

In Fleet Street, parts of the tabloid press screamed that I was Lord Haw-Haw reborn in Baghdad, a rookie in my first war, broadcasting treachery. My kind and wise editor, John Mahoney, kept the tabloid storm away from me, but one of my rivals loomed out of the gloom at the Al Rasheed Hotel to tell me his bosses had said that my reporting was being discussed at the highest levels in the BBC. His mind games didn't work and I stuck by my story, taking pains to report only what I saw and heard.

On the day the war ended, I was woken by bursts of gunfire and for a moment thought the Americans were attacking Baghdad. Then I realized that Iraqis around the hotel were firing their Kalashnikovs into the air, celebrating a ceasefire. Regime officials were triumphant and relieved. They had survived, and so had the regime.

The ceasefire talks were held in a tented village in Safwan, one of the towns captured by the Americans in south-eastern Iraq. Keen to show the Iraqis who was boss, Norman Schwarzkopf positioned at least forty American tanks on its rim and lined up dozens of helicopter gunships, forcing the Iraqi delegation to run the gauntlet of Apaches to remind them who was boss. It looked tough on TV.

The Iraqis had been crushed on the battlefield but came to the talks with a plan. Schwarzkopf fell for it, although he didn't initially realize what he had done. The head of the Iraqi delegation was Lieutenant-General Sultan Hashem Ahmad al-Tai, whom the Americans respected as a military professional rather than a Saddam loyalist. General Hashem agreed to the American requests and made just one of his own: he asked that government officials be permitted to use helicopters – they needed them to move around, as the

Americans had destroyed so much. Schwarzkopf agreed because, after General Hashem had said yes to so many American requests, 'I didn't feel it was unreasonable to grant one of theirs.'[6] It was careless, naive, deadly negligence.

The Iraqis were right to say the bombing had left their country's infrastructure in ruins – most civilians had no power and no running water – but I had seen for myself how the Americans had preserved crossings and routes they would have needed had they been ordered to press on to Baghdad. Bridges over the mighty Tigris were still standing and the roads were passable; when the regime expelled foreign journalists with only a few hours' notice, we drove out to Jordan along an intact desert highway. In a few places where the road was cratered, we bumped across the flat sand and gravel easily enough.

The helicopters were important because Saddam Hussein had a major rebellion on his hands. Kurds in the north and Shias in the south of the country rose up after the ceasefire because George Bush appeared to have given a clear signal that they should finish the job. On 15 February, Bush appeared at a Raytheon defence plant in Massachusetts and praised the factory as 'the home of the men and women who built the Scudbusters' – by which he meant the Patriot anti-missile system, celebrated at the time as one of the war's wonder weapons. He repeated that Saddam needed to pull his forces out of Kuwait immediately and then, in front of a squad of TV cameras, said, 'There's another way for the bloodshed to stop, and that is for the Iraqi military and the Iraqi people to take matters into their own hands to force Saddam Hussein, the dictator, to step aside.'[7]

Kurds and Shias had risen up before, only to be crushed by Saddam and earlier Iraqi regimes. Bush was not telling them anything they did not want to do, let alone issuing a direct order, but he strengthened a belief that this was their chance. Saddam, after all, had never been weaker.

However, two of their assumptions were wrong. The first was that they would get help from America's fully primed war machine. The other was that following the ceasefire, Saddam's forces had nothing left. They had suffered huge casualties and a humiliating defeat, but Saddam Hussein and his military had plenty of options remaining for dealing with internal rebels once the ceasefire had been signed.

In the weeks after he signed the agreement, in Schwarzkopf's own words, America 'discovered what the son of a bitch had really had in mind: using helicopter gunships to suppress rebellions in Basra and other cities'. He defended his decision to let them fly, but the Kurds and the Shias still believe that it was the helicopters that made the difference. It was a mistake that summed up America's failures in Iraq over the next quarter of a century – all the power in the world does not compensate for knowing an enemy and understanding a society.

News that Saddam's men were killing Shia and Kurdish rebels was slow to reach the outside world. With all foreign correspondents expelled, the regime did everything it could to close the country off, which in 1991 was still just about possible. The headlines were all about the occupation of Kuwait, where smoke from the burning oil wells, torched by the Iraqis as they left, blacked out the sun.

I crossed the border from Turkey back into Iraq alongside Kurdish fighters known as the *peshmerga*. They were relaxed about dozens of Soviet-made mines protruding in places from the soil, promising that we would be fine if we stuck to the path. Hundreds of thousands of Kurds were retreating to the mountains to escape Saddam's savage response to the rebellion. At the Turkish border, they were stopped by lines of commandos wearing their distinctive light blue berets. Instead of turning back to face Saddam and his men, thousands of them sat down where they were, on slopes clogged with mud and shit from people with dysentery. A few had tents, but many had no shelter at all. It was still winter in the mountains, cold and wet. Sometimes it snowed.

On that stretch of the mountain frontier, the only Iraqi Kurds allowed through were those carrying dead bodies. One cold morning I watched a gaunt Kurdish man walk through the mist with a small bundle wrapped in a red blanket. It was the body of his child, who had died in the night. The border was on the crest of a ridge, and a mile or so down a steep slope on the Turkish side was a village with a mosque, where they took bodies. A woman, perhaps the child's mother, tried to dash past the soldiers to follow the man with the bundle, only to be tackled to the ground and sent back to Iraq. Another man, with deep wrinkles and eyes full of tears, left his dead son at the mosque's door, hoping that he would get a decent burial. He arranged the blanket around the body to make sure the toes were covered, as if tucking his son in to keep him warm. Inside, families who had managed to avoid the soldiers and get into Turkey were sleeping in the prayer hall next to piles of wrapped corpses. A television was spluttering away in a corner, broadcasting fragments of life in the outside world that might as well have been another planet.

Back on the Iraqi side of the border, it was easy to see the differences between people from the towns and people from the countryside. I met a man who had worked in the oil business in Kirkuk, who spoke good English, wore Western clothes, had one dead child and was terrified of losing the others. They had abandoned everything in an attempt to escape Saddam Hussein's men, but death followed them into the mountains. An education, a middle-class job and a good grasp of English were not much help there.

The Kurds who were doing best were mostly peasants, wearing traditional clothing that protected them from the cold. The men staked out compounds for their families with twigs and rigged up shelters with plastic sheets. The women had buckets and cooking pots and sent their children out to find firewood. When I walked past their fires, they would offer to share their food, while more educated, less capable people died in the mud.

Eventually, the Americans and the British were embarrassed into dropping aid to the Kurdish refugees in the mountains. The RAF lowered the ramps at the back of their C-130 cargo planes and their men pushed the aid out of the back. I flew with the Americans out of their base at Incirlik in south-eastern Turkey, on a plane carrying bales of battered-looking US Army combat jackets and sleeping bags along with the ubiquitous MREs, meals-ready-to-eat. The packages were strapped to pallets mounted on rails. The pilot opened the ramp at the rear, tipped up the nose of the aircraft, and they slid out and headed for earth.

In a valley deep in the mountains, around 20,000 Iraqi Kurds had gathered at a place called Uzumlu, a few hundred metres on the Turkish side of the border. It was a five-hour drive from our base at the border town of Hakkari and the only vehicle I could find to rent was a Suzuki jeep designed to cruise to beach cafes, not fight through muddy mountain tracks. A lot of the refugees were wearing the US combat jackets that I'd seen dropped from the sky. Young men chased the pallets of aid over the border when they landed in Iraq, ignoring Turkish soldiers with megaphones warning them that they were risking their lives in a minefield. Some were killed. A Kurd sat on a rock and told me, 'I think we will face our fate. We will die one after the other. We've escaped from Saddam Hussein and his death, and we are facing another death here.'

Families without young men to fight for food did very badly. If a lorry carrying supplies arrived at the camp, it would be set upon and stripped in minutes. Many Kurds were dying from exposure and disease. A queue of women holding babies stood waiting outside a tent to see the only doctor. One woman's face was hopeful as she handed over her baby, but she crumpled when the infant was examined and handed back to her. The child had died in the queue.

With the media coverage full of the slaughter of Kurds and Shias, President Bush defended his decision to withdraw without removing Saddam first. He admitted to feeling 'frustration and a sense of grief for the innocents that are being killed brutally', but explained that he did 'not want to see us get sucked into the internal civil war inside of Iraq'. Decisions that made sense in the Oval Office felt callous in the mountains and deserts. Bush and his people had concluded that removing a tyrant by force would not create an easy transition to peace. They had seen Iraq's fault lines and did not want them to crack open. Bush Senior also wanted to send reassuring signals to the Turks, who wanted no concessions to Kurds, and the Saudis, who looked on their own Shia Muslim minority as a potential fifth column for Iran. Some of the critics who believed Bush should have removed Saddam would advise his son, George W. Bush, when he became president nine years later. The catastrophic decision to 'finish the job' in 2003 shows that Bush Senior had a better understanding of the constraints the US faced in Iraq than the second President Bush, who faced the same issues and drew a different conclusion.

Deeper thinking might have saved thousands of Kurdish and Shia lives in Iraq in the months after the coalition's victory in Kuwait. Allowing Saddam space to attack his internal enemies was not an automatic consequence of letting him remain in power. The Bush administration itself reckoned that by April 1991, around one thousand Kurds were dying every day. Around a million and a half Kurds fled, and Saddam's forces are believed to have killed around 20,000 who did not escape in time.

Saddam's actions to preserve his regime had created a serious political problem for Western governments. The Americans, the British and the French were shamed into acting, and a series of resolutions flew through the UN Security Council. It was too late for the Shia rebellion, which was crushed by late March. Although several hundred thousand coalition troops were nearby, the allies decided that helping the Shias was not possible. It was also an area of southern Iraq that could not be reached by foreign journalists, so there was no threat of on-the-spot news coverage, to tarnish the victory in Operation Desert Storm. The Kurds, on TV screens every night, were a different matter. Troops from Bush's coalition were sent across the border from Turkey to protect the Kurds, with military engineers providing shelter and clean water. The government of Saddam Hussein in Baghdad was warned to leave the Kurds alone, and coalition warplanes patrolled throughout the 1990s to make sure he did as he was told.

Without the threat of Saddam's return, Iraq's Kurds were able to start building their homeland. Had Iraqi politics been different, it might have been a state in waiting; it had oil and a certain amount of Western goodwill. Erbil, the capital of Iraq's Kurds, now a modern city with shopping malls, running water and restaurants, was grim and down at heel in 1991. My hotel room was so filthy I couldn't work out the least bad place to put my sleeping bag. In the end I chose the floor, which had more dirt than the bed but fewer visible insects.

A generation after Saddam's purge announced the start of his regime, and more than a decade after a masked executioner ended his life, his regime continues to cast a shadow over Iraq. In Mosul, the country's second city, a grassy mound was a strange, informal memorial, appropriately ugly, to the Iraqi people who had been tortured by their leaders and by the world, standing out in an ocean of broken brick and concrete in the heart of Mosul's old city. The old man who showed me the strange green island said it was caused by American bombing during the war to remove Iraq from Kuwait. We were talking in the spring of 2018, a year after the end of the war to root out Islamic State and twenty-seven years after Desert Storm. Lumpy grass covered the mound, like a dressing over the badly broken bones of an old fight. A few scrubby bushes had new shoots, but destruction from the war against the jihadists still swamped the city. The dead lay where they had been killed, their corpses rotted and shrivelled in the ruins. A few people were moving buckets of rubble by hand, trying to clear patches of ground to rebuild their houses and shops. Mains water and electricity were memories they had turned into jokes, certainly not part of anyone's new lives.

I can still hear Rory's home-recorded cassette of the *German Requiem* hissing through a weak speaker in the BBC office at the Al Rasheed Hotel, as we watched green and red tracer arcing lazily through the sky. The music will always take me back to that war, and to the surprising courtesy of Iraqis whose families had been slaughtered in the Amiriyah shelter. Two years later I was in another war, in Bosnia, when I heard that Rory had been killed filming an attempted coup in Moscow. I played the music and remembered my friend Rory before trips to Baghdad during the long, isolated years that Iraq faced until its next nightmare: invasion, occupation and more war.

4.

Jerusalem: God, Power, Possession and Loss

The first time I visited Jerusalem, I got lost. I'd rented a car and was trying to drive to Bethlehem, which is just down the road, but I took the wrong turning and ended up in a Palestinian village I now know is called al-Azariyeh. In the Bible its name was Bethany, and it was the place where Jesus is said to have raised Lazarus from the dead. But on a dark night in 1991, as I looked for somewhere to turn around, the modern Holy Land intruded, and it is a place without miracles. A group of teenage Palestinian boys waited in an alleyway for an Israeli army jeep to pass and pelted it with stones. I've seen much more violence between Palestinians and Israelis since then, with weapons much more lethal than stones, but the incident was a soft introduction to the hard reality of life in Jerusalem, the 'city of peace' according to the Hebrew meaning of its name. In real life, it is hard to think of a city with a bloodier history.

Jerusalem has been at the centre of more than a century of festering conflict between Jews and Arabs. The tectonic plates of religion and culture come together in the city and when they move, Christians, Jews or Muslims all over the world can feel it. The people who live there, whether they like it or not, find themselves at the sharp end of disagreements that span the globe. On my first trip in 1991, trying to find the road to Bethlehem was the easy bit; Jerusalem is full of wrong turnings, and reporting the Palestinians and the Israelis is a great way to make enemies. What happens in Jerusalem, the things they do to each other, can make people anywhere in the world angry.

In Jerusalem, it always starts with God, with power, possession and loss following close behind. Not all Israelis and Palestinians are religious people, but even non-believers respect and use the power of religious symbols. The best way to start understanding the lure, the sanctity and the toxicity of the city is to go for a walk inside its walls. The Old City is tiny, not even half a square mile, built on a series of steep hills. I used to jog around the outside of the walls in the morning; the gradient, not the distance, was the challenge. Even that was a journey through an intractable conflict. Palestinian women in village dresses would be sitting outside Damascus Gate selling herbs, vine leaves or olives, depending on the season; as Israel built walls and fences after the second Palestinian uprising in the early years of the twenty-first century, fewer of them were able to get into the city. On the opposite side, devout Jews streamed in and out of Dung Gate to get to the Western Wall. Just as the Palestinian women's embroidered dresses showed which village they came from, the headgear and costumes of the Jews revealed their affiliations. Depending on which part of the ultra-Orthodox world they were from, men wore either velvet skullcaps or hats made of black felt, which some swapped for fur on the Sabbath. Their wives covered their hair with scarves, hats or wigs, or sometimes a combination of all three. Religious Zionists wore multicoloured knitted skullcaps. Just as when General Allenby and the British arrived in 1917, Jerusalemites were still identified by their hats.

Up a steep hill further along the wall was Zion Gate, pitted with hundreds of bullet holes from Israel's war of independence in 1948, the event Palestinians call al-Nakba, the catastrophe. Israel declared itself independent on 14 May, as Britain left Palestine. In the months before that, Jerusalem had been a battlefield as Arabs and Jews fought for control. The new Israeli state suffered its only serious defeat in the Old City; its forces were ejected from the Jewish Quarter following a siege, and Palestinians and Jordanians burnt down its synagogues. The following year, the armistice left Israel with all of West

Jerusalem, which had been a patchwork of Arab and Jewish suburbs and villages. Jordan controlled the east and the city remained divided by walls, wire and a strip of no man's land. Until Israel captured the entire city in 1967, the gates in the walls of the Old City facing Israel were closed and barricaded. Streets and alleys were turned into cul-de-sacs by rusting corrugated iron, concrete blocks and barbed wire. Windows in the honey-coloured stone buildings overlooking the other side were blocked up and turned into strongpoints or sniper positions. The only crossing point between the two worlds was known as the Mandelbaum Gate. Diplomats, pilgrims and journalists were allowed to use it, as long as they had the right papers.

The two sides, the Jews and the Arabs, went about their business and the weight of the conflict never lifted. Israelis scrabbled to build a new state while Palestinians mourned the loss of the one they never had. Hundreds of thousands of Palestinians languished in refugee camps, sometimes in sight of homes and fields they had lost, while thousands of new Israeli citizens lived in transit camps for immigrants. Many had been displaced by Arab pogroms and the European Holocaust. In the 1960s, well-off Jordanians and Palestinians motored down from Amman to have lunch at the newly built Intercontinental Hotel on the Mount of Olives, looking across the valley at wealthy Israelis on the terrace of the King David Hotel in West Jerusalem. Palestinians owned houses and businesses on the other side that were by then in the hands of Israelis. Just below the Intercontinental was the Jews' most holy cemetery. Some of the gravestones were desecrated. The Israeli writer Amos Oz, who grew up in Jerusalem, wrote that the landscape was 'pregnant with suppressed violence'.[1]

Another war was certain. When it came, in June 1967, it was not like the hard fighting of 1948. Israel had a lightning victory, sweeping through the whole city and the West Bank, the area of Palestine that had been controlled by Jordan, in less than three days. David Ben-Gurion, by then in semi-retirement but still a big political figure as Israel's founding prime minister, argued that the walls of the Old City should be pulled down to unify Jerusalem, but his suggestion was ignored.

Inside the gates, Jerusalem is dense with a past that shapes the present. In 1998, as Israel celebrated fifty years as a state, I walked into the Old City through Damascus Gate and got talking to a group of middle-aged Palestinian men who were drinking small glasses of sweet tea in the vegetable market just inside the walls. On Israel's significant birthday, I asked them what defeat felt like. Temporary, one of them said. The Crusaders were here for a century, but the Israelis have only managed half that. The men used their version of history to block out what they could see with their own eyes: the Israeli occupation of the land captured in 1967 was deep and determined, and violent resistance had not stopped them. The men took from their history the lesson that staying put was their best strategy; their chance would come when Israel went the way of every other conqueror of Jerusalem. Israelis are just as determined to press the point that they are not going anywhere. Jerusalem, they insist, is the Jews' eternal capital, a place they founded and then prayed and longed for during centuries of exile. That its other conquerors did not stay the course, they say, does not mean that they cannot.

Jerusalem and its holy places sit at the heart of the Middle East like a time bomb. Amos Oz described how the city had swallowed its conquerors: 'Jerusalem', he wrote, 'is an old nymphomaniac who squeezes lover after lover to death before shrugging him off her with a yawn, a black widow who devours her mates while they are still penetrating her.'[2] Jerusalem has had many lovers: not just Palestinians and Israelis, but Jewish kings, Roman emperors, Byzantines, Persians, Muslim caliphs, Christian Crusaders, Mamluks, Ottomans, British and Jordanians.

The holy sites enclosed by the walls are the beating heart of Jerusalem. They make the pulses of believers race, often dangerously. Religious sites should not automatically generate strife, but Jerusalem's uniqueness lies in the fact that three monotheistic world religions dream of the same small area, the power of which lies in the high-voltage fervour generated by nationalist fury and religious passion.

A crucial detail that surprises most people when they see Jerusalem for the first time is that the three religions' holiest sites are just the length of a demonstration away from each other, part of the same confined physical space. The most important place for Muslims and Jews is the most contested piece of ground in the world, a

35-acre compound that was built more than two thousand years ago. It enclosed the Jewish Temple until it was torn down on the orders of the Emperor Titus in 70 CE after the Jews rebelled against Roman rule. Six hundred years later it was chosen as the site of the Dome of the Rock, one of the first and most beautiful Islamic buildings, and al-Aqsa, the holiest mosque for Muslims after Mecca and Medina in Saudi Arabia. In Arabic the area is al-Haram al-Sharif, the Noble Sanctuary, in Hebrew Har HaBayit, the Temple Mount. A short walk away, through a tunnel and an Israeli security checkpoint, is the Via Dolorosa and the greatest Christian shrine, the Church of the Holy Sepulchre.

Around 20 BCE the Jewish king Herod the Great started building a new temple. His labourers dug into the bedrock, levelling out the hilly terrain to create an esplanade that is still there more than two thousand years later. The Ottomans built most of Jerusalem's walls, but stretches of Herod's original survive, stone ashlars weighing hundreds of tons. Some Palestinians prefer to believe that the Jews never had a temple there, despite decisive archaeological evidence. Archaeologists have uncovered the infrastructure of the Jewish city of biblical times, but the Temple site itself has never been excavated. Both religious Jews and Muslims would be outraged. Sending in the archaeologists would be an easy way to set off Jerusalem's time bomb.

The western section of wall, which was part of the supporting structure of the Jewish Temple, is the holiest place where Jews can pray, by custom and by law. Once it was known as the Wailing Wall, the place where Jews would mourn their loss of the Temple, but modern Israel prefers 'Western Wall' – better than a word that is lachrymose and, even worse, weak. For many Israelis, not just the religious, this wall and the Temple Mount are at the core of their claim to the city.

The Christian claim is rooted in the life and death of a dissident Jew. It was an era when would-be Jewish Messiahs drew large crowds as they awaited the Kingdom of God, one of whom was named Jesus. Whether or not he was the son of God is a matter of religious faith. He died on the cross as a Jew, and Christianity emerged gradually; it became the dominant religion in Jerusalem after it was adopted by the Romans. Within a hundred years, pilgrims were visiting the places associated with Christ's life. In the fourth century, the Emperor Constantine built a church to commemorate the resurrection of Jesus on the site of a quarry where Christians believed he had been crucified; it became the Church of the Holy Sepulchre.

In 638, Arab followers of the new religion of Islam besieged Jerusalem. It was a peaceful conquest, at least by the city's blood-soaked standards. Early Muslims faced Jerusalem, not Mecca, to pray. The Quran tells how the prophet Muhammad travelled through the night from Mecca to Jerusalem, flying on a winged horse before ascending to heaven.

Fifty years after the Muslims arrived in Jerusalem, the Umayyad caliph Abd al-Malik wanted to show that Islam was the worthy successor of Judaism and Christianity. He commissioned the Dome of the Rock for the site where the Jewish Temple once stood. It was a triumph, as he intended. The dome rears up above the rooftops, glinting in the sun. In the 1980s, Jordan's King Hussein is reported to have sold a country estate in England to give the dome a new covering of gold leaf. It is architecturally harmonious because its proportions follow mathematical rules. That is where the harmony ends.

Jews had prayed for a return to Jerusalem since the Temple was destroyed, and by building on its ruins Abd al-Malik sent a message that history had moved on. He also had a message for Christians inscribed around the top of arches that support the Dome of the Rock. Sternly, a verse from the Quran reminded them of the oneness of God. Allah could not be split into a Trinity, as Christians believed; neither could he father a son or be resurrected.

Christians, undeterred, continued to pray at their greatest shrine, even when a pilgrimage there could have ended in death or slavery. In modern times, the Church of the Holy Sepulchre is noisy and chaotic, packed with pilgrims elbowing their way to the holiest parts of the sprawling building. The church is shared between the main Christian sects, who each guard their part of it so jealously that disputes between rival clergymen sometimes descend into punch-ups. The distrust is so deep that the same two Muslim families have looked after the great iron keys that lock the church's mighty door ever since Saladin captured Jerusalem from the Crusaders, in 1187. The Christian sects do not trust each other with them.

The indigenous Palestinian Christians have been weakened by centuries of emigration. For a beleaguered community, religious festivals are also statements of national identity and of the Palestinian Christians' right to be there — as they are for Jews and Muslims. The biggest festival is the Orthodox Easter, when at least ten thousand worshippers pack into the church for the ceremony of the Holy Fire. Over more than a thousand years, the crowds have only been prevented from gathering twice — in 1349 during the Black Death, and in 2020 because of the Covid-19 pandemic. They crush together, waiting for the moment when the Greek Patriarch goes into an ugly nineteenth-century stone kiosk known as the Edicule that Christians believe marks the tomb of Jesus. He emerges brandishing two thick handfuls of flaming wax candles, which the faithful believe have been miraculously kindled by the Holy Spirit to mark the resurrection of their saviour. The excitement in the congregation turns to frenzy. They yell and hoot, as noisy as a football crowd, as the flame is passed around the church in clumps of candles, a confusion of thick smoke and melted wax and burnt fingers. Some worshippers rush to the doors and pass the holy fire to worshippers outside, who carry the flame in lanterns to Christian churches in the Old City and the West Bank, and via the airport to Orthodox congregations around the world. Back inside the Holy Sepulchre, I've seen people exhausted by the experience, clutching lit candles, collapsing against the walls. It is religious passion on a grand scale, but for Palestinian Christians it is also a way of reminding themselves, Muslims and Israelis of their rights to the city.

Capturing the Wall on the third day of the Six-Day War in 1967 was a climactic and unifying moment for Israelis. On the final day of the war, as Israel sealed its overwhelming victory by capturing the Golan Heights from Syria, three men went to the Wall to make plans for the future. They were General Uzi Narkiss, who had led the attack on the Old City; Teddy Kollek, the Israeli mayor of Jerusalem; and General Chaim Herzog, the military governor of the West Bank. The Wall was in a narrow alley, separated from the Jewish Quarter by a small, densely packed Palestinian neighbourhood called the Mughrabi, or Moroccan Quarter. The three Israelis decided then and there to demolish the houses and open up a plaza to connect the Wall with the Jewish Quarter. An important Jewish holiday was about to happen, and tens of thousands of Israelis were expected. They needed space, and the crumbling houses of the Moroccan Quarter were in the way. As always in Israel's wars, they knew the world was watching closely and that their actions might only be possible if they worked fast. As Herzog said, 'We were concerned about losing time and the government's difficulty in making a decision. We knew that in a few days it would be too late.'[3]

The Israeli state has made the area around the Western Wall a national as well as a religious shrine. New Israeli paratroopers are sworn in at floodlit night-time ceremonies in the plaza, during which they pick up a Bible and then a rifle. Jerusalem's Jews never stopped praying at the Wall, but the Holy City had not been at the forefront of the minds of the Zionists who had come, mostly from Russia and Eastern Europe, to create a state for the Jews. They were mostly secular and wanted a new start, which meant creating a state populated by a new Jewish archetype: strong and suntanned from manual labour, utterly different to Jews in the countries they had left behind.

The army that captured Jerusalem in the 1960s was dominated by men who had grown up on collective farms that placed as much emphasis on building a nation as they did on growing crops. Mostly they were not religious, but when they reached the Wall they found emotions that they were not expecting and a symbol upon which they could agree. Yoel Herzl, the adjutant of General Uzi Narkiss, was an immigrant from Romania, a survivor of the Holocaust who had never felt accepted by native-born kibbutzniks. But when he saw the Wall, Israel felt like a part of him for the first time. 'From that second,' he told me, 'it took a big part of my heart. I will always be ready to fight for it.'

As Israel grew stronger in the 1960s, American and British military intelligence reported that Israel could beat all its Arab enemies. During the crisis that led to war in 1967, Israeli generals, who were confident they would win, pushed hard against cautious political leaders. General Itzhak Rabin, chief of staff and future prime minister, was caught between the two sides and suffered a temporary nervous collapse that he put down to nicotine poisoning. Israeli civilians were alarmed by blood-curdling threats from Egypt and feared another

Holocaust. The younger survivors of the genocide were still of fighting age. David Rubinger, an Israeli photographer on assignment for *Time* magazine, was with the paratroopers when they reached the Wall; the photographs he took of a scene that left him dazed would become iconic. 'We were all crying. It wasn't religious weeping. It was relief. We had felt doomed, sentenced to death. Then someone took off the noose and said you're not just free, you're king. It seemed like a miracle.'[4] Rubinger was secular, but at that moment he was prepared to believe in miracles. In the eyes of religious Israelis, God had intervened to grant them victory. A bolt of messianic energy turbo-charged a new movement, to complete the Zionist project by settling Jews in their historic homeland of Judea and Samaria. It was the stretch of land that the rest of the world knew as the West Bank, and which many Palestinians called home.

When negotiators were trying to make peace between the Israelis and Palestinians in the 1990s, the Americans suggested that both sides should control their holy sites, with overall sovereignty vested in God. This creative thinking was not sufficient to produce agreement about a place that was so loaded with history, religion and emotion. Perhaps that is why Jerusalem is typically won, held and kept by force. Uzi Narkiss, the general who led the attack in 1967, recorded that Israel's victory marked the thirty-seventh time the city had changed hands violently. Israel's swashbuckling defence minister General Moshe Dayan, famous for wearing an eyepatch, made a deal with the Waqf, the Muslim trust that administers the sacred mosques, that non-Muslims could visit the Temple Mount but not pray there. Dayan was a fierce fighter and Israeli nationalist, but he recognized that the other side existed, whether he liked it or not.

Some Jewish extremists would like to raze the Muslim sites flat and build a third temple. A group called the Temple Mount Faithful have made the incendiary suggestion that the Dome of the Rock and al-Aqsa Mosque are 'signs of Islamic conquest' and should be demolished and rebuilt in Mecca. They are a small group of extremists; but the idea that Jews should have more freedom within the walls of the mosque compound has gained a lot of ground on the Israeli right. Although the government of Benjamin Netanyahu repeatedly denied that it wanted to increase the Jewish footprint on the Temple Mount, more Jewish extremists entered the site during authorized visiting hours to pray while he was in power.

I have never been to a city where history is so important, along with the memory of death. The Israeli writer Amos Elon called Jerusalem a 'necrocracy', a place where the dead have a vote. Religion, power, loss, longing and violence are hopelessly entangled there. The Palestinian poet Mahmoud Darwish, whose work was considered threatening enough by Israel in the 1960s to earn him a spell of house arrest, wrote about being accosted by an Israeli:

> A woman soldier shouted:
> Is that you again? Didn't I kill you?
> I said: You killed me . . . and I forgot, like you, to die.[5]

5.

Guns and Olives

From dawn, lines of people, mostly men, walked through the streets of Ramallah towards the place where Yasser Arafat was going to be buried. Some carried Palestinian flags, others posters with portraits of his face, its stubbly beard framed by his trademark black and white keffiyeh, his headscarf. It was 12 November 2004; Arafat had died in hospital in Paris twenty-four hours earlier. A state funeral had already been held in Cairo and now a helicopter was bringing his body home to the West Bank.

Arafat, leader of the Palestinians since the 1960s, was one of the world's most famous – or notorious – people, depending on your view of Palestinian nationalism. He was the personification of Palestine, its tragedies, struggles and pain, given as well as received. Even his keffiyeh carried a nationalist message. He always wore it pushed back behind his left shoulder and down the front of his chest on the right, broad at the top and tapering towards the bottom, shaped like historic Palestine.

I arrived from Paris, where I had joined legions of journalists outside the Hôpital d'Instruction des Armées Percy, a military hospital in the suburbs where Arafat was being treated for a mysterious blood disease. Many Palestinians believe the Israelis poisoned him, which they deny to this day.[1] The crowds in Ramallah made it hard going to get close to the Muqata, his battered headquarters, once a British police fortress. He had been isolated there in the last three years of his life, blockaded by the Israeli army on the orders of the prime minister, his old enemy Ariel Sharon. In 2001, at the height of the second Palestinian intifada or uprising, Sharon spoke for most Israelis when he called Arafat 'a murderer, a pathological liar'.

Everybody who was there on the day of the funeral wanted to get into the Muqata, as the helicopter carrying Arafat's body, accompanied by the chief mourners, was going to land there. The crowds enveloping the perimeter lurched forward and my face was shoved into the back of a young man's head, his hair crunchy with coconut-scented gel. Near where I was standing, hundreds of men pushed towards a break in the wall made by some Israeli shell or tank and competed to climb over the rubble. I jostled my way in with them. In death as well as life, Arafat was the symbol of the Palestinian struggle for independence, much more than just their leader. The mourners were highly emotional, saying that Abu Ammar, as Palestinians call him, would remain in their minds and their hearts.

The funeral was chaotic, with mourners sending volleys of bullets into the air. Terrible scenarios raced around my head: what if they hit a helicopter, or fell back to earth and killed someone? The disorder was somehow appropriate. Arafat had often tried to create a little tactical confusion.

Frenzied uniformed Palestinian police and soldiers managed to keep a landing zone open, but mourners surged towards the helicopter carrying Arafat's body even while its rotor blades were still moving. The chief Palestinian negotiator Saeb Erekat stood in the doorway of the helicopter, begging the crowd to give Arafat 'the honour he deserves'. Later Erekat also condemned the attitude of Israel and some of its American allies to his dead leader's part in the Palestinian struggle for independence. Many Israelis regarded Arafat as an unreformed terrorist and blamed him for the suicide bombs that had killed hundreds of Israeli civilians in his last few years. 'I'm afraid if Mother Theresa were to be our president, Nelson Mandela were to be our prime minister, Martin Luther King to be our speaker and Gandhi to be our chief negotiator, the Israelis will find a way to link them to terrorism and some voices in Washington will echo that. The question wasn't Arafat,' he said.[2]

The question was the collision between the rights of Palestinians and the success and legitimacy of Zionism, the movement founded in Europe to create a homeland for the Jews in Palestine. Erekat's denunciation came from angry frustration about the reality the Palestinians faced. The creation of an independent state for his people had been Arafat's life's work. He died without achieving it, and by the time Erekat himself died of Covid-19 in 2020, independence looked even further out of reach.

In the 1990s I lived in Jerusalem, not far from a hill called Mount Herzl that is a national symbol of modern Israel. Israelis who have served the state are buried there, in cemeteries with lovingly tended gardens and air that on hot summer afternoons carries the scent of wild herbs, cypress, pine and cedar. Alongside soldiers are the graves of the great and the good of the Israeli state. One of them is Theodor Herzl, the man after whom Israelis named the hill. He was only forty-four when he died, in Switzerland, from heart disease in 1904, and his remains were brought to Jerusalem for reburial in 1949, months after the armistice that ended Israel's war of independence.

After Herzl's only visit to Jerusalem, he wrote in his diary: 'When I remember thee in days to come, O Jerusalem, it will not be with pleasure.' But the new Israeli government needed to strengthen its claim to the city. Herzl was not reburied because he loved Jerusalem, but because he founded Zionism, the political creed that created modern Israel.

Anti-Semitism had deep roots in Europe, and in the late nineteenth century it was flourishing in a continent that was also saturated with nationalism. Herzl was born in Budapest and although he was fully assimilated into Austro-Hungarian society, he was drawn to a new idea emerging in Europe that the Jews were as much a nation as the Czechs, the French or the Germans and therefore deserved their own homeland. Herzl made his living through writing. He reported the trial of Alfred Dreyfus, the Jewish French army officer who was wrongly convicted of spying for Germany and sent to Devil's Island, the notorious French penal colony. Although Herzl's articles and his diaries did not dwell on the fact that Dreyfus was a Jew, he later he wrote an essay titled 'What made me a Zionist was the Dreyfus trial'.[3] For him, the necessity of having a state for the Jews was clear;

the question was where it was going to be. In his book *The Jewish State*, published in 1896, he flirted with the idea that it might be in Argentina and was not enthusiastic about a suggestion by the British government that they might settle Jews in Uganda. For a while Herzl favoured the barren scrub of the Sinai desert, but Eastern European Jews with an attachment to the biblical land of Israel managed to talk him round to the idea of Palestine, then part of the Ottoman Empire.

Herzl was not the first European to discuss Zionism, but he turned it into a big idea and made himself its charismatic leader. In 1897 he organized the first World Zionist Congress in the Swiss city of Basel, declaring triumphantly, 'I founded the Jewish State . . . In five years, perhaps, and certainly in fifty years, everyone will perceive it.' He was only a year out – it was fifty-one years before Israel's declaration of independence.

Zionism's challenge was always that Palestine was not empty. Rabbis who went there after the 1897 Congress cabled back to Europe, 'The bride is beautiful, but she is married to another man.'[4] Herzl's plans caused some alarm in Jerusalem. Yusuf Diya al-Din al-Khalidi, a Palestinian scholar and former mayor of Jerusalem, wrote to Herzl. He expressed his admiration for the Jews, condemned their persecution in Europe and accepted their right to live in Palestine, but asserted that 'brutal circumstances' made it 'folly' for Zionists to plan an entirely new state for the Jews in Palestine, 'an integral part of the Ottoman Empire, and more gravely, it is inhabited by others'.[5]

Herzl's reply showed that as well as being a Jewish nationalist, he was a man of his times. The 1890s were the high point of European colonialism, and he had absorbed the idea that settlement equalled progress. His letter ignored the points that al-Khalidi had made and promised a people's dividend: 'In allowing immigration to a number of Jews bringing their intelligence, their financial acumen and their means of enterprise to the country, no one can doubt that the well-being of the entire country would be the happy result.'

Palestine had well-established Jewish communities long before Herzl formulated his idea of political Zionism, part of the Ottoman Empire's religious mosaic. Although Palestine as a whole was overwhelmingly Arab at the beginning of the twentieth century, Jerusalem had a Jewish plurality. Unsurprisingly, a people whose own presence on the land went back millennia saw Zionism as imposing an alien European creed on their land, but the Jews argued that their claim was older and had greater moral force. Jews had prayed for a return to Jerusalem ever since the Romans destroyed their temple in 70 CE. Synagogues, wrote one eminent rabbi, 'became the home in exile of a scattered people. Every synagogue was a fragment of Jerusalem.'[6]

The Jewish immigrants who arrived in waves from the end of the nineteenth century were unlike the religious Jews who lived and prayed in Jerusalem. The most dynamic, arriving either side of the First World War, had an ideology of Hebrew labour, a belief that the Jews would build a homeland in farming colonies and redeem a lost land with their own sweat and, if necessary, blood. They bought land from absentee Arab landlords, to the consternation of Palestinian farmers who had worked it for centuries, which caused competition and clashes about possession and control. Jewish farmers who employed experienced Palestinian farm workers were encouraged, and sometimes forced, to replace them with Jews.

One of the leaders of the campaign against employing Arabs was David Ben-Gurion, an immigrant from Poland who thirty years later would be Israel's first prime minister. Although the conflict has many other layers, at its heart is a long and violent saga between two peoples competing for one piece of land. From the very beginning, Zionist thinkers discussed the 'transfer' of the Arab population from the land needed by the Jews for their new country. In 1895, Herzl wrote, 'We shall try to spirit the penniless populations across the border by procuring employment for them in the transit countries, while denying them employment in their own country.'[7] The word 'transfer' still surfaces in contemporary debates. For the Zionists, a Jewish majority was a necessity in their future independent state, and it was clear from early on that the Arabs were not going to agree.

By 1929, when Yasser Arafat was born, the conflict was well established. He spent most of his childhood in Cairo and fought in the 1948 war, which ended with Israeli independence. The new state meant catastrophe for the Palestinian Arabs, whose society of farmers, traders and a growing middle class was ripped apart. From Jerusalem in the hills to Jaffa and Haifa on the coast, hundreds of thousands of people lost their homes and possessions. More than

700,000 fled or were forcibly expelled, with only a handful allowed to return. Israel passed laws that transferred the houses, land and businesses of Palestinians into the possession of the new state if the owners were considered to have become absentees; since they were not allowed back to claim them, the result was the mass seizure of Palestinian assets.

The events of 1948 created decades of violence, and their consequences are still felt daily in the Middle East. But conflict had also been built into the British mandate by a single line in the text of the Balfour Declaration; Britain promised to 'view with favour the establishment in Palestine of a national home for the Jewish people', while also making sure 'that nothing shall be done which may prejudice the civil and religious rights of existing non-Jewish communities in Palestine'. The British never managed to contain the tension and outbreaks of violence between Zionist Jews and Palestinian Arabs, with various commissions and enquiries trying and failing to find a way through their conflicting promises.

Under the terms of the mandate the British had from the League of Nations, they granted the Jews in Palestine autonomy to run their own affairs and police their own communities, giving them an opportunity to prepare for the time when they were given – or could seize – independence. The Arabs were a different matter. When they revolted against British rule and Jewish nation-building in 1936, they were crushed with the tried and trusted methods the British Empire used against recalcitrant subjects: executions ordered by judges, or summary killing by troops, attempts to divide and rule, and the authorization of the punishment of civilians with draconian emergency laws – which Israel later inherited and used.

The revolt convinced the British that the two communities could not live together. In July 1937, a Royal Commission headed by Lord Peel recommended partitioning Palestine into two states; around one-third of the land would be given to the Jews and the rest to the Arabs, with Britain retaining control of Jerusalem and a corridor to the sea. Sixty years later, during the failed peace process of the 1990s, a 'two-state solution' with a territorial split much less favourable to Palestinians was proposed by would-be peacemakers. In 1937, Palestinians outnumbered Jews, and Peel decided that 200,000 Arabs would have to be moved from the area that was to be allocated to the Jewish state.

When the Arabs rejected this plan, Ben-Gurion, the Zionist leader, took a longer view. Borders more acceptable to Zionism would come later – the important thing was that the British had recognized the principle of a Jewish state and had proposed moving the Arabs out of it. Ben-Gurion angrily rejected the next set of British ideas in 1939, which rejected partition and instead proposed a homeland for the Jews within an independent Palestine shared by the two sides. To create what Britain believed would be a workable balance, it proposed another five years of Jewish immigration, until Jews made up around one-third of the total population. After that, Palestinian Arabs would be able to veto the arrival of any more Jews. Britain's battle with the Zionists was sharpened by the moral pressure to accommodate refugees from Nazi persecution. During the Second World War, the most prominent Palestinian leader, the Grand Mufti of Jerusalem Haj Amin al-Husseini, allied himself with Germany, hoping in vain that Hitler would attack the Jews and the British in Palestine.

After the Second World War, Britain was bankrupt, exhausted and in decline. The Holocaust had resulted in unprecedented sympathy for the Jewish people, and British attempts to turn back refugee ships made headlines and enemies. British forces in Palestine fought Jewish militias, hitting back hard after the bombing of the heavily guarded British headquarters at the King David Hotel in Jerusalem in 1946, which killed ninety-one people, Jews and Arabs as well as British. But they never imposed on Jews the repression they had used against Arabs in the 1930s.

The British Empire was in full retreat; compared to the momentous decision to quit India, it was not a big step for the government to renounce its mandate to rule Palestine and hand the problem to the newly established United Nations. In November 1947 the UN voted to partition Palestine into two states, with Jerusalem and its holy places under international control. The Arabs rejected the idea, while the Zionists accepted it.

Both sides knew that the departure of the British meant war, but the Jews were better prepared than the Palestinian Arabs. Their leaders created effective fighting units, brought in more weapons and ammunition and even organized a fledgling air force. By comparison, the Palestinian militias were disorganized, badly armed and weakened by the damage done by the British in the 1930s. Their best commander, Abd al-Qadir al-Husseini, was killed in a key battle on the road to Jerusalem in April 1948. Palestine was deep in civil war in the months before the last British troops drove their armoured vehicles onto ships at Haifa. Over footage of relieved soldiers marching up gangplanks on 14 May 1948, bringing Britain's unhappy three decades of rule to an end, even the usually gung-ho Movietone newsreel commentator had to concede that 'the last British troops leave Palestine, and very few of them could have been sorry'.[8] The same day, David Ben-Gurion declared the independence of Israel in Tel Aviv.

Its Arab neighbours invaded to try to destroy the new state at birth. The Israelis faced a fight for survival, as they were under attack by the Arab invaders from all sides. In terms of numbers, the two sides were well matched. The Israelis won because they were better armed, educated, organized and led than their invaders, with more friends abroad. Just three years after the end of the Holocaust, the Zionists were ready to die to grab their chance of a state. The Arabs were disunited, suspicious of each other, and unwilling to coordinate their plans. King Abdullah of Jordan did not want the Palestinians to have their own state. He had his own plan to absorb parts of Palestine populated by Arabs into Jordan.[9]

Like all wars, it was a brutal business. In April 1948 two of the war's most notorious massacres happened in the space of a few days. Jewish forces attacked Deir Yassin, a Palestinian village on the edge of Jerusalem, killing 110 people. A few days later, a Jewish medical convoy was ambushed on the road to a hospital in Jerusalem, killing seventy-nine. More than seven decades later, more details are emerging from Israeli archives of several dozen massacres by Israeli forces as they advanced, expelling thousands of Palestinians from their homes. They include accounts of Arab prisoners who surrendered under white flags being shot out of hand, of massacres of civilians, and other brutality, including rape. Some Israeli ministers expressed their horror at what was happening in cabinet meetings of the new state. One of them called it a 'plague . . . all our moral foundations have been undermined.' Ben Gurion, the prime minister, shut down attempts to investigate the killings.[10]

Deir Yassin was the most notorious massacre, but it is clear that all of them accelerated the flight of Palestinians. In July 1948 Israeli troops forced virtually the entire populations of the towns of Ramle and Lydda (renamed Lod by Israel) from their homes at gunpoint. Yitzhak Rabin, then an officer in his twenties, led the forces who carried out the evictions. Around 250 Palestinians were killed in the assault on Lydda, including dozens of unarmed detainees who were being held in the church and the mosque. Rabin was not proud of what he did but he considered it necessary; as he later said, 'we could not leave Lod's hostile and armed populace in our rear'.[11] In 1995, when Rabin was prime minister, a Jew assassinated him for attempting to make peace with the Palestinians.

In 1948, Israel was the stronger side. Its Arab enemies were able to inflict many casualties, but they were incapable of winning a war against a determined adversary that was prepared to do anything in pursuit of victory. Shimon Peres, later prime minister and the father of Israel's nuclear force, wrote a book called *David's Sling* about the rise of the Israeli armed forces. He started his career as a young protégé of David Ben-Gurion, working indefatigably to buy weapons and ammunition for the 1948 war, and promoted the idea of a Jewish David against an Arab Goliath. It was far from accurate, but it helped with Israel's image in the West.

Palestinians call the defeat the Nakba, the catastrophe. Its details still cause fury, and the memory of 1948 is a fundamental driver of the conflict. Many Israelis refuse to accept clear evidence that so many Palestinians were forced out, clinging to a belief that they were ordered to leave by their leaders. The events of 1948 turned an Arab majority in the land that became Israel into a Jewish one. David Ben-Gurion put it succinctly: Israel was 'a captured land' and 'war is war'.[12] He had no scruples about doing what was necessary to win.

Neither did Yasser Arafat. He was one of a group of Palestinian nationalists who founded a movement known as Fatah that had the aim of destroying what they condemned as the colonialist occupation of Palestine. He did not care that the Israelis were much stronger – he wanted to take them on. Some Palestinians called him the 'madman'.[13] His first attacks, in the mid-1960s, were no more than pinpricks. His moment came in 1967, in the months after Israel inflicted the crushing six-day defeat on the armed forces of Egypt, Jordan and Syria. As Israelis settled into their occupation of the West Bank, including East Jerusalem, Arafat took the fight to them, collecting discarded weapons from battlefields, moving round in disguise and organizing hundreds of attacks. Israel hit back in 1968 with a major military operation at the Karameh refugee camp in Jordan, which had become a big Fatah base. At least twenty-eight Israelis, sixty Jordanians and one hundred Palestinians were killed in a day of fighting. The battle established Arafat's legend and put him on the cover of *Time* magazine. The young revolutionary gave countless interviews while dressed in his combat jacket and keffiyeh, with stubble and sunglasses. The story that accompanied the *Time* cover, published in December 1968, reported that Arafat was 'enthusiastically portrayed by the admiring Arab press as a latter-day Saladin, with the Israelis supplanting the Crusaders as the hated – and feared – foe'.[14] The writer captured the essence of his lifelong leadership style.

> When a guerrilla comes in to report a successful raid, Arafat's eyes, bulging almost to the panes of the dark glasses he wears day and night, dance with delight. He speaks softly and turns aside all questions about himself: 'Please, no personality cult. I am only a soldier. Our leader is Palestine. Our road is the road of death and sacrifice to win back our homeland. If we cannot do it, our children will, and if they cannot do it, their children will.'

Arafat did not mean what he said about a cult of personality. It was a crucial part of how he increased his grip on Palestinian nationalism. He created one of the most recognizable political brands in the world. Posters of him appeared wherever there were Palestinians, who had never had a leader with his charisma. He was a living, fighting antidote to the dull and defeated generation that he succeeded. Thousands of recruits signed up to join armed Palestinian guerrilla groups, including many young men who had grown up in refugee camps surrounded by stories of the Nakba, with their elders venerating bunches of iron keys for lost homes as if they were holy relics. During the ethnic cleansing of Lydda and Ramle in 1948, an Israeli intelligence officer called Shmarya Guttman watched as long lines of Palestinians were forced to walk from their homes at gunpoint until they had crossed the front line into Jordanian-held territory: 'Occasionally you encountered a piercing look from one of the youngsters . . . and the look said: we have not yet surrendered. We shall return to fight you.'[15] These were the men who queued up to fight for the Palestinian Liberation Organization twenty years later.

Arafat caught the imagination of Arabs, and their governments provided generous funds. His activism was not what Egypt's President Nasser had planned when he founded the PLO. He wanted to use it to control Palestinian nationalists, not to let them loose. Nasser wanted to decide when to confront Israel, but when war came in June 1967 it was another disaster for the Arabs. Arafat turned the PLO into his own vehicle for confronting the Israelis; by the summer of 1969 he was its chairman, and Fatah was its biggest faction. He used the PLO as an umbrella to force a degree of unity on the other Palestinian factions, to campaign for international recognition and to fight Israel. Fatah and the other factions shot, bombed and hijacked their way into the headlines, killing civilians as well as the military and the police. In 1972, Fatah gunmen calling themselves 'Black September' killed eleven Israeli athletes and a German policeman at the Munich Olympics.

The Middle East was at boiling point, and another full-scale Arab–Israeli war happened in October 1973. Syria and Egypt launched a surprise attack when Israel had closed down for Yom Kippur, the most important Jewish holy day. Intelligence reports that it was coming had been ignored; the crushing defeat Israel had inflicted in 1967 had induced hubris in its leadership. Israel narrowly came out ahead, while Egypt still considers the war a victory.

The war once again demonstrated that the Arab–Israeli conflict was a battlefield for the superpowers, who set up airlifts to support their Middle Eastern allies. In Washington, DC, the war coincided with the Watergate scandal that submerged President Richard Nixon and his administration. The moment of maximum danger for the superpowers came when Washington believed that the Soviet Union might intervene in the war.

As the crisis deepened on the evening of 24 October 1973, President Nixon was asleep in the residence at the White House, possibly drunk, or, as Henry Kissinger, the secretary of state, tactfully called it, 'distraught' about the wreck of his career. Kissinger and Alexander Haig, Nixon's chief of staff, decided not to wake him for the crucial meeting in which they decided to move the US military, including the nuclear strike force, to DEFCON 3, indicating maximum readiness for war.[16]

Arafat's ruthless pursuit of Palestinian freedom shaped Palestinians' views of themselves as well as the way they were seen abroad. He was also a pragmatist who became more aware with the passing years that a bigger political strategy was needed alongside the fight. Many Palestinians were faced with the same inner decisions. Was it more effective to use reason to persuade the world that their cause was just, or to pick up guns like revolutionaries in Algeria, Vietnam or Cuba? At his most effective, Arafat used both tracks, making headlines around the world for the Palestinian cause while also sealing his position as the human embodiment of Palestinian hopes for independence. His big moment came in 1974, when he was invited to address the United Nations in New York. Arafat swaggered into the General Assembly wearing a cream suit, keffiyeh and dark glasses to deliver his most famous lines: 'I come to you bearing an olive branch in one hand and a freedom fighter's gun in the other. Do not let the olive branch fall from my hand.' He repeated it three times.

Arafat was offering Israel a choice of peace or war, and the General Assembly gave him a standing ovation – though he also had plenty of enemies among Arab leaders. Jordan's King Hussein had fought a war against the Palestinians in 1970 when they looked close to taking over the country. For Israelis, Arafat was a terrorist, and his olive branch was a joke. In 1982 they invaded Lebanon, where the Palestinians had established what amounted to a mini state after they were moved on from Jordan. Arafat was forced into another exile, in Tunis. He sided with President Saddam Hussein after the invasion of Kuwait in 1991, appearing in Baghdad during the war to offer support against the American-led coalition. Every time Arafat, complete with keffiyeh, khaki jacket and entourage, moved through the halls of the Al Rasheed Hotel in a chaotic procession, journalists tried to ask questions. My plan was to corner him in a narrow corridor that was lined with the plate-glass windows of the hotel's barber. His bodyguards swept me aside and I was slammed into the window so decisively that I thought I might end up being thrown through it, surrounded by broken glass.

Arafat's decision to support Saddam was a major reason why the Americans did not include him in a peace initiative after their victory in 1991, which began with a conference in Madrid. But then another, secret track, organized by the Norwegians, changed the equation. For a while, the vision of a Palestinian state and an end to decades of conflict seemed to be coming into focus – until assassination, the killing of civilians and a renewed fight for the land ended that hope for another generation.

6.

Tell Them He's Dead

Jerusalem is high in the hills and its winters are short and cold, but Jerusalemites treat them as a nasty surprise. We had rented a house in West Jerusalem, the side of the city that has been part of Israel since 1948. It was cold and I needed a heater. Jewish Jerusalem shuts down during the Sabbath, from Friday evening to Saturday evening, so I drove to East Jerusalem and bought one. Gas in Israel and the West Bank comes in cylinders; when the Israeli gasman turned up at home with new ones for the cooker, I asked him for one for the heater too. He took a look at it. Impossible, he said. I sell Jewish gas and you need Arab gas. He meant that the East Jerusalem heaters still had the type of fittings they used in Jordan, almost thirty years after the Jordanians lost the city. The Israeli ones were different.

I carried the empty cylinder around in the car for weeks, trying to find time to go to a Palestinian gas dealer in East Jerusalem. When I saw one in Ramallah in the West Bank, the problem still wasn't solved. I can't sell you gas, he said. You have Israeli gas. We sell West Bank gas. The problem this time was the colour of the cylinder. The cylinder that was delivered to my house was painted Israeli blue. East Jerusalem was annexed by Israel after it was captured in 1967, so its cylinders are also blue. The West Bank was also occupied but was not annexed to Israel, so its cylinders were silver, but the Ramallah gasman was prepared to repaint my cylinder to make it West

Bank gas. I drove back through the checkpoint into Israel and a few hundred yards later, I overtook an army jeep. Then I saw it in the rear-view mirror, accelerating fast. I let it pass, but it screeched to a halt and a couple of soldiers leapt out, pointing their rifles. They had spotted I was taking West Bank gas into Jerusalem, and that made me a security risk. It might have been a bomb. When they realized I was just a dumb foreign journalist, they relaxed and made me promise to get the cylinder painted the right colour.

Every part of life was touched by the conflict. It was exhausting. It might have been more fun to live in Tel Aviv, a hedonistic, mostly secular city on a Mediterranean beach. In Jerusalem winters I've scraped the ice off my car only to find an hour later that people in Tel Aviv are in short sleeves. Israelis who live in Tel Aviv sometimes say that it's easier to forget the conflict, or ignore it, but Jerusalem is the opposite. Although I grew to love it along with all its imperfections, the hatred in the city was oppressive. Everything was infected by struggle and conflict, even the gas. At low points, whenever I drove past Ben Gurion Airport and saw the tailfin of the next British Airways flight to London, I fantasized about boarding.

Peace ought to be the answer. In the 1990s, an attempt was made to end the conflict. Had it succeeded, hatred and suspicion would not have evaporated overnight. But a fleeting glimpse of a better life meant that when it failed, the removal of hope made everything worse. Years of negotiations, meetings, memos, draft texts, summits and agreements were given a deceptively smooth name: the peace process. It took important steps, but did not get close to overcoming everything that makes the conflict enduring and toxic.

The peace process emerged from the end of the Cold War and an explosion of Palestinian anger that swept away any complacency that they were resigned to living under a military occupation. The uprising that began the next phase in the conflict did not come from Yasser Arafat, who was struggling to energize Palestinian nationalism from his distant exile in Tunis. It started in December 1987, after an Israeli truck collided with a car in occupied Gaza, killing four Palestinians. Years of resentment ignited. The Arabic word for it, *intifada*, also stuck in English. Images of Palestinian children throwing stones at Israeli tanks became emblems of oppression and put the conflict back on the world's agenda.

The end of the Cold War and victory in the war with Iraq convinced President George Bush that a new era was there for the taking. As he basked in victory in 1991, Mikhail Gorbachev was fighting for the survival of the Soviet Union. He managed to ride out an attempted coup in the summer, but the USSR was doomed, and the hammer and sickle flag was lowered over the Kremlin for the final time on the last day of that year.

Bush, president of the world's only superpower, had unprecedented freedom to act. Days after the end of the Gulf War, on 6 March 1991, he told a joint session of the US Congress in Washington, DC that the planet was full of new possibilities: 'We can see a new world coming into view. A world in which there is the very real prospect of a new world order.' It would start, he said, with peace in the Middle East: 'The time has come to put an end to Arab–Israeli conflict.'[1]

It would be done by swapping land for peace. Israel would give up territory it had captured in the 1967 war – Bush did not specify how much – in return for security and recognition, while Palestinians would get 'legitimate' political rights. Equating Palestinian political rights with Israeli security was a big change for an American president. Bush had based the legitimacy and legality of the war with Iraq on UN Security Council resolutions; now it was time to respect the key resolutions passed at the end of the Arab–Israeli wars of 1967 and 1973.

Some Security Council resolutions are straightforward, like the ultimatum to Iraq to leave Kuwait or face the consequences. Others are compromises and require creative drafting. Resolution 242, passed after the 1967 war, is ambiguous because of the absence of a three-letter word, 'the'. The text says the 'acquisition of territory by war' is inadmissible and calls for the 'withdrawal of Israel armed forces from territories occupied in the recent conflict'. The use of 'territories' rather than 'the territories' has spawned more than half a century of debate. The resolution states clearly that belligerents should not be allowed to keep territory they have seized, but Israel and its supporters highlight the absence of the word 'the' before 'territories' as proof that they can keep some of it.

In 1984, Lord Caradon, the British diplomat who drafted the resolution, said that he'd had 'constant discussions' with the rest of the Security Council including Muhammad Farra, a Palestinian who was Jordan's ambassador, and Abba Eban, Israel's foreign minister. Eban had warned about the dangers of occupation – holding onto the territory captured in 1967 was for him 'not a guarantee of peace but an invitation to early war'.[2] According to Caradon, 'we all agreed that the occupation was holding up any prospects of future peace'.[3] He said he had expected some border adjustments, but it is clear that the absence of the definite article was not intended to give Israel permission to carry out a vast programme of land confiscation and Jewish settlement that began in 1967 and continues more than half a century later.

The Americans went ahead with a peace conference in Madrid in 1992; its main achievement was to establish the principle of negotiation. While follow-up talks went on, parallel secret meetings between Israelis and Palestinians started in a castle outside Oslo. Norwegian officials performed a psychological high-wire act to keep them talking. One of them, a diplomat called Mona Juul, recalled that 'A huge part of their lives depended on the outcome of these negotiations, not only for the representatives, but for their whole people. It was very emotional as they worked around the clock, sometimes bursting out in the middle of the night, yelling, "This is hopeless, I can't stay here any more."'[4]

The talks were labelled the Oslo Process, and they led to a deal, which was signed on a sunny day on the lawn of the White House in September 1993. President Bill Clinton beamed and clapped as Yasser Arafat shook hands with Israel's prime minister, Yitzhak Rabin, and its foreign minister, Shimon Peres. It was not perfect, but it was an agreement, which in the long struggle between Israelis and Palestinians was a moment of real hope.

The first phase of Oslo allowed conditional Palestinian self-rule in Gaza and gradually in cities and towns in the West Bank, beginning with sleepy Jericho in the Jordan Valley. Arafat made a triumphant return from exile to preside over a new headquarters in Gaza. The idea was that the Israelis and Palestinians would start with deals on the small stuff, to build enough goodwill to get them through the really difficult problems: what to do about Jerusalem, Palestinian refugees, and how to work out the border between Israel and an independent Palestine. The objective was two countries – the two-state solution. It was controversial and difficult because it involved making concessions and accepting that the other side had rights, too.

Two years later, the process that had started with such hope was under severe pressure from Palestinians and Israelis who believed it was a wrong-headed, dangerous betrayal. Measured Palestinian critics warned that Arafat had given Israel the gift of recognition in return for a basket of illusions that allowed Israel to continue colonizing the occupied territory that Palestinians needed for a state. Palestinians in militant Islamist movements set about trying to wreck the Oslo Process by sending suicide bombers to kill Israeli civilians.

Israeli faith in the chances of peace declined with every Palestinian attack, which was the intention of the men who sent the bombers. Israeli militants were whipped into a fury by the prospect of giving occupied land to the Palestinians. An early flashpoint was Hebron, in the heart of the occupied West Bank, which had an especially militant Jewish settlement in the heart of a big Palestinian city. On 25 February 1994, a Jew called Baruch Goldstein burst into the Cave of the Patriarchs, the site of the tomb of the prophet Abraham and his family and the holiest site in Hebron for Jews and Muslims. He opened fire with an automatic weapon, killing twenty-nine worshippers and wounding more than one hundred before he was beaten to death by men he had not been able to kill. The Oslo Process was damaged by bloodshed, but it went on. Rabin and Arafat went back to Washington at the end of September 1995 to sign the second part of the Oslo agreement, with Bill Clinton as their witness.

On 3 November, as Jewish Jerusalem was closing down for Shabbat, I stopped my car at a red traffic light near the King David Hotel in Jerusalem and a demonstrator shoved a leaflet through the open window on the passenger side. Boaz Paldi, an Israeli colleague, read it out as the lights turned green. A big rally was planned for the central square of Tel Aviv the following night, to support the peace process. Boaz asked me if I wanted to go, but I wasn't very interested. The hope and fanfare of the handshakes on the White House lawn had faded into the hard graft of negotiations. We were expecting guests for dinner on Saturday and I had done a lot of stories about the peace process. I told Boaz not to worry, quipping that it would only be a story if the prime minister was shot. A BBC colleague, Asher Wallfish, had told me a few weeks earlier that the Israeli security service had briefed the Hebrew press about talk of assassinating Yitzhak Rabin. He said they weren't taking it too seriously, putting it down to right-wing chatter rather than hard planning.

In Israel, right and left in politics are a measure of how much land and control Israelis are prepared to concede to Palestinians. Left-wingers offer more, right-wingers offer less, or nothing. This divide goes back to the 1920s. The roots of the Israeli far right lie in the Revisionist movement, which was founded in 1925 by Ze'ev Jabotinsky, a Zionist writer born in Russia who had established Jewish units in the British army in the First World War. Jabotinsky believed that the Jewish homeland should be on both sides of the River Jordan – in other words, including present-day Israel, Gaza and the West Bank, as well as much of the modern kingdom of Jordan on the East Bank. In the 1920s, the other extreme of the *yishuv*, the Jewish community in Palestine, pushed for a binational solution, which would mean one state for two peoples. By the end of the twentieth century the far left was a tiny minority while Jabotinsky's heirs were thriving, driven on by what Abba Eban, foreign minister in 1967, who was thoroughly secular, called 'great gusts of theological emotion' generated by the return of the Jews to their biblical homeland, the area known as the West Bank.[5]

I was having dinner with some journalist friends in our house on Saturday night, 4 November 1995, when all our pagers erupted with messages that the prime minister had been shot and was on his way to hospital. At first Rabin was conscious, telling his driver and bodyguard that the wound was not too serious. As he lost consciousness, the panicking driver, who didn't know Tel Aviv, got lost and had to pick up a policeman to direct them to the hospital. The dinner party broke up in seconds. I rushed to our studios in Jerusalem and did a short report with the few things we knew. Then I sat in a studio in front of a camera, wired to a microphone, being fed scraps of information as they emerged. While I was doing another live update, I could see my colleague Boaz swapping intense whispers with the Israeli cameraman, who was listening to Israeli army radio on his headphones. Boaz advanced on me. 'He's dead,' he mouthed, getting closer. 'Tell them he's dead.' He was so near to the desk that I thought if I didn't say something, he would. So I reported to millions of BBC viewers around the world that Rabin was dead.

Rabin's assassin was a Jewish extremist, Yigal Amir, who killed him because he believed that his decision to trade land for peace made him a traitor to the Jewish people. Rabin had spent the evening on stage at the rally in front of Tel Aviv City Hall alongside Shimon Peres, his longtime political rival, who had helped to persuade him to embrace the idea that peace was possible with the Palestinians. Peres and the rally organizers were worried that Israelis, increasingly frightened by attacks by Palestinian suicide bombers, were losing faith in the idea. A low turnout would have damaged their cause. Some of Rabin's advisors were worried that standing alongside peace campaigners, who many Israelis felt were soft on the Palestinians, might damage his reputation as Mr Security. On the night, though, the square was packed. Rabin, a gruff former soldier, even did his best to sing along with the Song for Peace, the anthem of Israel's peace movement.

Rabin made a quick exit from the stage and walked down a flight of steps to street level, where his car was waiting. He was about to get in when Yigal Amir shot him in the back. Rabin's security team had not cordoned off the area, which later caused a string of conspiracy theories. Amir had been casually waiting close to the car, chatting to security men who had challenged him. A slim young Israeli, Amir did not register as a threat with bodyguards, who were looking for suspicious Palestinians, but his T-shirt covered his Beretta 84F semi-automatic pistol. He had loaded it with hollow-point ammunition, which expands inside the victim and causes more damage than conventional bullets. Amir killed Rabin because he believed he was putting Jews in danger by turning land over to the Palestinians that had been given to the Jewish people by God.

Rabin's decision to back the Oslo agreement had made him a target for fierce political attacks from right-wingers who believed he was giving away not just their security, but their birthright as Jews. He faced daily abuse and accusations of treachery, and was portrayed on posters in Nazi uniform. Rabin's supporters believed the leader of the opposition, Benjamin Netanyahu, was inciting and rabble-rousing against him; Netanyahu chose his words carefully, but was present at rallies where others defamed and threatened the prime minister.

It was clear that the assassin wanted to kill the peace process as well as Rabin. I reported on the night of the assassination that 'he was the leader Israelis trusted most with their security. Without him, concessions to the Palestinians would have been unworkable. This is a defining moment for Israel and for the peace process.' From that night, hopes of peace died a slow and steady death, just as Amir had intended. No twentieth-century political killing was more successful. In his first interrogation following his arrest, Amir toasted his own achievement. He told the police, 'I approached him before he got into his car and shot him with three bullets.' Two of them hit Rabin, ripping into his spleen and puncturing both lungs, while the other wounded a bodyguard. Amir's interrogators asked him if he had any regrets about the murder. 'God forbid,' he responded. His plan was to kill Rabin and 'silence him politically'.[6]

Amir said during his interrogation that the foreign minister, Shimon Peres, who along with Rabin and Arafat was awarded a Nobel Peace Prize for Oslo, had been a secondary target – killing Rabin was what mattered. The vitriol had not stopped most Israelis believing that Rabin would never let them down. He had been a national hero since his twenties, when he commanded an elite unit in the 1948 war of independence. By 1967 he was chief of staff, commanding the armed forces that crushed Jordan, Egypt and Syria in six days. Reluctantly, he had agreed that Israel's future depended on peace; if he said a deal was worth doing, it had a chance.

In the early hours of the morning after Rabin's murder, Shimon Peres convened the Israeli cabinet. Every face showed their horror at the killing and the daunting scale of the task that remained. If Rabin had lived, the Oslo Process might still have failed – after all, it had serious flaws for both sides. Some Israelis argued that the Palestinians would never accept a Jewish state. They didn't trust Arafat and loathed Hamas and Islamic Jihad, two groups that wanted to destroy Israel. Many Palestinians accepted Israel's existence but rejected Oslo as a bad deal, arguing that Israel was deceiving them with token concessions while it tightened its grip on the occupied territories.

Both Palestinian and Israeli sceptics found plenty that reinforced their fears in the tumultuous years that followed. Oslo was flawed, but it was all they had, and until Rabin was killed it had been working. No one has had a better idea about peace than splitting the land between Israelis and Palestinians – it goes back to Lord Peel's Royal Commission in 1937.

Rabin and Yasser Arafat were enemies who seemed to be turning mutual hatred into the beginnings of a grudging respect. Rabin's widow received Arafat at her home after the assassination. Allowing him to travel to Tel Aviv was an unprecedented gesture by the Israelis. For the only time I could remember, Arafat allowed himself to be photographed bald and bare-headed, with no keffiyeh or military forage cap, as he sat with Leah Rabin talking about his shock at 'an awful and terrible crime against one of the brave leaders of Israel and the peace makers'. World leaders came to Rabin's funeral pledging redoubled efforts for peace, while across Israel, young people lit candles and wrote poems about a man many had taken for granted.

The Oslo peace process staggered on for a few years, mainly thanks to the energy of American negotiators. In the last months of Bill Clinton's presidency, an ill-conceived summit was held at Camp David, the US president's hideaway in the hills of Maryland. By July 2000, the negotiators on either side of the table knew each other well, sharing meals and even becoming friends. As the talks floundered, the US secretary of state Madeleine Albright tried to change the mood. To relax the delegates, she showed two films – *Gladiator* and the US submarine film *U-571* – but it didn't work. The summit ended in failure, ushering in a second intifada and years of violence.

A generation on, Palestinians are disunited and Israelis are more right-wing. The loudest voices on both sides come from those who believe they are doing the will of God, not those who are trying to find give and take on otherwise intractable issues. Attempts to revive the peace process during the Obama administration failed; Israel's determination to keep settling its citizens in the occupied territories in defiance of international law, escalating Palestinian violence and the built-in violence of the occupation, sucked out trust and hope. A generation after Oslo, it is often said that the chances of a two-state solution have disappeared because Israel has taken so much of the land Palestinians wanted for a state. Perhaps if the will was there it could still be done, but it seems not to exist. Perhaps Jerusalem, and the land they both want, can never be bargained away. If there was ever a moment for peace, it came and went.

7.

Death on the Nile

Some journalists spent a lot of time trying to track down Osama bin Laden, but I wasn't one of them. On one of the rare occasions that I hit the Bin Laden trail, in 1998, it was in Sudan, with a small herd of Friesian dairy cattle on the banks of the Blue Nile. The cows were in an air-conditioned shed on a farm in a place called Soba, around an hour's drive outside Khartoum. Bin Laden had lived next door for four years from 1992; he owned a lot of property in Sudan, until it was confiscated by the government when he was told to leave.

I was trying to find out what Bin Laden had been like as a neighbour. He had moved to Sudan, with four wives, many children and his entourage, after he turned against the Saudi regime, which had concluded that he was a threat. The regime stripped him of his Saudi citizenship while he was in Sudan. At that time in his life, although Bin Laden was immersed in the politics of radical jihad, he was not yet entirely consumed by building al-Qaeda, the violent jihadist group that transformed global politics in a single morning on 11 September 2001.

While he was in Sudan, Bin Laden had other business interests. Like his father, he built roads, and the impoverished Sudanese government bartered with him, paying for them with huge grants of land. In 1996, he showed a correspondent from *Time* magazine work in progress on a highway from Port Sudan to Khartoum. According to the correspondent, Scott Macleod, 'he was trying to present the image that – look, I'm a businessman. I have my problems with the Saudi government, I won't deny them – and he ran through a litany of why the Saudi government was corrupt or illegitimate. But he said, "The way of fighting this is not violent. We're politicians." He was at pains to show me the non-military side of Osama bin Laden.'[1]

The tour he gave *Time* magazine also included a factory for tanning leather and a sunflower seed plantation. Bin Laden believed Sudan could produce much more food, and he was involved with experimental agriculture. So was his former neighbour in Soba, who explained that the Friesians had much better milk yields than the scrawny Sudanese cattle that foraged outside in the dust. The only trouble was that without air conditioning, the Friesians died. He wouldn't say whether he had discussed his cattle-breeding plans with Bin Laden, insisting that they had never been friends. Bin Laden, he said, was always distant, a rich man with a modest lifestyle. He kept horses and would go for long rides. I peered over the wall from the cowshed. The Bin Ladens had not left much behind. One of his former followers later said the farm was used for weapons and explosives training, though no triggers were pulled or bombs detonated.

Sudan in the 1990s offered jihadist radicals such a warm welcome that US president Bill Clinton believed the Sudanese government had let Bin Laden set up a plant to produce VX nerve gas, which was why I was in the country. Bin Laden himself had been forced to move on to Afghanistan in 1996, where he became a much more serious adversary of the United States. I was visiting the farm on the Blue Nile, which might have been an idyllic spot were it not for its associations with its former owner, because al-Qaeda had just perpetrated its first deadly spectacular. On 7 August 1998, suicide bombers had attacked the US embassy in Nairobi, the Kenyan capital, killing 213 people, almost all of whom were Kenyans, and injuring 4,500. Nine minutes later in Tanzania, another al-Qaeda bomber blew himself up in a truck at the American embassy in Dar-es-Salaam, killing eleven and wounding eighty-five. Part of the retaliation ordered by President Clinton was the destruction of the Shifa pharmaceutical factory in Khartoum, the plant US intelligence believed was developing VX. Not for the last time in America's war on al-Qaeda, their intelligence was wrong; a watchman at the factory was killed in the attack and the country's capacity to manufacture medicines was crippled. I went to the bombsite, where thousands of packets of aspirin were scattered in the rubble.

That summer was the first time that the names of Osama bin Laden and al-Qaeda became familiar to people who were not expert in the growth of radical jihadist violence. Reports on the BBC website at the time referred to him as 'Mr Bin Laden, an exiled Saudi dissident'; in an interview with the BBC just before President Clinton ordered the strike, he had denied any involvement in the embassy attacks. A few years later, an interview with Osama bin Laden would have been a huge world exclusive; in 1998 it was a throwaway line. I looked to see what the BBC said about him when it reported his death in 2011, but by then there was no need for a description. Everyone knew his name. The BBC was no longer calling him Mister.

Osama bin Laden was born in 1957, a scion of the richest Saudi family without a royal title. His father was Mohammed bin Laden, an immensely wealthy and well-connected construction tycoon. Bin Laden Senior was born into poverty in Yemen and never properly educated, but prospered thanks to talent, hard work and an eye for a deal. He made billions building highways and public buildings, grafting the infrastructure of a modern state onto a country that was still running on camel power. Most important of all, Mohammed bin Laden had the trust of the senior members of the Saudi royal family. His work came in on time and on budget, and he did not flaunt his vast wealth. The family connection continued into the next generation. In the 1980s, King Faisal's son Prince Turki was head of Saudi intelligence, while Osama was in Afghanistan sponsoring fighters and even carrying a Kalashnikov in the jihad against the Soviet Union. At this stage in his progress towards being the world's most wanted man, he was an ally of the Saudi state. The sons were useful to each other, just like the fathers had been, and Osama became a source for Prince Turki.

Osama bin Laden could not have had much of a relationship with his father. Apart from his business empire, Mohammed bin Laden had more than fifty children from perhaps twenty marriages. A pious man, he made sure he respected Islamic law, with regular divorces ensuring he never had more than the four permitted wives. Mohammed bin Laden was awarded the most important contract in Saudi Arabia, to modernize and maintain Mecca's Great Mosque. Looking after mosques became a Bin Laden speciality; his firm was hired by King Hussein of Jordan to maintain the al-Aqsa Mosque and the Dome of the Rock in Jerusalem, until Israel captured them in the 1967 Middle East War. When Osama was ten his father was killed in a plane crash, leaving behind a huge business and a vast fortune. Mohammed's old patron King Faisal made sure the family's companies were looked after until Osama's brother Salem was old enough to take over.

Then came 1979; its consequences roared around Saudi Arabia, the Middle East and the world. It was bookended by the Islamic revolution in Iran and the Soviet invasion of Afghanistan. On 20 November 1979, Saudi Arabia faced its greatest upheaval so far. Hundreds of radical Islamists seized the Great Mosque in Mecca, and held out until they were defeated in a protracted and bloody siege. Guns were smuggled into the mosque in coffins borne by men masquerading as mourners. Their leader, Juhayman al-Otaibi, a wild-haired former Saudi national guardsman, urged them on. A dozen or so worshippers and clerics were killed as al-Otaibi's men locked the gates. Snipers stationed themselves in the mosque's minarets and repelled the assaults of the authorities.[2]

Salem bin Laden, Osama's older brother who was now running the family firm, tracked down detailed blueprints of the mosque, which the authorities needed to clear out the passages and prayer rooms in the basements. It took two weeks for the Saudis, using the blueprints, brute force and potent tear gas supplied by French special forces, to drive out the rebels. In that time, hundreds were killed. Sixty-three rebels were captured and later beheaded.[3] Osama bin Laden watched what was happening from a few miles away in Jeddah on the Red Sea coast, where he was a devout young university student. When he joined the Afghan jihad, one of his associates said he praised the rebels as 'true Muslims . . . innocent of any crime . . . killed ruthlessly'.[4] Later, after he broke with the Saudi regime over its collaboration with the Americans, Bin Laden echoed al-Otaibi's demands: stop exporting oil to the West, expel Westerners and dethrone the Al Sauds.

After the literal decapitation of the rebels — sixty-three of them were beheaded in public squares — the conservative, elderly men who ran the country decided that the way to stop a repeat of the siege was not to root out extremism but to return to an even more austere reading of Islam's teachings. It was given a name — Sahwa, meaning 'awakening' — but it was, in fact, part of an exercise in official forgetting. Mentioning al-Otaibi's name in the papers was forbidden, and Saudi Arabia returned to a puritanical and intolerant interpretation of Islam. The royal family, however, continued to live in splendid luxury, jetting between European capitals in lavishly fitted-out Boeing airliners and even visiting the fleshpots of the countries their clerics condemned. Everyone else was at the mercy of the angry men in robes, the religious police.

A generation later, the millennial Crown Prince Mohammed bin Salman insisted that the events of 1979 had interrupted Saudi Arabia's march of progress. It had never been any sort of liberal paradise, but Saudi Arabia was more relaxed in the 1970s than it was in the 1990s. After the siege of the Great Mosque, the cultural and religious barricades went up and the religious police went on the offensive. Female singers were banned from television, though not from radio; the sight of a woman was considered more dangerous than her voice. The religious police smashed musical instruments, burned books, shaved heads and ordered floggings. Cinemas were closed, not that the Saudis had ever enjoyed the full popcorn-and-blockbuster experience. According to Jamal Khashoggi (the Saudi journalist who years later was killed, the CIA said, on the orders of the Crown Prince), this depiction of life before 1979 was exaggerated. Khashoggi wrote that when he was a teenager in Medina in the 1970s cinemas were 'makeshift, like American drive-ins except much more informal. The movie was beamed on a big wall. You would pay five or ten riyals (then approximately $1.50–$2) to the organizer, who would then give a warning when the religious police approached. To avoid being arrested, a friend of mine broke his leg jumping off a wall.'[5]

Osama bin Laden was not the sort of young man who would go to any kind of cinema. Family and friends who knew him as a teenager in Jeddah say he was unusually religious, more so than his brothers, who were mostly educated abroad.[6] He was not the only young Muslim who was attracted to the messages he heard in the mosques. The crushing defeat inflicted by Israel on its Arab neighbours in 1967 had deflated the bombast of secular Arab nationalism. When the rebels seized the Great Mosque in 1979, religious radicalism was already bubbling up, not just in Saudi Arabia but across the Muslim world. Inspiration came from the Islamic revolution that had overthrown the shah of Iran at the beginning of the year.

Ayatollah Khomeini returned from exile in France and Shia clerics outmanoeuvred the secular democrats who had thought it might be their revolution. Religious Saudis liked the way the world was transfixed by Khomeini's display of the power of Islam, even though the Sunni Wahhabi clergy condemned Shias as heretics.

By the time Iraq was ejected from Kuwait, the young man who had watched the tumultuous consequence of the events of 1979 was influencing a new generation. The Saudi intelligence services decided that Osama bin Laden had become a threat. He was rich enough to cause a lot of trouble, had potentially violent veterans of the jihad in Afghanistan on his side and had condemned the House of Saud. He was angry that his plan to fight for Saudi Arabia had been ignored, which compounded a resentment shared with other veterans of jihad in Afghanistan that their efforts were not appreciated.[7]

After the American-led forces had done the job that Bin Laden insisted could have been done by Saudis, he was confined to his house in Jeddah by the authorities. He managed to persuade them to let him travel to Peshawar in Pakistan, the jumping-off point for thousands of fighters heading to Afghanistan during the jihad against the Soviet Union. But the focus for jihadists had switched to the Middle East, and Bin Laden needed a new base. He found one in Sudan, where Islamists and their sympathizers in the army had seized power in 1989. The leading Sudanese Islamist, Hassan al-Turabi, was the ideologist of the new regime of General Omar al-Bashir and planned to turn Sudan into a radical pillar of the Sunni world. For Bin Laden, his wives and his entourage, it was time for a new start.

If religious solidarity was not enough, Bin Laden was more than a jihadist star. He was also one of the few rich foreigners to invest in the country. He splashed money into a series of businesses, providing jobs for Afghan veterans who had followed him into exile, as well as thousands of Sudanese. When his businesses were not successful, he complained that local workers were lazy, but testimony from his associates suggests that he was spending more time on what mattered most to him – al-Qaeda.

One of Bin Laden's earliest followers, Jamal al-Fadl, was part of his advance guard in Sudan, going back to his native country to rent houses and farms. Al-Fadl did not share Bin Laden's ascetic lifestyle; in the 1980s, he had fled Saudi Arabia when the police arrested his flatmate for possession of marijuana, and moved to the USA on a student visa. At a mosque in Brooklyn, he was recruited for the Afghan jihad. By the time the Bin Laden caravan was established in Sudan, al-Fadl was looking after the payroll, resenting that others earned more money. So he awarded himself an unofficial pay rise. When Bin Laden found out, al-Fadl threw himself into the arms of the Americans in return for witness protection and immunity. He was their best jihadist catch so far, claiming to be the third person signed up by al-Qaeda.

A strange symbiotic relationship developed between al-Fadl and his FBI handlers. They moved a dozen members of his family from Sudan to the US and spent over a million dollars looking after them. Al-Fadl was nicknamed 'Junior' and they teased him about loving fast food. In return, he testified against Bin Laden and some key followers in the 2001 trial of four men for conspiracy to bomb the US embassies in East Africa.[8] In court, al-Fadl described the tradecraft of an international jihadist. When he travelled for al-Qaeda, he was instructed not just to shave his beard and wear Western clothes, but to spray himself with cologne, 'smelling, you like women, you look for women . . .' and to carry cigarettes. Devout Muslims do not smoke.

During his years in Sudan, Bin Laden cemented his alliance with an ally from his time in Afghanistan. Ayman al-Zawahiri, an Egyptian doctor, became the al-Qaeda number two and its leader after Bin Laden was killed by American commandos in 2011. His education had been completed in an Egyptian prison. In his cell he studied the works of Sayyid Qutb, an Egyptian radical who wrote that that Muslims had a duty to fight for God. Al-Zawahari was tortured, like so many other radicals, and emerged ruthless and angry into an organization called al-Jihad. They killed Anwar el Sadat, the president of Egypt, in 1981, for making peace with Israel, and by 1995 they wanted to kill his successor, Hosni Mubarak. Their priority was still the 'near enemy', the ungodly and repressive rulers of their country. The United States, the 'far enemy', was not yet the main target.

An ambush was set for the airport road in Addis Ababa as Mubarak's motorcade swept into the city on an official visit on 27 June 1995. An SUV rammed the convoy and armed men leapt out firing, while others who had lain in wait opened up with weapons smuggled into Ethiopia by Sudanese diplomats. The armour on the president's Mercedes stopped the bullets, and a rocket-propelled grenade that would have made short work of the vehicle jammed.[9] Mubarak, who had been splattered with blood during the assassination of Sadat, ordered his driver into a screeching U-turn back to the airport. Back in Cairo in one piece, quipping at a news conference that 'I was cool all the time,' Mubarak turned his security services on jihadist groups. The extremists around Zawahiri were targeted in Egypt and Sudan. Two sons of Zawahiri's senior operatives, barely teenagers, were blackmailed by Egyptian intelligence into spying on Zawahiri. When he found out, he had them dragged in front of an improvised Sharia court, convicted and shot, with the proceedings filmed as an example to anyone else contemplating treachery.[10]

Al-Turabi, Sudan's chief Islamist ideologist, was horrified by the execution of children and by the over-mighty behaviour of Zawahiri and his jihadists. They were told to get out. Bin Laden followed soon afterwards, stripped of most of his Sudanese business and property. Zawahiri led a peripatetic life before heading back to Afghanistan; Bin Laden took the direct route in a Soviet-built aircraft provided by Sudan, and Mullah Omar, the leader of the Taliban, welcomed him. They were in position for the years of preparation that would go into the attacks on the United States on 11 September 2001, and the years of war that would follow.

8.

Gaza

One hot afternoon in Gaza I retreated to my room, muttering something to my colleagues about background reading. I lay on my bed and closed my eyes, trying hard to fool myself that the breeze coming off the Mediterranean and the waves slapping the sides of fishing boats meant Gaza and I could have a peaceful moment. I dropped off, until gunfire, lots of it, interrupted my dreams. A wedding hall was next door. I assumed the shooting came from guests who were celebrating, not trying to kill each other. Palestinians are not the only Arabs with a nasty habit of marking significant moments by firing hundreds of rounds into the air. I rolled over and went back to sleep. After all, interruptions happen in Gaza; once, I had just got out of the shower when a huge explosion from an Israeli air strike blew in all the hotel's windows.

The gunfire continued outside, and it started to sound less like a wedding. When a waiter knocked on the door to tell me to stay in my room, I went downstairs to take a look. A wounded man was lying in the hotel foyer and a cleaner was mopping up his blood. In the street, armed men were taking cover behind plant pots and in doorways. It was 2007, not long before the two main Palestinian factions, Hamas and Fatah, engaged in a brief and brutal war over control of the Gaza Strip. Shoot-outs in the street were quite common. They had a fundamental and often deadly disagreement about the best way for

Palestinians to deliver themselves from their tragedy of being out-muscled by Israel.

The elements that make the long struggle between Palestinians and Israelis toxic and destructive are all visible, active and growing on both sides of the wire that separates Gaza from Israel. In Gaza the human spirit, despite everything, is strong. People laugh and make jokes about their predicament. Gaza is slightly smaller than the Isle of Wight, which has plenty of room for its 150,000 residents, plus tourists. More than two million Palestinians live in Gaza, and they don't get many visitors. It runs eastwards along twenty-five miles of coastline from the top right-hand corner of Egypt, and is called a 'strip' because it is no wider than seven miles, often narrower. Apart from the short border with Egypt, it is entirely surrounded by Israel. The beaches are Gaza's parks, where Palestinians can walk, swim, relax a little and wonder about a much bigger world most of them can never visit, somewhere out beyond the horizon.

Gaza was one of the historic towns of Palestine, a small place surrounded by fields and sand dunes. When Israel won its war of independence in 1948, Egypt ended up with Gaza and hundreds of thousands of Palestinian refugees, who had taken refuge there after they either fled the fighting or were forced from their homes at gunpoint by Israeli troops. Israel took Gaza, and the refugees, from Egypt in the 1967 war.

Palestinians are the most politicized Arabs. Gazans follow what is happening on the other side of the wire closely, fighting the isolation that shrinks their own lives and turns them inward. About two-thirds of Gaza's Palestinians are descended from the original refugees, and they mostly live in eight large refugee camps. One of the biggest and most overcrowded is Beach Camp, which started with 23,000 refugees in tents and now has nearly four times as many people living in breezeblock houses separated by alleys so narrow that it is easy to reach out and touch both sides. Gaza is one of the most densely populated places on the planet. Most people are never alone. The poorest families live in two or three rooms, with a small yard if they are lucky. Family ties are strong; three or four generations live together, and refugee children know the names of the villages that their great-grandparents came from in 1948.

The main gateway to Gaza is the Erez Crossing from Israel. Palestinians need permission to use it, which is hard to get. Permission to work in Israel is prized because it means an income. It also means rising in the small hours to get through security at Erez to arrive on time at the farm, building site or restaurant that has employed them. Movement restrictions were still relatively new when I crossed Erez for the first time in 1991. Bored Israeli soldiers checked documents in a small wooden hut, and when they finished I drove in with an Israeli TV crew, past the barbed wire and machine guns. Thirty years on, the only Israelis allowed into Gaza are under military orders. Foreigners with permits, journalists and aid workers are usually allowed to cross, but only diplomats can take a car. Not far from where the hut used to stand, in a gleaming terminal like an international border, Israeli conscripts still look bored as they check documents. Footsteps echo around empty halls big enough to handle thousands of people, as few can satisfy Israel's security requirements.

Once when I got up early enough to drive down from Jerusalem at dawn, I arrived to find that the door marked 'Gaza' was locked. A security guard from a private company came trotting over. He was in his mid-twenties with sunglasses perched on his head, a short-barrelled M16 assault rifle bumping against his hip as we walked to the gate. He had the keys to Gaza, the home of more than two million people, in his pocket, next to his cigarettes. He unlocked the door, smiled again and wished me a good day.

Once you have passed that first door, you are still in the terminal but there is no more direct contact with Israelis – though they watch everything through CCTV. More security guards with automatic weapons look down from platforms that jut out of the offices where the gate operators sit at their screens. Moving through the narrow, winding corridors feels like being a mouse in a laboratory experiment, under the eyes of controllers who reward good behaviour and block the path of anyone who breaks the rules. Almost at the end of the line, a distant finger presses a button to open one more grille and the travellers pass down a ramp. Once the grille has closed and the lock clicked shut, a steel door in a high concrete wall slides open and Gaza stands on the other side.

It is hard to disagree with Palestinians who call Gaza the world's biggest jail. Many of them have never been able to leave. The path to the first Palestinian checkpoint is wired in and roofed with steel, running through a wasteland where orange groves and wheat fields on one side and a factory on the other stood until they were bulldozed to give Israeli soldiers an unobstructed view of anyone approaching. On the Israeli side of the fortifications are the lush fields of kibbutz Yad Mordechai, named after a Jewish fighter in the Warsaw ghetto. The kibbutz is famous in Israel for its Holocaust museum, its honey and because it was where in 1948 the new Israel stopped the advance of the Egyptian army. British weapons from the 1940s are concreted into the old trenches to commemorate the battle, pointing across the generations at cutouts of Egyptian soldiers.

Israeli soldiers fire at anyone who gets too close to their positions – sometimes to warn, sometimes to kill. Once I saw them shooting over the heads of boys scavenging for scrap metal in the rubble. My Palestinian colleague was waiting at the tea stall next to the Palestinian checkpoint, a broad grin on his face. 'Welcome to Gaza,' he said. 'They're just shooting to impress you.' He drove us into Rimal, the closest there is to downtown Gaza, squinting past the old bullet hole in the windscreen of the BBC's armoured Land Rover.

When the Oslo peace process was inaugurated in the 1990s, Gaza was the first place that was turned over to Palestinian self-rule, along with Jericho in the Jordan Valley. While there was hope that the agreements would work, I managed to get permission from the Israelis to take an old lady and her grandson from Gaza back to Jaffa, now part of Tel Aviv but once the leading port of Palestine. The idea was to mark the fiftieth anniversary of the Palestinian catastrophe of 1948, when Israel won its independence war and Palestinian society was destroyed and dispersed. It was the first time that the grandson had left the Gaza Strip, and to start with there was some excitement. The boy saw a train and asked what it was – Gaza has no railways. The trip turned into a bad idea. The grandmother could not find where she had lived. We went to a Palestinian restaurant where the waiters were friendly – Jaffa has a small population of Palestinian Arabs with Israeli citizenship – but our guests did not want to eat. The grandmother perked up when we found an overgrown Muslim graveyard, but was downcast when she could not locate any familiar names.

Everything in Jaffa had changed since she had left with thousands of other Palestinians in 1948. They were relieved when we dropped them at the Erez checkpoint, and did not glance back.

Palestinians were divided by the Oslo peace process. Leading Palestinian intellectuals opposed Yasser Arafat's increasingly uncomfortable accommodations with Israel, railing against the agreement that they believed was a betrayal. The poet Mahmoud Darwish, who had written his nation's symbolic declaration of independence in 1988, resigned from the PLO in protest. He wrote a poem dismissing the signing ceremony that Bill Clinton had directed on the White House lawn as a 'technicolor movie'.[1] Resistance, he concluded, had to continue.

The Palestinian American political scientist and essayist Edward Said devoted much of the creative energy left in his life to condemning Oslo. In the *London Review of Books*, he attacked 'The fashion-show vulgarities of the White House ceremony, the degrading spectacle of Yasser Arafat thanking everyone for the suspension of most of his people's rights, and the fatuous solemnity of Bill Clinton's performance, like a twentieth-century Roman emperor shepherding two vassal kings through rituals of reconciliation and obeisance: all these only temporarily obscure the truly astonishing proportions of the Palestinian capitulation.'[2]

Some of the most reasoned criticism of the Oslo agreement came from Haydar Abd al-Shafi, a doctor in Gaza who was repelled by the compromises and corruption that came with it. He was a veteran nationalist and one of the founders of the PLO, but was cut off from Arafat's exiled magic circle during the years of occupation in Gaza. After Oslo was signed, the exiles came home and found that home-grown nationalists who had fought the first intifada resented any attempt to lord it over them. Not long before the assassination of Israel's prime minister, Yitzhak Rabin, in 1995, Haydar 'Abd al-Shafi declared that Oslo had already failed, due to Israeli violations: 'By now it is obvious that Israel is determined to maintain its presence, its control over the territories, the settlements. In fact, what has gone unnoticed is that Israel has never given up its claim to the occupied territories in its entirety, in keeping with the Zionist programme.'[3]

The essence of the conflict never changes. At its heart is the desire of two peoples for the same small piece of land that lies between the Mediterranean and the River Jordan, but it is more than a dispute over real estate. The religious and national identities of the two sides, and their past histories, are connected intimately to the land they both want. The Israelis are stronger than the Palestinians by every military or economic measure, but the Nakba of 1948 has taught the Palestinians that if they leave, they will not make it back. Israelis are troubled by the legacy of centuries of Jewish persecution and the knowledge that, however loudly they proclaim the land is theirs, while Palestinians remain and assert their own claim they will never be able to trust the foundations on which they have built their state.

The Oslo agreements deepened the rift between Fatah, Yasser Arafat's faction, and its biggest rival, Hamas, whose name is an acronym for Islamic Resistance Movement. Hamas is an offshoot of the Muslim Brotherhood, a group that was established in Egypt in the late 1920s to put Islam at the heart of political and social life. While Arafat's people negotiated, Hamas set out to destroy the agreements by killing Israelis. At that time, whenever I was stuck behind a bus in Jerusalem or Tel Aviv, I wondered if it was about to blow up. Bombers would get on crowded buses or enter restaurants and detonate explosive belts, killing themselves and as many Jews as possible. The number 18 bus route in Jerusalem was hit twice inside eight days in early 1996, killing a total of thirty-three civilians and twelve Israeli soldiers. Whenever shoppers heard more than one ambulance siren, they would look around nervously. The attacks convinced many Israelis that the Palestinians did not want peace and helped the right-wing leader of the Likud Party, Benjamin Netanyahu, score a narrow electoral victory over Shimon Peres.

The same spring as the bus bombs, Arafat agreed to crack down on Hamas at an emergency summit convened by Bill Clinton in Sharm el-Sheikh in Egypt. Back home, Palestinian security forces kicked down doors and locked up large numbers of activists. I would later meet one of them, who was physically and mentally scarred by what happened to him in one of Arafat's jails. As we walked around Gaza's Commonwealth War Cemetery, an oasis of peace and shade a world away from the dusty, noisy city, the man told me it was the only place he could think since Arafat's men tore out his fingernails with pliers. They had regrown as horny little stumps.

After that, Hamas supporters harboured deep resentment and talk of national unity was thin. Yasser Arafat's stature among Palestinians as the leader who had put them on the world political map meant he was just about able to hold his people together, but relations between Fatah and Hamas deteriorated rapidly after he died. The Arafat side accepted Israel's existence and cooperated with Israel's security forces, while Hamas had a charter calling for its destruction and was classified as a terrorist group by Israel and the West.

The mutual dislike hardened when Palestinians held elections in Gaza and the West Bank in 2006. President George W. Bush had declared his support for Arab democracy as part of an attempt to justify the invasion of Iraq three years earlier. His secretary of state, Condoleezza Rice, had made a speech in Cairo accepting that 'the United States had for sixty years pursued stability rather than democracy... throughout the Middle East the fear of free choices can no longer justify the denial of liberty. It is time to abandon the excuses that are made to avoid the hard work of democracy.'[4] It was the thought of this hard work that made Fatah nervous. The more realistic officials working for Arafat's successor Mahmoud Abbas, known to Palestinians as Abu Mazen, realized that they might lose.

Palestinians were sick of Fatah's excesses, corruption and ineptitude. Like Israelis, they were cynical about any talk of peace. The barman in the American Colony, the Jerusalem hotel frequented by journalists, said he could tell an electoral upset was coming when Christian Palestinians had told him, over glasses of whisky, that they would be voting for Hamas. The sight of Palestinians who usually followed Johnnie Walker declaring an interest in the Islamic Resistance Movement showed the depth of Fatah's problems.

Fatah were aghast about the victory of Hamas. So were the Americans. I visited one of the most senior diplomats at the State Department in Washington, DC. 'Of course,' he said, 'it's the wrong result. We're going to have to overturn it.' The Bush administration was only prepared to do Dr Rice's 'hard work of democracy' if voters chose the right candidates. The US, the UK and their Western allies backed Israel's policy of isolating Gaza to put pressure on Hamas, and it was no surprise that the crisis led to bloodshed.

I went to see Mohammad Dahlan, the Fatah strongman in Gaza who had started as a street-level leader during the first Palestinian intifada in the late 1980s. Dahlan was a tough and ruthless operator who was rapidly acquiring a smooth exterior. After years in Israeli prisons, he spoke fluent Hebrew, and he was close to the Americans. In his office, he explained that things were difficult but optimistically suggested that Palestinian unity would assert itself.

When the Americans helped Fatah prepare a coup against the newly elected government, Hamas fighters unceremoniously ejected their rivals from the positions of power they still held in Gaza. Fatah never forgot the defeat, or the humiliation. Top men in Fatah, Dahlan included, rushed to the Israeli checkpoint to escape. Back in London, I watched pictures of Hamas fighters firing their Kalashnikovs into his desk, in the office where I'd spoken to him a few weeks earlier. Dahlan would become an advisor to Mohammed bin Zayed, the man who ruled Abu Dhabi. Years later, I talked to him in a luxurious hotel suite lined with fine walnut panelling, overlooking Hyde Park in London. When I asked him whether he would ever return home, he sipped mineral water from a cut-glass tumbler and was coy about his political ambitions. It was clear he was waiting for his moment. Since his childhood in a refugee camp in Gaza, he had become a rich man in a life that was like a mini-series.

Gaza's new bearded masters included Ismail Haniyeh, a beefy man with a charismatic smile. Mahmoud al-Zahar, a generation older, was the last surviving co-founder of Hamas – all the others had been assassinated by the Israelis. When I met him, he brushed aside my questions about the Hamas charter's clauses about destroying Israel, instead picking up a globe from his desk and tracing his finger from Nigeria to Indonesia. 'All this,' he said, 'is Muslim, and that is why we will win.' The walls of his salon were lined with chairs separated by small tables for the obligatory glasses of sweet tea, but less usual was a big up-and-over garage door at one end, and two parked SUVs. I asked why he shared space with his cars. It was obvious, he said – to escape the Israelis.

Israel pulled its soldiers and settlers out of Gaza in 2005, blowing up their homes, synagogues and bases as they left. It was no act of charity, but because the Israeli prime minister, Ariel Sharon, a strong believer in the power of physical force, had decided that the time had come for Israel to impose its own solution. After fighting in the 1948 war as a teenager, Sharon made his name leading devastating reprisal raids into Gaza and the West Bank in the 1950s. Some Israelis, and even Palestinians who had seen him as a bloodthirsty killer, hoped briefly that his approach might be another route to some sort of peace. They never found out, because Sharon suffered a devastating stroke a few months after the Gaza withdrawal; it left him in a vegetative state and he died eight years later.

Sharon's withdrawal left Israel still in control of movement in and out of Gaza with the exception of the single crossing into Egypt, which was also restricted. Israel rejects the UN view that controlling Gaza's borders means it still has responsibilities as an occupier.

To punish Hamas and try to force them out, Israel imposed a blockade on Gaza, with the full support of its allies. In an attempt to beat it, a network of smuggling tunnels was dug under Gaza's southern border into Egypt. The diggers would sink a shaft about fifteen metres into the sand and gravel before tunnelling around 300 metres into Egypt. The Egyptian authorities promised the Israelis that they would close the tunnels down, but their pursuit of smugglers was generally half-hearted. Arms were smuggled in alongside fuel, soft drinks, cigarettes, food and anything else that could be sold, with the trade becoming so established that Hamas taxed the imports. For Eid al-Adha, the annual Muslim feast of the sacrifice, calves, sheep and goats were led through the tunnels to be slaughtered.

As always in sieges, most people did very badly, especially the men who suffered death by suffocation under tons of sand in collapsed tunnels. A few made a lot of money; the tunnel entrepreneurs were the closest thing Gaza had to oligarchs. I used to guess the intensity of the blockade by looking at the rubbish on the streets. The writing on drinks cans was a clue: Hebrew meant the Israelis had loosened up and let in Coke and Fanta from their bottling plants, while Arabic meant the crossings from Israel were tighter and Egyptian soft drinks were back on the menu.

Hamas, Israel, the blockade and generations of conflict combined to cause a series of wars. Tensions would wax and wane depending on whether Hamas or other armed groups were firing missiles and rockets into Israel, and whether Israel was bombing Gaza or sending in raiders. Israel's firepower always inflicted many times more death and destruction than the Palestinians could manage. It is pointless to try to disentangle the starting point of each escalation, because the combustible mix had produced a conflict that was just waiting for a spark: these regularly blew up into serious wars, and the makings of the next one were always left behind in the rubble.

Living either side of the border wire can be difficult and dangerous. Israelis are much better protected; their homes have strengthened walls and safe rooms, and they have missiles that can shoot down other missiles. Even so, experiencing a single rocket attack on the Israeli side, let alone dozens in a day, is terrifying. In Israeli towns and villages along the border, concrete structures were erected in playgrounds, bus stops and anywhere citizens might need to take cover in seconds, when the red alert was broadcast from loudspeakers.

It would be wrong, though, to suggest there is any kind of equivalence between the experiences of Israelis on their side of the wire and Palestinians inside Gaza on the other. Statistics say a great deal about the weight of fire Israel has directed at Gaza, the destruction it has caused, and most of all the numbers it has killed. The first major war between Israel and Hamas began on 27 December 2008 and lasted three weeks. Tension had been rising steadily, with exchanges of rocket fire and air strikes – it was clear that both sides were ready for a fight. Israel called it Operation Cast Lead, while Hamas called it al-Furqan, meaning separation or salvation. The Israeli human rights group B'tselm recorded that Israeli security forces killed 1,398 Palestinians, including 345 children. The Palestinians killed five Israeli soldiers and no civilians.

One night during the campaign, Shlomi Eldar, a reporter for Israeli television, was in the studio to present the evening news when his phone showed a call from a Palestinian doctor inside Gaza. Izzeldeen Abuelaish was one of the few Palestinians who had a permit to move freely through the Erez Crossing – he worked as a fertility expert in an Israeli hospital. He lived with his family in the Jabaliyah refugee camp in Gaza. Four months before the war, his wife had died from cancer.

A prominent peace campaigner, Izzeldeen was fluent in Hebrew and had many Israeli friends. Shlomi Eldar put the call on speaker, broadcasting Izzeldeen's anguish to viewers who had tuned in for news of the war. An Israeli tank had shelled his home, killing three of his five daughters and his teenage niece.

When the Israelis lifted a ban on foreign journalists entering Gaza, I saw the tank tracks just yards from Izzeldeen's badly damaged home. He told me, 'I thought I'm protected. They know me, no armed people in the house.' The ruins of that building contained all the pain, powerlessness and frustration of Palestinians. Izzeldeen showed me photos of his meetings with Ehud Barak, Israel's former prime minister and chief of staff of the armed forces. His campaign for peace had taken him right to the top. Then he showed me his daughters' room, burnt from the blast of the shells. It was full of the remains of their lives, Barbies from when they were smaller, schoolbooks, smashed computers, magazines, broken bunk beds. Mayar, aged fifteen, and her cousin Noor, were decapitated in the attack. The doctor's twenty-one-year-old daughter Bessan, his eldest, survived the first shell, and her thirteen-year-old sister Aya was injured but alive. Two or three minutes later, a second shell killed them both.

Israelis often say that they have the most moral army in the world, with their soldiers under orders to do all they can to protect non-combatants. Israel denies it uses disproportionate force in Gaza, but using heavy weapons in densely populated areas makes civilian casualties inevitable. When I asked a senior Israeli government minister who he thought was responsible for the deaths of civilians in Gaza's wars, he said the answer was simple: Hamas.

It staggered me how Izzeldeen Abuelaish was able to talk rationally about what happened to his family. Many Israelis as well as Palestinians listened, even if they disagreed with him. The election of Hamas, he told me, was 'a result of a long, long process, since Oslo – even before'. The fundamental reason why his family was destroyed was the conflict between two peoples, Israel's punitive treatment of Palestinians and everything that stemmed from the closure of Gaza to the outside world. I asked him if he thought resistance against Israel and the occupation is justified. 'I believe in resistance by word. A word can be stronger than a bomb . . . any military action is a waste of time, it will make it more difficult to create peace. It creates more victims, more killing. We are living here, both. We were created to live together and to find the way to live equally with respect and cooperation. Side by side, that is the only way.'

Gaza's petri dish of conflict contains endless stories of appalling suffering. In that 2009 war, a sixteen-year-old boy called Ahmed Samouni told me how he was trapped for four days in the ruins of his home, where at least thirty members of his extended family were killed after the Israelis attacked it with missiles. Ahmed was trapped with his six-year-old brother Abdullah, who also survived. The two boys spent four days with the bodies of their mother, their uncles and two brothers, and two of their other brothers bled to death as they lay with them. His brother Is'haq took two days to die. When he crept from the house to find water, soldiers shot at him. 'I think about it every day,' he said. 'I tell the Jews, we have a God and he may take revenge for me.'

Ahmed was treated by Gaza's best-known psychiatrist, Dr Eyad el-Sarraj, who pioneered mental healthcare in Gaza, especially for children. He was a brave man, who spoke out against the abuses committed by both sides, and spent time in a Palestinian prison for his courage. Before he died of cancer in 2013, Eyad and I talked in his garden over a beer. Ahmed and the other children who had suffered so badly, he told me, had lost the three most basic needs for a child: security, the care of a parent or a trusted adult, and pleasure. As a result, they faced 'a very painful journey . . . They can cope with this over the years with the help they can get, but I don't think anyone can assume that they will be fully recovered.'

Eyad recalled the previous generations of traumatized children he had treated: 'I don't want to be presumptuous, but from experience we have seen children growing up from stone throwers into suicide bombers.' Like many of his countrymen, he believed that Israel wanted to sow hatred in new generations of Palestinians, in order that they would always have an excuse not to make peace. 'For Israel,' he said, 'peace is the most dangerous thing, not war.'[5]

Israel could recapture Gaza in days if it wanted to, but then it would be responsible for more than two million people. Palestinians cannot destroy a state as strong as Israel, but Israel has proved that it cannot bludgeon Palestinians into submission. Until matters change in Gaza, there will be wars between Hamas and Israel. Change would require a new attempt at peace, with the participation and consent of all sides, and there is currently no chance of that.

9.

The Final Frontier

Once the 1991 war in Iraq was over, so was the fear of being turned into charred carbon by an American missile during the long drive across the desert to Baghdad. Without air strikes, the scariest part was when our driver Abu Ali made tea, because he kept on driving while he did it. We travelled in GMC Suburbans, sleek, fast American monsters. Petrol was cheaper than water in Iraq, so no one minded how much gas they guzzled. Abu Ali had a small kettle that plugged into the cigarette lighter. Once it had boiled, he poured water onto a teabag and around an inch of sugar in his tannin-tinted glass. He steered with his knees during the tea ceremony, the speedometer never falling below 100 miles per hour. The highway was straight, with very few other vehicles as collision targets.

As the kettle bubbled away, I would block out the thought that a splash of boiling water could end very badly and stare out of the passenger window at the flat, rocky desert that stretched to the horizon. It was spotted with the remnants of war, destroyed bridges and the burnt-out skeletons of trucks. The Suburban hurtled forward and Abu Ali returned a hand to the wheel while he held his tea glass with the other. We never stopped to check out the war debris – the regime's rules for travel did not allow diversions. I didn't want to find some unfortunate's bones in the blackened cabs of the lorries, and besides, something might still be sitting there waiting to explode.

We sped across the desert, straight arrows flying through a flat rocky landscape that seemed through my half-closed eyes by turns lunar and interplanetary. Abu Ali's only cassette, a collection of Lionel Richie's love songs played on Andean panpipes, wormed its way into my mind as the scrubby, stony desert passed by. It was 900 kilometres from Amman to Baghdad, but it felt like light years. Baghdad was at the other end of the galaxy, with Saddam's actions and the world's response consigning the city – and the country – to isolation. Fierce restrictions on the economy and on imports were imposed to punish the regime into either changing its behaviour or collapsing, but the sanctions were destroying not Saddam and his cohorts but the Iraqi people.

The victorious allies wanted Saddam out, and they did not expect him to last long after President George Bush ordered a ceasefire. Saddam was a strongman, went the argument. The humiliation of defeat would cut through the miasma of fear and he would be ousted. In Washington and London, they denied repeatedly that they had any desire to hurt Iraqis who were already his victims. But no amenable strongman emerged to oust Saddam, so the Americans and British went for a policy of containment and applied military and economic pressure. In Washington, London and in the UN Security Council, the line was repeated throughout the 1990s that Saddam Hussein could solve all the problems at a stroke by obeying the resolutions of the UN Security Council. Any suffering in Iraq was his fault.

Saddam's dictatorship was as brutal as ever. His equivalent of bread and circuses was candyfloss and a roller coaster. As the sanctions hit Iraqis, he abolished admission charges at the Baghdad fairground. Night after night, it was full of people trying to forget their troubles. It was better than the war, when the streets were empty and dusty with the fallout of soot from burning buildings, but also worse, because they had lost the hope that Saddam's time might nearly be over. For the leader, it was almost business as usual, once he had crushed the uprisings by Kurds and Shias at the end of the 1991 war. George Bush had encouraged them, then ordered his military not to intervene as perhaps 20,000 Shias and the same number of Kurds were killed. Responding to the invasion of Kuwait had been the easy bit, but the end of the war was messy for the Americans, who didn't want the responsibility of overthrowing Saddam.

General Norman Schwarzkopf, US commander during Desert Storm, wrote that taking all of Iraq would have left America stuck 'like a dinosaur in a tar pit', but they did not want an unrepentant Saddam to continue behaving like a dictator. The seed of unfinished business settled in some American minds and germinated into a dangerous sense of failure. By August 1998, with the temperature in Baghdad nudging fifty degrees, the visible damage to the city had been repaired. Bombed-out ministries were rebuilt exactly as before, and the same Saddam posters were replaced. The city's restored telephone exchange was decorated with exactly the same mural of Saddam flashing his white teeth as he made a call on what my memory says was a pink telephone. War and sanctions had left Baghdad battered, exhausted and impoverished, like so many of its people.

To contain Saddam's regime, the UN Security Council passed three resolutions in the 1990s intended to destroy Iraq's presumed stockpiles of weapons of mass destruction and its ability to produce them. Iraq, under pressure in the ceasefire talks, had agreed to let in UN weapons inspectors. Although they destroyed a great deal, there were constant rows about where they could go and what they could see. Saddam cultivated the swagger of a man who had been attacked by the world's most powerful nations and survived. I watched a sculptor putting the finishing touches to the president's latest statue. Beating America was Saddam's greatest achievement, the sculptor said, avoiding the eye of the ever-present regime minder.

Having an honest conversation with Iraqis was difficult. Indoors, they assumed the room was bugged. Anywhere they could be seen by others, the worry was being betrayed. Talking to a foreigner made it even worse; if that person also had a television camera and a microphone, it came with a certain interrogation by the security police, so we were never short of fervent expressions of love and admiration for Saddam. The regime had tortured and killed enough people by the 1990s for all Iraqis to know the risks of doing anything that resembled opposition. In Baghdad's markets, narrow lanes lined with small shops and open-air stalls, worn-down people, once comfortably off and now virtually destitute, sold their remaining valuables. Mr

Jassim's shop sold gramophones with veneers of walnut and teak, and old records, but they were not cheap. Nothing was in Iraq, thanks to huge inflation caused by sanctions on top of an economy destroyed by war.

In response, the government printed money. In a drawer at home, I still have a thick wad of worthless Iraqi banknotes from the 1990s. The head of Saddam Hussein stares balefully at my socks. The paper is thin and Saddam's image smudges easily. Money was weighed rather than counted; inflation wiped out savings, and everyone who relied on a fixed salary was impoverished. Shopping needed a carrier bag full of Iraqi dinars, but most traders, like Mr Jassim the gramophone man, preferred dollars.

Mr Jassim tried, unsuccessfully, to sell me a wind-up gramophone complete with a brass trumpet-shaped horn. I thought about the original owners, maybe middle-class merchants, swaying to crackling dance tunes in the 1930s. Perhaps they were Jews, a prosperous community who had been forced to leave in a hurry after the birth of Israel in 1948. Or a British officer might have imported it to remind him of what he was missing back home. Mr Jassim had a more successful line in nervous flattery of the all-seeing and all-knowing Saddam Hussein. Sanctions were, he said, without doubt the worst thing in Baghdad, 'but they won't affect us as long as the leader is here. He has done a great many things . . . he is rebuilding almost everything – bridges, the infrastructure – all these things.'

People did what was necessary to survive in a country where politics were turbulent and often violent. After Saddam launched his disastrous war with Iran in 1980, young men were conscripted into the army with no release date. When the war ended in 1988, Saddam was left with a vast army that might have turned against him if he failed to keep the men and their families clothed and fed. The treasure houses of Kuwait were just over the border, but the reckless decision to invade, occupy and loot Kuwait brought not just humiliating defeat, but crushing sanctions.

Dealing with a dictatorship involves making nasty compromises. You have to work within their system to get the chance to look in, and sometimes that means doing it their way. After Saddam was saved by George Bush's decision to stop the advancing armies before they reached Baghdad, he rebuilt his regime. In the twelve uneasy years before the next war, it kept tabs on foreign journalists by forcing us to rent offices at the Ministry of Information. We assumed everything was bugged, and a bespectacled official made weekly rounds to collect wads of dollars from our cubbyholes, which had been carved out of a conference room.

Another compromise was agreeing a 'programme' with the ministry. Just off the main ministry newsroom, where the minders sat and smoked, was a small office with a more senior official sitting in a fug of tobacco. Requests for visits from an interview with the president (impossible) to visiting a nuclear site (almost impossible) had to be carefully calibrated, but the thing that you included in your request (knowing that it was absolutely possible), would be a visit to Saddam Hussein Children's Hospital, because they had a legitimate point to make about the impact of sanctions. Before 1990 Iraq had first-world standards of health care, but after nearly a decade of sanctions, the hospitals had slipped back into a different age.

Sanctions imposed restrictions on so-called 'dual use' products that could be used in Iraq's weapons programme. Medicines were supposed to be allowed in under sanctions, but the process was slow and UN agencies complained that they did not get what they needed. The doctors and nurses were demoralized and depressed, and I took to apologizing to the doctors for the fact that our intrusions changed nothing. Dying children were in every ward, and parents crushed by life. One doctor's answer was to show me how they did not have disinfectant to clean the floors, before pointing out a small boy who was being slowly killed by acute myeloid leukaemia. His eyes were swollen and puffy. In countries without sanctions he might have survived: not in Saddam's Iraq.

Many families knew the hospital could not save their children. They would bring their birth certificates when they were admitted because they knew they would be needed for the death certificate. A scheme existed to allow Iraq to sell oil to raise money for food and humanitarian supplies, but the process of clearing funds to buy what was needed moved slowly and there was never enough cash. At the same time, the Security Council turned a blind eye to a huge black market in oil exports from Iraq to Turkey, partly because the Kurds, allies of the West, depended on it. They needed the money to fund their enclave in northern Iraq.

The sanctions were supposed to back up the UN inspectors' search for weapons of mass destruction. The regime was forced to let them in, then tried to slow them down, relieving the international pressure from time to time by letting them get on with their jobs. By the start of the new century, Iraqis not in the regime were sick of the impact that the standoff between Saddam and the outside world was having on their lives. I suggested to one man that the best way to end the agony would be to let the inspectors get on with what they wanted to do, finish the process and then have the chance of a new era. His answer was full of frustration: 'We've had them for the last nine years. Haven't they done their job yet? Believe me, the expression is that they're looking for a black cat in a dark room where there is no black cat.'

UN officials in Iraq were shocked and angered when they saw what sanctions were doing to the Iraqi people. Denis Halliday, a UN assistant secretary general and humanitarian coordinator in Iraq, resigned in protest after a year and began campaigning against a policy he called 'genocidal'. In a speech on a US college campus in October 1999 he declared: 'We are now in there responsible for killing people, destroying their families, their children, allowing their older parents to die for lack of basic medicines . . . We're in there allowing children to die who were not born yet when Saddam Hussein made the mistake of invading Kuwait.'[1] Halliday's successor in Baghdad was Hans von Sponeck, another veteran of three decades at the UN. Before he took the long drive into Baghdad, Halliday told Von Sponeck that his job would be to administer 'a criminally flawed and genocidal UN Security Council Iraq policy'.[2] Halliday's contention was that deliberately punitive limits had been put on the humanitarian programme to use the misery of the people to destabilize the Iraqi government.

Von Sponeck did not last much longer than Halliday as the UN's humanitarian coordinator in Iraq. He resigned in 2000, sick of running a programme that he believed was deeply flawed and highly politicized.[3] During his last few weeks in Baghdad, he went with me to the Saddam Hussein Children's Hospital, where we saw children dying who could have been saved. Just like all the Iraqis I met, Von

Sponeck and his UN colleagues were horrified by what sanctions were doing. As we walked through wards of doomed children, Von Sponeck told me he would no longer administer a system that penalized the people and helped the regime. Trying to control Saddam was, he said, 'like trying to catch a tiger. In the process you're killing a beautiful bird.' It was not enough, he told me, to say that the fate of Iraq was in the hands of Saddam Hussein. 'We cannot wish away the impact of sanctions on the life of the common civilian population in this country. We have evidence. We have very hard evidence. For example, UNICEF keeps saying that if the maternity trends for children in the eighties had continued into the 1990s, 500,000 children would not have died. Now that is a fact. It's not that it's not an emotional argument. It simply is a fact.'

Von Sponeck's criticisms were hitting home, but the US State Department spokesman James Rubin waved them away, saying about him, 'This man in Baghdad is paid to work, not to speak.'[4] When Von Sponeck resigned, Rubin's response was that the US was 'very pleased . . . Mr Von Sponeck was a humanitarian affairs coordinator. He was not the arbiter of national or international security for the world.'[5]

The Americans and the British refused to accept any responsibility for the suffering of the people. Saddam's regime spent money rebuilding palaces that could have been spent on food and medicines. But sanctions were a blunt instrument. Twenty years on, they are still used as a way of exerting pressure. Since Iraq, the UN, the US and the European Union have tried to target sanctions — with the Syrian leadership, for example — so far, without any noticeable effect.

Jutta Burghardt, who had worked alongside Von Sponeck on the UN World Food Programme, resigned the day after him, for the same reasons, fed up that American and British hawks ignored her protests. Before she left Baghdad, she told me that she had assumed the UN operation was in Iraq to protect the human rights of the Iraqi people. Instead, she said, 'It's a screen, a veil to hide a situation where under complete embargo people are living in misery, increasing impoverishment — real human tragedy. Maybe the world doesn't really know what's going on here.'

Sanctions did not really touch Iraq's elite, some of whom made fortunes from busting sanctions by importing goods they could sell at huge profits. Some of them used to come to enjoy the pool and the tennis courts at the Al Rasheed Hotel, an oasis in Baghdad's broiling summer. The only impact of sanctions on the hotel's leisure facilities that I noticed was an occasional shortage of chlorine in the pool. Journalists also had to stay at the heavily bugged Al Rasheed, and sometimes in the evenings, when the temperature was down to forty degrees or so, I used to play tennis with a senior official at the Ministry of Information called Naji al-Hadithi, regarded as friendly by foreign journalists. Later on, as Naji Sabri, he was Saddam's last foreign minister. He was rarely hostile, except when Baghdad was being bombed and he would swap his Italian suit for the olive-green uniform and black beret of the Baath Party. Naji had a mean slice, and a liberal approach to line calls. He would hit it out and announce that it was in. All his opponents who valued their next visa or interview would agree.

It is impossible to be a foreign correspondent in a dictatorship without working with the regime. It is the price of lifting the edge of the curtain to throw light on what's happening. But there are limits. It bothered me that it was easy to report the impact of sanctions, but much harder to report the brutality of the regime. People were scared to talk about it, but I had to find ways to remind my audience that Iraq was, to borrow the title of a book about it, a republic of fear. On one trip in 1993, the US Congress published a report that talked about repression and coercion in Iraq. I quoted from it extensively, and a couple of hours later found myself summoned to the offices of a senior official and ordered to leave for the border immediately, or else.

I went to see my old tennis partner Naji, who was under pressure in the complex game of palace politics and fighting to protect his position in the regime. Naji turned up the classical music he always had playing in his office, and went to his bathroom. He stood halfway out of the door, with the taps going full blast to confuse the hidden microphones, and mouthed that he couldn't help and that it was time for me to break for the border. Naji's life was complicated. He has repeatedly denied reports that he worked for the Americans in the last year or so of Saddam's rule, by which time he had grown a bushy Saddam-like moustache to go with his relaunch as foreign minister. I suspected that he had some kind of deal with Washington that allowed him to escape to Qatar via Damascus, and never appear in the deck of cards featuring the faces of wanted men that was issued to US forces.

The regime's main link with the outside world was the deputy prime minister, Tariq Aziz, a Christian with a fondness for a good cigar. In an encounter broadcast on Iraqi television, negotiations between the regime and UNSCOM, the agency charged with disarming Iraq, broke down. Tariq Aziz berated its head, Richard Butler. 'You always speak in an imperial, pompous manner. That we decide, we decide what is right and what is wrong. We decide what is enough and what is not enough. And you forget that you are not an imperial force.'

Butler replied, mildly, 'Well, I guess that concludes our meeting.' The weapons inspectors pulled out and it was clear what was coming. Just before Christmas 1998, the intergalactic highway across the desert was busy with journalists arriving and humanitarian workers and weapons inspectors leaving. The Americans, assisted by the British, were going to punish Saddam's regime for the deadlock over weapons inspections. It was the heaviest bombing since the 1991 war. Bill Clinton, in a live broadcast from the Oval Office, said that Operation Desert Fox would 'protect the national interests of the United States and indeed the interests of people throughout the Middle East and the world'.

In four days and nights, the Americans and the British dropped 415 cruise missiles and 600 bombs. The news teams in Baghdad decamped from their cubbyholes at the Ministry of Information and set up on the roof. The city shook as clouds of fire exploded from the buildings that had been chosen for destruction. Cruise missiles tracked across Baghdad's night sky, hitting palaces, security buildings, suspected weapons sites and parts of Iraq's air defence system. Although I could feel the blast waves, it felt fairly safe up on the roof. The explosions were real, but it felt as if the crisis was made for TV; since we would be putting it on the world's screens, and the Americans knew where we were, we assumed we would not get bombed. After the experience of 1991, we knew that modern weapons are accurate to a couple of metres. When it was all over, a colleague in Jordan told me that the Pentagon had suggested a time that his network might want to go live. The bombing started punctually in the early hours of the morning, at the same time as the satellite they'd booked after the Pentagon tip-off. It coincided neatly with prime-time evening news eight hours back on the east coast of the United States.

The action was not enough for a small but influential lobby in Washington, DC that had never stopped calling for regime change in Baghdad. Some of them went on to be architects of the invasion of Iraq in 2003. The Americans were infuriated that Saddam was still in power – it felt as if he had got away with defying them. Deputy Prime Minister Tariq Aziz appeared before journalists in Baghdad and compared what was happening to the days after the First World War, when the fledging RAF bombed recalcitrant Iraqi villages. The regime had taken on most of the world's most powerful countries in 1991 and been emboldened by the experience, realizing that the blunt force of sanctions was having consequences that many people in the US and Britain found uncomfortable. Not only were the people of Iraq suffering, but Saddam's regime, the real target, was pushing back hard. It could see the cracks sanctions were causing in the alliance and was doing all it could to make them worse.

After four days, the Americans declared victory, although Saddam beat them to it in his own broadcast to the nation.[6] He was shown surrounded by close advisors hanging onto every word of his wise counsel. The image presented to the Iraqi people and the outside world was of solidity and calm. We fought, he told his audience, a holy war of glorious and immortal conquest. 'History will be proud of these days and those who make them – the great Iraqi people and their bulwark and sword, the heroic army, which records these days with letters of light.'

Britain's prime minister, Tony Blair, had formed a strong political friendship with Bill Clinton. At home, Blair had concentrated hard on winning power for Labour, delivering victory with a landslide majority in 1997. Like any leader, he had to make domestic policy a priority in order to win power. In office he defaulted, as a foreign policy novice, to the standard position for British leaders since the Second World War: get close to the Americans and stay there. He gave Bill Clinton all the support he could. The whole world, Blair said, would rejoice if Saddam Hussein fell. In the absence of that, four days of bombing had 'put him back in his cage'.

It was all over in time for Christmas. Before we all went home, Tariq Aziz told the journalists assembled in the Ministry of Information that the allied bombing had wounded 180 and killed sixty-two. As for Blair's choice of words: 'This is the old rhetoric of a liar. He accused my president of being a serial liar, but it proves that he is a serial liar and many honest British MPs and people have strongly condemned his position.'

Life and art seemed too close for comfort. The year before Desert Fox, Robert De Niro and Dustin Hoffman starred in *Wag the Dog*, a film about a made-for-TV war with Albania to rescue a beleaguered president accused of sexual shenanigans in the Oval Office. When Bill Clinton ordered the bombing of Baghdad, he was in deep trouble for his own sexual antics in the White House with Monica Lewinsky, a twenty-four-year-old intern. A former US secretary of state, Lawrence Eagleburger, supported the attack but acknowledged that its timing 'smells to high heaven'.[7] As the planes and missiles hit Iraq, the president was being impeached for 'high crimes and misdemeanours'.

The attacks bought Clinton a day's delay in the impeachment proceedings, but Congressional Republicans pressed ahead, outraged by what seemed to be a cynical ploy. Clinton's aides later wrote about how distracted he was by the storm over his affair, but no American leader looks more presidential than when orders are issued in the Oval Office to go to war.[8] The timing of the attacks might have been more to do with looking presidential as his private life imploded than a lunge towards an alternative future without the shadow of Ms Lewinski.

Although the timing might have been useful for Clinton, assumptions that it was as much an act of political theatre as an act of war were overblown. The bombing dealt a severe blow to what was left of Saddam's special weapons programmes. After he was overthrown by the 2003 invasion, Iraqi weapons experts told American interrogators that Desert Fox had destroyed the few parts of their research that had escaped the UN weapons inspectors. Saddam had five years left. When I could, I travelled back and forth across the desert to Planet Baghdad, as Iraq's isolation deepened and slid towards catastrophe.

10.

In the Name of God

The first time I met my colleague in Tehran in 1990 she was wearing a black chador, as all Iranian women did at the time, with a black headscarf that showed not a single strand of hair. It's probably best I don't name her, but she was a most elegant woman. I could tell from the quality of the silk and the stitching that she cared about how she looked.

The woman dealing with foreign journalists at the Ministry of Islamic Guidance in Tehran wore a chador made of something that looked like thick black gabardine. She was about my age and slightly scary, not because of her clothes, but because she spoke perfect English and had a sharp understanding of the mind of an average Western journalist. I was on my first trip to Iran, and struggling to do the right thing. The guidance office demanded that all visiting journalists submit a programme of requests. I noticed that the hotel restaurant menu started with the words 'In the name of God', and someone suggested I put that at the top of my letter. I thought if it was appropriate for *fesenjan*, the classic Iranian chicken stew with pomegranate, it might help with filming requests. The scary lady in the thick chador held my letter between her finger and thumb and read out the words, a contemptuous smile on her lips. 'In the name of God? Do you really mean that, Jeremy?'

Dress codes for women in Iran were liberalized during the

presidency of Mohammad Khatami, a moderate who was elected in 1997. Women can wear bright colours if they want, and outfits can be quite figure-hugging as long as flesh is not displayed. Headscarves are still mandatory. In poorer areas and villages not much has changed, but trendy young women in middle-class North Tehran position their scarves somewhere toward the back of their heads and don't try too hard to stop their hair spilling out.

By 2009, my elegant female colleague would wear Western-style clothing in the office before grabbing a headscarf and a garment, known in Iran as a manteau, a bit like a trench coat, to go outside. One day we were off to a demonstration. The Basij, the regime's hardline militia, were going to be out in force. It was summer, and my colleague was wearing strappy sandals. Before we left, she sat down to put on a pair of trainers. I asked her if we were going to have to run for it. No, she said, but if we get arrested and the Basij see I've painted my toenails dark red, we're going to get into even worse trouble. She was one of many Iranians who wanted more openness, better connections with the West and more personal freedom. The Basij who might take exception to her nail varnish were social conservatives, men who believed women's place was at home. Painted toes were a tiny symbol, but enough to enrage a religious militiaman.

Outside, the streets of Tehran were in ferment. The presidential election had delivered another victory for the hard-line populist Mahmoud Ahmadinejad, and hundreds of thousands of people had been protesting for days that the result was a fraud. The Islamic Republic allows elections, but they are not fair or open. A certain amount of free speech is allowed, as long as it is not directed at the Islamic system, but the candidates have to be vetted before they are allowed to stand. The Supreme Leader is the most powerful person in the country, but the president has a big impact on the way Iran goes.

A couple of weeks after the election, the regime was cracking down hard. The big demonstrations had stopped, but small ones, mainly by students, continued. They would set fire to rubbish skips before the riot police and the Basij arrived to break their heads. Basij were standing every ten yards or so along Tehran's broad avenues, armed with thick clubs or rubber truncheons. Behind them, never far away, were squads of armed police.

A stern voice on the phone from the Ministry of Islamic Guidance had warned me that there would be serious consequences if I tried to report from the streets, even more serious than simply being deported. I presumed he was threatening arrest, maybe even prison. But my colleague and I reasoned that banning reporting didn't mean we couldn't walk down the street and watch what was happening. I did not carry a microphone or camera, and in 2009 I didn't have a smartphone.

When a young woman called Neda Agha-Soltan was shot dead on the edge of a demonstration that summer, someone filmed what happened and posted it online. Social media was just starting, but images of her last few minutes rocketed around the world. Millions watched her die and drew their own conclusions about a regime that would shoot its citizens dead in the street. The digital revolution was making it impossible to close a country down, and it was a sign of things to come. A year later, the Iranian government jammed satellite broadcasts to stop Iranians seeing a documentary about Neda. Two years later, in 2011, videos on social media and satellite TV played a big part in spreading the Arab uprisings.

It rankled when the BBC warned viewers I wasn't able to report from the streets. Every day I went for long walks with my Iranian friend and wrote up what was happening when I got back. In the evenings people would go to their rooftops to chant 'Allau Akhbar' – God is greatest. It was a form of protest that they had used against the shah before he was overthrown in 1979, and now it was being turned on the Islamic Republic. It echoed around the middle-class apartment buildings where the BBC office was based, in North Tehran, a well-off area that in places felt as calm and wealthy as a quiet corner of a city in Germany. My elegant Iranian colleague did not stay beyond five in the afternoon because the presence of so many police and Basij on the streets made her nervous about getting home safely. I spent every evening on my own, recording the neighbours' chants, trying to operate equipment to send over pictures, and attempting piece-to-camera selfies on the balcony.

In the end, the Islamic system survived the challenge in 2009, but the regime had been given a bad fright, and since then has used more subtle ways of manipulating elections. In 2021 victory was guaranteed for the hardliner Ebrahim Raisi by banning all other credible candidates from standing. An irony of the Islamic Republic is that the heirs to the 1979 revolution behave in ways that resemble the old regime of the shah. The state denies its people agency and the right to speak freely; it is backed up by security organizations that do not hesitate to kill to intimidate, control and punish the people; corruption lurks at every level; and the regime has a propensity for expensive foreign adventures that are unpopular at home.

Iran had a powerful empire at a time when Europe was still a patchwork of primitive, warring tribes. Iranians have a rich culture, a keen eye for the intricacies of life and a hatred of the Western stereotype that portrays them as a mass of chanting fanatics. Many Iranians are suspicious of the intentions of foreign governments. At the top of the list are America, Israel and Britain. The first few times I was in Iran, I was surprised by the influence Britain is still believed to have there. Many people in the UK have forgotten about their country's long history of meddling in Iran's affairs, if they knew about it in the first place; Iranians learn about British imperialism at school. Iran's dysfunctional relationship with the Western world is rooted in the interventions of Britain and America. As always with powerful nations, their actions were designed to protect and promote their own interests.

Britain took control of the waters of the Gulf between Arabia and Iran in the 1820s, to stop pirates attacking shipping on the route to India. The discovery of oil in southern Iran in 1908 changed everything, putting the Middle East front and centre in the minds of the leaders of the great powers, where it has stayed ever since. In the years before the First World War, Middle Eastern oil began to power a world that was racing into a revolution in mechanization, transportation and communications. It was another reason for the big powers to intervene; oil was a strategic resource as important as steel or coal had been in the nineteenth century, much too precious to be left to the people who lived on top of it.

It started with three men in London. Winston Churchill, First Lord of the Admiralty, and Admiral Sir John Fisher, the First Sea Lord, were determined to turn the Royal Navy into a fleet propelled not by coal, but oil. Fisher was so enthusiastic about the new fuel that he was known as 'the oil maniac'. Most of the oil pumped commercially in the early years of the twentieth century came from the Gulf of Mexico, too far away and too American; the world's leading maritime power needed its own supply. Churchill and Fisher backed the plan of William Knox D'Arcy, a speculator and entrepreneur who had made a fortune in the Australian gold rush, to prospect for oil in southern Iran.

D'Arcy extracted a concession from the shah of Iran to exploit oil reserves across the whole country except the five provinces that bordered Russia, in return for £20,000 in cash, £20,000 in stocks and just 16 per cent of the profits. Six years later, D'Arcy was staring at bankruptcy. His men could not find the lakes of oil he was convinced lay somewhere underground in the province of Khuzestan. Gloomily contemplating the loss of his house in Grosvenor Square in Belgravia and his neo-Gothic country mansion, Stanmore Hall in Middlesex, with its splendid pre-Raphaelite tapestries, D'Arcy raised enough cash for one last attempt. On 26 May 1908, on a plateau in the Zagros Mountains, oil gushed high into the Iranian sky.[1] D'Arcy's new enterprise, the Anglo-Persian Oil Company, spawned two mighty parts of the modern petrochemical industry: BP, and the Iranian Ministry of Oil.

From the beginning, investors smelled profit. When the shares were first offered for sale on the stock markets in London and Glasgow, buyers jostled five deep at the trading desks. A 140-mile-long pipeline was built from the oil fields in Khuzestan to supply a refinery on Iran's Gulf Coast. The Royal Navy switched to oil; Churchill bought 51 per cent of the company's shares for the British government on the eve of the First World War. He regarded Britain's near monopoly of Iranian oil as one of his greatest achievements. The deal D'Arcy had made in 1901 netted him another fortune as well as providing bundles of money for Britain's exchequer and cheap oil for the Royal Navy. It was a disaster for Iran, and not just financially; Britain's outsize influence distorted Iranian politics for decades.

The British needed Iranian oil to fuel the British Empire, and protected their investment with tried and trusted imperial methods. Indian sepoys guarded D'Arcy's expedition even before it had struck oil, and by 1916 they were reinforced by a new militia recruited from friendly tribes called the South Persian Rifles, based in Bandar Abbas.[2] British officers commanded militiamen in dozens of skirmishes with unfriendly tribes, while the Rifles arrested German and Austrian agents who recognized the strategic importance of oil and were doing all they could to whip up nationalist passions.

As more oil fields were developed in the mid-twentieth century, the British stuck to D'Arcy's original deal, even extending it in 1933. The company, now renamed the Anglo-Iranian Oil Company, paid more in taxes to the UK government than it paid in royalties to Iran. Abadan was its company town, built around the world's biggest oil refinery. The town was built on strictly segregated lines and Iranians were not trusted to do the company's big jobs. Senior Europeans lived in recreations of English suburbia on the coasts of the Gulf, in big and airy villas or bungalows surrounded by lawns and hedges, while workers had terraced houses with high walls and tiny courtyards. They were built out of modern materials rather than the cooler mud bricks they might have used in their home villages, which meant the workers roasted in the summer.[3] The worst place was a shanty town known as Paper City, which was 'without electricity or running water . . . The unpaved alleyways were emporiums for rats.'[4] The oil industry created Iran's first industrial working class. In the winter of 1978–9, Abadan was one of the cities that rose against the shah.

Behind high walls in a scruffy Tehran neighbourhood, with a lion and a unicorn on the pillars of the main entrance, is Britain's fourteen-acre embassy compound, a tangible reminder of its imperial power in Iran. In the embassy's grand dining room, next to plasterwork inscribed with 'VR', the monogram of Queen Victoria, a brass plaque commemorates the table settings for a lavish dinner in 1943 that celebrated Winston Churchill's birthday. It was held during a conference at which Churchill and the US president Franklin D. Roosevelt agreed to Stalin's demand that they open a second front in Europe against Nazi Germany. Iran was a vital supply route for American military aid to the USSR, and its oil was a crucial part of the allied war effort. In 1941, the British and the Soviets invaded and removed

Reza Shah — they suspected he was a Nazi sympathizer — replacing him with his son Mohammad Reza Pahlavi. The young shah was not invited to the dinner or the conference.

After 1941, a generation of Iranian politicians managed to open up an era of relative political freedom. Iran's political institutions were raucous and full of intrigue, but they were functioning. The great powers' minds were elsewhere, which offered a chance to regain sovereignty. After the war, they faced down an attempt by Stalin to swallow Iran's northern oil fields. Britain's domination of Iranian oil was an obvious target for Iranians who were fed up with meddling foreigners making fortunes at their expense, and the British were horrified when the Americans agreed to share the profits from Aramco, its equivalent of Anglo-Iranian Oil, with Saudi Arabia. Losing control of Iranian oil would kick away another leg of Britain's increasingly rickety pretensions to world power.

The British were struggling to preserve their position in the Middle East against a wave of protests. The world was changing. Iranians, like Egyptians, and the feuding Arabs and Jews in Palestine, did not want foreigners telling them what to do or helping themselves to their wealth. Political life in Tehran was turbulent and sometimes violent: a prime minister was assassinated by an Islamist who shouted, 'Long live Islam, death to the oil company.'[5] Iran's factions ranged from royalists who supported the shah, to leftist fellow travellers with Moscow, to clerics and nationalist parliamentarians. Despite their fierce disagreements, the importance of breaking the hold of Britain on their country's oil industry and natural resources was something they could all understand.

By the time the Anglo-Iranian Oil Company offered to split the profits with the Tehran government, it was too late. In 1951 the company was nationalized by a vote in parliament. The prime minister appointed to see it through was Mohammad Mossadeq, an elderly, long-serving politician from an aristocratic family who had been educated in Switzerland. Two years of crisis followed as the British fought to regain some kind of control. Mossadeq was a disruptor who made enemies at home as fast as the British and the Americans vilified him abroad. His habit of playing up his infirmities, taking to his sickbed and fainting at moments of high emotion was a gift for

British newspaper cartoonists, who lampooned Mossadeq as a hysterical foreigner.

He did not make many friends in America, either. *Time* magazine named Mossadeq their 'man of the year' for 1951, with the caption, 'He oiled the wheels of chaos' and an article that ridiculed his performance:

> In a few months he had the whole world hanging on his words and deeds, his jokes, his tears, his tantrums. Behind his grotesque antics lay great issues of peace or war, progress or decline, which would affect many lands far beyond his mountains . . . In his plaintive, singsong voice he gabbled a defiant challenge that sprang out of a hatred and envy almost incomprehensible to the West.[6]

The pressure on Mossadeq told. Iran had suffered so much from foreign intervention that his critics at home used the views of the great powers as ammunition against him. The British appealed to the international court in The Hague and then deployed the Royal Navy to blockade Iran's oil exports. As the economy shrank, Mossadeq's enemies gathered, from Moscow-aligned communists to important generals.

By 1953, the British and the Americans decided the time had come to end Iran's democratic experiment. The Eisenhower administration saw the Middle East entirely through the prism of the Cold War with the Soviet Union, and as far as they were concerned Mossadeq was no kind of ally. The White House ordered the CIA to plot a coup, in concert with MI6, to restore the status quo in Iran – they had allies in the Iranian military that had also seen enough of Mossadeq. The shah was persuaded to dismiss him and fled to Rome when the first attempt at a coup failed; the second did not. One of the American plotters was H. Norman Schwarzkopf Senior, father of Stormin' Norman who led Operation Desert Storm in 1991.

Once Mossadeq was ousted, the shah returned and imposed arbitrary and increasingly authoritarian rule, setting Iran down a path that led to revolution in 1979. Iranians and critics of the US and its allies point to the 1953 coup as the epitome of mid-century imperialism.

The removal of Mossadeq had consequences that were still felt seventy years on. Opponents of the Islamic Republic believe the coup snuffed out Iran's chance to develop a democracy. The wound in the Iranian psyche caused by foreign meddling was deepened by the memory of the United States removing Mossadeq in league with the fading British imperialists.

The shah embarked on a plan for ambitious modernization once he was back in power. His 1960s 'White Revolution' brought in land reform, and oil money paid for the construction of highways and airports. He cultivated his image. In the glossy magazines, the man on the peacock throne was always at the pinnacle of Sixties jet-set glamour: skiing at St Moritz, enjoying state dinners at the White House and country life at his estate in England. He was handsome, athletic and brave, flying his private plane in the thin air of the mountains. His empress Farah was beautiful and their children were charming. Only later would lurid tales emerge of his taste for European prostitutes, and corruption in his court.

The shah was an autocrat at the head of a vicious police state that allowed no political freedom. Like Arab leaders of his era, he tried to create a compact with the people to deliver some prosperity in return for them doing as they were told; he was less successful than Arab dictators. As Iranians pushed back, the nasty fantasy that his dictatorship was benevolent was exposed. The SAVAK, the secret police, was notorious for brutality, arbitrary arrests and the disappearance of the regime's opponents. The shah's enemies presented him as an American puppet, imposing an American plan on a country with a proud history and culture.

It made him an uncomfortable ally for Jimmy Carter, the champion of human rights who was elected as America's president in 1976. The United States had built a strategy around the alliance with Iran and its modernizing leader, who had enough oil money to keep the American arms industry busy. Iran also had diplomatic relations with Israel; the US found it useful to have two non-Arab regional powers straddling the perpetually troublesome Arab world. Little more than a year before the revolution, Jimmy Carter visited Tehran and

1. Operation Desert Shield, 22 November 1990. President George Bush eats Thanksgiving dinner with US soldiers in Saudi Arabia. Their presence lit a fire in the minds of jihadist extremists. One of them was Osama bin Laden.

2. American troops on Iraq's border with Kuwait in 1991. Saddam Hussein's looming presence was inescapable. Dictatorship, invasion and war trapped Iraqis in a long nightmare.

3. Iraqi Kurds fight for food. More than one million fled to the mountains after Saddam Hussein crushed their uprising in the spring of 1991. Desperate men stripped vehicles of relief supplies when they arrived in improvised camps. The scenes shamed the US and its allies into a big relief operation.

4. Bill Clinton pointing to a peaceful future at the signing of the Oslo 2 accord at the White House on 28 September 1995. With him from left to right: King Hussein of Jordan, Prime Minister Yitzhak Rabin of Israel, Palestinian President Yasser Arafat, and President Hosni Mubarak of Egypt. Five weeks later Rabin was assassinated by a Jewish extremist who wanted to destroy the peace process.

5. Reporting on the presidential referendum in Baghdad in October 1995. Saddam Hussein, the only candidate, won with 99.96% of the vote.

6. In August 1998 Osama bin Laden declared a holy war against the United States. Two weeks earlier al-Qaeda had killed more than 200 people in attacks on the US embassies in Kenya and Tanzania.

7. The power of religion in Jerusalem. A Christian believing she is in the presence of God during the Holy Fire ceremony in the Holy Sepulchre church. Jews and Muslims in the city have the same religious passion. Mixed with nationalism, it can be explosive.

8. The power of religion in Najaf, Iraq. Millions of Shia pilgrims come to pray at the shrine of Imam Ali, who they believe was the rightful heir of the prophet Muhammad. Sunni Muslims disagree. The dispute over the succession started the schism in Islam.

9. The epicentre of Jerusalem. An ultra-Orthodox Jew reads psalms facing the Western Wall. Above it is the compound sacred to Muslims that encloses the Dome of the Rock and al-Aqsa Mosque. The Christian Holy Sepulchre church is a few hundred yards away to the left.

10. US Marines pulling down Saddam's statue in Firdos Square as they enter Baghdad on 9 April 2003. Years later the Iraqi who started the attack on the statue told me nothing Saddam did was as bad as the murderous chaos set off by the American-led invasion.

11. Jewish settlers leaving the Gaza Strip in August 2005. Israel's decision to withdraw from Gaza allowed Hamas to claim a victory.

12. The people want the fall of the regime. Eighteen days of protests in Tahrir Square in Cairo at the start of 2011 ousted President Mubarak. Hope surged around the Middle East, until the counter-revolution began.

13. Children were often bussed to 'spontaneous' demonstrations supporting Colonel Muammar al-Gaddafi in the months before he was overthrown. This was outside the UN headquarters in Tripoli in April 2011.

14. President Bashar al-Assad of Syria in Damascus in 2010, about nine months before his forces opened fire on demonstrators. It took five years to get another interview, when he denied all accusations that his regime was killing thousands of Syrians.

15. With rebels from the Free Syria Army in Saqba, a Damascus suburb, on 27 January 2012. In the first year of the war they looked set to overthrow the regime of President Bashar al-Assad.

16. Morning coffee in Douma, one of the rebel-held satellite towns of Damascus in December 2012. The man who owned the American M4 assault rifle was later arrested in France for war crimes.

17. Bashar's boys. Young Alawites in Mezze 86 in Damascus in September 2013. The Assad regime would never have survived without the support of its own Alawite sect and other Syrian minorities. It wasn't blind loyalty. They feared Islamist extremists might kill them.

18. Christian militias joined the fighting on the regime's side in Maaloula in 2013, against the Nusra Front, a splinter group of al-Qaeda. Residents of the mainly Christian town outside Damascus still speak Amharic, believed to be the language used by Jesus Christ.

unwisely praised the shah's 'island of stability' and the people's 'admiration and love' for their leader. Months later, as millions marched against the shah, Jimmy Carter's envoy advised Iran's generals to aim at the protestors' chests if shooting over their heads did not work.[7] By then the demonstrations were too big to be crushed, and their tone was more Islamic. Anger boiled over.

The shah left Iran for the last time on 16 January 1979, tears pouring down his face, stooping at the last moment to stop a guard kissing his feet[8] – a belated flash of humility for a doomed autocrat. His departure was billed as an extended 'vacation', starting in Egypt. He was, in fact, dying of cancer and would never return.

Ayatollah Ruhollah Khomeini had been in exile for sixteen years, mostly in Najaf in southern Iraq, until Saddam Hussein expelled him at the request of the shah in October 1978. After Kuwait refused to let him in, he travelled back across the desert to Baghdad and on to Paris, where his entourage set up a temporary headquarters in a villa on the edge of the city. The revolution in Iran was major global news. In Paris, Khomeini was much more accessible than he had been in Najaf, and a cleric most non-Iranians had never heard of quickly became a world figure. He would often hold court, sitting cross-legged under an apple tree in the garden, impressing Western journalists who decided he was stern, learned and sincere. Many Iranians were just as taken with the contrast Khomeini made with the opulence of the shah and his court.

Khomeini's advisors recorded their leader's sermons on cassette recorders, played them down the phone to sympathizers and sent tapes to revolutionaries back home. With the shah already in exile, they chose 1 February for a triumphant journey back to Tehran on an airliner chartered from Air France. Millions lined the route into the city. Eleven days later, the government appointed by the shah, led by Prime Minister Shahpur Bakhtiar, was deposed. In the months that followed, liberals and leftists who had also laid claim to the revolution were outmanoeuvred, squeezed out, imprisoned and sometimes killed. The Ayatollah and his revolutionary council were in control. Shahpur Bakhtiar lived as a political exile in France until 1991, when he was killed, along with his secretary, by an Iranian hit squad who tricked their way into his apartment.

Iran's Islamic revolution was more than a shift in the political, religious and cultural terrain of the Middle East; in 1979, a year of momentous consequences, it changed the entire landscape. The revolutionaries showed that Islamists could sweep away a regime and turn Iran from a friend of the West to its enemy in a matter of months. They inspired the Saudi zealots who occupied the mosque in Mecca. By the end of the year, Afghans responded to the Soviet invasion by embarking on a holy war. And Iran's new masters inflicted a series of humiliations on the Americans that were so traumatic that they resonate forty years on.

The former shah, Mohammad Reza Pahlavi, cut a sorry figure in exile without his grand titles, his palaces and his power. Jimmy Carter immediately offered America's ally asylum in the US, but Pahlavi decided his best chance of a route back was to stay in the Middle East, first in Egypt and then in Morocco. In Iran, Khomeini and his supporters were consolidating their hold on the country. The shah had given women the vote; female students at Tehran University marched through the winter slush to protest, unsuccessfully, against new rules demanding that they wore Islamic dress. The clerics did not budge, and it took a while for Iran's erstwhile Western friends to work out the enormity of what had happened.

Anti-American feeling raged in Iran. A few weeks after Khomeini's return, some of his supporters stormed the US embassy and took diplomats hostage. The Iranian government still contained ministers who had been negotiating with the Americans, and they persuaded the radicals to end the siege. Jimmy Carter realized that giving sanctuary to the hated Pahlavi would inflame Tehran's revolutionaries. He withdrew the offer of asylum. But some of the most powerful men in America believed the shah deserved better. They included Henry Kissinger, not long out of office as secretary of state and still the world's most famous diplomat; David Rockefeller, chairman of Chase Manhattan bank; Richard Helms, a former US ambassador to Iran; and John J. McCloy, who was so well connected that he was known as 'the chairman of the establishment'.[9] Together they formed an old boys' network they called Project Eagle to get the shah to the US. They succeeded, with consequences so calamitous for their country that the documents were kept sealed until *The New York Times* saw them after David Rockefeller's death, aged 101, in 2017.[10]

The behind-the-scenes influencers of Project Eagle were determined to offer a mooring to the shah, who had become the world's most notorious nomad. After Egypt and Morocco he went to the Bahamas and then Mexico. Henry Kissinger told a Harvard Business School dinner in New York that America's friend should not have to be 'a flying Dutchman looking for a port of call'.[11] The shah stopped concealing his cancer, which he had kept a secret for six years; President Carter was persuaded that he needed life-saving treatment that was only available in America. Outside his hospital in New York, Iranians prayed for him to die as soon as possible. Much more significantly, the US embassy in Tehran was surrounded by enraged demonstrators. Khomeini made a speech in Qom, Iran's holy city, on 1 November 1979, calling the shah 'that corrupt germ' and threatening that the US 'will be confronted in a different manner by us if they continue'.

Three days later, it became clear what he meant. Radical students climbed over the gates of the embassy and occupied the building, taking the staff hostage. Khomeini ordered the release of female diplomats because 'Islam reserves special rights for women' as well as African Americans; he explained that they might have been press-ganged into service, as 'blacks for a long time have lived under oppression and pressure in America'.[12] Fifty-two American citizens were held for more than a year, and often paraded in public for the TV cameras. Crowds marched along the former Roosevelt Avenue outside the embassy, chanting 'Death to America.'

Back in America, there was outrage. Walter Cronkite, anchor of the CBS *Evening News*, took to ending his bulletin with a running total of the days the Americans had been held hostage. Anti-Iranian protests were held across America. Sales of Iranian caviar plummeted. Some Iranian Americans were sacked from their jobs and their children bullied at school. In April 1980, an attempt to send commandos to rescue the hostages ended in a deadly fiasco that killed eight Americans, rubbing in the humiliation. Only four years earlier, Americans had cheered on the Israeli commandos who rescued their hostages at Entebbe Airport in Uganda. America, the superpower, could not manage the same trick.

The hostage crisis poisoned the end of Jimmy Carter's presidency; it was one of the reasons why Ronald Reagan won the 1980 election. The hostages were released after 444 days, moments after Reagan's inauguration; Algeria helped to negotiate a deal that released billions of dollars' worth of frozen Iranian assets to buy their freedom. It later emerged that Reagan's team had held secret talks with Iran to make sure Carter received no credit for their release. The Islamic Republic of Iran turned out to be highly resilient, surviving America's fervent opposition and a war with Saddam Hussein's Iraq so bloody that it recalled the slaughter on the Western Front in the First World War.

The hostage crisis, like William Knox D'Arcy's oil concessions, the nationalization of the Anglo-Iranian Oil Company and the 1953 coup, lies behind the dysfunctional relationship that still exists between Iran and the United States and its Western allies. Forty years on, the contest between America's camp and Iran's continues to drive conflict in the Middle East.

11.

Ground Zero

It was easier than I'd expected to get to Ground Zero in New York City a few days after the attacks of 11 September 2001. I walked downtown from my hotel near Times Square, gradually getting closer to the place where the twin towers of the World Trade Center had stood. I assumed I would be stopped, but at a police barrier just below Houston Street I waved my BBC pass at an officer, who let me through. Inside the cordon there were no more challenges, and I walked right up to the steaming, smoking wreckage that filled the World Trade Center's 18-metre-deep basement and went about five storeys high. Firefighters, ironworkers and salvage experts laboured in the ruins, searching for bodies. Dust from the collapse of the towers still clogged the air. To keep out of their way, I went to a bar a few blocks away, ordered a beer and watched. When the shifts changed, the people who lived in the neighbourhood clapped the firefighters in and out of the terrible, tangled pile of rubble, steel and human remains. At some point in the next few days, security was tightened and it became harder to reach Ground Zero, as the world was learning to call the site: part of a new vocabulary that included 9/11, al-Qaeda and Osama bin Laden. I didn't really want to return. It felt like intruding into a private bereavement.

It had taken me a few days to reach New York. The United States and Canada had closed their airspace to all traffic apart from the military, and Britain did the same. It did not need much insight to recognize that this was a different kind of attack, by a different kind of foe, on the world's biggest powers, and that there would be long-term consequences. I tried to find the right words, telling viewers of *BBC Breakfast* that 'the reverberations of this story will clearly not be going on for weeks or months but for years . . . we'll be feeling the repercussions of this for a long time to come'. I wasn't the only one on air the morning after to compare its impact on the United States to the surprise attack on Pearl Harbor in 1941. A generation later, that seems self-evident, but on 12 September 2001 we all had a lot of adjusting to do.

One of the first aircraft to come in across the Atlantic was an elderly chartered Boeing 747 with several hundred British journalists on board. We landed at Montreal Airport – Canadian airspace had been first to reopen. The journalists squabbled over hire cars before driving six hours or so south to New York City. When we got there, one of the world's busiest places was stunned and silent. The sense Americans had of being safe at home from anything less than a full-scale nuclear attack was gone. The US air force was patrolling the skies above Manhattan. The low-flying F-15 warplanes were supposed to be reassuring, but in fact highlighted how much had changed. The attacks set off a chain of consequences for America and for the rest of the world that are still unravelling, centred on the Middle East. Radical Islam had been maturing and flexing new muscles for much of the twentieth century; it has shaped most of the first two decades of the twenty-first.

Not far from Ground Zero, sprouting into the waters around Lower Manhattan, are piers that were built for transatlantic liners. In 1948, a year that was as pivotal for the world as 2001, almost everyone crossing the Atlantic arrived on a ship. Millions of refugees were moving across Europe and Asia, driven from their homes by war and struggling to survive. One of the century's worst winters hit Europe just as the continent was plunged into the deep freeze of the Cold War. The Soviet Union blockaded land routes into West Berlin to try to squeeze out their former allies, who responded with an airlift that lasted almost a year. At its height, a transport aircraft was landing in West Berlin every thirty seconds. The United States was settling into a new role as a global superpower while Britain and France, the old imperial powers, were in full retreat.

At the same time, the Middle East was being torn apart, with Arab countries fighting to destroy newly independent Israel. The wounds created by that war and by the Arab defeat have never healed properly. In November 1948, a ship docked on one of New York's piers, and down the gangplank came a man whose intellectual legacy had profound global consequences.

Sayyid Qutb was an Egyptian in his early forties who had started his career as a poet and literary critic. In the time he spent in America after arriving in New York, he developed a view of the world that made him the intellectual inspiration of the men who, much later, perpetrated the 9/11 attacks. He had studied American literature, but it did not prepare him for what he found. He saw a colossal clash of cultures and concluded that the US, the new giant, was a moral wasteland. Qutb spent time studying in Greeley, Colorado – a university town founded on temperance – and saw degradation everywhere. In an article in 1951 called 'The America I have seen', Qutb condemned everything from haircuts to clothing, and even the way Americans made gravy. He saw a primitive country saturated with greed, lust and violence. Spectators at a football game were 'enthralled with the flowing blood and crushed limbs . . . destroy his head. Crush his ribs. Beat him to a pulp.'

Men used their muscles to obtain 'submission' of women, who knew 'seductiveness lies in the round breasts, the full buttocks, and in the shapely thighs . . .' Qutb was appalled when he saw a minister playing records at a Sunday student dance in a church hall. When he put on 'Baby It's Cold Outside', a duet sung between a man and woman as he tries to persuade her to stay the night, Qutb's description dripped with disgust:

> They danced to the tunes of the gramophone, and the dance floor was replete with tapping feet, naked legs, arms wrapped around waists, lips pressed to lips, and chests pressed to chests. The atmosphere was full of desire.[1]

When he boarded a liner to go home, Egypt was boiling following the unexpected defeat by Israel. In the beaten Arab countries, the old order of nationalist politicians and kings was being blamed for making deals with British and French imperialists. It was a time of demonstrations and strikes, and a new answer: Arab unity.

In Egypt, the first job was to get rid of the British, who had been forced to grant a form of independence but still stationed thousands of troops in the country. Egyptians were proud of their country's antiquity, and the presence of the British was humiliating and enraging. In Cairo, a few elite Egyptian families were allowed into the Gezira Sporting Club, a walled and leafy enclave around a grand pavilion on an island in the Nile; but it was mostly a British preserve, where they could order drinks at the Lido bar overlooking the swimming pool, or play polo, croquet, cricket, tennis and even watch horse racing. Cairo was replete with the agreeable trappings of imperial life. In the broad boulevards of the city's European Quarter, British officers, businessmen and their ladies ordered tea or whisky on the terrace of Shepheard's Hotel, one of the grandest in the British Empire. A few minutes' stroll away was the all-male, all-British Turf Club.

Controlling the Suez Canal was a fundamental part of Britain's self-image as a world power. British India was gone; the Canal balanced out undeniable evidence of decline. Towards the end of 1951, Egypt's prime minister Mostafa el-Nahas had had enough. After negotiations failed, he abrogated the treaty that allowed the British to station 80,000 troops in the Canal Zone. When that did not persuade the British to go either, Nahas and his ruling Wafd Party encouraged guerrilla attacks and a blockade of the British base in the Canal Zone. Anti-British anger deepened into riots and strikes as radios crackled with politicians' furious appeals to Egyptian patriotism.

The British hit back in January 1952, occupying police stations in the Canal Zone that they said were being used for attacks on their forces. When they tried to seize government buildings in the city of Ismailia, the government urged the police stationed there to resist. British tanks and artillery bombarded them for hours; forty-six policemen were killed, with seventy-two wounded. As the news spread, furious crowds marched into Cairo's European Quarter, smashing and setting fire to the symbols of foreign domination along its boulevards. By the end of the day the smoking ruins included bars, nightclubs, cinemas, casinos, the Turf Club and Shepheard's Hotel itself. When film of what happened arrived back in London, the Movietone news report headlined 'Results of Cairo's Black Day' condemned 'appalling' riots, 'a thoroughly organized attack on the property of British and other foreign nationalities', shameless arson in 'a big city with fine streets and modern buildings, many of them of course products of foreign interests'.[2]

Egypt was reeling, but King Farouk, a socialite who was out of his depth, preferred to look away. On 'Black Saturday', as the European Quarter was burning, Farouk hosted a banquet to celebrate the birth of his son and heir.[3] Egyptians were in the mood for change, fed up with the corruption of the Wafd and the king and his courtiers. Six months later, the army overthrew Farouk in a classic coup d'état, seizing public buildings and the radio station, where a young officer called Anwar Sadat came to the microphone to announce that the Free Officers had taken over. Their figurehead was a popular general, Mohamed Naguib, but mostly they were younger men who had served in the lost war in Palestine and were fed up with the old order. The real leader was Colonel Gamal Abdel Nasser, who went on to dominate the Arab world and still casts a long shadow over Egypt. At the height of his powers, even hard-bitten journalists felt Nasser's charisma. The British foreign correspondent Sandy Gall wrote:

> Physically he was an impressive man, tall for an Egyptian, well built, handsome and with a film star quality that turned heads and made him the centre of attention. But his most noticeable feature was his smile. It came on and off like an electric light, the shiny white teeth flashing on and off.[4]

Farouk and his family were packed off on the Egyptian royal yacht *Mahrousa* to sail into a gilded exile. The elegant vessel, built on the Thames in 1863, dropped anchor on the island of Capri in the Bay of Naples, an appropriate refuge for the portly monarch who was one of the most photographed celebrities of the 1950s. Egyptian naval ratings lined the *Mahrousa*'s rails to wave goodbye. An officer in an immaculate white uniform extravagantly wiped away tears as Farouk and his family boarded a humble tourist boat and were ferried ashore. Without its royal cargo, *Mahrousa* steamed back to Alexandria for a new career as Egypt's presidential yacht.[5]

For a while, opposition to the British brought together the two wings of Egyptian nationalism. On one side was the new secular breed of officers and technocrats, personified by the dashing Gamal Abdel Nasser, who rejected the idea of any more deals with the old imperial powers. The other kind of nationalism came from the Muslim Brotherhood, which since the late 1920s had been building a network dedicated to the creation of a state ruled by the laws of Islam. The Brotherhood's founder Hasan al-Banna believed that Islam was always political because it was about every part of life. The alliance between the two tendencies was convenient – Sayyid Qutb even advised the military for a while – but it was temporary. Once the Free Officers were in power, a clash began between the military and the Muslim Brotherhood and its offshoots. It is a feud that has never ended.[6]

The military grabbed the sinews of power in Egypt in 1952 and has never let them go. Anwar Sadat, the officer who broadcast news of the coup, became president when Nasser died. Sadat was assassinated by disciples of Qutb. When a Muslim Brotherhood government was elected after the Arab uprisings of 2011 to replace direct military rule, it did not last long. The generals removed the president and did all they could to break the Brotherhood, whose leaders were soon in exile, imprisoned or dead. General Abdul Fattah al-Sisi became president and imposed a police state as vicious as any in Egypt since the Free Officers overthrew King Farouk. Sisi portrays himself as Nasser's heir. He has the yacht *Mahrousa* but lacks his charisma.

Nasser and his military successors, including Sisi, saw the Muslim Brotherhood as a threat. The reach and influence of their network made them the military's only serious rival for power. When in 1954 a member of the Brotherhood tried to kill Nasser, the armed forces threw its former allies, including Sayyid Qutb, into jail. Long years behind bars and sharing cells strengthened the bonds within the secretive culture of the Brotherhood. It gave Qutb plenty of time to write, to build a legacy for al-Qaeda and the world created by 9/11.

Qutb's most influential book, *Milestones*, describes how violent struggle could build a religious state under the sovereignty of God, not the ruler. God's everlasting rule required an everlasting war against apostates and infidels. Qutb wrote about an idea that was well known in Islam called *jahiliyya*, which describes the 'ignorance' of the time before the prophet Muhammad received the message of God. Qutb was influenced by the ideas of Abu Al'a Mawdudi, an Islamist scholar in British India and then Pakistan, who argued that jahiliyya was not just the time before Islam; it was ever-present. The ignorant, the jahili, were not just Christians, Jews and the other non-believers, but also Muslims who were traitors to their faith and could therefore be killed. That included a godless elite and its followers.[7]

Nasser saw correctly that he was high on Qutb's list, and had him executed in 1966. Qutb's manuscripts were smuggled out of jail and were hugely influential in shaping the development of radical Islam. An early convert was the young Ayman al-Zawahiri, who went on to be Osama bin Laden's number two. Qutb's books, his life in prison and his death in a hangman's noose still inspire radical jihadists.

The great Egyptian novelist Naguib Mahfouz, whose early work Qutb had championed as a young literary critic, fell foul of one of Qutb's followers. In 1994, when Mahfouz was an old man, an Islamist militant stabbed him in the neck as he left his home in Cairo. His crime was to have written a book that al-Azhar, the highest Islamic authority in Egypt, had banned many years earlier for portraying the prophet. When Mahfouz won the Nobel Prize for Literature in 1988, Sheikh Omar Abdel Rahman, one of Egypt's most prominent radical clerics, said the author deserved death for encouraging a mood of blasphemy. In the end, Mahfouz died peacefully in old age; the sheikh, on the other hand, took his last breaths in 2017 while serving a life sentence in the US for his part in the conspiracy in 1993 to bomb the World Trade Center in New York.

Despite Qutb's contempt for the US, he did not believe that the West should be the first target for righteous Muslims. Instead they should start with the 'near enemy', the leaders of their own countries; the 'far enemy' would come later. It was al-Qaeda who took Qutb's jihadist ideology to the global stage. On 11 September 2001, earning the eternal favour of God by martyring themselves and killing others was on the minds of the men who hijacked four aircraft to turn them into lethal weapons. Fifteen of the hijackers were Saudis. The rest included two Emiratis, one from Lebanon, and a single Egyptian, Mohammad Ata, their leader. Qutb's ideas didn't just live on. They exploded into the world.

The attack on America by al-Qaeda showed Americans that they were vulnerable in the places where they felt safest. Social media was still a few years away, so New Yorkers used drawing pins and tape to post photos of missing friends and relations. Noticeboards of the missing sprang up outside hospitals and photos were pasted to shop windows, lines of happy snapshot smiles and grieving messages. Union Square in New York was full of shrines and messages for the dead. The families' grief and the outrage of the nation powered an almost unanimous desire in the US to hit back. Shock knocked the wind out of the US government and its allies. President George W. Bush, not long in office and no expert on foreign affairs, declared that the US had been hit by an act of war and would fight back with a war on terror. America was under attack. It had no other choice.

Perhaps there was one. The world might have been spared the worst of the hard years that followed if the attacks had been treated as the actions of a dangerous but small group of conspirators. Instead America entered an open-ended war without an easy-to-define victory. It was not difficult for the Americans to crush al-Qaeda as a coherent network or to drive Bin Laden into hiding, but it was much harder to tackle al-Qaeda's attraction to a small but significant number of Muslims. The excesses that went with the war on terror delivered recruits into extremist groups. When al-Qaeda's organization was smashed, its ideology had a second life.

President Bush made a quick decision to go after Bin Laden and al-Qaeda in Afghanistan. By the end of the year, the Taliban, al-Qaeda's hosts, had been driven out of Kabul, but they were never beaten. Bin Laden escaped into hiding. The other country on the US agenda was Iraq. Most of the 9/11 hijackers were Saudis, born, educated and radicalized in the kingdom, but Saudi Arabia was an ally and Bush had appointed to powerful positions people who believed that America had unfinished business with Saddam Hussein. The most influential of the group who came to be known as the 'neoconservatives' was Paul Wolfowitz, the number two in the Pentagon, who had seen Saddam

Hussein as America's main enemy in the Middle East since the invasion of Kuwait.

Everyone could agree that 9/11 was a huge intelligence failure, but the crucial next step was to make sure nothing like it could happen again. Wolfowitz and his supporters argued that it did not matter that there was no evidence that Saddam Hussein had supported al-Qaeda; they were convinced that he had weapons of mass destruction and wanted a bigger arsenal. What if he gave terrorists the wherewithal for another 9/11, or for something even worse? The neoconservatives saw other reasons to remove Saddam. It would be a giant step towards remaking the Middle East, taking away the toxic fuel that powered Islamist extremism. Democracy would replace dictatorship. Israel would be safer.

In the United States, estimates of the job they faced were expanding. Our breakfast television programme for the UK went on air at one in the morning New York time, and I spent my evenings watching news shows that endlessly discussed the consequences of the 9/11 attacks. A young pundit mused about the chances of matching the achievements of 'the greatest generation', the Americans who had grown up in the Great Depression and fought against the Nazis and the Japanese. Could we, the young man asked, live up their legacy? The mood, in those first days after 9/11, was of hyper-patriotism and a sense that they were on a new road that would be long and hard. It was soon clear that evicting the Taliban regime by force from Kabul was not going to be enough to satisfy the desire in the US not just for revenge, but to make sure America could never be threatened again.

The consequences of 9/11 were starting to shake the Middle East. America and President George W. Bush had Iraq in their sights. Naji Sabri al-Hadithi, my former tennis partner at the Rasheed Hotel in Baghdad, was now the country's foreign minister. By 2001 he had outmanoeuvred his enemies in the court of the dictator, cultivated a Saddam-style moustache and emerged with a top job. A few days after 9/11, Naji knew Iraq was in America's sights. He stood in front of TV cameras to say that the regime in Iraq had no connection with the attacks and did not harbour or sponsor al-Qaeda. He insisted the Americans and the British knew that was true. Perhaps looking for support outside Iraq, he told the cameras that the Bush administration could be bad for Muslims:

> There is a need for a quiet approach to address this problem; for a reasonable and careful one, away from warmongering, away from this desire to unleash a field of hatred against Muslims and against Arabs inside the United States and against Muslim and Arab nations outside the United States.[8]

Unlike other leading members of Saddam's government, Naji al-Hadithi was never declared a wanted man. A top CIA official claimed that he was their man on the inside, but when I phoned him years later, by which time he was a professor at Doha University in Qatar, he insisted it was all 'a dirty lie'.

Israel responded to 9/11 with a declaration from its prime minister, Ariel Sharon, that 'all Israelis stand as one with the American people'.[9] Sharon was dealing with an armed Palestinian uprising, the second intifada. The first President Bush had regarded him as an extremist, and Sharon was concerned that the second would adopt his father's view. Sharon was already under pressure in the West for his forceful response to the new intifada. After 9/11 Sharon and his advisors worried that 'Bin Laden would tell the Americans they were paying the price for the Middle East conflict' and the Americans would believe them.[10] The opposite happened. Sharon moved quickly to identify Israel's fight against Yasser Arafat and the Palestinians with America's fight against Bin Laden and al-Qaeda. Palestinians played into his hands when small groups of them celebrated 9/11 by dancing in front of television cameras. When Arafat said Palestinians were 'completely shocked' at the attacks, most Americans didn't trust his sympathy. One of his closest advisors, Nabil Sha'ath, saw trouble ahead. Six months after 9/11, he warned that unfettered use of American power could make the problems faced by the Middle East and the world worse, not better. It was, he said, 'like seeing the cub of the lion being eaten by the hyenas and knowing that the lion is going to roar and go mad at everything that moves in the forest'.[11]

President Bush delivered a State of the Union speech warning of an 'axis of evil' that included Iraq, North Korea and Iran. In the summer of 2002, Dr Javad Zarif, Iran's representative at the United Nations, met Britain's prime minister Tony Blair to relay the message from Iran's reformist president Mohammad Khatami that a clash between Islam and the West would be bad for both sides: 'we see this very serious exacerbation of Islamophobia in the West, and this will have implications that are far greater than 11 September and the tragedies that that ensued'.[12]

The decision to include Iran in Bush's axis of evil killed the chances of building a rapprochement to help stabilize the Middle East. After 9/11, it might have been possible. The Iranians had passed helpful intelligence to the US to use against the Taliban, who were their enemies too. When the US arrived in Afghanistan it tapped into the common interests of Iran, India, Russia and the Afghan Northern Alliance, which had been fighting the Taliban in different ways for the best part of a decade. The big US contribution was its massive air power.[13] Cooperation continued after the Taliban were driven out of Kabul, with negotiations to create a new government and what naive observers hoped would be a better Afghanistan. According to Trita Parsi, a leading Iranian American analyst, 'The United States had not only won the war, but thanks to Iran, it had also won the peace.'[14] Consigning Iran to the axis of evil was a missed opportunity.

A week after 9/11, Bush was preparing Americans for what lay ahead. America's enemies had 'roused a mighty giant', he said. 'Make no mistake about it, we're determined. This administration, along with those friends of ours who are willing to stand with us all the way through, will do what it takes to rip terrorism out of the world.'[15]

12.

Mission Unaccomplished

I kept dreaming about burying the cameraman in a shallow grave in the grounds of the Rasheed Hotel. Night after night, I was in Baghdad as the Americans advanced towards the city, watching him being killed by the same piece of shrapnel the size of a baby that had hit the Rasheed while I was there during the 1991 war. The earth was rock-hard and in my dream I could only scrape out a narrow trench. It was the ground where, in real life, I'd found the shrapnel in 1991, a fragment of a cruise missile that flattened the conference centre across the road.

When that explosion shook the mighty concrete-and-steel Rasheed, I found myself on the floor as the plate-glass windows quivered and alarms went off. I agreed to go back to Baghdad for the coming war when the BBC asked me before the 2003 invasion. But every night I was there in my dreams, with that grave, the arid earth and the dead body of my friend, so I changed my mind. My daughter Mattie was a toddler, and my partner Julia was pregnant with our second child. I sat with Mattie, watching Postman Pat videos, envying his simple life and wishing I did not have to risk mine. In 1991, aged thirty, I had not hesitated for an instant. Twelve years later, my brain was telling me something else.

Kids' TV was a break from a witches' brew of war talk. When pundits talked up the capabilities of Saddam's Republican Guard, I remembered what had happened when one of our drivers in Baghdad, an amiable, unwarlike Kurd, was conscripted into it. He bribed his way out for a few hundred dollars but before he returned to civilian life he felt so sorry for his comrades, who lived in a barrack room with broken windows, that he bought them some meat. Unscientifically, I concluded that a regime that had been isolated and sanctioned for more than a decade, that wasn't even feeding its supposedly elite troops properly, could not be building weapons of mass destruction.

Saddam's arsenal was the reason Bush and Blair most often gave for going to war, but the Americans had others. They needed more revenge than the Taliban could provide. Influential advisors of the president had believed before 9/11 that the 1991 war would not be over until Saddam was removed. In London, Blair's formidable powers of persuasion were being tested. A big proportion of the British public was queasy about the way he had tied himself to Bush and his plan for war. Cartoonists lampooned Blair, showing him tucked into Bush's pocket like a grotesque pet. However, Blair's reasons were more complicated than simply staying close to his friend. He believed that Britain's alliance with the US depended on supporting it during its darkest hours. Number Ten chartered Concorde to fly to Washington, DC so he could stand shoulder to shoulder with Bush. Successful interventions in Sierra Leone and Kosovo had convinced Blair that powerful nations should not hesitate to use force if it was the only way to make the world better.

Our driver's farcical military career was not the only reason why I doubted Iraq had weapons of mass destruction. Saddam was so weak after the 1991 defeat that he was forced to allow UN weapons inspectors into Iraq. They stripped out layers of deception that the regime had wrapped around his military ambitions, then dismantled and destroyed stockpiles of chemical and biological agents and the beginnings of a nuclear programme. In the 1990s the inspectors institutionalized international intrusion in Saddam's regime, along with sanctions and the no-fly zones patrolled by the Americans and British. The inspectors spent years in Iraq, rooting around the regime's storehouses and bases, destroying anything suspicious and sending great spirals of smoke into the sky every time they blew something else up. The traces they found of a nuclear weapons programme did not mean it continued; in 1997 they reported that there were no 'indications that any weapon-useable nuclear material remained in Iraq'.[1] UN nuclear inspectors went back in to Iraq in the run-up to war. On 14 February 2003, Mohamed ElBaradei, the director of the UN's International Atomic Energy Agency, begged the Security Council for more time, telling them, 'We have to date found no evidence that Iraq has revived its nuclear weapon programme since the elimination of the programme in the 1990s.' El Baradei persuaded some influential people, including the retired General Norman Schwarzkopf, but not George Bush or Tony Blair. In Britain, the government should have sensed that trouble was ahead when it ignored the protests of over a million people who attended an anti-war march in London. But in Downing Street and the White House, the war drums were beating so loudly that Bush and Blair ignored the protests, the UN weapons experts and those who knew Iraq and its complexities.

Since 1990, when I'd watched them landing the contents of their military warehouses in Saudi Arabia, military intervention in the Middle East had become a habit for the United States and its British ally. But this time, according to the Bush administration, they were playing for keeps. The neoconservatives around George W. Bush were zealots for imposing democracy by force. They did not want to miss a second chance to remove Saddam Hussein. Regime change, the neocons insisted, would be a major victory in the war on terror. It did not matter that there was plenty of evidence that the Iraqi dictator did not provide a home for al-Qaeda; Saddam was a clear and present danger, they insisted, because he had weapons of mass destruction.

False intelligence came from Rafid Ahmed Alwan al-Janabi, an Iraqi who had been granted political asylum in Germany. The Americans codenamed him 'Curveball', a baseball term for a pitch that spins and deceives. He told German intelligence he had seen mobile laboratories for developing biological toxins in Iraq. The Germans did not believe him, and Britain's MI6 had serious doubts, but Curveball's information was too good for the British and American governments to pass up. Later, he admitted he had made it all up.

Curveball had connections to Ahmad Chalabi, another Iraqi exile who had spent years campaigning for regime change. Before he had the ear of politicians, Chalabi tried to cultivate journalists. After

I came back from the war in Baghdad in 1991, Chalabi somehow found my home phone number and used to ring to ask when I was going back to Iraq, offering interviews about his new movement to overthrow Saddam. Journalists are often approached by exiles from authoritarian states who dream of a return. Chalabi could appear energetic and charming, as well as implausible and untrustworthy. I thought he was a fantasist, but I should have taken him more seriously. To my amazement, he found a receptive audience in Washington among those who were still fighting the 1991 war in their minds. Secretary of State Colin Powell did not trust him, but he became Vice President Dick Cheney's favourite Iraqi. Chalabi helped push the US Congress into passing the Iraq Liberation Act in 1998, with a hefty regime change budget from which his own Iraqi National Congress received more than $100 million.

In London, Tony Blair's job would have been easier had he been able to extract a resolution explicitly authorizing an invasion from the UN Security Council. He could not talk his way past the French president, Jacques Chirac, who told him that military service in Algeria had convinced him that war was the worst option and the Middle East did not need another one. Chirac warned that overthrowing Saddam would lead to disaster. In an interview on French TV, he threatened to use his country's veto in the Security Council: 'France will vote no because we believe tonight that there are no grounds to wage war to achieve the objective that we have set, the disarmament of Iraq.' According to one of Blair's top advisors, the prime minister did not have much respect for Chirac's opinion. 'Tony Blair never paid any attention to what Chirac said . . . He'd kind of come out rolling his eyes and say: "Oh dear, dear old Jacques, he doesn't get it, does he?"'[2]

Chirac's refusal to go to war made waves. The committee that ran cafeterias in the US House of Representatives ruled that French fries and French toast would be renamed 'freedom fries' and 'freedom toast',[3] and the White House made the same change on the Air Force One menu. The more serious consequence was that Bush, Blair and their allies would be going to war without the specific legal authorization of a UN Security Council resolution. The UN Charter authorizes war only in self-defence, or to enforce decisions taken in the Security Council under Chapter VII of the Charter. A year later, the UN secretary general Kofi Annan explained in an interview with the BBC that the invasion was 'not in conformity with the UN Charter, from our point of view, and from the Charter point of view it was illegal'.[4]

Five years later, Britain's ambassador to the UN in New York Sir Jeremy Greenstock said that Blair had been 'extremely disappointed not to have specific UN backing'.[5] The White House and Number Ten relied on an unconvincing argument that existing resolutions were enough. Another UN resolution would not have made the invasion any less catastrophic for Iraq and the Middle East, but its absence meant that the international system designed to restrict the ability of big powers to go to war had failed.

I didn't buy the arguments about weapons of mass destruction, and I recalled the warnings I'd heard in Baghdad in 1991 about the certainty of bloodshed when an Iraqi leader was removed. In March, two days before the invasion, I watched Tony Blair seeking parliamentary approval for the war. He was a brilliant politician who spoke so well that I started to wonder whether his arguments were, after all, the truth. One of his predictions still stands out. Blair told the House of Commons why he believed Britain was doing the right thing by joining America:

> It will determine the way in which Britain and the world confront the central security threat of the twenty-first century, the development of the United Nations, the relationship between Europe and the United States, the relations within the European Union and the way in which the United States engages with the rest of the world. So it could hardly be more important. It will determine the pattern of international politics for the next generation.[6]

It did all of those things, but not in the way that Blair expected, because Saddam did not have weapons of mass destruction. Blair won the vote, though he had been deeply worried that he might lose it. Sir Jeremy Greenstock recalled in a BBC documentary that Blair and his team were not packing their bags, but they were checking desk drawers in Downing Street to see how much was portable.

As the Americans and British massed their troops on the Iraqi border, it was assumed that Saddam Hussein had a plan to deal with them. But according to his CIA interrogator, he was fatalistic on the eve of war. He knew, even if Tony Blair did not, that sanctions, weapons inspections and international pressure had stopped him modernizing his conventional forces, let alone creating an arsenal of weapons of mass destruction. He marched his men through Baghdad's triumphal arch made of two giant swords, commissioned to commemorate the war with Iran in the 1980s, but they were facing the might of the Americans. The CIA interrogator concluded Saddam was out of touch, without a plan for the storm that broke over his regime.[7]

The US military called the first raids on 20 March 'shock and awe'. Huge explosions lit up the sky in direct line of sight from the journalists' hotels. The Americans were also taking care of the media battlefield, vital in modern war. Their troops drove for the capital while the British took care of Basra. On 9 April, the Americans captured Baghdad. Without the regime, law and order collapsed. Government buildings and private property were looted and priceless artefacts were pillaged from the National Museum.

Weeks after the fall of Saddam and his disappearance into hiding, Iraq was not respecting the easy scenario laid out by American neoconservatives. Vice President Dick Cheney quoted predictions in a speech the previous summer that 'after liberation, the streets in Basra and Baghdad are sure to erupt in joy in the same way throngs in Kabul greeted the Americans'.[8]

The Bush administration had dismissed repeated warnings that replacing Saddam and occupying Iraq would be difficult and dangerous. They ignored plans for the day after made by the Pentagon and the State Department. Instead, President Bush sent a diplomat, L. Paul Bremer III, to be his viceroy, along with pallets laden with millions of shrink-wrapped dollars. Bremer dissolved the Iraqi armed forces, leaving tens of thousands of trained soldiers, already smarting from the humiliation of defeat, unemployed and impoverished. He also purged the ministries of civil servants who had been members of Saddam's ruling Baath Party, despite the fact that for many Iraqis a party card was a matter of necessity rather than belief. The

Americans might have used Iraqi soldiers to help secure the streets and civil servants to run the country, but they did not, and they soon found that they didn't have the troops or the expertise to do it themselves.

Just after the regime collapsed, my curiosity got the better of me and I went back to Baghdad. Ill-prepared American civilians occupied Saddam's palaces, living on camp beds in marble halls that sweltered until the air conditioning was fixed. Frustrated reservists told me that they had been happy to do their patriotic chore at weekends, but not for a year in Iraq. On the streets, Iraqis were terrified by looting and violence and I joined American patrols struggling to hold back the chaos. A Captain Stacey from the US 2nd Cavalry talked about trust: 'We're here to help them . . . we're not those people Saddam made us out to be.' It wasn't working. The captain in his Humvee tried to chase down intelligence that insurgents were planning to attack his patrol, but all they could do was cruise the streets, sometimes stopping to show some presence.

The insurgency took off quickly. Fallujah is a hot and dusty town on the edge of the desert, around an hour's drive from Baghdad. The US 82nd Airborne had entered the town easily, but within days they opened fire on crowds that were protesting against their presence, killing seventeen people and wounding more than seventy.[9] The paratroopers claimed that they were shooting back; they were front-line troops, untrained for crowd control in a volatile and angry town. The Iraqi protestors insisted they were unarmed. They weren't on 1 May, the day President Bush declared the end of major combat operations. Someone tossed two grenades over a wall into a compound occupied by the US 3rd Armored Cavalry, wounding seven US soldiers.

I went to Fallujah a couple of weeks later. As usual in Iraq, most people were welcoming, but collectively the town was seething with anger. A Palestinian journalist friend overheard young men in the market boasting that they would kill Western news teams. Before the end of the year, well-armed and trained Iraqi insurgents had embedded themselves in Fallujah and many other towns. An American soldier I spoke to on a street corner was still wondering what had happened to the cheering crowds they were told to expect. 'I don't have any hard feelings against the Iraqis,' he said. 'We try to liberate them, but some of them don't like us. It's just the same as anywhere you go, right?'

An Iraqi man who was looking on was already making comparisons with the Saddam years: 'America claims it's given us freedom but under Saddam we had water, electricity and security, which we don't have any more.'

In Washington, the neocons were still celebrating. Ken Adelman, a friend of Vice President Cheney, had used his column in the *Washington Post* to predict that removing Saddam would be a 'cakewalk'. In a triumphalist post-invasion follow-up headlined 'Cakewalk Revisited', he castigated defeatists, explaining that the absence of gratitude on Iraq's streets was because dictatorship had removed their ability to party. America should have predicted 'how a totalitarian regime could so pulverize its people and military as to intimidate them, at least for a time, out of celebrating even their own liberation'.[10]

President Bush had a victory to sell. He was flown onto the deck of the USS *Abraham Lincoln*, an aircraft carrier steaming along the Californian coast on its way home from the war. A 'Mission Accomplished' banner was draped across the carrier's bridge. It was premature. Saddam was gone, but the weapons of mass destruction had not been found and Iraq was falling apart. Ahead lay the catastrophic consequences of the invasion, for Iraq and for the region.

Tony Blair was the first leader to visit Iraq, jumping across the Kuwaiti border to the palace in Basra that the British had requisitioned as their headquarters. I drove down from Baghdad, past long American supply convoys transporting vast amounts of stores and equipment, from tanks and bulldozers to food. As soon as I arrived, I could see that the British would struggle to control a city as big and restive as Basra without the troop numbers and logistics of the Americans. Blair's bodyguards made sure he stayed in the British base, but I went into a dangerous city that might have given him pause for thought. At the General Hospital, they were treating people who had been shot and stabbed on streets that were getting meaner by the day. I asked a wounded man what he would say to Tony Blair if he had the chance.

'I will say to him, number one, provide us with security, electricity, water. Please. Don't guard only the oil wells – please guard us. Please try to reconstruct Iraq, not to take oil only. And please, if Iraqi government started to work, please go out as early as possible.'

The invasion of Iraq was a catastrophic error that set off a chain of disastrous consequences that still thunder around the Middle East. A sectarian civil war between Shia and Sunni Muslims spread from the Gulf to the Mediterranean. Hundreds of thousands of Iraqis died, and soldiers who had been told they were fighting to protect their families back home died in a country that their leaders didn't understand. Far from eliminating al-Qaeda, the invasion and occupation turned Iraq into an incubator for violent Islamist extremism. Many people in the Middle East believed Islam faced a new crusade. The war became a recruiting sergeant for young men who became jihadist killers.

When Syria was ripped apart by war after 2011, the fear of making the same mistakes left the West paralysed. Back in 2003, during Blair's triumphant visit to Basra, I had been looking forward to asking him about weapons of mass destruction – which still hadn't been found, because there weren't any. After he had praised the troops, it was my turn for a question.

'What about this business about weapons, prime minister? What about weapons of mass destruction?'

Tony Blair looked at me for a moment, then turned and walked away without answering.

13.

One Thousand Saddams

The citizens of Baghdad had a deep affection for Abu Nawas Street, an avenue lined with eucalyptus trees that ran along the River Tigris. During the 1950s and 1960s, Baghdadis could eat and drink alcohol in marquees pitched on strips of sand along the river, or on boats moored to the bank.[1] Bars lined the other side of the road. Even during the 1990s, when sanctions were hitting the country hard, Iraqis with enough money would head for the open-air restaurants of Abu Nawas Street to eat *masgouf*, Iraq's national dish of grilled fish. Huge, muddy-looking carp were kept swimming in pools until they were needed. Once they'd been stunned, scaled, sliced and staked upright next to a wood fire, hungry Baghdadis would dig into the charred, crispy monsters with flatbread and salads.

Getting a drink became more difficult after 1993; Saddam banned alcohol in restaurants as part of the 'Faith Campaign', his tactical decision to shore up his regime with displays of public piety. But in the late 1990s, discreet diners could still drink *arak*, the spirit made from distilled aniseed that is an excellent accompaniment to the food of the Levant. I used to eat *masgouf* and drink *arak* on Abu Nawas Street with a friend who was a senior United Nations official. She said the UN had told their staff to avoid the dish, because the fish were bottom feeders and the dictatorship could be dumping heavy water and other traces of weapons programmes in the Tigris. But like the restaurant's Iraqi customers, we kept on eating *masgouf*, hoping that their fish came from farms, not the river.

When dictatorships die, poison is released as well as relief. Law and order collapsed once the Baathist boot came off the throats of Iraqis after more than thirty years, and the streets of Baghdad became very dangerous. As Iraq sank into civil war, going out at night carried the risk of running into sectarian death squads. Hundreds of bodies were dumped into the Tigris. The *masgouf* restaurants closed and fishermen struggled to sell their catch; the combination of dead bodies floating down the Tigris and the omnivorous, plump carp was not appetizing. Clerics issued fatwas ruling that it was dangerous to eat river fish. The fish farms boomed.[2]

When I returned to the city just after the fall of Saddam, the Americans had put a tank on Abu Nawas outside the Palestine Hotel, where journalists and other foreigners were staying, and cut the street off with a tangle of wire. The reason was on the other side of the river: the former presidential palace, now the American headquarters at the heart of the fortified district of Baghdad that they called the Green Zone. They hardened their defences, separating it from the rest of the city with concrete blast walls, machine-gun towers and thousands of feet of razor wire. It was an echo of the old regime; Saddam Hussein had also made sure that the Abu Nawas waterfront was well guarded, to keep potential attackers away from his sprawling complex of palaces and brutalist public buildings across the Tigris. Inside the Green Zone, the invaders and their trusted Iraqi allies worked in relative safety.

Returning British diplomats hoped for a while to resume a separate diplomatic existence from the Americans. Just after the invasion, I went to an impromptu drinks party to celebrate the repossession of the British embassy. Generals and Foreign Office diplomats clutched gin and tonics and talked about moving back into the elegant Ottoman building on the banks of the Tigris. The last time I had seen in it, in the run-up to the first Gulf War, several dozen British workers had been camping in the grounds while the regime refused them permission to leave the country.

The embassy had a ballroom with a sprung floor and a river yacht, until it was damaged in the 1958 revolution. The building was closed when diplomats pulled out of Iraq as war approached in 1991. Twelve years later it was a small time capsule, with calendars for 1990 still on an office wall and yellowed typewritten instructions about heightened security in the Kuwait crisis stuck up with drawing pins. Britain's bid for diplomatic independence in Baghdad did not last long. As the insurgency gathered force, they put up the shutters again and moved into the Green Zone. In 2021 they were still wondering what to do with the shuttered building.

The Americans could protect the Green Zone from everything except mortars, which insurgents lobbed in when they could get close enough, but they did not have enough troops to secure the rest of the city. They took stringent security precautions before venturing into the badlands of what they called the Red Zone. The US defence secretary Donald Rumsfeld believed the highly trained, high-tech American armed forces did not need as many boots on the streets as his generals wanted. He was right when it came to beating the weak Iraqi army on the road to Baghdad. But it became clear very quickly that the Americans did not have enough troops to keep order in the country for which they had just become responsible. It was open season for criminals – women were raped, cars were hijacked and homes were ransacked – and they didn't have the resources to stop it happening. 'Stuff happens,' was Rumsfeld's response in Washington: 'freedom's untidy'. He put the chaos down to 'pent-up feelings' after decades of repression.[3]

In the early summer of 2003, I drove past government buildings that had been so comprehensively stripped by looters that even the copper electricity wires in the walls and water pipes in the floors had been removed and carted away. My destination was the Canal Hotel, a low concrete building from the 1960s that was now the Baghdad headquarters of the United Nations. During the dictatorship I had gone there to talk to the brave people who were trying to help the Iraqis; it was one of the few places we had been allowed to visit without asking permission in writing and taking a guide from Saddam's goon squad. The journey was also a chance to drive around the city relatively unobserved – although I assumed the drivers reported everything about where we went. In the 1990s, the Canal Hotel was a reassuring place in a city without reassurance. I hoped, wrongly, that it could be the same in the new Iraq.

On that day in 2003 I was going to see Sergio Vieira de Mello, head of the UN operation in Iraq following the invasion. De Mello, a Brazilian in his mid-fifties, was the handsome superstar of the United Nations who had been given its toughest job. He was talked about as a future secretary general. In August, a few months after our meeting, a suicide bomber drove a truck full of explosives into the hotel, killing himself and twenty-two people, mostly aid workers. De Mello was trapped in the rubble and died before he could be rescued. Later in the year, the International Committee of the Red Cross was also attacked, a signal that no one was off limits for the insurgents. Most other international aid groups followed them out.

Behind the wire in the Green Zone, the Americans were digging a deeper hole for themselves. Having purged the ministries of civil servants who had been members of Saddam's ruling Baath Party, Paul Bremer, head of the Coalition Provisional Authority, signed Order No. 2, the 'Dissolution of Entities'. It abolished all the old regime's military and security services. Bremer wrote later that his intention had been to send a firm signal that Saddam and the Baathists were gone for good.[4]

Very quickly it became clear that disbanding the military was going to backfire. Three weeks after Bremer signed the order, the International Crisis Group judged that Baghdad was 'in distress, chaos and ferment'.[5] They predicted, accurately, that the order threatened 'to put hundreds of thousands of mostly young men on the streets without serious prospect of work or, thus far, promise of a pension. Many, it is feared, will join the gangs of thieves who roam the streets virtually unchecked or form the nuclei for future armed resistance to what is referred to as the American occupation.' Around 350,000 men were cut loose. No one in the Green Zone could claim they had not been warned.

The breakdown of law and order had long-term consequences. The failure of the mighty American war machine to stop looting, arson and killing was a sign that it had vulnerabilities that could be exploited. Saddam was in hiding and his men had disappeared from the streets, but isolated attacks on US troops escalated rapidly into a fully-fledged insurgency.

Occupying and administering Iraq became a deadly business. For a while, supporters of the invasion could cling onto one dramatic televised moment. It starred Kadhim al-Jabbouri, a beefy weightlifter and wrestler who was fed up with Saddam Hussein. He could not wait for the Americans as they entered Baghdad on 9 April 2003, and to hurry things up he decided to destroy the large statue of Saddam Hussein that stood on a dusty traffic island in Firdous Square near the Palestine Hotel. A few hours before the Americans arrived, Kadhim grabbed his sledgehammer and began thumping at the statue's concrete plinth.

Kadhim had not always hated Saddam. For a while, the sunlight of the regime's favour shone on his business, a motorcycle workshop specializing in Harley-Davidsons. Saddam even chose him to look after his cherished collection of motorbikes, which included the one he had used to escape Baghdad in 1959. But Kadhim's position as the president's chief biker did not stop the regime killing fourteen members of his family. After that, Kadhim refused to do any more work at the palace. The regime's response to his effrontery, Kadhim told me as we sat sipping tea in his oily workshop, was to put him in jail for two years on trumped-up charges. He was eventually released in one of Saddam's periodic amnesties, but on the morning of 9 April 2003 he wanted his own personal moment of revenge. He found it with his sledgehammer.

Journalists watched what was happening from the hotel and sent pictures around the world. Kadhim says their presence protected him from Saddam's secret policemen, who melted away as the sound of American guns came closer. When the Americans arrived, combat engineers looped a steel cable round the bronze Saddam's head and used a crane to finish the job, live on television. The statue tumbled unceremoniously from its plinth onto the scrubby earth and broken paving of the traffic island. Saddam's delighted former subjects tore off their shoes to slap the graven image of their former leader. Scenes of them belabouring the bronze Saddam flashed around the globe, the symbol for which the journalists, invaders and Iraqis had all been waiting.

In 2003, Kadhim was proud to learn that his story had reached George W. Bush in the Oval Office, but when I met him in 2016, he wished he'd left his sledgehammer at home. Like many Iraqis, he blamed the invasion for starting a chain of events that destroyed the country. He longed for the stability of Saddam's time. First, he said, came the realization that it was going to be occupation rather than liberation. Then he despised the corruption, mismanagement and violence that crippled the new Iraq. Like most Iraqis, he hated the arbitrary lawlessness of the country; carrying a gun for a corrupt wannabe warlord was one of the few areas of employment open to young men. Death could come quickly – from getting too close to an American patrol or, as Iraqis turned on each other, from being the wrong sect at a checkpoint. Kadhim was despairing.

> Saddam has gone, and we have one thousand Saddams now. It wasn't like this under Saddam. There was a system. There were ways. We didn't like him, but he was better than those people. Saddam never executed people without a reason. He was as solid as a wall. There was no corruption or looting, it was safe. You could be safe . . . Iraq was taken from us. Baghdad was taken from us.

Nostalgia for Saddam's brutal stability started with the hubris that lay behind the mistakes made during the invasion. The White House and the Pentagon had prepared to destroy the Iraqi state, but they had not planned how to take over the governance of the country. The next mistake was an over-simplified view that Iraq's political future was a zero-sum game between Shias and Kurds on one side and Sunnis on the other. When the Coalition Provisional Authority tried to set up an interim governing council to change the way the occupation looked, seats were allocated based on the relative size of the sects, embedding sectarianism in the new Iraq's political DNA.

Iraq has a rich mix of religions, sects and ethnicities. Among Muslims, the fault line that matters most is between Shia and Sunni Arabs. In Iraq, the majority are Shias, though they are a minority in most

Muslim countries. The schism goes back to the wars over who should succeed the prophet Muhammad as leader of the Muslim community after his death in 632. One group believed that his family should inherit his position and power. They became Shia Muslims. Their rivals became Sunnis. They wanted Muhammad's closest associates to lead the rapidly expanding Muslim world. The third significant group in Iraq are Kurds; most of them are Sunni, but they are not Arabs and have their own language and culture.

The politics of sectarianism in the Middle East has the same power as European nationalism to generate anger and mobilize communities. In the Middle East I had flashbacks to the wars of former Yugoslavia, of neighbours killing neighbours and death at checkpoints for carrying the wrong identity card. Shias and Sunnis, like the Yugoslavs, would not have descended into sectarian killing without unscrupulous leaders whipping up communal hatred to strengthen their own power.

Iraq's communities were not fated to end up at war with each other; like the other Middle Eastern states that emerged from the Ottoman Empire, Iraqis had forged a national identity. They supported the country's football team, which even reached the finals of the World Cup in 1986. Uday Saddam Hussein, the dictator's sadistic son, was put in charge of Iraqi sport. At the offices of the Iraqi Olympic Committee, he kept a private jail equipped with full torture facilities. When I went to a big football match in the 1990s, in a stadium dominated by a portrait of Saddam, I had no idea that if the team lost, Uday would impose punishments on the players ranging from head-shaving to beatings.

Saddam was a Sunni. His own sect, and his tribe, dominated his regime, giving it a sectarian undercurrent. So did his war with Iran, the leading Shia power. But being Sunni did not guarantee safety. Saddam killed people from all of Iraq's communities, from his own tribe and even his own family. In 1995, Lieutenant-General Hussein Kemal, once one of the most powerful men in the regime, defected to Jordan with his wife, Saddam's daughter Raghad. With them were Kemal's younger brother and his wife, Raghad's sister, as well as their children and an assortment of relatives.

Kemal spent months being debriefed by Jordan intelligence and the

CIA. At a meeting with the UN, he recognized a man he had sent to infiltrate the weapons inspectors. He told him, 'Get the fuck out of here. You have been working for me. I refuse to be debriefed by one of my own agents.'[6]

But as the drama of his defection receded, Kemal was miserable in Jordan and made the mistake of believing a promise by Saddam that if he brought his family back to Iraq, he would be forgiven. It was a remarkably bad decision for a man with first-hand knowledge of Saddam's attitude to disloyalty, who was complicit in some of the regime's dirty deeds. The murderous Uday was waiting at the border; the Kemal men were separated from their wives and children and allowed to drive to Baghdad for an angry meeting with Saddam. After that they retreated to a house where their father and another brother, as well as their sister and her children, joined them for the inevitable showdown. They were all killed after a thirteen-hour gun battle. Uday, dressed in traditional tribal robes, led the mourners in the funeral for the dead from his side. Years later, Raghad gave a series of interviews to the Saudi-owned television network al-Arabiya insisting, unconvincingly, that their clan and not her father decided that her husband had to die. Even in death she was trying to please her unyielding father. For Saddam Hussein, loyalty was everything.

The violence that seeped from every part of Saddam's regime continued to shape Iraq after he was captured. Like every authoritarian leader, he used the power of his security services to crush any political activity that did not pay him homage; the resulting absence of civil society and rival parties meant there was a power vacuum once his regime had fallen. Paul Bremer and his fellow Americans made it worse by abolishing what was left of the Iraqi state, believing that the solution lay in empowering the Shia and Kurdish majority. Abolishing the Iraqi military and the security services and sacking Baathists from state jobs was intended as a positive signal to Shias and Kurds, but it also alienated many Sunnis. Some of them picked up guns to join the insurgency, and many more supported it.

It was not inevitable that Iraq would become a sectarian battleground, but the actions taken after 2003 made it happen. By the time Saddam was executed, on a bitterly cold morning in December 2006, Sunnis and Shia were killing each other in large numbers. His masked Shia executioners chanted sectarian slogans as Saddam went to his death, staring at them with disgust in a display of courage that his followers in the insurgency must have found inspiring.

The failure to find a coherent system to replace Saddam meant that the Iraqi state – or what was left of it – stayed weak. The new political system was intended to impose, as the historian Toby Dodge puts it, a 'victor's peace'.[7] Shia politicians returned from exile in Iran or Europe and together with their Kurdish allies – and with the permission of the Americans – they wrote a constitution that was designed to seal their control of Iraq for sectarian parties. Secular nationalists of all confessions lost out.

It was hardly the democracy that had existed in the fantasies of neocons in Washington. Worse from their point of view, the removal of Saddam Hussein handed a world of opportunities to the Islamic Republic of Iran, the country regarded by America as the greatest purveyor of state terror in the Middle East. Saddam had revelled in his self-appointed role as the strongest Arab obstacle to Iran; now that he and his regime had gone, Iraq went from being an Arab bastion against Iran's ambitions to a playground in which they could build alliances with Shia leaders, organize militias and deliver blows to their American enemies.

Neither could the Americans say convincingly that they had scored a victory in the war against the perpetrators and ideology that had brought 9/11. Before the invasion, they claimed that Saddam Hussein's Iraq was a refuge for al-Qaeda, but his downfall strengthened the jihadist killers by transforming Iraq into their land of opportunity. The chaos of the occupation turned Iraq into a magnet for violent Sunni Muslim extremists. Syria let more extremists cross the border, as the Assad regime wanted to make trouble for the Americans.

Many extremists also crossed into Iraq from Jordan, the most notorious of whom was a veteran of the jihad in Afghanistan who called himself Abu Musab al-Zarqawi. He was a Jordanian who had been tortured and radicalized in jail in his home country. Zarqawi built up a savage al-Qaeda franchise. In 2005, he sent suicide bombers into three hotels in Amman. I raced across the border from Jerusalem to see the devastated lobbies and ballrooms. At least fifty-seven people were killed, many of them families and friends celebrating a wedding. Their blood congealed on the floors, studded with fragments of broken glass.

Like all of his kind, Zarqawi had no hesitation in killing anyone who got in his way as he attacked a government that he believed was breaking God's law. He sent dozens of suicide bombers to kill Shias in marketplaces and mosques, and Shia death squads retaliated by killing hundreds of Sunnis every week. Their dumped bodies often showed signs of torture. Some Shia militias were attached to the Iraqi government; an American officer serving in a Sunni neighbourhood of Baghdad called the National Police 'sectarian murderers . . . You had what could only be described as liquidation missions.'[8] Sectarian violence, already increasing, exploded exponentially after Zarqawi's gunmen killed nearly four hundred people at the Shia Askari Mosque in Samarra in February 2006.

Zarqawi was killed by a US air strike in June 2006, but the damage was already done. The worst of it was in Baghdad. Murderous sectarian warfare caused thousands to flee to areas where their sect was the majority. The failure of the Americans and their allies to establish law and order after they removed Saddam's regime led to ethnic cleansing and made it easier to kill with impunity.

The impact was still felt a decade later. During the fight to drive the extremist killers of Islamic State from Mosul, Iraq's second city, I met a man who had moved back into his family home after the fighting had passed through his area. The battle continued not far away, and our conversation was punctuated by helicopter gunships firing missiles towards the old town where IS fighters dug in. The man had been an officer in the Iraqi army under Saddam, but he lost his job, pay and pension when the United States dissolved the armed forces. After that, life was a struggle for his family. His son, barely a teenager, made some money selling scrap metal with a friend, but the two boys came to blows over how to split the cash. I asked the former officer what happened to his son and he replied that the fight had got out of hand, and his son had killed his friend. He told me the boy was still in jail, and turned back to his bricklaying.

14.

The People Want the Fall of the Regime

On the day that the people of Egypt became a threat to President Hosni Mubarak, I was in a back alley in Cairo in the middle of a noisy, jostling crowd. Everything hurt. Everyone hurt. Some people around me were bent double, coughing, spluttering, clutching at streaming eyes and faces. My skin felt like it was on fire. Somewhere near the heart of the crowd was a well. Or perhaps it was a tap, a bucket or a plastic bottle. I couldn't see as I was half blind and opening my eyes was an agony. We were all supplicants, with fingers cupped, waiting for the salvation of the water. It wasn't holy. It just wasn't tear gas.

Everyone there had been given a good gassing, a face and both lungs full, by the security forces of the President of the Republic. Rivers of snot were pouring out of my nostrils. Someone I couldn't see poured water into my hands and splashed more into my face, rubbing it in, which only made things worse. I had two small videotapes stuffed in my sock, hidden ever since the police had spotted us filming from the roof of a nearby building and had come crashing up the stairs. It was just after the noon prayer on 28 January 2011, and it was getting clearer with every passing minute that Cairo was in the grip of an uprising that was accelerating towards revolution.

The alley was just off Giza Square, which is normally a scruffy, traffic-choked interchange on the road to the pyramids. On that Friday, the fourth successive day of demonstrations in Cairo, it was packed with people, not cars. I had been under the flyover that ran along one side of the square, waiting for the end of the prayer at a big mosque about one hundred metres away. Lines of riot police were on the other side of the square. The fight started when the worshippers left. Among them was Mohamed ElBaradei, Egypt's most famous international diplomat, a Nobel Peace Prize laureate for his work with the United Nations to stop the spread of nuclear weapons. As the square was overtaken by violence, ElBaradei, casually dressed and wearing sunglasses, made a tactical retreat surrounded by a phalanx of supporters. He had been a popular figure since the run-up to the invasion of Iraq in 2003, when he had tried to disprove the claims that Saddam Hussein had weapons of mass destruction. Now he was back from his job in Vienna, offering to lead a transitional government if Mubarak stepped down; Egyptians, and the regime, took him seriously, for a while.

More people arrived to join the fight against the police, pouring out of minibus taxis in Giza Square. The police fired arcs of tear gas and high-pressure jets of stinking water into the crowd. In the square, protestors smashed police vehicles, torching some as they turned them over. By mid-afternoon, tens of thousands of angry and excited people were on the streets of Cairo, demanding the end of the thirty-year rule of President Mubarak. I had become cynical about demonstrations in Egypt, which generally consisted of small groups of brave advocates for democracy, human rights and the rule of law, all dangerous beliefs to parade in public in Mubarak's Egypt. Mostly they were middle class and educated, which meant they inhabited a different world to the majority of Egyptians. They would pop up with placards and slogans for as long as it took for the police to get there to give them a beating. One of the organizers of the protests still could not believe what had happened when we talked three weeks later: 'To be honest, we thought we'd last about five minutes. We thought we'd get arrested straight away. I reckoned I'd end up in the back of a police van . . . it had happened before.'[1]

On that day, however, it was different: Cairo's poor were on the streets. You can't have a revolution without the urban poor. It's not just us, one of the middle-class protestors crowed triumphantly when he saw them, it's not just the Rolex brigade. They threw stones, yelled slogans and threw the police's tear-gas canisters back at them. Old men were punching the air. Young men took on the police with stones and pieces of broken-up pavement. Crowds fought for control of the bridges across the Nile as clouds of tear gas belched across the river. The police fired buckshot into the demonstrations. The men who were hit retreated, blood pouring from small holes in their faces and bodies, and others took their places. By the evening, demonstrators had taken over Tahrir Square, Cairo's equivalent of Piccadilly Circus.

A few months later, with Mubarak dethroned, I sat at a tea stall in Tahrir Square with Wael Abbas, one of Cairo's best-known bloggers. He left his glass of sweet tea on an upturned plastic crate as he talked about how the uprising started. The last straw, Wael said, was an election in December 2010. Everyone knew it would be fixed, but when the fix went in it was blatant, egregious and so violent that the regime seemed to be showing absolute contempt for the people. 'They didn't care. We are going to forge the elections, motherfuckers.' Then came the revolution in Tunisia that in early January 2011 removed the country's president, Zine al-Abidine Ben Ali. 'It gave people courage to do something similar,' Wael explained. 'Because they saw that it was possible. Other people did it. This small country that beats us in football in African tournaments has removed its president. Why the hell can't we do that?'

Anger takes years to build, but it can overflow in a moment. The biggest political explosion in the Middle East for a generation was unleashed by a single act, driven by humiliation and rage, that caught the imagination of millions. It happened on 17 December 2010 in Sidi Bouzid, deep in the interior of Tunisia: the kind of dusty, forgotten town where people talk about injustice as if it was one of life's immutable facts, like growing old, or the weather.

Mohamed Bouazizi was a market trader in his mid-twenties selling fruit and vegetables. He was pushed over the edge when inspectors from the local council demanded to see his licence. Like most of the traders, he did not have one. Six months later, Feyda Hamdi, the inspector who was seen as his chief tormentor, sat alongside three male colleagues and told me how most of Bouazizi's colleagues had made a run for it when they arrived. But something in him broke and he stood his ground, yelling at the injustice. The inspectors confiscated his produce and, more seriously for a poor man, his cart and his weights, the only capital in his business. Bouazizi set fire to himself outside the offices of the regional governor. Local protests went national after one of Tunisia's powerful trade unions organized rallies and tipped off the pan-Arab broadcaster Al Jazeera. The demonstrations reached the capital, Tunis, and the army was deployed – but instead of protecting the regime it sided with the protestors, keeping them away from the president's loyalists in the police.

The target of the protests was Zine al-Abidine Ben Ali, Tunisia's corrupt president. The president, his wife Leila Trabelsi and their extended family were so grasping that two years before Mohamed Bouazizi's self-immolation the US ambassador to Tunisia, Robert Godec, had called them 'a quasi-Mafia'. In a cable released by Wiki-Leaks, Godec reported that corruption was getting worse: 'Whether it's cash, services, land, property, or yes, even your yacht, President Ben Ali's family is rumoured to covet it and reportedly gets what it wants.' The yacht in question belonged to a French businessman. Two of Ben Ali's nephews liked the cut of its jib and helped themselves.

While Ben Ali and his clan grew richer – in 2008, *Forbes* magazine estimated that he had salted away five billion dollars – Tunisians were getting poorer. Unemployment rose. Investors stayed away, scared off by corruption. Ben Ali had taken over as president in a bloodless coup in 1987, pushing aside his ailing patron Habib Bourguiba, the man who led Tunisia to independence from France in 1956. He kept links with France strong; a deep gulf separates Tunisia's francophone havens on the Mediterranean coast from the have-nots in the Arabic-speaking interior. The residents of Sidi Bouzid were the very model of a people not just overlooked, but disregarded.

Mohamed Bouazizi embodied the frustration not only of Tunisians, who felt disenfranchised from any chance of making their lives less difficult, but of Arabs across the Middle East. Ben Ali had the gall to visit him in hospital; the president's men released a grim photograph of him standing uneasily next to a dying man swathed in bandages. Many Tunisians saw the bedside visit as a cynical attempt to blunt the protests: the perpetrator was taking advantage of his victim one last time. Ten days after Bouazizi died of horrific burns on 4 January, with the streets of Tunis jammed with protestors, President Ben Ali fled to

Saudi Arabia with his family. The Saudis refused to extradite him. Six months after their escape, Ben Ali and his wife were tried in absentia in Tunisia and handed thirty-five-year sentences for corruption and embezzling public funds. Ben Ali died in exile, of cancer, in 2019.

Arabs like to chant, and the favourite slogan of the protestors in Tunisia was 'The people want the fall of the regime'. Its pleasing drumbeat rhythm in Arabic became the soundtrack of the year as others rose up against their national despots. In Egypt, the uprising began ten days after Ben Ali's escape to Saudi Arabia. Anger with the brutal regime of Hosni Mubarak had been growing and built steadily from June 2010, when two plainclothes policemen beat a young man called Khaled Said to death in Alexandria. At first his mother was told that her son had swallowed the contents of a bag of drugs he was trying to sell, but witnesses said that the police had picked on him in a cafe, slammed his head into a marble table and left him for dead.

In the mortuary, Khaled's brother saw that his face had been smashed and most of his teeth were missing. Standing over his brother's body, he took a photograph with his mobile phone and uploaded it to the internet alongside another one of Khaled alive, with a hopeful smile. It went viral, and Khaled Said became a martyr and a symbol that every Egyptian could understand. 'It was Khaled Said's wretched luck', wrote the author Alaa Al Aswany, 'to be born Egyptian at a time when Egyptians are slaughtered like stray dogs, with impunity and without any impartial investigation or even a word of apology.' Aswany, whose international fame meant he could not be silenced by the regime, took to ending his prolific newspaper columns with the words 'Democracy is the Answer'.[2] Wael Ghonim, an Egyptian working for Google in Dubai, started a Facebook group called 'We are all Khaled Said' that soon had hundreds of thousands of followers. At the Tahrir Square tea stall, the blogger Wael Abbas laughed about how long it took the police to catch on to the power of smartphones and the internet: 'They thought that we were some kids in pyjamas sitting in our bedrooms and trying to say smart stuff and talking to people of our kind and we had no audience.'

Eighteen days of demonstrations ousted Hosni Mubarak, who had been an immovable part of the political landscape of the Middle East for nearly thirty years. At least 800 people were killed during the protests. Some journalists called it 'the Facebook revolution', but that was only part of the story. Most Egyptians could not afford a smartphone or a computer and in some poor areas, around 40 per cent were illiterate. But every cafe had a television that was tuned to news channels. The people saw what was happening on Al Jazeera, and joined in.

Mubarak did not go easily. His political party mobilized support, including a hard core of thugs known as *baltagi*, a term that comes from a Turkish word meaning 'axe man'.[3] The *baltagiya* existed before the uprising, criminals given a licence to break the law in return for doing jobs for the security forces. Mubarak turned them onto his opponents, and anyone else in the vicinity. One of them pulled a knife on me in the streets behind Tahrir Square. I hoped that he had not noticed my flak jacket, and that if he used the knife (in the end he didn't) he would stab one of the bulletproof carbon-fibre plates.

At the height of the battle for Tahrir Square, a miasma of tear gas hung over Cairo. At night, it drifted in through my open window a couple of miles away, along with the distant roar of revolution. To stay in the square, the protestors had to fight off Mubarak's security forces, the *baltagi*, and a bizarre cavalry charge by men on camels. Not every day was violent; sometimes Tahrir was a carnival, with platforms for speeches and music, men with handcarts selling sweet potatoes baked in wood-fired ovens, and a sense of solidarity among Mubarak's opponents that was unusual in Egypt. On violent days, bleeding protestors were treated at an improvised dressing station in a mosque on one of the streets behind Tahrir in what used to be Cairo's European Quarter, surrounded by crumbling apartment houses built to emulate Haussmann's Paris, with tall windows and balconies.

On the streets, bandaged students sitting in the gutters made the place look like a tableau of some Parisian insurrection, *Les Misérables* on the Nile. During the worst stoning and brawling, casualties came in every thirty seconds or so on improvised stretchers made of corrugated iron or doors torn from their hinges. Young protestors wore bloodstained bandages long after they were needed, campaign medals to commemorate their revolutionary moment.

* * *

Across the Middle East, Arabs could not take their eyes off live broadcasts from Tahrir Square. Tunisia is the smallest country in North Africa, squeezed between Libya and Algeria, but Egypt was a different proposition. One in four Arabs are Egyptians, and for much of the twentieth century their country was the political and cultural leader of the Arab Middle East. Mubarak's moribund years had taken away a lot of the shine, but Egypt and the Egyptians were back at the centre of events. Uprisings followed in Libya, Bahrain, Yemen and Syria, and discontent bubbled across the region. Millions identified with the anger of Mohamed Bouazizi and wanted to taste the freedom that Tunisians and Egyptians seemed to have seized.

It did not happen overnight. Arab states in the Middle East had been in the grip of authoritarian regimes rooted in the armed forces, monarchies or sheikhdoms since the 1950s, and by 2011 almost all of them were not delivering lives that their people wanted. The failure of governance ran deep. In Egypt, power had been in the hands of the military since Gamal Abdel Nasser's Free Officers overthrew the king in 1952, imposing an arrangement that was copied by other authoritarian Arab regimes. The government would improve the people's lives, as long as they left politics to a small group of generals and their cronies. It gave them some legitimacy, until economies were outpaced by rising populations. By 2011, only the oil states of the Gulf had the money to maintain the old social contract, at a time when the digital revolution made it impossible for Arab regimes to block evidence from the internet and TV that there were better ways to live.

Arab regimes built up big police states to control discontent. Octopus-like domestic intelligence agencies spied on the people, building and maintaining a barrier of fear. In 2011 that barrier crumbled for a while; a traumatic moment for Arab authoritarians. Since then, they have worked hard to restore it. Arab police states worried obsessively about threats to their power but they could not stop what turned out to be the biggest threat of all: the rising population.

The pressure came from young people. Around two-thirds of Arabs were under thirty and they wanted jobs and freedom, not authoritarian and corrupt leaders who diverted national wealth to their cronies or their own offshore bank accounts and were prepared to jail or kill anyone who was a critic, let alone a threat. Years of corruption and under-investment had produced mass unemployment, sucking the hope from the young along with their fear of the regime.

To make matters worse, the old dictators across the region were grooming their sons to take over. In 1999, Syria's president Hafez al-Assad died and was succeeded by his son Bashar. It was a tribute to the strength of Assad Senior's regime that he was able to impose his will from the grave to stop the Syrian military reviving its long tradition of coups. In Libya, Colonel Muammar al-Gaddafi was grooming his son Saif al-Islam. And in Egypt, Hosni Mubarak was preparing the succession of Gamal, a businessman with an MBA from the American University of Cairo, known in the family as 'Jimmy'. Many of those who rose against the old order in 2011 took action when they realized that not even the death of their ageing despots would free them.

In the end, Egypt's generals removed Mubarak because it was the only way to preserve the power of the military as the country's ruling institution. As a former air force general, Mubarak was one of their own, but he had become a liability. President Obama wanted him out; the armed forces would not jeopardize $1.3 billion of annual American military aid. The evening Mubarak stepped down, the news roared across Tahrir Square. It felt as if the whole of Cairo was on the streets. In reality many were not, hated the lack of order, and worried about the future.

The next day, tens of thousands of Egyptians celebrated their elevation from subjects to citizens by cleaning up the square. They brought brooms, buckets and paintbrushes and set about demonstrating that they owned Egypt. The writer Alaa Al Aswany lit a cigarette and tossed the empty packet aside, only for a woman in her seventies to come over and tell him how much she liked his work before politely asking him to pick up the litter he had just thrown on the ground. 'We're building a new and different Egypt now,' she said. 'We have to keep it tidy.'[4]

Around the fringes of the square, a shingle beach of rubble and rocks had been deposited during eighteen days of protests, thrown in spiky black clouds by thousands of hands at supporters of the former president who had tried to break in to stop their revolution. It was carted away, except for the granite cobblestones that had been Tahrir's heavy artillery, which were put back in their original spots.

That dawn, there was an extraordinary sense of the possible. A tented village stayed at the centre of Tahrir Square, where the protestors sheltered from the winter rain and held endless meetings about the future. They did not manage to make coherent political plans; the excitement was too much, and they were hampered by petty rivalries. The lack of political organization would hurt them in the next three years.

January and February 2011 were tumultuous. Ten days after Tunisians deposed Ben Ali, the uprising started in Egypt. Four days after Mubarak was ousted, it was Libya's turn; protestors surrounded a police station in Benghazi, the second city, and the authorities opened fire. From the start, events in Libya felt more like a civil war than an uprising. Rebels in Benghazi stormed the military garrison and seized its arsenal of weapons; the city was in their hands by 20 February.

Five days later, Gaddafi's son Saif al-Islam decided that letting in journalists might help their cause. I flew to Tripoli, more than 1,000 kilometres west of Benghazi, on a wet and freezing night. The airport was packed with people trying to board planes out of the country, and tens of thousands more were waiting outside in the rain and the mud. Well-organized countries issued their citizens with hi-vis jackets and led them onto special evacuation flights, but the unlucky citizens of other countries had to wait many more days. The Nigerians were still outside the airport weeks later, camping miserably in ditches, scavenging through abandoned luggage, surrounded by refuse and human sewage. Many of them said their wages had not been paid and employers had disappeared with their passports; the only alternative to waiting for salvation was to get to the Tunisian border, thirty frightening checkpoints away.

Far to the south, protestors took over the Pearl Roundabout, the main square in Bahrain's capital, Manama, and tried to recreate what had happened in Tahrir. This was the first uprising to be infected by the sectarian poison that had become increasingly toxic since the US invasion of Iraq in 2003. In Bahrain, the royal family and the elite are Sunni, and the Shia majority were demanding equality. The Sunni royals and their big brothers in Saudi Arabia were convinced that Iran was reasserting an old claim to Bahrain. The Saudis and the Emiratis sent troops across the 25-kilometre causeway from the mainland to help Bahraini forces crush the uprising. An independent report into the violence, commissioned by King Hamad of Bahrain in a gesture to the protestors and his Western allies, concluded that the authorities had deployed excessive force, extracted false confessions under torture and used 'terror inspiring behaviour' against its own citizens.[5]

In December 2012, a year after the report was published, the populations of the Shia villages around Manama were still protesting. I rode in the back of a police SUV one night and it felt like being with an occupying army. Hostility and contempt have a way of getting through the bulletproof glass and the armour plate, even when the stones bounce off. One of the officers I was riding with claimed the problem was teenagers 'pushed by higher leaders', but the evidence showed that state repression was to blame. On another night I went to Shia villages, without the police, where people of all ages took to the streets in the evenings to demand the fall of the regime. The security forces would scatter them, leaving young men to throw stones or petrol bombs. These villages were the very opposite of the shopping-mall glitz that the oil states of the Gulf like to project. To the demonstrators, Iran represented some kind of salvation, but Bahrain's Shias did not need to be told to protest. They had seen revolution across the Middle East, and they wanted their own. The Bahraini state crushed their hopes, helped by the Saudis and what Amnesty International called the 'shameful silence' of its Western allies, especially the UK and the US.[6]

The power of the Egyptian example reached Yemen. A big camp at the university in the capital, Sana'a, was the Tahrir equivalent. Yemen's veteran leader, President Ali Abdullah Saleh, had plenty of enemies after so long at the top. He too had been grooming his son to succeed him. He lost the support of key military and tribal leaders, the army split, and Saleh began the fight, not just for his job, but his life.

I was in Libya, trying to get the interview that mattered most at that time, with Muammar al-Gaddafi. It happened at an Italian restaurant overlooking the sea, where I was whisked by the son of one of Gaddafi's close associates in an armour-plated BMW with a built-in Kalashnikov rack, upholstered in suede fine enough for an Italian jacket. Mohammed Abdullah al-Senussi, son of the Libyan regime's feared intelligence chief, turned round in his seat: it's a James Bond car, he said happily. Like all of the regime's royalty, Mohammed kept a close eye on his image. Most days he was a designer urban guerrilla, with thick stubble and an elegant combat-style jacket teamed with expensive jeans, a black cashmere beanie and blue suede boots. He was a close friend of Khamis Gaddafi, the colonel's youngest son; the pair were captured and killed by rebels about forty miles south-east of Tripoli in August 2011, in the brutal confusion that followed the fall of the regime.

We lined up outside the restaurant to shake hands with Colonel Gaddafi, who arrived wearing flowing ochre robes with matching headdress and aviator sunglasses. I was sharing the interview with Christiane Amanpour, then working for the US network ABC News, and Marie Colvin of the *Sunday Times*. The man I had seen so often on front pages and in cartoons settled himself down and produced a five-star display of defiance, dismissing the uprising as the work of drug-addicted young people and blaming the West for wanting to recolonize Libya. He looked disbelieving when I told him I'd seen people demonstrating against him in the streets.

Since that night in Tripoli, I've replayed the recording of the interview, pausing it on close-ups of Gaddafi. The disbelief that flickers across his face looks genuine, as if he could not understand how there could possibly be demonstrations against him. I do not doubt that he believed what he was saying; the suede-lined armoured BMW had transported me into the bubble of heroism that Gaddafi had inflated in forty years as Libyan leader.

Gaddafi had not taken the title of president – part of the pretence that he was a leader who had opened himself to the authority of the people. He had seized power at the head of a junta of young officers in 1969, when he was in his late twenties. Since then, he had rarely gone anywhere inside Libya without meeting a crowd hysterical with joy that he had arrived in their lives, however briefly. Perhaps by the end he had forgotten or did not know that many of the crowds were paid loyalists, bussed in to cheer and shout.

During the months of the rebellion in 2011, I started seeing the same faces at the endless, ritualistic demonstrations in Green Square next to the ramparts of Tripoli's walled old town. An old man offered a handshake at one of the rallies and pressed into my palm a used cartridge case from a Kalashnikov rifle, discreetly, like a black spot delivered to curse the regime.

The ritual of paying homage to Gaddafi would always include an alarming moment when guns were drawn and dozens of bullets were fired into the blue day or the dark night. Women would join in, ululating, as they pulled heavy-looking automatic weapons from under their hijabs and opened up at the sky. Their favourite chant was *Allah, Muammar, Libya wa bas* – 'God, Muammar, Libya and that's all we need'. Dancing, chanting crowds would block roads to dance and blaze away the day, and after dark their chants would drift into my hotel window with the night air.

Reaching districts of the capital lost to the regime meant evading roadblocks manned by Gaddafi's frightening militiamen. Demonstrators would march out of the mosques until they came up against the regime's men, who would open fire, wounding and killing unarmed civilians. Gaddafi swore he would hunt the rebels alleyway by alleyway. Someone set the speech to music, adding pictures of a dancing girl to Gaddafi's rant. *Zenga*, the Libyan word for alley, went viral as the video was downloaded by hundreds of thousands of Arabs, even after it emerged that an Israeli had made the video.

Gaddafi threatened to open his arsenals and arm his supporters to crush the rebellion. When I spoke to senior members of the regime, they insisted that this was rhetoric, that Gaddafi would sit down with leaders of Libya's tribes and thrash out a deal the Libyan way. The British prime minister David Cameron and the French president Nicolas Sarkozy decided that he was serious. Western politicians and diplomats, blindsided by the speed of events in Tunisia and Egypt, were determined to stay ahead of Libya's revolution. Some of Barack Obama's most influential advisors agreed that Gaddafi was bent on spilling a great deal of blood, and set to work to persuade a reluctant president that action was needed.

Gaddafi's men were well armed and in tanks, pushing aside chaotic rebels who were firing wildly from guns mounted on pick-up trucks. The regime's forces advanced rapidly eastwards towards Benghazi, while Gaddafi's son Saif al-Islam swaggered around the foyer of the five-star Rixos Hotel in Tripoli predicting imminent victory.

The rebels were the least of his father's problems. Much more serious for him was that his enemies in Paris, London and Washington were winning the argument that Gaddafi was plotting a genocide. The Libyan delegation at the UN defected to the rebels, pulling down the green banner of Gaddafi's Libyan Arab Jamahiriya at their mission in New York and flying Libya's original red, black and green flag instead. On 12 March, the Arab League voted to ask the Security Council to impose a no-fly zone on Libya. Gaddafi needed as many friends as he could find, but he had burnt all his bridges with his fellow Arabs with his aggressive, erratic behaviour. He had even plotted to assassinate King Abdullah of Saudi Arabia when he was still Crown Prince.

The Security Council, with the support of the Arab League, passed a resolution stating that 'all necessary measures' could be taken to protect Libyan civilians. The wording of the resolution, in which Britain played a big part, signed two death warrants. One was for the Gaddafi regime; the other was for the chances of finding a diplomatic solution to the crisis that was building in Syria. The US, UK and France treated the resolution as a charter for regime change; the Russians, outmanoeuvred, swore that the same thing would not happen to their Syrian allies.

In Libya, Western powers and their allies soon started air strikes; the super-rich, ambitious rulers of Qatar sent in troops, weapons and advisors. The Gaddafi regime claimed that it wanted to talk, but was always told that the colonel and his cronies would have to leave power first. My new friend Fouad Zlitni, a lugubrious diplomat who had spent years translating for Gaddafi, sighed with resignation: 'Negotiating with the leader is like making love to a beautiful woman . . . you don't just say "come to bed". You ask her if she wants a cup of coffee. It's the same with Gaddafi. If you want to make a deal with him, you don't tell him what to do. You just say, "Let's talk . . ."'

The NATO-led air strikes became part of Tripoli's daily drumbeat, a counterpoint to night-time gun battles. Many civilians died in the raids, though NATO – as ever – insisted that they worked hard to protect non-combatants. The trouble is that bombing a heavily populated city always kills people who are not targets.

On 20 June 2011, NATO flattened the country estate of Lieutenant-General al-Khuwaylidi al-Humaydi, who had been one of Gaddafi's closest advisors since seizing power with him in 1969. My guess was that NATO must have had information, which turned out to be wrong, that Gaddafi was staying there. It was a private house, though it may have been used for meetings away from Gaddafi's Tripoli compound. Five children were among thirteen dead, including three of Humaydi's grandchildren and his pregnant daughter-in-law. At the local hospital their remains were laid out in beds made up with starched white linen. I tried to count the dead, but it was hard to tell from the gnarled, burnt fragments that had been tucked into the beds how many bodies were there. A nurse cradled the corpse of a boy who looked as if he had been two or three years old. A man held up a blackened torso with a child's arm still attached. The attack was no accident. NATO called it 'a precision strike on a legitimate military target'.

Back in Tripoli, the Russian consul, a man called Viktor, was in a furious mood as he drove me to his embassy. The Russians believed they had been deceived by the West's interpretation of 'all necessary measures' in the Security Council resolution. Viktor took his frustrations out on the Tripoli traffic and his car's screaming clutch. He drove jerkily, sucking furiously on his cigarettes in a massacre of nicotine and tar, complaining about life in Libya (nothing to do but eat, no films, no theatre, no booze) and the hypocrisy of Western countries that found it easier to bomb than talk. I pointed out that Gaddafi had done some pretty bad things to his own people.

'Yes, but that happens in Saudi Arabia and Bahrain, too. Maybe there are more people in jail there – we just don't know.'

The embassy was hosting a meeting with Russia's top envoy to the Middle East, Mikhael Margelov, in a wood-panelled room decorated with oil paintings of snowy forests. Margelov was impressive, fluent in Arabic and English as he explained how he would square the impossible circle and persuade Gaddafi to stand down by offering a chance to stay in Libya, protected by his tribe.

It would have been better to negotiate the end, rather than let Gaddafi create his own *Götterdämmerung*. The chaotic and violent collapse of Gaddafi's regime, and his brutal death, created a disastrous power vacuum in Libya. The way he governed meant that Libya's institutions were as hollow as film sets. Gaddafi and his family became the state. When they were gone, nothing was left except militias fighting for the spoils in a protracted civil war that was still killing people ten years later.

The UN Security Council resolution was the beginning of the end for Gaddafi, setting in motion the events that culminated with a full-scale rising in Tripoli in August 2011. By then, the rebels were much stronger than in the chaotic first months of their revolution, thanks to arms shipments, Qatari instructors and NATO air strikes. They rose in Tripoli to drive out the colonel, his family and loyalists, who escaped to Sirte, the coastal town where Gaddafi had grown up.

It took two more months to find and kill Gaddafi. As the noose tightened around Sirte he tried to escape to the Jarref Valley, where he was born. Afterwards, one of his inner circle told the BBC that it amounted to a suicide mission; no country was prepared to shelter Gaddafi, and he was ready to die by Libyan hands. Perhaps if he had sneaked out at night he might have made it, but he left in a convoy of seventy-five cars, which was soon attacked by the French air force. Gaddafi survived the strike and took refuge in a drainage pipe until he was dragged out by a mob, beaten, shot and stabbed until he died a horrific death. Every Libyan I met was pleased that Gaddafi was dead. When I suggested that a trial might have healed the country, they laughed or cursed. The vision of Gaddafi haranguing Libyans from the dock was powerful political magic that could only be expunged with his own blood.

The violence of the regime's collapse cursed the future. After basking in the cheers of the delighted citizens of Benghazi, David Cameron and Nicolas Sarkozy went home without a plan to stabilize Libya, happy to accept the insistence of Libyan allies that they did not need any foreign help to rebuild the country from the ground up. Ten years later, Libya was a warring mess of city-states, tribes, jihadists and militias.

The Russians nursed their grievances, determined not to make the same mistake when it came to Syria. Deadlock in the Security Council crippled any hope of a united international response as war began to break Syria into pieces. Arab authoritarians drew their own lessons from the end of the regimes of Ben Ali and Mubarak, who had made the mistake of not killing enough of their enemies. For them, Gaddafi was half right: he used force, but he did not have a strong ally to back him.

The counterrevolution was on, and by the end of the year, 30,000 Arabs were dead. The protestors in Cairo and Tunis who were swept up with joy about what they had done seemed not to notice, and nor did many in the West, who made a snap judgement that a happy, democratic ending was on the way. It was the same illusion that liberal democracy was unstoppable that had followed the end of the Cold War.

I had known the Middle East long enough to be horribly aware of the trouble ahead. I tried to offer some caution in my reporting, avoiding the phrase 'Arab Spring' because it made what was happening sound quick and easy, and it was neither. Without a doubt, 2011 was a major turning point in the history of the Arabs: the biggest challenge in the six decades of autocracy that had defined the Middle East since the 1950s. The only trouble was, the autocrats were not going to go quietly.

15.

The Road to Damascus

One evening, on a dark and cold back road, an armed man walked out of the wet fog. I was not sure which side the fighter was on. Shapes loomed behind him with the glowing tips of cigarettes marking the whereabouts of a few faces, but it was hard to tell how many of them there were. The rich smell of a cowshed drifted in through the car windows, already opened for a nervous listen for gunfire or explosions. 'Watch out, Saul went blind on the road to Damascus,' someone who knew the Bible had warned me a few days earlier, on my way into Syria from Beirut over mountain roads banked with snow.

I couldn't see much driving up to that unknown, unlit roadblock. Some torches flashed and for a nauseous moment I thought they were from one of the regime's armed units, perhaps the Shabiha, the militias it used to do dirty work. Their name translates as 'ghost', but what they meant was thug. I knew Assad's enforcers were busy. At the end of the dark January afternoon we drove slowly past a man in a civilian's black leather jacket standing in sleeting, slanting rain, directing around twenty soldiers in full combat gear who were piling out of the back of a bus. He was bald and looked as if cruelty was his business, his Kalashnikov bumping casually against his tan trousers as he sent the soldiers down the lanes that led to Douma, one of an arc of satellite towns making up an area called Eastern Ghouta that rebels had seized.

The man at the checkpoint was not Shabiha. His walkie-talkie crackled and fizzed, and he pulled back his hood to show a mask made from the green, white and black version of the national flag, the banner of the uprising. His men were from the local militia, claiming affiliation to the Free Syrian Army, which was less a coherent military formation and more an expression of belief. In the first year of the war, rebel groups were mostly local men and defectors from the Syrian military. More of them appeared, with guns and black balaclavas with slits for mouth and eyes. Some had Kalashnikovs they had stolen from the army when they changed sides. The rest had an assortment of hunting rifles, pistols and pump-action shotguns and were delighted to see people from the outside world. They started chanting 'Freedom' and 'Welcome BBC'.

In the first few years of the Syrian war, it was just about possible to cross from regime areas into rebel territory. Around Damascus, much of it was close to the city centre and the heavily guarded compounds that were the heart of Bashar al-Assad's regime. In the short, dark days around Damascus in January 2012, we nibbled around the edge of Eastern Ghouta, looking for a way in. The rebels were active and confident. From Douma they had cut the main highway to Aleppo, forcing traffic going north onto mountain roads encrusted with army checkpoints.

After only a few months of shelling, Ghouta was already badly damaged. It held out for another seven years, until entire neighbourhoods were rubble and artillery, air strikes and starvation forced its defenders to surrender in return for safe passage to what was by then Syria's last rebel-held enclave, the north-western province of Idlib. But that was years away. In 2012, Douma was dark and cold; the regime had cut off the power. Dozens of death notices were pasted to the walls of a mosque that were tattooed with bullet holes. Empty streets looked like scenes from a dystopian video game, lined with rubble from broken buildings, with boys going half-wild burning plastic to fight a freezing wind. It felt as if death had swept through a few times and was coming back soon. The killing was happening somewhere close that night. Ragged bursts of gunfire and explosions came from the edge of town, but in Douma, morale was solid. A nightly rally, which the rebels managed to stream live on the internet, was held in a square in the centre, with speakers and lights powered by a generator. Men made speeches from a stage. Teenage boys did a war dance, waving swords dangerously. The only women there were in my team, except for a few small girls holding their fathers' hands. A baby's face was decorated with a slogan, carefully drawn, that said, in Arabic, 'Go, leave us, step down Bashar.' The men who had gathered kept saying that President Bashar al-Assad had to die, and were cheerfully discussing the options. Hanging was popular.

The secretive, ruthless Assad family has ruled Syria since 1970; Bashar inherited the job when his father, Hafez, died in 2000. I have a fridge magnet that I bought in one of the narrow lanes of the old city of Damascus. It shows Hafez, his wife Aniseh and their children posing with their bicycles. Just another family, except that their dad was redefining the words 'iron grip'. In 1982, a few years after the photo was taken, Hafez and his younger brother Rifaat crushed a rebellion by the Muslim Brotherhood revolt in Hama, a city known for its deep Sunni piety and towering waterwheels on the Orontes River. As many as 25,000 people were killed.

Bashar did not grow up expecting to be president; the job was reserved for his eldest brother, Bassel, whose official portraits show a dashing army officer in sunglasses and an immaculate uniform, often on horseback. Bassel was killed in 1994 when his Mercedes hit a roundabout as he drove to Damascus Airport, late for a plane on a foggy morning. Bashar was a doctor, training in London to be an ophthalmologist. He was called back to Syria to take up his duties as heir to the presidential throne. It cannot have been easy. Hafez had made sure that the Syrian people knew Bassel as his eldest son and heir, and Bashar now found himself having to lead the pack.

When he inherited in 2000, Bashar presented himself as a different kind of Arab leader, more modern and open than his hard-faced predecessors. His father believed mobile phones and the internet were such dangers to his regime that only the elite was allowed to use them. Bashar opened up the digital world to the whole country. The family took a big stake in Syria's mobile network through Bashar's maternal first cousin, Rami Makhlouf, deepening a pattern of corruption that put billions of dollars in the Assads' coffers.

In the year that he succeeded his father, Bashar met a young woman from London who was on holiday in Damascus, and they quickly married. Asma Akhras was born in London and brought up in suburban Ealing by Syrian parents; her mother was a diplomat and her father was a cardiologist. She had a first-class degree in computer science from King's College London and a job at an investment bank. Her presence made some Westerners assume that the new generation of Assads would break with the family's bloodstained and repressive past. Bashar promised reforms, repeatedly. Many Syrians believed him, even as he found more ways of explaining that he was still waiting for the right time to deliver them. Some Western journalists found Asma's intelligence, elegance and beauty so compelling that they helped enthusiastically to build her image. In February 2011, as protestors marched across the Middle East, a lavish *Vogue* profile headlined 'A Rose in the Desert' gushed: 'Asma al-Assad is glamorous, young, and very chic – the freshest and most magnetic of first ladies . . . She's breezy, conspiratorial, and fun.'

Many Syrians did not fall for the propaganda. For a generation they had watched the Assad regime oppressing and intimidating its subjects. Bashar had, however, acquired a certain personal legitimacy, even popularity, because of his harsh words for Israel and his support for their most obdurate enemy, Hizbullah in Lebanon. He was tall, thin and quietly spoken, with a certain diffidence that reinforced the idea that he was not a typical Middle East strongman. He looked like a doctor, not a warrior. His later behaviour suggests it was a piece of typecasting he hated.

I interviewed Bashar twice in the years before 2011. He was friendly and extravagantly polite, allocating around ten minutes before the meeting for a private chat during which he enquired solicitously about my health, family and journey to the palace. One of the interviews happened during the war between Israel and Hamas over the New Year of 2009. He knew I'd travelled to Damascus from Jerusalem and asked what I thought was happening between Israel and the Palestinians, nodding attentively as I answered. Appearances were wrong. Bashar was not diffident. He radiated self-belief, and insisted he would do whatever it took to make sure Syrians were safe and prosperous. I did not expect him to share his inner doubts with a visiting reporter, but he seemed confident to the point of self-delusion.

In January and February 2011, Syrians watched transfixed as protests overthrew the presidents of Tunisia and Egypt, and uprisings started in Bahrain, Yemen and Libya. In January, I could hear Bashar al-Assad's complacency in an interview he gave to the *Wall Street Journal*.[1] The uprisings, he explained, showed that the Middle East was polluted by political stagnation. What was happening, he said, was as bad as a plague of microbes, but Syria would not be troubled by it. 'Whenever you have an uprising, it is self-evident to say that you have anger, but this anger feeds on desperation.'

Dr Assad's diagnosis was wrong. He might have been right if he had brought in the reforms he had been promising for ten years. Syria was not immune to the virus of change. But when Assad's authority was challenged, he ordered his men to reach for their guns – just as his father had in Hama in 1982.

I was in Tripoli reporting the uprising against Gaddafi in March 2011 when tweets started to appear about demonstrators being shot dead in Deraa, a city in southern Syria. It was not a surprise; Syria was a convincing candidate for an uprising. The Assad family, in power since 1970, had created a highly repressive police state. The population was young, angry and frustrated, just as in other Arab countries. Protests started in Deraa after a group of boys was arrested by the Mukhabarat, the regime's terrifying security apparatus, for spray-painting revolutionary slogans on their school, including the words they must have heard on TV in the endless live coverage of Egypt and Tunisia: *ashaab yurid isqat an-nizam* – 'The people want the fall of the regime'. The boys, aged between eleven and sixteen, were detained, beaten and tortured.

Some of Bashar's advisors counselled restraint. Deraa city and the surrounding province were traditional, patriarchal and tribal. An approach to Deraa's elders, and keeping promises to reform his corrupt regime, could calm matters. After ten years of war and killing, Syrians from the first protest movements told me that might have worked. One organizer of student protests in Aleppo in the north, now exiled in New Zealand, told me that a reformist Assad could have a won a fair election, if he had risked it.[2]

Many Syrians who were hoping that the moment had come for the regime to display some sort of olive branch waited anxiously for a speech Bashar was due to make on 30 March. He entered the parliament chamber to rapturous applause, smiling indulgently as much older members competed with each other to praise their leader. One found the superlative of the day. It was not enough that Bashar was Syria's president; he should be the leader of the whole world. But his speech disappointed any Syrian who still hoped he was not like his father. He told them that although the uprisings across the Middle East were justified responses to stagnation, the protests in Syria were not legitimate, because their country was modernizing and dynamic, the sternest opponent of Israel and the West in the region. Syria's enemies were exploiting the turbulence in the Middle East. They were foreign conspirators, forcing their way in to destroy the country. If they wanted war, he would lead the fight.

Syrians who had clung to Bashar's promises of reform were horrified by the speech. They had hoped he might pull back; instead, he had effectively declared war on the protestors.

Jihad Makdissi, a Syrian diplomat I was friendly with, was deeply depressed. A couple of months later, with the regime killing demonstrators, he opened up to me over a coffee in London, well away from the risk of bugs in the embassy in Belgrave Square: 'He's got to get rid of the old guard, or the ship is going to sink. This isn't Egypt. Syria doesn't have a political system, it has a family system, and the Assads don't have a long history of making concessions. The more you corner the regime, the more stubborn it will be . . . Either the president will ride the wave of reform – and pretend it's his agenda – or get swept away by the tide.'[3]

Makdissi was hoping Assad would try to make a deal to stop the country being destroyed: 'I believe in the survival instincts of Assad. It's not too late.' But it was. He was called back to Damascus for an unhappy spell as foreign ministry spokesman, saw the reality, and slipped out of the country with his family.

In case anyone had any doubts left, Bashar al-Assad was proclaiming that he would stick to his father's methods. Simon Collis, British ambassador in Damascus as the war started, told me that the best way to understand the family's methods was to watch films about the Mafia. As the regime's atrocities piled up, Britain closed its embassy and withdrew its diplomats in protest.

Bashar's local boss in Deraa was his first cousin, Atef Najib. Family members had key positions in the regime's departments of coercion and repression. When tribal elders and the fathers of boys who had been arrested for spraying slogans went to ask him for their freedom, Najib told them, 'Forget you have children ... and if you want new children in their place, then send your wives over and we'll impregnate them for you.'[4] Arrogant and violent, Najib could claim the dubious distinction of being the first official in Assad's regime to order his men to shoot and kill protestors. Two other regime tough guys – Maher al-Assad, Bashar's younger brother, and his cousin Hafez Makhlouf – arrived to help Najib look after the family's interests. Maher commanded a crack armoured division, the descendant of the 'Defence Companies' which were commanded by Rifaat, the younger brother of the first President Assad, in the murderous operation against the Muslim Brotherhood in Hama in 1982.

Bashar's decision to use the iron fist inside an iron glove turned a series of peaceful protests into a war. When I managed to get to Deraa months later, local people, still defiant, were desperate to talk to outsiders about the regime's atrocities. Roadblocks surrounded the city, while in the centre soldiers had set up sandbagged positions at main road junctions. It felt like an occupied Palestinian town on the West Bank, with Assad's Syrian Arab Army playing the part of the Israelis.

Young people came to talk to me about the people killed by the regime's men. 'They're slaughtering us every day,' one said. 'This is a street full of martyrs, there are eighteen martyrs in this street. Come and see for yourselves.' The faces of people killed in what they called a revolution were everywhere. The chubby, innocent smile of thirteen-year-old Hamza al-Khatib was on many posters all over Syria. Hamza disappeared during a demonstration in Deraa at the end of April. His bloated, battered body was returned to his parents around a month later. Hamza had been shot and stabbed and his penis had been cut off. The regime claimed that protestors who were attacking the security forces had killed him, and Bashar al-Assad met his family to offer condolences. In a brutal and grotesque charade, Hamza's haunted-looking father appeared on Syrian state TV and praised the generosity of the president, who 'engulfed us with his kindness, graciousness and promised to fulfil the demands which we've called for with the people'.[5]

Angry protestors were soon shooting back after mass demonstrations in the spring and summer of 2012 were met with bullets. Picking up guns against the corrupt regime made them feel liberated, and they thought they had the Assads on the run. I spent a day at a hospital in Homs as a steady procession of muddy and battered military Land Rovers and vans brought in regime casualties from the front line. Wounded men were rushed into the operating theatres, where organs shredded by bullets and high explosive piled up in kidney dishes, cut out by exhausted surgeons standing in pools of blood. Parked outside the surgical block were more trucks and vans loaded with soldiers' bodies in a tangle of blood, mud and mutilation, all men who had not survived the long drive from the front line. A military band in the car park played a wheezy send-off as families took their dead to be buried. Tens of thousands of Syrian men who wanted no part of Assad's war defected to the rebels or escaped abroad. But there were always soldiers in the Syrian Arab Army who were prepared to give their lives. Many echoed the president, telling me that they were fighting a conspiracy to destroy the country. They had heavy weapons and could take ground, but did not have the numbers and reinforcements to hold onto it when they went off to fight the next battle.

In the first winter of the war, at the start of 2012, Damascus was stuck in a nightmarish tale of two cities. It was possible to pass the last regime checkpoints around central Damascus and drive only a few hundred metres before running into rebel positions. Barricades of burnt-out cars and trucks protected by sandbags were defended by a blend of local men and army defectors. On 27 January 2012, I drove to the suburb of Saqba. The air was thick with insults directed at the Assads. 'God curse your soul, Hafez, for your child the donkey.' The streets filled with several thousand men for the funeral of a man killed by the regime's soldiers. When word went round that soldiers and Shabiha were nearby, they scattered. Men cocked their weapons and prepared to fight. A heavy-set man in a camouflage tunic told me he had been a general in the army. 'Stay with me, don't be afraid, our resistance is strong,' he said. We left, and getting back to the city centre took some doing. Although the Free Army controlled a big piece of Damascus, they were also surrounded.

That winter, thousands of people piled into squares in areas controlled by rebels and chanted for the downfall of the regime. During a brief ceasefire, the besieged town of Zabadani opened up for a few days. It was battered and broken, but in better times it was a summer resort in the hills between Damascus and Beirut. As it was getting dark the rebels stretched out a huge independence flag and sent fireworks into the sky to tell the people to gather in the town square to celebrate a moment that was not victory, or anything like it, but was a break from the war. A woman told me, 'It's enough for me to have these two days of freedom, and it doesn't matter if I die tomorrow.' Armed men, local heroes, poured out of civilian cars. I asked them what chance they had against the regime's heavy weapons and warplanes. They grinned as one of them said, 'God willing, we will win. We're ready to die for the women and children and to defend our honour.'

All but one of the young fighters I met that night were killed in the five years they held out in Zabadani against the Syrian army and Hizbullah, Assad's allies from Lebanon. In 2017 they made a deal, an honourable surrender after a medieval siege, to exchange the mainly Sunni population with a besieged Shia village in Idlib Province. The man who told me what had happened had also been in the town square that night, cheering for the Free Army. He suffered his own tragedy: his eighteen-year-old son was killed by a barrel bomb, just as he was about to get out to study somewhere safe.

The first year or so of the war was the optimistic time for rebels. A bearded commander in Qaboon, a Damascus suburb where the frontline positions were a few yards apart (I visited both sides), told me that he hoped Syria could be Islamist but not extremist, 'like Turkey'. When I tried to find him ten years later, I was told he had been killed. But in that first year, even when it was clear that the regime's forces were going to keep on killing until the regime was safe, it never took long for someone to say that Bashar al-Assad's time was up. It seemed logical that he would go the same way as Ben Ali in Tunisia, Mubarak in Egypt and Gaddafi in Libya. All of them, me included, were wrong.

Bashar al-Assad had been right when he said Syria was different; the difference was the iron-clad legacy left by his father, who did all he could to make his regime coup-proof. Hafez al-Assad favoured key families from the Sunni majority, but he gave a crucial stake in the system to Syria's minorities: Christians, Ismailis, Druze and most of all, his own Alawite sect. Alawites dominated the armed forces and the police state because they were the people he trusted most. Throughout the years of war after 2011, the regime never lost the loyalty of most of its Alawite commanders. In Egypt the loyalty of the senior officers was to the military, not to a family. President Mubarak was cut loose to save the institution's power. In Syria, the vast majority of the officer corps associated their own fate with that of the Assad family.

Hafez al-Assad knew all about the dangers of instability and disorder for rulers and their families. Military coups happened regularly in Syria after independence from France in 1946; there were three in 1949 alone. He wanted stability and imposed the system he hoped would guarantee it. The Assad family's rise to power began in Qardaha, a poor village in the Alawite heartland in the mountains on the Mediterranean coast. Syria's Sunni majority generally regarded the Alawites with suspicion; they were a breakaway sect from Shia Islam, with secretive rituals and beliefs. Many Alawites are secular. A general broke off from directing the shelling of the rebel-held side of Aleppo to give me some home-made *arak* that he said with pride came from Qardaha, the Assad birthplace. It was in an old Jack Daniel's whiskey bottle, complete with original label.

Hafez and his younger brother Rifaat were the first in their family to get a secondary education, which meant leaving their village for Latakia, now the big city on the coast but sleepy and small in the 1940s. It was still large enough for Hafez to see and resent the power of property-owning Sunni businessmen, who gave their people lives that impoverished Alawis could only dream about. He listened to Baath Party activists talking about Arab unity and socialism, liked what he heard, and plunged into student politics.

Hafez wanted to get to the top. He chose the best route for poor and ambitious young men in Syria in the years after independence, applying to the national military academy in Homs. The officer cadets were not just paid but fed, an important perk.[6] Hafez al-Assad did well. He was sent to learn to fly fast jets in the USSR. He also made a lifelong friend, Mustafa Tlas, a Sunni from an equally poor background who became his closest ally. The rise of people like Hafez and Mustafa was bad news for the traditional Sunni landed classes. As Assad's biographer Patrick Seale noted, the Syrian elite made a historic mistake: 'scorning the army as a profession, they allowed it to be captured by their class enemies who then went on to capture the state itself.'[7]

They learned the art of the coup d'état. Assad's first taste of power was as a junior member of a military junta dominated by Baathists that took power in 1963. Their rule dripped with blood. Troops and tanks crushed an uprising by an alliance of Sunni landowners and supporters of the Muslim Brotherhood who believed that Islam, rather than the junta's brutal, secular Arabism, was the answer. The uprising ended with rebels trapped in a mosque in Hama, a town renowned for fierce Sunni piety. The Baathist regime shelled it until its minaret collapsed and then sent a tank to break down the door.

Assad was ruthless. He learned to use power, manipulate loyalty, and eliminate rivals and traitors. In 1966, he and his top officers purged their own side. The founder of Baathism, Michel Aflaq, was allowed to leave the country, but they settled matters with the others with a day-long gun battle. The losers were tortured and killed. Assad rose to be minister of defence, in time to bear his share of responsibility for the disastrous and humiliating defeat in the 1967 Middle East war that left Israel occupying the Golan Heights, the plateau in southern Syria that it later annexed. Since the entire leadership shared ownership of that disaster, the face-off between the junta's most powerful members, Assad and Salah Jadid, was postponed. Tension between them increased as Assad outgrew his role as Jadid's apprentice. Jadid was a disciplined and honest officer who lived a simple life and forced ministers to swap their Mercedes for more modest cars. He was tough and ruthless, until Hafez outmanoeuvred him.

The Assad–Jadid power struggle came to a head in 1970, when Syria's southern neighbour, King Hussein of Jordan, fought a war known as Black September to stop Yasser Arafat's Palestinians taking over his country. Assad the pragmatist viewed Arafat as an out-of-control troublemaker. Jadid, a much more radical Arab nationalist, saw the Palestinian leader as an ally against the Israelis and Hussein as an untrustworthy dupe of Israel and the West. During an acrimonious party congress in 1970, Jadid accused Assad of treachery and tried to strip him of his rank; his crime was not ordering the air force to support the Palestinians. Hussein had a secret guarantee from Israel and support from the US. Had Assad done as Jadid wanted, Syria would most likely have been handed another beating. Assad was shrewd enough to realize that, and he expected Jadid to make his move at the congress. He ringed the venue with his loyalists, and Jadid and his followers were arrested.

Syrians who were on the losing side in palace coups were often sent into exile, perhaps to a congenial diplomatic post, but Salah Jadid was a bad loser. Reportedly, he told Assad, 'If I ever take power, you will be dragged through the streets until you die.'[8] Jadid's reward for his defiance was incarceration for life in Mezze Prison in Damascus. His body left the prison in a coffin in 1993. One of his allies, Nureddin al-Atassi, who held the figurehead position of president when Assad seized power, was locked up in Mezze and released to fly out to Paris for medical treatment only when Assad knew he was dying of oesophageal cancer.

Hafez al-Assad never forgot an enemy, and he only forgave those who were no longer a threat if it suited him. He became the dominant Arab leader during his thirty years in power. Before Assad, Syria was a pawn in the calculations of others. Assad restored national pride, though not the Golan Heights, when he joined Egypt in a surprise attack on Israel in 1973. The American secretary of state Henry Kissinger went to Damascus to negotiate; afterwards, Assad's palace was a vital stop in any round of Middle Eastern shuttle diplomacy. In marathon meetings, waiters plied visitors with round after round of sweet Arab tea, thick coffee and fresh lemonade. Assad would not offer bathroom breaks, forcing the Americans to show weakness by requesting them. When James Baker was US Secretary of State in the administration of the first President George Bush, he called it 'bladder diplomacy'.[9] Hours into a meeting in 1991, he waved a white handkerchief in surrender when he could take no more. Until almost the end of his life Hafez al-Assad was manoeuvring around the Americans, trying to find a way to get the Golan Heights back from Israel without giving away too much in return.

During the Assad years, Syria became a family business, but it was not a happy one. When Hafez had a heart attack, his brother Rifaat attempted a coup, only for the president to rise from his sickbed and pack his brother off into a lucrative exile. Long after Hafez was dead, I visited Rifaat in his huge mansion on the Avenue Foch in Paris. Loyalists who had been banished with him guarded the ground floor, and I had the feeling that guns were not far away. Rifaat smiled modestly when I complimented him on his property portfolio, which include some of London's best addresses. 'You know how it is.' Rifaat waved a hand airily around his huge rococo salon. 'It's all mortgages.' In 2020 a court in Paris disagreed, sentencing him in his absence to four years in prison for money laundering and stealing Syrian state funds to pay for his property empire.

The rift in the Assad family was passed down to the next generation. For a while in the early 1990s Rifaat was allowed back to Syria. His son Ribaal had a blazing row with his cousin Bashar in the car park outside the summer pizzeria at the Damascus Sheraton, a playground for offspring of the Syrian elite. It was like rival branches of the Soprano family facing off outside a New Jersey steakhouse. That wasn't the end of it. When Ribaal was about to fly out to study at Boston University, his father was warned to expect trouble at the airport. Ribaal told me they arrived to find 200 uniformed and armed men: 'So they come and surround the plane. Passenger buses come in again with many soldiers . . . and started shooting in the air, you know. On the runway you could see many red berets from the Republican Guards . . . the plane was full of people, passengers, and they start shooting in the air . . . They heard this guy telling him in Arabic, telling another – an officer telling a soldier in Arabic, "Quickly, shoot him, that's him."'[10]

Ribaal was not shot, but he had to go back to Damascus with them. Rifaat, still respected as one of the regime's hard men, told the officer in charge he'd fight in 'every street in Damascus' if his son was hurt. The next day he was allowed to leave, but Hafez had made his point. Do as you're told, and respect the boss and his boys. Bashar had learnt a lesson too. Don't show weakness, don't tolerate rebellion – and if it comes, crush it without hesitation.

16.

The Mosque on Makram Ebeid Street

Every August, the people of Cairo fight a battle against the red-hot summer. In 2013, another fight was going on, between the military and the Muslim Brotherhood. At the Iman Mosque on Makram Ebeid Street, men crowded towards the main door carrying slabs of ice wrapped in brown paper on their shoulders. It melted on their shirts, dripping down their backs as they entered the building and were slapped by a fug of putrefaction. The heat was beating the living and the dead.

The smell came from the bodies of supporters of the Muslim Brotherhood, laid out in neat lines on the floor of the mosque. The police and army had killed them the day before as they crushed two sit-ins that were occupying entire neighbourhoods. Egyptians were in the last act of an attempted revolution. For two and a half years I had watched as they swung from wild optimism following the removal of president Hosni Mubarak to street violence and political chaos. Just over a year earlier, the dead people in the mosque had supported Mohamed Morsi, the Muslim Brotherhood's candidate for president. The Tahrir revolutionaries were so divided that they failed to get a candidate into the final round of the election. It came down to Morsi against the candidate of the military, a former general. Poor governance is at the root of many problems in the Middle East, and Morsi was very bad at being president. After twelve calamitous months in office he was removed and imprisoned by the armed forces six weeks before the massacre on 3 July 2013. Cairo was in turmoil; the hopes of 2011 had come down to a fight for the future of Egypt between the Muslim Brotherhood and the armed forces.

The coup happened in slow motion. Morsi ignored an ultimatum from the generals. Forty-eight hours later, they put thousands of men, squadrons of armoured vehicles and coils of razor wire on the streets of Cairo. By any definition of the word it was a coup, but the army denied it, claiming the troops were simply following the wishes of the people. It was the start of a merciless and brutal round-up of Morsi and everyone who mattered in the Muslim Brotherhood, and plenty who didn't.

The Brotherhood's biggest counter-protest took place in the squares and avenues around the Rabaa al-Adawiya Mosque. Thousands of Morsi's supporters pitched tents, blocked the streets and swore to stay put until the military went back to the barracks and Morsi had his job back. Some of them talked about becoming martyrs for their cause; in the Iman Mosque and other temporary mortuaries, their families were sinking into the reality of what that meant.

I followed the ice-men up the steps into a broiling building that had not been designed for the storage of corpses. Some of the bodies were unclaimed, lying lonely on the floor. Others had families around them, cradling the wrapped bundles, stroking the shrouded shapes of faces and shoulders and crying as they waited for the paperwork they needed to bury them. Even the death certificates were hostages in the fight. Families complained that they were only being granted if they agreed that suicide was the cause of death, not the bullets of the security forces.

I counted around 200 bodies in rows on the floor of the main prayer room, wrapped in white cotton stained with blood and the fluids that drain from humans when they die. In an investigation published the following year, Human Rights Watch calculated that 257 victims were taken to the mosque, out of at least 817 dead. The report concluded that 'The indiscriminate and deliberate use of lethal force resulted in one of the world's largest killings of demonstrators in a single day in recent history.'[1] The massacre might even have been a crime against humanity. Apologists for what happened compared it to a surgical procedure to cut the cancer of Islamism out of Egypt. Reputable analysts pointed to evidence that armed supporters of Morsi had fired first; even if that was true, the lines of dead bodies in the mosque showed that the response of the military and the police was out of all proportion to the threat.

It was only a day since they had been killed, but unrefrigerated bodies putrefy quickly in Cairo's high summer, especially in an unventilated room without air conditioning that is crowded with the living as well as the dead. Lumps of ice were placed around the corpses to try to slow down the rot and they melted into the shrouds, covering the floor with puddles of bloody water. A man went around the room squirting brown antiseptic. It soaked into the ooze of blood and melted ice. A woman wearing black hijab with a headscarf covering her face and a stethoscope around her neck walked around spraying an air freshener with one hand and waving lighted incense sticks with the other. With no one left to save, fighting against the smell must have felt like a useful thing to do.

A man wanted to talk to me. He said his name was Ahmed Badir, and he stood with his arm around his distraught mother, over the wrapped body of his brother. They had packed his shroud with ice and topped it with the Quran. Blood was soaking through the area around the dead man's head and chest. Ahmed was middle-class, middle-aged and educated, like many of the Brotherhood's supporters. Tears spilled from his eyes and into his neatly trimmed beard.

'You're not going to get away with this murder,' he promised the military. 'You can't kill your own people and get away with it. There's a law. And there are international courts. And people will pursue all peaceful means to hold these people accountable. Everyone who's in this government should be held accountable for the massacres that are happening right now.'

But the military, its commander General Abdul Fattah al-Sisi and his tame politicians did get away with it. Sisi was a short, uncharismatic general who was not prominent before the 2011 uprising. His rise started when he became military intelligence chief; Morsi promoted him to head of the armed forces. Morsi needed a military ally and the gambit might have spread the blame aimed at a government that was struggling with unfamiliar and unresponsive levers of power.

It failed. Like his predecessors since 1952, Sisi was prepared to lock up, torture and execute opponents. He added to that a willingness to shoot hundreds of people in the streets.

Ahmed Badir and the families in the mosque were never going to get the justice they wanted. There were, as Ahmed said, laws and international courts, but Sisi chose which laws to respect at home, and he had powerful allies in the Gulf and the West who protected him from any sort of international tribunal. Hosni Mubarak and his sons, thanks to Sisi, were rehabilitated and freed from jail. Sisi was not just the new sheriff in town. He was also the new law, and less than a year later he was president.

Many more Egyptians would be killed in street battles before the bodies that lay in the Iman Mosque had been buried. The Brotherhood prided itself on its ability to put huge crowds on the streets. The next day, 16 August 2013, was a Friday, which made it a focus not just for prayer but for protest. I couldn't see any way they could keep it peaceful – I wasn't sure anyone wanted it that way. The morning was quiet, but if there is going to be trouble it is usually after the noon prayer. I went to the Tawhid Mosque in the centre of Cairo and it was overflowing. Men were lining up for prayer on the pavement outside and spilling onto the street. When they finished praying, the chants started. One of them, ominously, went, 'We don't care about life, we sacrifice ourselves for religion.'

The Brotherhood's plan was for twenty-five marches to converge on Ramses Square in the centre of Cairo, including one that started at the Tawhid Mosque. As usual, the organizers had neat beards, often with their moustaches shaved to expose a gap between mouth and nose. Higher up their faces, most of them also had the dark, raised callus on their forehead known as a *zebiba*, literally 'raisin'. They believe it is a sign of piety, caused by prostrating themselves and resting their heads on a mat a minimum of thirty-four times during the five daily prayers. Other Muslims, no less pious, believe that grinding your forehead into the floor is painful and unnecessary.

Many young men, ready for a fight, demanded the death of Sisi. One made a throat-cutting gesture as he marched past our camera. Military helicopters clattered over the enraged marchers, who screamed curses into the sky that were drowned out by their rotor blades. During the uprising against Hosni Mubarak, the army had been seen as the protector of Egypt's civilians. It still was by the millions who opposed Morsi and the Brotherhood, but not by the other side of Egypt. The protestors piled into Ramses Square, uprooting steel railings to make barricades, until the killing started.

The Interior Ministry had warned that any attacks on police stations would be answered with live bullets. I stood on the Sixth of October Bridge, one of the elevated highways that cut through central Cairo, watching what was happening on the roof of the local police station. The official story was that protestors opened fire. Perhaps they did, but all I saw outside the station was a crowd of men emerging from clouds of tear gas to throw rocks. From the bridge, I could see police officers looking down from the roof. Some were wearing white summer uniforms, next to plainclothes men in T-shirts, jeans and flak jackets cradling small submachine guns. Next to the bridge where I was standing, bursts of live bullets fired from the police station hit the wall of a crumbling building, bringing down a small avalanche of plaster and brickwork. The watchers on the bridge retreated, with some people shinning down ropes and cables to get out of the line of fire.

Too many bullets were flying around Ramses Square. We retreated back to the Tawhid Mosque, which had been turned into a casualty dressing station after the prayer. Motorcycles pulled up outside it, with bloody, groaning men sandwiched between the rider and a frantic passenger. The quiet ones were already dead or dying. Motor scooter pick-ups buzzed up and down to the square, some of them with paramedics in the back who were putting intravenous lines and saline drips into the wounded. The main prayer floor of the mosque was crowded with casualties and the people who were trying to save them. When they died, they were carried up a staircase that was slippery with blood, on stretchers or the backs of men, to a room where they were prepared for burial. As they counted as martyrs, the bodies were left unwashed, but they soon ran out of white cotton for burial shrouds and sent out for more.

Every few minutes, I had to press against the wall to let another body get past. I kept thinking that if supporters of Sisi and the military saw our pictures it would just confirm their belief that the

Muslim Brotherhood and Morsi had brought disaster on themselves. Across the city, Sisi loyalists were celebrating at the ruins of the Rabaa al-Adawiya sit-in. Blood had congealed on pavements and workmen were clearing the debris of burnt-out barricades and tents from the streets. A few portraits of Mohamed Morsi that had somehow survived were fished from the rubbish and laid out in the road and on the pavements for cars to drive over his face and pedestrians to tread on it.

All of Egypt's illusions and broken dreams since the revolution of 2011 were tangled up in the wreckage of the sit-in, the lines of bodies in the mosques and the street battles. Life had been cheapened. Everyone knew the security forces would fire into crowds of unarmed protestors without hesitation – I had seen it myself two days after the coup, on 5 July, when Morsi supporters protected by men with clubs took over Rabaa al-Adawiya Square, the occupation that ended with the massacre. On a stage outside the mosque, an unusually charismatic figure in the leadership was making the crowd cheer. Mohamed el-Beltagy was renowned for his fiery speeches. Afterwards he denounced the coup to me, his blue checked shirt sticking to his chest and his voice hoarse: 'It is a coup against ballot boxes. It is a coup against the will of the people. Millions will stay in the square of the revolution to stop the coup and bring back the elected president.'

Beltagy was the only member of the Brotherhood's leadership with some crossover appeal to secularists. Unlike most of his colleagues, he praised the pro-democracy activists in Tahrir Square during the January 2011 uprising. Weeks later, his seventeen-year-old daughter Asmaa was killed when the Rabaa al-Adawiya sit-in was crushed. The crowd listened, their fury rising. After a mass prayer, they marched on an army base about a mile away where Morsi was imprisoned. An officer shouted at them through a megaphone to keep back from the perimeter wire. When the crowd surged forward, the soldiers opened fire – in the air for the first thirty seconds or so, and then they lowered their weapons and fired directly at them. A man near me fell down dead, the back of his head missing. I was knocked down by something that felt like a punch in the head. I was convinced it was a tear-gas canister, until I saw blood on my shirt and more coming out of a hole below my right knee. Buckshot had hit my left temple and buried itself in my leg. After I was shot, Egyptians queued up to apologize and to offer me tissues to wipe blood away. Decent people, in a country that was in a terrible mess, and getting worse. Someone even offered me a lift to my hotel or the hospital.

Egypt's disaster was a slow-speed crash. Everyone could see it happening, but they could not stop it. Mubarak's removal was the single most important moment in that spring of Arab uprisings in 2011. If he could go, the reasoning went, so could anyone, however well established and powerful they seemed. The euphoria did not last, with any hope that Egypt's future belonged to the democratic will of the people disappearing in the confusion. The revolution had a fatal flaw: it was incomplete, and in the end most of Egypt's elite stayed in place. President Hosni Mubarak was made to step down by the armed forces so they could retain their power. The generals calculated that he had to go because of the weight of popular protest, following the abrupt decision by President Obama to end his support for the man who had been America's number one Arab ally only a few weeks earlier.

The revolution of illusions left the military untouched, even though it was the institution to which Mubarak owed his power. It was even strengthened, because idealistic young revolutionaries welcomed the soldiers to Tahrir Square. One of their favourite chants was 'The army and the people are one hand.' Perhaps ordinary soldiers were on their side, but the generals were not. The army protected itself, and Mubarak was dumped because his presence at the top was no longer sustainable. He had to go to preserve as much as possible of the status quo. That left the generals taking the decisions, through the Supreme Council of the Armed Forces.

The Tahrir revolutionaries tried to continue the spirit of the square, where they had spent the days debating, speechifying, making music and chanting. They were proud that they had created the Egypt they wanted in the Tahrir bubble, and they fought to protect it from Mubarak's thugs. Inside the square, there was a tolerance of other faiths and individuals that is rare in Egypt. Women were, with the exception of a few terrible cases, generally respected and not insulted, groped or worse. Muslims protected Coptic Christians when they were praying. Free speech ran riot. The protestors believed they had captured their tomorrow, but it was an illusion. They were busy all day, but never managed to offer a coherent and convincing political plan to Egyptians who needed a new constitution as well as elections.

A smooth transition to democracy was never going to happen in an authoritarian system that been controlled by ex-generals who many believed had been backed by a sinister deep state for more than half a century. During those years, what passed for politics was not for the people. Instead it was reserved for the alliance between the military and a small and corrupt elite. Honest politicians were frozen out.

During most of 2011, the generals in the Supreme Council of the Armed Forces showed no urgency about keeping a promise that civilian rule would be restored with free elections and a new constitution that set out rights and responsibilities in the new Egypt. The joy of Tahrir evaporated, and the country was looking more like the old Egypt. By November, anger exploded after the security forces broke up a protest in Tahrir Square. The main battlefield was Mohamed Mahmoud Street; for most of a week, fierce street battles were fought there. It was a straight road that ran between Tahrir Square and the hated Ministry of the Interior. The square was peaceful as mostly middle-class activists tried to recreate the old harmony. Half a minute's walk away, young men who would have been called working class if they had jobs took on tear gas and sometimes bullets with stones and petrol bombs. During the January events that ousted Mubarak, one of the most popular chants from crowds that contained many students had been 'Silmiya', which means 'peaceful'. By the end of the year the young men on Mohamed Mahmoud were there to fight, for dignity and identity as much as politics. The backbone of the new street fighters were Ultras: organized groups of football fans, mainly from Cairo's two big clubs, al-Ahly and Zamalek. The authorities used so much tear gas that local residents complained it was invading their homes and choking their children.

The young street fighters did not welcome outsiders. One day, a man draped in his team's colours loomed out of the fog of tear gas at the BBC cameraman Nik Millard and me. 'You leave now,' he said, jabbing his finger at us, 'or I swear I will kill you.' Maybe he was planning a beating rather than murder, but we went back to Tahrir

Square, only a few hundred yards away and a bizarre counterpoint to the mayhem on Mohamed Mahmoud. Well-behaved protestors were waving flags and running through their repertoire of chants. Proud mothers and fathers bought excited children ice cream, popcorn and candyfloss. Street vendors, sensing that the crowd was getting hungry, wheeled in their carts. Revolutionary fuel included liver sandwiches and *kusheri*, an Egyptian national dish of lentils, rice and pasta topped with fried onions and spicy tomato sauce.

At the top of Mohamed Mahmoud Street, medical helpers were ready with a range of tear-gas remedies from lemon juice to bottles of milky indigestion remedy, supposedly useful because it was an alkaline solution. Anyone choking on a lungful of gas would get it sprayed without request into their faces. After a shift on the front line, young men would march proudly back into the square. I took out my phone and tapped out a tweet:

> Ultras – organized football fans – just marched back into #Tahrir. Been fighting police and now behave like conquering heroes #Cairo

The battle of Mohamed Mahmoud Street ended with a truce after five days. The renewed revolutionary passion convinced the military that it could not avoid elections. Dozens of new parties emerged, full of talk but without credible or coherent plans for winning elections. They had no chance against Egypt's two long-established and highly organized centres of power: the military and its old enemy, the Muslim Brotherhood.

Beards and headscarves were relatively scarce in Tahrir Square during the revolution, which helped to create an assumption that what came next would be secular. In fact, political Islamism was about to get the chance it had been waiting for – and not just in Egypt. The Brotherhood's leadership had kept a low profile, which infuriated younger activists who wanted the legitimacy that came from being part of the uprising. The older ones who had spent their lives in and out of prison were cautious. Their advantage was that years of opposition to the regime gave them a reputation for good organization, and clean hands.

One veteran of years behind bars was Essam el-Erian, who became the head of the Brotherhood's Freedom and Justice Party. He stayed in his old office, on a quiet island in the Nile, above a workshop where a pair of white songbirds harmonized with rhythmic readings of the Quran coming from the radio. El-Erian was a cheerful man, laughing about the way he had escaped after only sixty hours of his last incarceration. The street outside the prison gates, he said, had filled with the families of criminals as Mubarak's authority ebbed away, and the guards slipped away as they felt the regime crumbling around them. Gangsters and their families pulled down part of the prison wall, and the political prisoners followed the thugs and thieves out onto the street.

The first tangible sign that political Islam could be the big winner of the Arab uprisings came from Tunisia, where the revolution had looked even more secular than Egypt's. Ennahda, the local offshoot of the Brotherhood, won a democratic election; its leader, Rachid Ghannouchi, came back from more than twenty years of exile in London, insisting that he would protect Tunisia's social freedoms and would not destroy the tourist trade by imposing restrictions on bikinis or beer.

In Cairo, the amiable el-Erian assured anyone who would listen that if the Brotherhood won an election in Egypt it would not cancel the next one: 'The Arab Spring is going to continue. Arabs can convince the whole world that they are ready for democracy, that their civilization, their culture is compatible with democratic principles and it is time to accept this Arab Spring and accept the results of the democratic process.'[2]

Plenty of secular Egyptians who felt the freedoms won in Tahrir were now part of their DNA did not believe a word that el-Erian said. For every misleadingly friendly Islamist democrat, there were, they argued, those who were closer to the teachings of Sayyid Qutb, the Egyptian writer and Brotherhood member who had helped inspire the ideology of al-Qaeda.

Certain their moment had come, the Muslim Brotherhood swaggered into Egypt's new era. Three months after the fall of Mubarak they opened a new headquarters that smelled of fresh paint and was adorned with their symbol, the Quran flanked by two curved swords.

Outside were the shiny, expensive cars of the businessmen who signed the cheques. Veterans of the Brotherhood's struggles talked discreetly on ornate sofas under golden chandeliers. Younger men paid court to a former leader who had spent thirty years in prison. Since Hassan al-Banna founded the movement in 1928, declaring that Islam was always the answer, it had been forced into a semi-clandestine existence. Now it looked as if al-Banna's dream of power was coming true.

Egyptians had their chance to vote for a new president in May 2012. By the time the top two candidates faced a run-off in June, it was the fifth time Egyptians had voted since the revolution. Voters were still enthusiastic in the queues, despite some nagging doubts about whether the military would give up power to an elected president. The Tahrir revolutionaries, squabbling and sidelined, did not have a candidate in the final round. Organization and power mattered most, which was why it came down to the Muslim Brotherhood against the military. Mohamed Morsi scored a narrow but clear victory over retired air marshal Ahmed Shawfik, Mubarak's last prime minister and a former commander of the air force.

Morsi became the new president. During the revolution the Brotherhood were cautious, watchful, keeping their distance. I had talked to him after a news conference that was deliberately held miles from Tahrir Square in an outer suburb. Morsi was an engineer, educated in America, devout, stolid and uncharismatic. He was only on the ballot because Khairat al-Shater, a wealthy businessman who was the real power in the organization, was disqualified as a candidate because of trumped-up convictions dating back to Mubarak's time. Egypt's attempt at democracy was becoming a festival of broken promises and accusations of bad faith. The Brotherhood dropped an unconvincing pledge not to run for office because it said the generals had broken their own promise to share power. From the start, the omens were not good.

Very quickly, any remaining vestiges of euphoria turned bitter, chaotic and then nightmarish. A country with no experience of democracy was unable to create one. It was crippled by the decision to go to elections before a new constitution could be agreed. The exact relationship between the powers of the president and the generals was not worked out. Egypt's attempt at democracy was built on sand, not steel.

On the streets, law and order broke down. The police, vilified during the revolution for brutality, stayed at home. The starkest tensions were in Cairo's poorest areas. One of these was Imbaba, a slum inhabited by more than a million people. It has acres of towering concrete tenements, separated by dark canyons so crammed together they are barely wide enough for a donkey cart. Children play near piles of foul garbage where goats and dogs root around for food. The place throbs with human energy, with bakers' boys on bikes with great wooden trays of bread balanced on their heads, dodging through the crowds of people fighting through another day. Education and decent health care are for other people. Imbaba exploded with joy when Mubarak was ousted, but then life became even harder. Food prices doubled. Jobs were badly paid, and around a third of young people did not have one. Economic pressure fed sectarian tension as Islamist extremists targeted and killed Christians, who make up around 10 per cent of Egypt's population. Churches were burnt out. Sectarian violence scared people, as it suggested their hard lives were getting worse.

The Muslim Brotherhood had built a huge following in Egypt by providing welfare services to the poor in Imbaba and all the places like it. The Brotherhood could organize clinics, but not a government. In office, President Morsi floundered. They turned the moment they had dreamt about since the 1920s into a disastrous failure. They were inept administrators who alienated people who were not hardcore supporters, widening Egypt's divisions. Places like Imbaba, which should have been their salvation – it supported Islamists against Mubarak in the 1990s – concluded that democracy did not work. The fear on the streets caused by the absence of police and the breakdown of order bothered Egyptians most of all. The 'party of the couch', a silent majority that was sick of turmoil, forgot the stagnation of the Mubarak years and grew nostalgic for the certainties of authoritarian rule.

One day, I sat drinking tea in one of the streets leading off Tahrir Square with a couple of taxi drivers. It was a pavement cafe, but not the kind you get in Paris. A few dirty wooden chairs were lined up along a wall full of political graffiti. Waiters brought glasses of tea with half an inch of sugar in the bottom, along with shisha pipes. The men told me that they would prefer Mubarak to Morsi any day because at least under the old regime their families had been safe.

Morsi dug a deeper hole. In November 2012 he issued a decree giving himself much more power. He said it was to speed up the process of getting a new constitution; his enemies said the Muslim Brotherhood was building a new dictatorship. By the time he reached his first anniversary as president, huge demonstrations organized by a group called Tamarod, or 'Rebellion', were demanding his resignation.

In July 2013, the generals made their move. State television broadcast a military communique giving Morsi forty-eight hours to respond to 'the people's demands' or it would impose its own road map. It sounded like a coup foretold. I watched the broadcast with Amr Moussa, one of Morsi's most prominent critics, a former foreign minister who had just stepped down as secretary general of the Arab League at its palatial headquarters on the edge of Tahrir Square. Moussa, a grandee in his seventies with presidential ambitions of his own, hopped up and down like an excited teenager as he watched.

Mohamed ElBaradei, former head of the UN's nuclear watchdog, the International Atomic Energy Agency, was another elder statesman who had supported democracy and now wanted the elected president out. On the day that General Sisi made good on his ultimatum, I found time to visit ElBaradei at his elegant house near the pyramids, a calm refuge from the turmoil on the streets. When ElBaradei returned from Vienna in 2011 with the Nobel Peace Prize, he had stuck out his neck for democracy and told Mubarak it was time to go. The Mubarak regime's tame media gave him a roasting, condemning him for spending so much time abroad that he was no longer a proper Egyptian. It was strange to hear him justifying the army's move against a democratically elected president. Even the White House, with its severe misgivings about the Muslim Brotherhood, had welcomed the result in July 2013.

ElBaradei took issue with my suggestion that putting tanks on the streets to remove an elected president fitted every definition of the word 'coup'. Courteously as ever, he explained that this time it was different because 80 per cent of Egyptians (he estimated) supported what they had done. It was, he said, the best way to get Egypt's revolution back on track; civilians and new elections would be back soon, and if the new political line-up did not include the Muslim Brotherhood, he would be the first to complain. The military had saved Egypt; ElBaradei warned that Morsi left in office would have provoked civil war and Egypt would be the new Somalia.

After a few days and dozens of deaths it was clear that a new, toxic and bloody mix had been injected into Egypt's divided society. The shiny new Muslim Brotherhood headquarters was attacked, burnt and looted a few hours after Morsi was given his ultimatum. The mob carried off air-conditioning units, the golden chandeliers, desks and even the office door of Khairat al-Shater, the man who might have been president. They tore the Brotherhood's Quran and swords emblem from the building and brandished it triumphantly over their heads as if they were footballers that had won the cup.

Morsi managed to post a plaintive message on YouTube, filmed on a mobile phone just before the army came for him: 'There are deadly attempts to steal this revolution, we return to square one, so we can begin all over again. This is something I completely reject and I don't accept this . . . I am ready to sit down with everybody, negotiate with everybody.'

It was taken down a few hours later, and his spokesman, Gehad al-Haddad, managed to post a message on Facebook: 'They have broken the constitutional legitimacy of the state. They have arrested the sovereign leader of the state. This is a complete military coup. We've seen them on the television, in the tanks on the streets. If that's not a military coup, what is?'

Egypt's revolutionary turmoil lasted from the rising against Mubarak in January 2011 to the fall of Morsi in July 2013. After the massacres at the two Muslim Brotherhood sit-ins in Cairo in August, Mohamed ElBaradei resigned as vice president, little more than a month after he accepted the job. In his resignation letter he lamented the violent crackdown, warning of a 'state of polarization and grave division . . . the social fabric is threatened as violence breeds violence'. He left for his home in Vienna a few days later, complaining in exile that his phone was tapped. When he dared to offer a mild criticism of by then President Sisi in 2017, the military's claque called for him to be stripped of his citizenship.

Tahrir Square remained a good indicator of the political temperature in Egypt. After the fall of Morsi, his opponents had plenty to celebrate. The square had some carnival days, full of families grazing from the street food carts. However, Tahrir also showed the ugly side of Egypt. I saw the square at night because I had to be there at midnight to do live broadcasts on the BBC *News at Ten*. At its worst, crowds of youths and men rampaged around, shooting off fireworks and occasionally picking on and beating hapless innocents they suspected were spies. Women were often targets. One evening, there was a loud disturbance around the doorway of the building we were using for live broadcasts. The doorman had locked out a gang of men who had been trying to sexually assault a woman, who had run into the building for help. They had used a familiar trick, supposedly 'rescuing' her from another group. Luckily for her, she escaped, but as her tormentors hammered on the door, the streets around Tahrir looked like a set for an apocalyptic film about cities gone mad.

A year later, General Abdul Fattah al-Sisi hung up his uniform when he became president with 97 per cent of the vote. His regime was far more repressive than that of Mubarak, who was released from prison along with his sons. Convincing evidence indicated the regime was carrying out extrajudicial killings; it also imprisoned thousands of political prisoners, including leaders of the original Tahrir Square protests. Many of them were held at Egypt's most notorious jail, Tora 922, better known as al-Aqrab ('the Scorpion'). Its cells were overcrowded and infested with insects, and in summer the temperature in the pestilent cell blocks rose above forty degrees with no fans or proper ventilation.

The deposed president Mohamed Morsi initially faced a death sentence. This was quashed, but he was convicted of a string of serious criminal offences including torture, unlawful detention, conspiring with foreign powers and leading an illegal organization. After he shouted during his first trial that he had been the victim of a coup, the dock was surrounded by soundproof glass. As a string of reports from human rights groups made clear, the prosecutions were deeply flawed. In June 2019, during yet another court appearance, Morsi collapsed and died in the dock. Essam el-Erian managed a grin when he was sentenced to life imprisonment. He died of a heart attack in prison in 2020. The family of Mohamed Beltagy, the charismatic orator whose daughter was killed in the Rabaa al-Adiwiyah massacre, feared he might be the next Brotherhood leader to die in solitary confinement at the Scorpion, in cells 'designed to be ovens in the summer and fridges in the winter', as his wife posted on Facebook in 2021.

August 2013 was the final watershed between the hope that had burst from the Arab uprisings two years earlier and the region's descent into a deep, dark pit. As Egyptians were killed on the streets of Cairo, the jihadist killers who called themselves ISIS were gearing up for the offensive that would end with the declaration of its caliphate in Mosul less than a year later. In Iraq, ISIS started 'Soldiers' Harvest', a campaign of bombings and assassinations intended to ignite the country's sectarian tensions. Across the border in Syria, ISIS turned on its jihadist rivals, attacking Liwa al-Tawhid, Ahrar al-Sham and the al-Qaeda-allied Nusra Front.

I was in Cairo when President Bashar al-Assad gambled on using chemical weapons against the rebel-held eastern suburbs of Damascus. I had a Syrian visa in my passport, so rushed to Beirut and on to Syria. To the surprise and relief of Assad's closest advisors, President Barack Obama blinked first in the face-off that followed.

17.

The Pivot of War

Syria's catastrophe pivoted on the events of 2013. Damascus echoed with the noise of the war. I slept with the windows open, not just for fresh air. Blast is more likely to smash them when they are closed. Every morning I would get my first impressions of the war from the dawn soundtrack. Only the regime had weapons heavy enough to shake the city. The loudest thunderclaps came out of a blue sky, as air strikes were easier on a clear day. If machine-gun fire was mixed in with the explosions, it meant that men were fighting within a few miles of the hotel. One side of Damascus is skirted by steep, rocky hills, and the sound reverberated off the crags and back down into the city. Smoke drifted overhead, the smog of war.

   A government official mocked me when I was startled by a warplane roaring unexpectedly overhead. 'Don't worry,' she said. 'It's nothing, we're used to it.' Her insouciance could not hide the truth; the regime was under severe pressure. They strengthened the fortifications in the government quarter, a series of ministries where they took the decisions that flowed into the rest of the regime's ecosystem of prisons, barracks and bloodstained interrogation rooms. At the entrance to ministerial compounds in a leafy quarter of central Damascus, elaborate chicanes were installed to slow down would-be truck bombers, to give the guards a chance of shooting before they detonated. Armed men stood at sandbagged defences, on walls and in towers.

The pressure on the regime had been mounting since the summer of 2012. Assad had turned into 'a wounded wolf', according to Nawaf al-Fares, Syria's former ambassador to Iraq and then the most senior official to defect.[1] In July, rebels in the suburbs launched Operation Volcano, an attempt to break into the centre of Damascus. They shot up streets and squares near the Central Bank and blocked the airport road. Light weapons and determination were no match for the regime's firepower. As it drove the rebels back, aircraft and artillery hammered the civilian areas from which they had emerged.

Assad's enemies were convinced that the cracks in his regime were growing. Another blow came the same month when one of its pillars, the Tlass family, defected with the help of the French secret service. Mustafa Tlass, a former minister of defence, had been a lifelong friend and confidant of Hafez al-Assad and responsible for a lot of the regime's dirty work. His son Manaf Tlass was a brigadier in the elite Republican Guard; he was the first of Bashar al-Assad's inner circle to defect. They fell out when he tried in vain to persuade the president to try dialogue with the rebels rather than destruction. Once Manaf was sure his family were out of the country he linked up with smugglers who took him over the mountains into Lebanon, and French agents extracted him from there before Assad's allies in Hizbullah could pick him up. Back in Damascus, a mob looted his home.[2]

Two weeks after Manaf reached Paris, the tensions within the Syrian ruling family turned deadly. On 18 July 2012, official media announced that Assef Shawkat, the husband of Bashar's sister Bushra and one of the regime's top security officials, had been assassinated inside the Bureau of National Security along with the defence minister Dawood Rajha and his predecessor Hassan Turkmani. What was most remarkable was the assertion that a suicide bomber had somehow infiltrated a meeting in the regime's equivalent of the White House Situation Room.

It would have been a huge coup for a rebel group to get a bomb into one of Syria's most heavily guarded buildings. Liwa al-Islam and the Free Syrian Army both claimed credit for the attack, but it looked like internal family business. Shawkat had a fraught relationship with the president's combative brother Maher, who put a bullet in him during an argument in the 1990s. Only the Assads know what happens inside their clan, but Manaf Tlass told the journalist Sam Dagher that Maher had bawled out Shawkat so thoroughly for letting Operation Volcano happen that he asked Bashar if he could take his family to Moscow for a break.[3] Bashar told Shawkat not to leave his post in Damascus. What kind of man, the president might have asked, would want to leave Syria when the system that raised him up was in such danger?

The answer was a man who feared he was about to become a victim. Shawkat was an Alawite, a former head of the Mukhabarat security agencies, and was viewed by some diplomats and spies in Europe and the United States as a potential replacement for Bashar al-Assad. The president and his brother Maher were fighting fires across the country throughout the first year of the war, as more territory fell to armed rebel groups. Shawkat had to go, and all the evidence pointed to an inside job; another episode in Syria's version of *The Sopranos*.

The denial of reality was part of a relentless campaign of disinformation. One typical day, I glanced up as I was entering the Foreign Ministry and saw a black mushroom cloud from an air strike rising from a block of flats a mile or so away. The guards near me barely bothered to look up at the smoke spiralling into the sky. I was visiting the deputy foreign minister, Faisal Miqdad, one of the few senior officials journalists were allowed to meet with cameras and microphones. He was a well-educated, experienced diplomat and a dedicated loyalist for the regime, who never offered so much as a hint that it could be creaking. Miqdad smiled at my ignorance when I suggested that the Assad ascendancy was struggling. He denied there was even a real war in the capital, let alone any suggestion that Bashar al-Assad might step down. He said it was psychological warfare waged by Syria's enemies. 'The government is strong, the Syrian army is strong, and the Syrian people are still rallying behind President Assad. That's why President Assad and the political system is still surviving, and it will survive.'[4]

The regime was trying to obscure what was happening. In April 2013, President Assad denied on state TV that there was any such thing as a liberated area in Syria; two years of evidence showed that he was lying.

As territory fell to the rebels, movement that had been possible in the first year or eighteen months became much harder, often impossible. The front lines were hardening, clogging the arteries of the war. In April 2013, Matt Hollingworth, who ran the UN World Food Programme operation that was feeding two and a half million Syrians every month, took a journey that would be impossible for journalists, a road trip between Syria's two biggest cities, Damascus and Aleppo.[5] He counted around fifty military checkpoints, of which barely half were manned by government troops. The rest were guarded by some of the scores of rebel groups that had grabbed their own patches of land. That year, the Carter Center listed 1,050 rebel brigades and 3,250 smaller units.[6]

The reality was that the only contact the president's men had with large parts of his country was through the sights of a weapons system. A long and grinding fight was going on outside Assad's strongholds in the centre of Damascus and the Alawite heartland of Latakia and Tartous. I had seen the rubble left by the regime's air strikes, spoken to rebel fighters and visited the medical centres and command bunkers they had set up in cellars and underground car parks. The regime had flattened entire districts, Declarations that the war was going their way could not cover up the truth. They had lost around half the country and Aleppo was almost surrounded, with half the city out of their hands. The regime was being worn down.

The centre of Damascus looked at first sight to be relatively untouched. In the mornings, shops opened and children walked to school. Millions of other children had no education, from the urban battlefields a few miles away to villages cut off in countryside. The traffic was gridlocked because so many new checkpoints had been set up. But no city rumbling constantly with the sounds of war can be normal. By the end of 2012, the ragtag rebels were better organized; plenty still saw themselves as revolutionaries, but groups were emerging that embraced different Islamist futures. Over the next two years, the jihadists that would become Islamic State would emerge in full force.

An arc of the Damascus suburbs was in the hands of rebels, and the regime was working hard to reduce it to rubble. To my British ear, the word 'suburbs' conjured a vision of gardens, hedges, children playing, the sound of lawnmowers and the scent of Sunday lunch. Damascus suburbs were concrete jungles, expanded chaotically when poor people, mostly Sunni Muslims, migrated to the capital looking for work as life in the countryside just got too hard. Syria suffered the worst drought in its recorded history between 2006 and 2011, which the UN said wiped out the livelihoods of 800,000 people. The regime made matters worse by subsidizing big landowners who intensively farmed thirsty crops like cotton and wheat. The parched north-east became a stronghold of the rebellion; men who had seen their animals die of thirst and hunger in their fields picked up guns to overthrow the president. The poor burned with anger, had no stake in the status quo and were desperate enough to challenge it.

President Assad had never been under so much pressure, from rebels at home and hostile foreign powers abroad, but he continued to hang on. The former leaders of Tunisia, Egypt and Libya lasted, respectively, days, weeks and months after insurrections began, but Assad was still in power, with men fighting and killing and dying for him. At the United Nations, Russia was blocking any attempt to use the Security Council against the regime. Iran was providing financial and military aid. And Iran's most powerful ally, Hizbullah from Lebanon, entered Syria's civil war in 2013. The army had been weakened by defections and by young men leaving the country before they could be conscripted, but it could fight effectively at limited times and places, as I saw for myself around Homs and Damascus.

Syria's mosaic of peoples and religions was breaking up under the pressure of civil war and the resurgence of sectarianism since the invasion of Iraq. Sunni Muslims were the biggest single group, around three-quarters of the population before the war. Around 10 per cent of Sunnis were Kurds, who are not Arabs. The Assads' own Alawite sect made up around 12 per cent, with Christians accounting for another 10 per cent. The remainder was a microcosm of the Middle East, including Druze, Ismaili Shias, and Alevis.

Assad's own Alawite sect bled for their loyalty. Processions of coffins and wounded men kept coming back to Alawite communities in Damascus and on the coast. A doctor in the military hospital in Latakia told me that on a bad day they would receive up to two hundred casualties, and as many as a quarter of those could die. Blood pooled under operating tables, splashing onto the plastic clogs of the surgeons as they worked. The wards were full of young men who had lost legs and arms, sometimes both. Outside, soldiers waited to take their friends' bodies home. A young man with a uniform and scrawny beard proudly showed me a tattoo on his skinny right bicep of Bashar, wearing sunglasses, in front of the Syrian flag. As I followed a funeral procession to an Alawite village in the hills, men leant out of their car windows as they raced away from the coast, spraying bursts of Kalashnikov fire into the air. Grieving and angry people walking from smallholdings that grew grapes and tobacco packed into village squares; women dressed in black collapsing over coffins and portraits of dead sons, brothers and husbands; almost every man of military age, from boys who could barely shave to greybeards in their fifties or sixties, was armed and in uniform. They believed the regime was their best hope, so they would fight to save it, and themselves.

It was the same in Mezze 86 in Damascus, a poor Alawite district that was the hard essence of the regime. Cramped blocks of flats hemmed in narrow alleys with pasted-up posters of the president, printed death notices and portraits of dead soldiers. Almost every building had its martyrs. Local militias had set up checkpoints on the access roads; they had many enemies, and Mezze 86 was a target for Sunni rebels. On a cold, wet day in December 2012, they showed me buildings that had been torn open by a car bomb, killing fifteen. A woman called Hana al-Ibrahim took me the remains of the flat where her sister had died. We stood in a sitting room with the outside wall ripped away like the front of a doll's house. Hana said Assad was right to fight the jihadists, because they were killers.

Inside one of the flats, a young woman wearing black buried her face in the hair of the daughter she held on her lap, a toddler dressed all in pink. A portrait of her dead husband showed a man in combat fatigues, with cropped hair, wraparound sunglasses and the ubiquitous Kalashnikov, photoshopped with the national flag and a deep blue sky. She said, 'For the country, for us to live and for the children to grow up, he had to sacrifice himself – and the other men should sacrifice themselves for the sake of the country.'

Like most Alawite women, the widow wore Western clothes. Alawites are mostly secular. Plenty drink alcohol. Many Alawites outside the Assads' charmed circle are poor. They fought because they believed that the alternatives were worse – up to and including extinction. One evening, Mokhtar Lamani, an amiable Canadian-Moroccan who was the UN's top resident diplomat in Damascus, told me that the Alawites were correct to fear genocide at the hands of Sunni religious extremists, given the sectarian hatred that was rampaging around in Syria and the Middle East.

The Assads had elevated the Alawites from an impoverished minority to the most important sect in the country, but they retained a strong collective memory of persecution at the hands of Sunnis. The rise of the Assads had given Alawites modest incomes, often from jobs in the security forces, as well as protection and status. Even their accent could engender fear. An order from an armed man who sounded as if he was from the coast was to be obeyed. I knew a Sunni who said he would put on an Alawi accent if he wanted to get something done. Educated Alawis hated the assumption that they were all regime hard men – 'the idea that we are all hard at work torturing someone in a cellar', as Sami Khiyami, the former ambassador in London, put it to me. But as sectarian identities became a reason to kill, most Alawites in Syria felt that Bashar al-Assad was their only chance.

Some Sunnis still sided with the Assads, along with Christians and other minorities. Sunni businessmen had a stake in the system and many from their sect were alarmed as rebel militias became dominated by jihadists. In September 2013, I drove along the lonely road from Damascus to Maaloula, a Christian town carved out of the Syrian mountains that was studded with the domes of churches and monasteries. It was one of the last places where people spoke Aramaic, the language used by Jesus. The Nusra Front, Syria's al-Qaeda affiliate, had fought their way into the town, and Christian soldiers loyal to Assad were a big part of the battle to drive them out. Fresh men were arriving from the Christian quarter of Damascus in an assortment of uniforms. Most wore crucifixes, which they kissed along with the Syrian flag, chanting for Bashar as they warmed up for the fight by wasting hundreds of bullets in the blue sky. The West, they told me, was backing the wrong side. A big man with a lantern jaw covered in stubble, a moustache like a hedge and huge cross around his neck shouted, 'Tell the EU and the Americans that we sent Saint Paul to you two thousand years ago to take you from the darkness – and you sent us terrorists to kill us.'

The regime stopped publishing casualty figures. A military hospital I visited in Damascus was full, with a triage team always on alert for new casualties to arrive from the front. A doctor showed me a young soldier lying unconscious in a bed with his father sitting next to him, waiting and hoping. The boy had been shot through the head, and the doctor struggled to find the right words. In the end he said, 'I don't recognize this place any more. This is not our life, this is not our country.' He talked as if he had blundered into someone else's nightmare. He told me he used to work for the NHS. 'I used to tell my friends in Britain to come to Syria,' he said. 'It was safe, and wonderful.'

Law and order was breaking down. Before the war, Syrians in Damascus liked to go out to restaurants if they had the money, to bars if they were not religious, and there was an endless variety of street food. As the war pressed in, bars and restaurants in the Christian Quarter of the old city closed. At night Straight Street, where the Bible says the scales fell from Paul's eyes, went dark. Smaller streets and alleys were empty and threatening. People were not just closing their businesses early and hurrying home because war had revived atavistic fears of the night. Kidnapping for ransom was becoming a lucrative business. At a meeting of the local branch of the Baath Party in a well-off area called Mashroah Duma, the local member of parliament, a middle-aged woman with a white headscarf, tried to reassure a room full of worried locals. The government, she said, was executing kidnappers. The people grumbled that in their area alone there had been more than twenty kidnappings, and at least four had ended with the hostage dead. 'Multiply that many times across Damascus,' said Wael Mahmoud, a pharmacist in his forties. He was also a Baath Party official and a loyal follower of the Assads who had decided to leave for the US with his family because facing a mafia was no way to live. Wael and his neighbours had all bought guns.

The regime armed 'popular committees', local men who were officially sanctioned vigilantes. In the old city, the fiercely pro-Assad journalist Rafiq Lofte stalked his neighbourhood with half a dozen

Kalashnikov-toting bodyguards. Rafiq said they were on the streets every night: 'If we did not patrol, others would come here to kill. People are scared.' The regime's intelligence services were still rounding up thousands, who disappeared into Syria's jails and intelligence centres, but at street level, men like Rafiq had become the law in a society fractured by the war. They supported Assad, but it was another sign that the regime was losing its grip.

Rafiq took me to see Bassam Wahbh, a shopkeeper who had been kidnapped and held for fifty-three days. Bassam held up his hand to show a stump where his little finger had been. His kidnappers had cut it off and sent it to his family with the ransom demand. They included a video. Bassam played it to me, his face screwing up, remembering the pain. In it he was gagged and his hand was bound to a block. It took one of his captors half a dozen blows to chop his finger off with an axe. Bassam, a Shia Muslim, believed he was kidnapped not just for money but for sectarian revenge. He claimed his captors were Sunnis from the Free Syrian Army, 'who believe we are infidels who should be slaughtered'.

'They directed sectarian insults to me and my sect. There was a lot of blame. They said I was an infidel. I tried to say Shias were believers, who also prayed, but they wouldn't have it. They hold a firm belief that we are infidels who should be slaughtered and killed, that it's a duty. A religious duty. Of course, this surprised me a lot. I didn't expect that such ignorance existed, and such hate existed. You know, in the end they are a bunch of outlaws who picked up arms against the state.'

Bassam was a hospitable man, and as well as the usual sweet tea, he offered us ice creams. While I'm getting them, he said, do you want to see my finger? We keep it in the freezer too, in a plastic bag.

At the end of the summer of 2013 came a crisis that the regime's enemies hoped would finish the Assads once and for all. Instead they emerged intact, believing that if they could survive that, they could survive anything. When I arrived in Damascus from Cairo I stood in the sun outside the Umayyad Mosque, listening to the sounds of the old city, the cadences of the Quran mixed with the regime's artillery batteries rumbling as they hammered rebel positions. For everyone except the unfortunates on the receiving end, the shelling had become background noise. It would have been routine, except that everyone was expecting American air strikes, which could have changed everything.

The crisis began on 21 August, when Eastern Ghouta, the arc of rebel-held suburbs, was attacked with chemical weapons. Terrible videos posted on social media showed civilians struggling to breathe, choking, contorted and dying. Frantic paramedics were sluicing them down with hosepipes and buckets of water to wash away the deadly chemical agents. In a quiet corner, dead babies and toddlers were swaddled tightly and laid out in a neat line, as if they were sleeping. Nine days later, a statement from the White House declared that US intelligence agencies had 'high confidence' that the attack was the work of the regime of President Bashar al-Assad.[7] The regime denied any responsibility.

Horror went around the world, as fast as the videos were uploaded to YouTube. Millions were reminded of a pledge made by Barack Obama a year earlier, in August 2012. When asked what would it take for him to use military force in Syria, Obama had answered: 'We have been very clear to the Assad regime, but also to the other players on the ground, that a red line for us is we start seeing a whole bunch of chemical weapons moving around or being utilized. That would change my calculus.'[8] American presidents cannot easily row back from direct comments about using force, a fact that made some of Obama's staff queasy. In that first American report on the attack, the preliminary assessment was that 1,429 people had been killed, including at least 426 children. A strike by the US military looked certain; the question was not whether, but when. Commentators in Washington pointed out that the US military did not do lightweight attacks.

In Damascus, everyone I spoke to expected American bombing, with responses that went from deep fear to excitement among supporters of the uprising that the foreign help they had begged for was finally arriving. Others just got out of town. People with family in the countryside returned to their villages to get away from anywhere that might turn into an American target. Syrians without rural boltholes stocked up with provisions and water, ready to ride out a new, and perhaps decisive, chapter in the war.

I could hear my footsteps echoing when I walked through the usually teeming arcades of the Suq al-Hamidiye, one of the Middle East's great markets. It takes a lot to put the shopkeepers of Damascus off their work, but most of their customers were elsewhere. Children ran around feeding pigeons, playing games while boys not much older tried to sell bunches of balloons to parents. The worn paving inside the courtyard of the Umayyad Mosque shone in the sun like a marble sea. I stopped in front of the mosque to buy a glass of pomegranate juice from a man who stood proudly behind his cart and a heap of shiny red fruit in the shade of the ancient jumble of walls. He scraped flakes of ice into a glass and poured the foaming, pink juice on top, refusing to take any money. The juice was delicious, just sharp enough and presented with a gappy grin.

If it were possible to squeeze the history from the square as effectively as he extracted the juice from his pomegranates, the result would be the concentrated essence of Syria. I drank my juice at a place where men and women have prayed to their gods for four thousand years, facing the long western wall of the mosque, one of the greatest Islamic buildings since it was built in 715 CE. At the base of the wall are stone blocks carved by the Romans, who turned a temple dedicated to the Semitic god Hadad into a shrine to Jupiter. The triumphal arch they built at the entrance still stands, part of the fabric of the souk. Long red, black and white sheets, the colours of the Syrian flag, were draped over the columns to deflect the sun. If any of the traders still had the old independence flag, with a green instead of a red stripe, they kept it well hidden, as it had been adopted as an emblem of the revolution against the Assad regime. Lines of bunting, each pennant printed with the official flag or the face of Bashar, were strung up on arches that are a remnant of Byzantine shops from the third century.

My phone rang. It was one of President Assad's closest advisors, summoning me to the working palace. I had no idea why, but I hoped that the president wanted to give the BBC an interview about the mess he was in. 'Palace' was a grand name for a nondescript office building that started life as an apartment block. A proper palace stands on the high ground over the city, looking down on Syrians and reminding them that the regime is strong and always watching. The streets around the palace I was heading for were guarded by some of the regime's most trusted servants, men dressed in shabby business suits, grubby shirts and ties, who carried their Kalashnikovs with such familiarity that the assault rifles looked as if they were permanent attachments to their arms.

I breezed through the security checks. They were expecting me. In the senior official's office we shared the usual pleasantries and, once tea was produced, got down to business. There was no Assad interview, just one single question: 'Jeremy, what's it like to be bombed by the Americans? You were in Baghdad and Tripoli when they were bombing. I saw you on television. You must know.'

The official was scared. So were all of them, I reckoned, in their scruffy beige offices. The war was at a turning point. I explained that the American bombing would be accurate. The bombs and cruise missiles would not miss their targets. The explosions would be like huge claps of thunder, and the ground would shake. I suggested keeping clear of the palace, military bases or any other obvious targets. State media broadcast a Syrian version of the message 'Keep Calm and Carry On', which Britain prepared for a German invasion in the Second World War. An announcer warned the people not to believe reports that senior officials were fleeing the capital. But they were.

I went to the Sheraton Hotel to look for regime people in its big gardens and outdoor restaurants. They were almost empty. So was the huge pool, usually a favourite place for the elite on a hot summer day. Two women were topping up their tans as their children splashed around. Like every parent in Syria, they worried about the kids. 'I'm nervous, I put them in bed, hug them, pray that we wake up safely, just got to live day by day.'

Assad, they agreed, was not to blame. He might not be perfect, but he was better than anyone else on offer.

'What if he goes? Give me one person – give me one Martin Luther King so I can walk behind him. Give me one that says that I have a dream to make Syria like this and I'll be the first person behind him in this revolution.' Defiantly, they swore that the Americans would not dare to attack Syria, because they would land themselves in a mess that they would not be able to escape. The Syrian Arab Army, Assad's own, was not taking chances. Convoys laden with men and munitions rumbled from their bases, dispersing to places where it would not be worth sending a costly cruise missile. In Beirut, the families of British diplomats were evacuated in case of violent repercussions.

A few days later, a journalist asked the US secretary of state John Kerry what it would take to stop an American strike. Kerry answered, in a tone of voice that suggested that it would never happen, that Assad 'could turn over every single bit of his chemical weapons to the international community in the next week'.[9] Russia's foreign minister Sergei Lavrov leapt on the remark and took it seriously. Obama was hemmed in by his own threat – he faced opposition in Congress to air strikes and needed a way out. To make matters worse, the British government, usually America's reliable ally, lost a vote on military action in the House of Commons. I stood on the balcony of the BBC office in the Four Seasons Hotel waiting to go live, listening to the vote with incredulity.

Obama and Assad were ready for a deal. Obama was a prisoner of his own year-old ultimatum and felt he was being bounced into a war that was not in America's interests. Assad feared that the Americans could deliver a mortal blow to his regime and was ready to pay a price to stop it.

A deal was done. Syria would hand its chemical weapons to UN inspectors, who would make sure they were destroyed. America would declare honour satisfied, and would not bomb. In Damascus, Assad's officials could not believe their luck. They reminded me of their equivalents in Baghdad in 1991 when the Americans declared a ceasefire after liberating Kuwait, leaving Saddam Hussein in power. In Damascus Assad loyalists who had feared the worst were reinvigorated. The president of the United States, they crowed, had blinked first. Not long afterwards, I met the former US secretary of defense Bob Gates, who said he had given all the presidents he had worked for, including Barack Obama, the same advice: 'Never forget you carry a big gun. If you load it, and point it, be prepared to pull the trigger.'

Obama was slammed by opponents who believed he had made the United States look weak. The Republican senators Lindsay Graham and John McCain said he had been duped into showing 'provocative weakness' by Assad and the Russian president Vladimir Putin, allowing the Syrian regime to 'delay and deceive'.[10] Three years later, as he left office, the president claimed that he had defied the standard 'playbook . . . a trap that can lead to bad decisions'.[11] Obama believed he had liberated himself from a fetish of using force to create the wrong kind of credibility, and prevented America from drifting into another war in a Muslim state. He had, after all, been elected on promises to end the wars in Iraq and Afghanistan. Without firing a shot, he could argue that he had eliminated an arsenal of weapons of mass destruction that had been created as an answer to Israel's nuclear arsenal, and then had been turned on the Syrian people.

The prospect of military intervention led by the US had hovered in the background since 2011; Obama's decision not to enforce his own self-declared red line gave every sign that the moment had come and gone. It was bad news for rebel militias who were not religious extremists and hoped that the Americans were about to give them the muscle they needed to overthrow the regime. Russia, Assad's protector at the United Nations, saw a new range of war-fighting possibilities. In the next two years, Russia's support for Assad's Syria deepened. Bashar al-Assad and his regime lost their fear of Western intervention, and with it some more constraints on the force they could use. America's Sunni allies, Saudi Arabia and Qatar, were blindsided; they expected air strikes. Afterwards, they no longer felt they had to support rebel militias that the Americans might consider 'moderate'. They started looking more closely at rebels with deeper Islamist agendas and the capacity to harm the regime. Turkey let thousands more jihadist fighters cross its long border with Syria to join the fight.

The Americans chose not to take their chance to transform the war. It opened up space for others. The jihadists who called themselves al-Qaeda in Iraq had moved into the vacuum in Syria to lick their wounds and regenerate after taking a beating from Sunni tribal militias in alliance with the US military. By 2013, the jihadists were strong again. They fed off the chaos in Syria. A variety of names identified them. The best known were ISIS and Islamic State. The Syrian people were about to experience a whole new world of pain.

18.

The Road to Hell

In 2014, Damascus to Raqqa was the most frightening bus route in Syria. It ran from the Syrian capital, where war between the Assad regime and a variety of rebel militias boomed around the city, to the stronghold of ISIS, an extremely violent group that had just rebranded itself 'Islamic State'. That year ISIS fighters swept through parts of Syria and Iraq, grabbing territory while sponsoring and inspiring attacks far away from both countries.

Glum-looking Syrians stood around with their bags, heading north to see their families. The bus station had been moved to the edge of the city because its old site was on the front line. Now it was just a line of stops on the edge of a broad highway, next to a low wall where unhappy passengers could sit and wonder about the roadblocks and checkpoints they would have to cross, or which seat to choose to reduce the chances of getting killed if someone decided to fire at the bus. A propaganda poster peeling off a billboard looked as exhausted as the passengers after a miserable and cold winter, offering a chance to join the army to be a hero. The refugee camps in Lebanon, Turkey and Jordan were already full of young men who had decided not to take that advice. Thousands of others were unwilling conscripts, hoping for duty at a quiet checkpoint, not the front line.

A middle-aged man in combat fatigues carrying a Kalashnikov assault rifle announced that he was the inspector. He explained that before the bus crossed into territory held by the jihadists, the driver would stop to warn men about the acceptable length of beards and women about the need to cover up. I would never have got on that bus. I didn't even like getting near the door. Just looking at the sign for Raqqa made me shudder. The jihadists of Islamic State were Sunni extremists. They killed non-Muslims, Shia Muslims and Sunni Muslims who they claimed had betrayed God. Anyone could qualify.

When ISIS were tearing through Syria and Iraq in 2014, they fell in love with their own savagery, with lakes of blood, with severing the heads of their victims and the metaphorical decapitation of a world that they believed they could reshape. Their sophisticated media operation produced material that was vile, cruel and technically proficient. I sat through some of their videos, of beheadings, mass executions and a captured Jordanian pilot being burnt alive, because I couldn't report on their crimes without seeing them for myself. In between all the killing was a video called 'The End of Sykes–Picot', the ISIS take on the history of the Middle East. It explained their plan to reverse the carve-up of the Ottoman Empire by France and Britain a century earlier. A bearded man speaking good English, wearing a shin-length robe in jihadist style, showed the camera around a wrecked border post they had captured between Syria and Iraq. He leapt across a scrubby piece of sand, supposedly proving that ISIS had abolished borders forever, because the world was a single country and it belonged to Allah. Starry-eyed as he strolled around the wreckage, he said his leader Abu Bakr al-Baghdadi, who had just announced that he was the caliph of the Islamic State, was the 'breaker of borders'. At the peak of its power, the group that called itself Islamic State held a third of Syria and 40 per cent of Iraq.

That summer, ISIS seemed to be unstoppable. Horror was part of the plan. Their deeds, and the care they took to film them, were designed to eat into hearts and minds. It worked. In June 2014, five Iraqi divisions with modern American armour broke and fled in the face of less than a thousand jihadist fighters in pick-up trucks, who went on to seize Mosul, the second biggest city in Iraq. Abu Bakr al-Baghdadi walked up the steps to the pulpit of the Great Mosque of al-Nuri and announced that Islamic State was the new caliphate. He had chosen a nom de guerre that echoed the name of the first caliph,

Abu Bakr, a close associate of the prophet Muhammad. The new caliph wanted to revive an entity that went back to the dawn of Islam. In the death spasm of his caliphate, when his dreams were undone, he ordered his men to blow up the twelfth-century Nuri Mosque.

When the battle to drive ISIS out of Mosul was over, I walked through the narrow streets of its old city. Some were impassable, blocked by avalanches of masonry set off by shelling and American and British air strikes. Climbing over the rubble was not advisable because it contained unexploded ordnance and rotting bodies. All that was left of the mosque's famous leaning minaret was a stump. I had seen it from a distance at the height of the battle, floating in and out of sight through the bomb smoke, an Iraqi St Paul's. Only a few panels of its intricate brickwork survived, covered in graffiti. One of them said in English 'ISIS fuck off'.

Mosul is an overwhelmingly Sunni city, and in the first few weeks after three years of ISIS control it was hungry, broken and exhausted. Its citizens were in confessional mood, recalling that when the jihadists took over they hoped it might be good news. They were angry and frightened about the behaviour of the Shia prime minister, Nuri al-Maliki, and his aggressively sectarian government, which treated Sunnis as enemies. Maliki had arrested the bodyguards of the few leading Sunni politicians, leaving them vulnerable in a country where armed men often settle arguments. Scores of protestors, mostly Sunnis, were killed when Shia-dominated security forces fired on a protest camp in the town of Hawija in April 2013.[1]

Shia militias did not just scare Sunnis, who had seen them fighting the American occupation and spent years in fear of their death squads during the sectarian civil war. When the fightback against ISIS was starting, I went with a Shia colleague to meet fighters from one of Iraq's most fearsome militias, Asa'ib Ahal al-Haq, the League of the Righteous. Normally my colleague was a confident big man, but he hesitated at the gates to their headquarters.

'What's wrong?'

'You have to understand, Jeremy. These people kill without hesitation.'

Inside, a commander with one of the most penetrating stares I had ever seen more or less promised to do the same if we ever double-crossed him. I tried to explain how the BBC liked to be fair, and then trailed off into a spasm of nervous nodding as he kept his stare on full beam.

The militias, which preferred to be called 'popular mobilization forces', were kept out of Sunni Mosul after it was recaptured. The regular units allowed in were their better disciplined and trained first cousins, also mostly Shias, flying flags of their martyrs Ali and Hussein from the radio aerials of their Humvees. Mosul's Sunnis were nervous, but the regular soldiers and special police units weren't jihadists or militiamen, and they brought food and the closest they had to protection. Outside a kiosk that had a few boxes of vegetables, cigarettes and soft drinks on display, too expensive for most people, Haji Saad al-Jabouri, a fortysomething father of five, was waiting with his youngest daughter for the army to hand out armfuls of flat Iraqi bread and scoops of lentil soup from a steaming pail. The girl, who was around six or seven, was dressed in a mauve T-shirt with the word 'Princess' in the best Disney cursive. As soon as she saw our camera, she struck a pose like an Instagram influencer, left knee bent slightly over the right, left hand on left hip, with a sweet in her chubby right fist. Her father gripped her wrist, jumpy from the strain of keeping his family safe for three years. Their suburban street was lined with rusty cars burnt out during the fighting.

Haji Saad apologized for assuming at first that the ISIS takeover of Mosul was a Sunni uprising. He realized he was wrong when Iraqi tribal militias who had arrived too went home after a few weeks. Jihadists with accents from North Africa and Saudi Arabia started ordering civilians around, and the people of Mosul started 'to die a thousand times a day'.

'It was hell, with poverty and disease . . . indescribable. We were so scared we used to hide our children and wives from IS every day. People who didn't support Daesh, or pay allegiance to them, or who carried a mobile phone, were killed, hanged all day at traffic lights, then burned. They hanged them also on bridges for a month or two until you could see their bones.'

Many people had grisly stories about bodies left to rot on their gibbets. Jihadists would make passers-by stop and look at the swinging, rotting corpses while they delivered threats and lectures about following orders.

A man called Jabar Qassar Mohammad, rebuilding his house with his sons, saw men being killed by Islamic State fighters for being gay: 'I saw a big crowd gathering at the market. Two men in military uniform were holding a young man aged eighteen or twenty. They went into the tallest building in Mosul, and went up to the roof with the guy. He was handcuffed behind his back. They pushed him off the roof, and he was killed.'

ISIS had killing in its DNA. It grew out of the remains of al-Qaeda in Iraq, an organization that flourished in the chaos after the Americans deposed Saddam Hussein, led by the first notorious jihadist of the Iraq war, Abu Musab al-Zarqawi. A petty thug from Zarqa in Jordan, radicalized in its tough prisons, he saw possibilities in Iraq's chaos after the US invasion in 2003. Al-Qaeda in Iraq killed Sunnis as well as Shias, uploading horrific videos of ritualized beheadings of Western hostages dressed in orange jumpsuits to match the ones worn by the inmates of America's internment camp at Guantanamo Bay. Sometimes Zarqawi wielded the knife personally.

Al-Zarqawi's short and brutal career ended with an air strike in 2006, but more leaders emerged and al-Qaeda in Iraq went on kidnapping, killing and capturing territory. For a few years I stopped going to Iraq. After years of reporting wars, I understood the risks of being shot or shelled. Being kidnapped for public execution online was not worth the risk.

Zarqawi's al-Qaeda was beaten by an alliance of Sunni tribal militias and US forces. From 2007, the Americans sent in reinforcements for an offensive they called the 'surge'. It would not have worked without a revolt against al-Qaeda by Sunni tribes. American money and weapons made the decision easier, but tribal militias took on al-Qaeda because they were tired of the jihadists' arrogant and violent behaviour. As well as beating and killing anyone who offended them, they tried to ban smoking tobacco, a pastime for millions of Arabs. The tribes also wanted to preempt Shia death squads who carried out their own atrocities against Sunnis when al-Qaeda killed their people.

By 2010, al-Qaeda in Iraq was in retreat; the Americans claimed that three-quarters of its leaders had either been killed or arrested.

It was assassination season. Osama bin Laden himself was killed in Pakistan the following year. What happened next showed that killing leaders – 'cutting the head off the snake' – did not kill the organization. Young Sunnis trapped in hard lives in poor towns went on listening to jihadists and their preachers, whose ideology gave them simple answers.

The remnants of al-Qaeda in Iraq regenerated into ISIS from surviving cells of veteran jihadists with seven years' experience of fighting the Americans, on top of the skills many of them had learnt in Saddam Hussein's army. New leaders appeared every time one was killed, on a conveyor belt coming from the mosques and the streets that produced new men to replace dead men. Abu Bakr al-Baghdadi's turn to be head of the snake came in the spring of 2010; he strengthened its body the way they knew best, feeding it with blood by sending suicide bombers to kill Shia civilians and anyone else they decided was God's enemy.

Baghdadi needed his best men back, so he busted them out of prison. Operation 'Breaking the Walls' started with an attack in Tikrit, Saddam Hussein's birthplace, which freed around 100 men, nearly half from death row.[2] The most spectacular breakout freed at least 500 experienced killers from the notorious Abu Ghraib jail outside Baghdad in July 2013. It was well planned, bribing guards to open doors while suicide attackers drove truck bombs at the gates. Many of the men who escaped crossed into Syria to join ISIS cells.[3]

Men like Zarqawi and Baghdadi thrive in the spaces governments cannot reach and prosper best when states collapse. Iraq became a land of opportunity for jihadists after the invasion in 2003, as Syria did after war broke out in 2011. Tensions between Sunnis and Syria's minority sects were inflamed and tracts of territory, including entire cities, were there for the taking. As the peaceful uprising in Syria was becoming a war in 2011, President Bashar al-Assad stirred the pot by releasing hundreds of jihadists. He denied it when I asked him, but the evidence shows that he wanted to justify his assault on the protest movement as a war between his own secular Baathist regime and Salafi jihadists. In the end that is what much of Syria's war became, but it did not start that way.

Baghdadi, like Zarqawi a decade earlier, saw the possibilities. He relocated to Syria, joined the Nusra Front, the local al-Qaeda affiliate, and rebranded his group as the Islamic State of Iraq and Syria. In English, it was ISIL or ISIS; in Arabic, it was Daesh. Jihadist politics were complicated and deadly. Abu Mohammed al-Jawlani, the leader of the Nusra Front, broke with Baghdadi; a year later, Nusra was fighting with other opposition groups against their remorseless rivals.

A long way from the blood and death in Syria and Iraq, President Barack Obama tried to play down ISIS as a new enemy. Just after the capture of Fallujah in 2014, the Sunni town about an hour's drive from Baghdad, Obama suggested to David Remnick of the *New Yorker* that ISIS were wannabes. 'The analogy we use around here sometimes, and I think is accurate, is if a JayVee team puts on Lakers' uniforms, that doesn't make them Kobe Bryant.'[4] Translated from American sportstalk, he meant that they were nothing like the original al-Qaeda, which America had been fighting for thirteen years by 2014. 'I think there is a distinction between the capacity and reach of a Bin Laden and a network that is actively planning major terrorist plots against the homeland versus jihadists who are engaged in various local power struggles and disputes, often sectarian.'

Obama was clinging to a false distinction because he had promised to extract America from wars in the Middle East, not get involved in new ones. He was speaking not long after he had pulled back from his own red line over punishing the regime for using chemical weapons. In the end, Obama could not stay out of the fight against Islamic State. The jihadists executed hostages and put horrific videos of the killings online. An American journalist, James Foley, was beheaded. The Iraqi government asked for US military assistance as the jihadists closed in on the Yazidi community in Mount Sinjar. Air strikes helped Kurdish *peshmerga* fighters stop their advance, though not before they killed Yazidi men and took women as domestic and sexual slaves. It took almost three years and thousands of lives to destroy the Islamic State caliphate. Even then, its ideology lived on, as it had when its predecessor al-Qaeda in Iraq seemed to have been defeated.

Fallujah, the city Obama tried to overlook, has always been part of my reporting in Iraq. During the war to expel Saddam Hussein's forces from Kuwait in 1991, I drove through the city as air raid sirens were wailing and civil defence wardens shouted at people to take cover. I was there in 2003, not long after the first Americans to arrive in the town had made a lot more enemies by killing demonstrators, jump-starting the Sunni insurgency in the city. The reasons why Sunnis fought the Americans were double-strength in Fallujah: anger at losing the privileges given to them by Saddam Hussein, fear of a new and vengeful Shia ascendancy, and fury at the occupation. Men from Fallujah who had good jobs in Saddam's army and police force were unemployed after March 2003.

Summer was heating up the desert like a pizza oven when I went back to Fallujah from Baghdad in June 2016, as government forces were driving IS out of the city. The road going in was lined with Iraqi military Humvees, heavy with fifty-calibre machine guns and jubilant soldiers. Under the flyover above the crossroads in the city centre was the frightening emptiness of an urban battleground. Groups of soldiers roamed around, with a soundtrack of mysterious bursts of gunfire and explosions ringing around empty buildings with a pox of shell-hole scars. That day, I didn't see a single civilian in Fallujah.

ISIS emblems were stuck all over a small plastic shed that must have been some kind of guard post. I kept thinking about what it would have been like to be arrested by the men who put the stickers on the walls. Clumps of what looked like beard hair were in a bin. Perhaps a jihadist had a rapid shave before he tried to escape. A pile of black robes with something that had once been alive rotting among them was in the middle of the street. It was a body, with a cable tied to one ankle. I guessed it was an ISIS fighter, perhaps one of the men from the guard shed, killed by soldiers dragging him behind a vehicle and then cut loose. The battle had lasted four weeks, enough to force out the most nuggety civilians. It was clear that thousands of Fallujah's Sunnis had escaped early on, wanting nothing to do with the jihadist reality. Grass sprouted in side streets. The gardens of abandoned suburban houses were overgrown with parched banks of scrawny vegetation, and dirty sand banked up on front doorsteps that no one had stepped on since the residents left in a hurry when the jihadists took over in 2014.

US Marines fought two battles with insurgents in Fallujah in 2004.

My BBC colleague Paul Wood, who was there with a colonel called Gary Brandl, reported that he 'strode around like a Hollywood version of what a Marine Corps officer should be, cigar stuck between his teeth as he dished out orders . . . "The enemy has got a face," he said. "He's called Satan. He's in Fallujah. And we're going to destroy him."'[5]

Whether or not the enemy was Satan, he was still there when the Americans were long gone. The US Marines said Fallujah was their heaviest urban combat since Hue in South Vietnam in 1968. It was also as destructive and inconclusive. American firepower could not stop their enemies melting back into everyday life until ISIS regenerated, when they would dig their Kalashnikovs out of their hiding places and take back the city.

Beating them, the Iraqi soldiers boasted, was beyond the Americans, but without US air power it might have been beyond them too. General Abbas al-Jabbouri, commander of the Interior Ministry's elite troops, the Emergency Response Division, showed me the ruins of a big house next to the River Euphrates that had been pulverized by American air strikes. Outside it was a white saloon car with tan seats, smashed windows and doors and panels peppered with shrapnel. Big blocks of explosive were stowed in the boot and in the footwell by the back seats, connected by a wire to the detonator and firing pin of a hand grenade. The general leant in and grabbed it, stuck his finger into the round loop at the top and mimed being a suicide bomber pulling the pin, commentating on the last journey of an imaginary bomber: 'He approaches the Iraqi security forces and pulls it out and blows up all the vehicles with him.'

Bodies of IS fighters who might have planned to detonate the car lay decomposing in the rubble. I stopped counting at a dozen. In midsummer in Iraq, with temperatures either side of fifty degrees centigrade, it does not take long for dead flesh to stink and ooze. I could see a few more corpses caught on the riverbank. One was the bloated body of a woman. As I walked away from the stench with General Abbas, I wondered how many of the decomposing dead would even be counted. By 2014, estimates of the dead in Iraq since the invasion started at around 200,000. The corpses of IS fighters were left where they were killed, to be chewed by street dogs and vermin until Fallujah's new masters realized they were health hazards and disposed of them without ceremony. The heavy, sweet stench of decomposition lay still as a corpse on the blanket of heat. The general smoothed his neat, swept-back hair, brushed off his immaculate camouflage fatigues and stared at me through his wraparound mirror sunglasses. 'These men are trash, and they've ended up where they deserved to be.'

In a deserted school, two IS fighters had been shot dead and left to rot. Opposite was a pair of suburban villas containing another horrifying tableau of life and death in the caliphate. In what must once have been a good-sized living room in one of the houses, the furniture had been replaced by cages made of heavy steel bars. Five of the cages were just big enough for a man to stand, but not sit. Two others were roughly waist high and about the size of dog kennels. An adult male would have had to lie hunched up without even space to turn round. Someone had set fire to the room to dispose of papers or human traces. It stank of burnt plastic and radiated agony. Lieutenant Hassan, a tall, athletic-looking young officer, explained the crimes that ISIS believed deserved being chained up like a tortured animal. 'They punished the civilians,' he said. 'Even if you smoke one cigarette, they will capture you and put you in a cage like this.' The other house was used as a courtroom. Paperwork stamped with the IS logo was scattered all around it, charge sheets for offences that included smoking, the devilish crime against God. Food and filth coexisted in the kitchen.

The winners of the battle looked after their dead, ensuring their bodies made it back to their villages or neighbourhoods in Baghdad. Some took the long drive to the Shia holy city of Najaf and Wadi al-Salaam, the Valley of Peace, the biggest cemetery in the world, a burial site for 1,400 years and the last resting place for millions. Space is so scarce that bodies are buried standing up, in narrow graves hacked out of hard, stony sand.

Najaf's most revered resident was the most senior Shia cleric in Iraq, Grand Ayatollah Ali al-Sistani. He was born in Iran but moved to Najaf to study in the early fifties, where he stayed. From the start, Sistani saw ISIS as a threat not just to his Shia followers, but to the state. He issued a fatwa telling Iraqis it was their duty to fight ISIS – the first one against an invader for a century, since the British arrived. Sistani's stature meant that thousands of young Shia men signed up for the fight. I watched them training one evening on a sports ground not far from the golden dome of the shrine of Imam Ali, which Shias believe is the resting place of Muhammad's son-in-law. Shia Muslims believe he should have been Muhammad's rightful heir. The recruits were put through an evening of military activity: marching, tackling obstacle courses and throwing themselves over barricades of burning tyres. They paraded in front of turbanned Shia clerics and ran through their repertoire of chants, venerating Sistani and cursing Sunni jihadists. I watched them and realized what was missing: none of their slogans included the word 'Iraq'. Instead, their banners and flags were a tour of the Shia landscape, physical and mental, as they fought an enemy that wanted to kill them because of who they were in a sectarian war.

It took three more years to end Islamic State's rule in Mosul. Shia militias did a lot of the fighting, against Islamic State jihadists who preferred to die rather than surrender. An Iraqi sergeant told me about the bodies he had searched: 'They're mainly French and Saudi, with some Chechens. When we kill them, we find their identity cards.' For about ten days, I followed Iraqi troops from the same Emergency Response Division I had seen in Fallujah as the battle went from house to house. They were not like the corrupt, divided army that collapsed in Mosul when it fell to ISIS. They wanted to fight, and they were ruthless. The Americans stopped training them after they were accused of torturing and killing prisoners.

Street fighting means enemies are often on the other side of a wall, or across a courtyard. Rooms shook when they opened fire through windows and holes in the masonry. Automatic fire in a small room makes your ears sting. Spent cartridges piled up around the sofas and beds and pinged off my helmet. A soldier stood on a chest of drawers to fire out of a high window. Another man, wearing tight black gloves, passed up fresh magazines with his left hand and kept a grenade ready in his right. In the bedroom next door, a beefy soldier with his assault rifle on his lap sat primly on a double bed in a mess of pink sheets and scarlet blankets. He had propped a machine gun against it and laid a tin of ammunition on the floral duvet. A shelf was decorated with plastic flowers and a mug printed with a girl's photo. Spare sheets were neatly folded in the wardrobe, and a woman's nylon housecoats hung in a corner cupboard next to where the soldiers swung through a broken window. In another bedroom, rocket-propelled grenades were lined up on the bed, resting until they were needed. The major commanding the squad, Wissam Ammar, set up his HQ in the sitting room and told me, 'They're surrounded. Either they fight or surrender.' They fought until they were killed. So was the major a month later.

Ammar's men were brave, moving between houses through holes bashed through party walls. Open alleyways were killing grounds. Progress was very slow. 'It's a street battle,' said one young officer. 'We advance in teams, from house to house. The enemy is very aggressive, using snipers and car bombs. God willing, we'll win.' It took five months to clear the old city. To speed things up, the commanders of the coalition made it easier to call in air strikes, which killed more jihadist fighters, and more civilians who were corralled by front lines and trying to ride out the battle. In the sky, the US air force and the RAF led a bombing campaign, insisting they were working hard not to kill civilians. Iraqis who managed to escape said that was not true. By the end of 2017, estimates of the civilian dead ranged between nine and eleven thousand.[6] The coalition did admit killing more than a hundred civilians on 17 March, when they dropped a 500-pound bomb on a building used by two snipers in an area called al-Jadida. The dead were sheltering in the basement and were crushed when it collapsed. The Americans blamed IS, claiming its men had rigged the building with explosives.

Destruction clogged streets and alleys. Once I thought I had stepped on the face of a corpse, but it turned out to be a mannequin from someone's destroyed shop, still grinning as it lay there cut in half. You could smell the human dead, even in the winter. Mosul fell to a coalition that included Shia militias on the outskirts of the city, mostly Shia interior ministry and army units on the ground. US special forces rumbled around in their huge 'MRAPs', armoured trucks reinforced against mines. The Iraqi government feared that tens of thousands of people leaving the city would make the crisis even worse, so passed the word that they should stay put. Civilians had terrible choices to make, or none at all. Jihadists made it hard for them to leave the tight lanes of the old city; they were used as human shields until they escaped or were killed.

I sat on a roof on the edge of the old town watching the smoke rising, and came down to talk to exhausted people who had found a way out. A man arrived carrying his son of about twelve or thirteen, who had a wounded foot and couldn't walk. His father was pouring with sweat and pumped with adrenalin, fear and desperation. Like all the men, and boys who were old enough to fight, they were lined up at gunpoint for interrogation. The soldiers I saw seemed to be acting correctly, but in Fallujuah hundreds were taken away for questioning by the Shia militia Kataaib Hezbollah. The UN said at least fifty men and boys were killed, and many who lived said they had been tortured.[7]

The women who crossed the front line were left alone and were allowed to talk. An exhausted woman on 26 March 2017 told me: 'All destroyed, our homes, our cars, everything, they destroyed us. The families are under the rubble. Entire families, the air strikes destroyed us. The families are gone.' Next to her, a woman in her thirties said: 'It was hell. Daesh are war criminals. They are not Muslims. And don't connect them to Islam.' Were the air strikes justified, I asked. 'I swear to God, they are not justified, because so many are affected. Yesterday, I couldn't count how many people we buried who we'd dug out from under the ruins.'

In my flak jacket, with my first-aid kit, a bulletproof GMC Suburban, and cash, credit cards and a plane ticket home, I felt like I'd beamed down into another world. It was not just one tragedy, or a few months of bad luck. Generations had trouble heaped on trouble: families killed, children maimed, lives full of desperation and oppression.

During the summer that they lost Fallujah, Islamic State sent suicide bombers into Karrada, in the centre of Baghdad. It was the last few days of Ramadan, when families like to shop after the Iftar meal that breaks the fast. The explosions ripped through crowded pavements and started big fires in busy shops. The blast, and the flames, killed 340 people and wounded many more. Twenty-four hours later, families were setting up shrines, lighting candles, praying and calling for God's revenge while young men dug through the basement of one of the destroyed shopping centres. No one expected to find survivors. They were looking for human remains, but all they found were some shoes and a pile of black ash. The fires were still smouldering and the basement was hot. Warm, scummy water dripped from the ceiling. Outside, hundreds of people were sharing their endless sadness, crying and praying, consolation and defiance. Christian clergymen lit candles and made the sign of the cross. Young people chanted a Shia anthem for the dead. They didn't seem worried that a crowded, dark street in Baghdad was a potential target for another suicide bomber.

Just because so many Iraqi civilians had been massacred over so many years did not make senseless killing any easier to bear. A man called Ali said Iraqis had been fighting since the 1991 war. They wanted peace. 'No, we're angry,' another man interrupted, 'because Iraqis are like sheep with wolves.'

After that bombing, and so many others in Iraq and right across the Middle East, I asked people to tell me who the wolves were. They said they were the corrupt politicians, the jihadist killers, all the bad men with guns, the police who took bribes and didn't offer security, the foreigners who arrived to protect their own interests and made life worse for the people as well as those who got rich and powerful by collaborating with them.

In Mosul I went to collect my thoughts in the remains of the museum, which the jihadists smashed up just after they captured the city. The failed and fragmented state of Iraq was the place where human civilization first emerged, and the museum floor was covered with lumps of statues from the Sumerian civilization that existed five thousand years ago between the Tigris, which runs through Mosul, and Iraq's other great river, the Euphrates. Jihadists wrecked the statues because they considered commemorating any god from the days before Islam a heresy that needed to be punished by destroying the evidence and killing the guilty. That did not stop them looting valuable, small, portable artefacts. The destruction was part of creating a caliphate that would return them to the golden age of Islam. It turned into a brutal, vicious tyranny. Inside the building, I tried not to do any more damage by crunching ancient terracotta under my boots.

Outside, the war went on. I could hear the shelling and shooting and imagine the killing.

Islamic State made the mistake of uniting their enemies against them. Iraqi militias backed by Iran that had fought the Americans ten years earlier now fought alongside them — not exactly shoulder to shoulder, but against the same enemy. They destroyed Islamic State's caliphate but not its ideology, which was incubated by chaos, danger and sectarian hatred.

Foreigners keep reappearing in Middle Eastern tragedies I have seen over thirty years. Islamic State, its predecessors and successors would not have been able to expand and mutate without the invasion of Iraq in 2003 by the US and Britain. The failure to replace Saddam Hussein's dictatorship with an effective government, or even an effective occupation, broke Iraq open, giving jihadist extremists the chance to spin their stories, fire their guns and detonate their bombs.

19.

The Russians Are Coming

Bashar al-Assad looked well when I met him in February 2015. Surprisingly well. His regime had been at war for getting on for four years. Hundreds of thousands of Syrians were dead, and millions more were refugees abroad or homeless and impoverished inside the country. Assad had lost control of more than half of Syria. Vast areas of it were in ruins. I thought the strain would be showing, but it wasn't, at least not on his face.

I had been asking for an interview since the war started. Finally, after all the requests and months of negotiation, it was about to happen, in the same guesthouse in the grounds of the presidential palace in Damascus where I had interviewed him a couple of times before the war started. The man I met then was unfailingly polite, dressed in an expensive suit, white shirt and dark tie, with a small, closely trimmed moustache, a high forehead and a much more confident air than his awkward-looking official portraits suggested. He hadn't really changed; though he would soon turn fifty, the age at which George Orwell said every man has the face he deserves, Assad looked remarkably untroubled. Apart from a few extra lines, I couldn't see any mark left by the suffering he had brought down on his country, or the knowledge that a short drive from his residence were fellow Syrians who would love to see him dead. Perhaps it was a sign of some inner conviction that he had justice and patriotism on his side, which was the message of his regime's propaganda. It had not occurred to me that he might believe it.

Colonel Muammar al-Gaddafi was another authoritarian Arab leader who had believed his propaganda – or at least that was how it had seemed when I interviewed him on that chilly February evening at an Italian restaurant in Tripoli, at the height of the uprisings in 2011. Maybe it was because he had spent the best part of fifty years meeting cheering crowds, but Gaddafi seemed certain that the Libyan people really did love him. He was eccentric and quixotic, moving in a sentence from focused to distant and distracted. His delusions and lies had collapsed along with his regime in August of that year, when rebels captured the capital and he went on the run, until a mob killed him with their fists, boots, a bayonet and a bullet.

Assad must have seen the videos of Gaddafi's death and feared that millions of Syrians wanted to do the same to him – but he had genuine support from important sections of the Syrian public. He would not have survived the first four years of the war without it. They bought his argument that Syria had a choice: the Assad they knew, or Islamic State. Some Sunnis were with him, as were religious minorities. A Christian friend in Syria explained that when they didn't like the choice, they just stayed quiet and tried to survive, or leave.

Assad's bedrock was his own sect, the Alawites. In the narrow streets and alleys of poor districts like Mezze 86 in Damascus, they could work themselves into a fierce passion for their leader that was powered by fear and desperation as well as sectarian loyalty. They were right to believe that victory for Assad's enemies would become their disaster too, so they fought, sometimes with misgivings, and took the brunt of sacrifices on the regime side. At the front of crowds of Alawites supporting Assad was always a rank of grieving mothers holding framed portraits of their dead sons in uniform. I wondered if they had felt indestructible, as young men often do, when the shutter clicked, or just tried to cover their fear of what they knew was coming. The willingness of their own people to fight and die was part of the wall the Assads had erected around their regime, but Bashar still faced the implacable hatred of millions of Syrians. If he felt the strain of becoming a pariah, he hid it well.

The world inhabited by the other Syria started within sight of the palace gates. I have pages of death threats to Bashar from his subjects in my notebooks and tapes. This was an eighteen-year-old boy in Douma, the satellite town in Eastern Ghouta on the edge of Damascus: 'Every day the army, the security is killing us. Twelve men were killed last Sunday.' Then he moved on to the mantra they loved the best, egged on by his friends: 'We want to kill Assad. He has to be killed. Everybody wants to kill him. He killed our people, he killed our families, and he has to be killed.'

Assad's guesthouse was like a boutique hotel, with plenty of marble and big indoor fountains. It stood at the end of a long drive, a discreet half-mile or so from the presidential palace, which is a series of glass, concrete and marble modernist cubes looking down on the city from a crag. Gardeners kept the lawns and trees neat, except for untamed rocky outcrops that hinted it was still the windy hilltop that had dominated Damascus for millennia. For anyone wanting to control Syria, it was a hill to covet, and to spill blood to possess. Armed rebels were no more than five miles away. I had visited them on the other side of the front line, in tunnels they had dug for protection from air strikes. I knew they dreamt of the day that they could have the hill, the palace and the president in their sights. The war pressed in on Assad's marble guesthouse.

Syrian TV set up a studio's worth of lights, cameras and cables in the library. Part of the deal that secured the interview was that they would film it. For days, I had war-gamed the questions to ask and the way Assad might answer them. In need of a clear head, I poked around the library as the Syrian technicians checked the mics and the lights and waited for their leader. A first-generation Apple iMac desktop computer stood on a table. Bashar was a computer enthusiast, so he must have had a modern one in the place where he did his real work. I checked the bookshelves. The autobiography of King Juan Carlos of Spain, inscribed affectionately by the author, sat close to *Known and Unknown*, Donald Rumsfeld's memoir of his time at the Pentagon, and Piers Morgan's *The Insider*. I wondered if Bashar had read them, and what he thought about running a regime in Syria compared to the antics of royalty, politicians and celebrities in the West. Juan Carlos abdicated, which Bashar would never do. The Assads had a carefully curated presence on Instagram, but in the

19. Supporters of the Muslim Brotherhood's President Mohamed Morsi took over parts of Cairo after he was deposed by the armed forces in July 2013. Hundreds were massacred when the military and police broke up their protests.

20. Young Iraqi Shia recruits test their bravery in Najaf in June 2016. Thousands answered a call to arms from their spiritual leader, Grand Ayatollah Ali al Sistani, to fight the jihadist extremists of Islamic State.

21. Syrian children living as refugees in their own country in Aleppo in September 2016. Around half of Syria's population lost their homes in the first ten years of the war.

22. Sisters emerge in their best clothes in September 2016 from the rebel-held Damascus suburb of Daraya. It was starved and shelled into surrender after five years of siege. By then the Russians were helping the Assad regime topple rebel strongholds.

23. The rebel-held side of Aleppo after the Syrian regime and their Russian allies had finished with it. Their victory at the end of 2016 was a major turning point in the war. The devastation caused by artillery and airstrikes went on for miles.

24. Nael Abdallah, Christian warlord and supporter of the Assad regime in the town of Sqelbieh, on the front line in October 2018 as the Syrian war continued. He carried a bottle of Johnnie Walker as well as a Kalashnikov in his car.

25. Iraqi government troops in March 2017 reloading with ammunition and tobacco in a pause in the long battle to drive Islamic State jihadists out of Mosul. Three years earlier Iraqi forces fled as IS took huge areas of territory. These men were made of sterner stuff.

26. Iraqi sniper waiting for a victim during months of street fighting to drive jihadists of Islamic State out of Mosul.

27. Iraqi soldier resting during house-to-house fighting in Mosul in 2017. The apartment's owners left everything they had behind.

28. Desperation and courage. A father saving his wounded son during the battle for Mosul in 2017.

29. Palestinians in Ramallah on the West Bank commemorate seventy years since Israeli independence, the event they call al-Nakba, the catastrophe. Keys of homes lost to Israel in 1948 have become symbols of dispossession and the desire for independence.

30. Ultra-Orthodox Jews at an election rally in Jerusalem in September 2019. Two months later Prime Minister Benjamin Netanyahu was indicted for corruption.

31. Taliban in Lashkar Gar, in Helmand Province, Afghanistan, just after their victory in 2021. The Taliban of the 1990s banned photography. New generation Taliban were deeply attached to their smartphones.

32. Afghan girls at a school in Helmand facing a frightening future after the Taliban's victory in 2021.

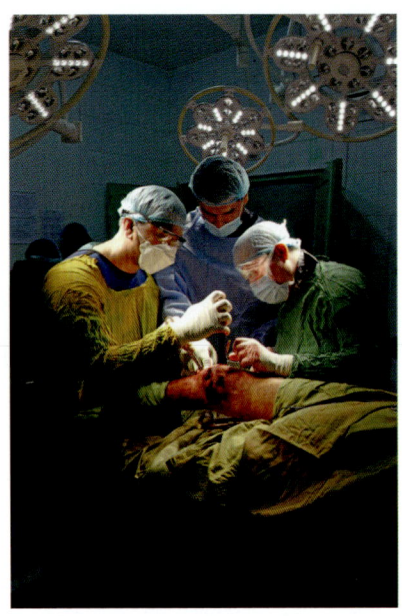

LEFT 33. Aftermath of an Israeli air strike in Beit Hanoun in Gaza in May 2021. Since Hamas took over Gaza in 2007 there have been many wars with Israel. RIGHT 34. British surgeons from the charity Action for Humanity operating on a victim of war in Marib in Yemen in 2021. Interventions by Western governments in the Middle East have mostly made life more violent and more difficult.

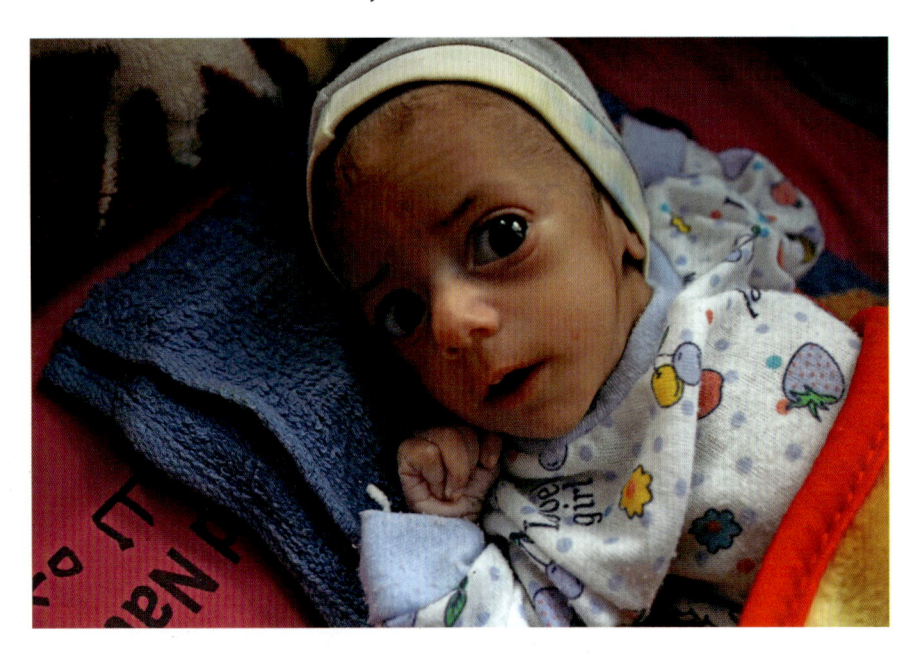

35. Yemen became the worst humanitarian disaster in the world in the years after 2015. Six-month-old Taqua Tarish was lucky enough to be treated in hospital in Marib for severe malnutrition. She still weighed 2.5 kilos, less than many newborns. It was a man-made crisis, caused by a struggle for power between Houthi rebels and Saudi Arabia and their respective allies.

hard years since 2011 Bashar would disappear from Syrian television for weeks at a time.

The president's aides whispered that Assad was in the building, and I was led across a polished floor to an anteroom where he was waiting. He leapt to his feet, still the polite host, which was when I noticed how little he had changed. No journalist wants to be accused of giving an Assad an easy ride, so I asked tough questions. Before the cameras rolled, I told him to expect them; not to warn him, but because a civil atmosphere produces the best interviews. Assad smiled and said, ask whatever you like. Do your worst. When I had met him before, he had displayed absolute certainty about the way things were in the Middle East. He was a stubborn man who wanted, I thought, to follow his father as the master manipulator of the Middle East. Leaders always want to project certainty, consistency and strength, but the best ones, brave enough to be peacemakers, are flexible, with supple minds. Assad didn't seem flexible, but perhaps that didn't matter, as the only ending he wanted was for the regime to survive and then press on to victory.

We had agreed that Syrian TV and the BBC would both broadcast the interview in full. This meant I had to keep it to twenty-three minutes, the slot that the BBC had available; Syrian TV would have taken as much as the president wanted. Agreeing to broadcast in Syria uncut did not damage our editorial integrity. The night before the interview, Assad's spin doctor was still refusing to drop a demand to join us in the edit room 'to help you select the best clips'. That would have seriously compromised the BBC, so we refused and I told her that we couldn't go ahead if she insisted. I felt sick, but there was no other choice. An hour later, her assistant rang to say she had changed her mind.

In the interview, Assad unleashed a series of preposterous points and stuck to them. The Western version of the Syrian war was just a collection of 'childish stories'. The uprising did not start with peaceful protests. The Syrian people had been under attack from terrorists from the start. He offered a flat denial that Syrian helicopters had attacked anyone with barrel bombs, metal containers packed with explosives and projectiles. I had seen the huge damage barrel bombs inflicted on rebel-held suburbs of Damascus, and told him so.

Hundreds of videos of the attacks and their consequences had been posted online. He denied everything, and tried to joke about it. The army, he said, 'use bullets, missiles and bombs. I haven't heard of the army using barrels, or maybe cooking pots . . . there are no indiscriminate weapons. When you shoot you aim, and when you shoot, when you aim, you aim at terrorists in order to protect civilians.'

Anyone who had followed events in Syria had seen video of barrel bombs smashing bricks and mortar and tearing human flesh. But the president was not going to waste time trying to change the minds of his critics. Everything was aimed at the Syrian audience watching at home. He was sticking to his story: Syria was facing a conspiracy hatched by an unholy alliance of enemies that included the West, Israel, Gulf Arabs and radical Islamists. All rebels were terrorists.

It was bizarre to remember that when Bashar succeeded his father, he was seen in the West as a potential bridge to the Arabs. Tony Blair considered offering him an honorary knighthood. During three days in the UK in 2002, the Queen received the Assads at Buckingham Palace. In the photos, everyone was smiling. Bashar's wife Asma was a Londoner and he did not behave like a man who had just inherited a police state. But he was never going to accept the price of better relations with the West, as it diluted the essence of the Assad regime. Glad-handing in Paris and London was not worth dropping his opposition to Israel and his support for its enemies. Everything was aimed at preserving his family's rule and his father's legacy, even taking Syria to war with every catastrophic consequence except the one the Assads feared most, which was losing power.

Away from the cameras, the president ushered me to a cluster of sofas and armchairs at one end of the room. He wanted to talk about Saudi Arabia, just one of the countries that had intervened in the war. Assad blamed the Saudis and their Wahhabi variant of Islam for everything bad that had happened in Syria. The Wahhabis gave the jihadists their ideology, he said, and the Saudi royals followed up with money and weapons. The Saudis' own arrests of extremists were simply a sign that they had lost control of their own creation, which would in the end destroy them. Assad delivered his views with a smile, as quiet, polite and certain as ever.

Rival Islamist groups were by then dominating the armed

opposition to the Syrian regime. Assad was right about some things. The Wahhabi view of Islam was close to the ideology of al-Qaeda, Islamic State and the smaller Salafist militias that at times fought the regime, or each other. He was also correct that many Saudis supported, helped finance and died fighting for al-Qaeda and IS. The rest of his analysis, delivered politely and with confidence in that anteroom, was wrong. The House of Saud's alliance with Wahhabi clerics was centuries old. It did not mean, as Assad claimed, that the Saudis were trying to replace him with Abu Bakr al-Baghdadi, the leader of Islamic State. Baghdadi was the enemy of the Saudis. His Islamic entity had no room for kings and, as a self-declared caliph, a successor to the prophet Muhammad, he had elevated himself above mere monarchs. As for al-Qaeda, it had regarded the Saudi royals as renegades ever since King Fahd rejected Osama bin Laden's plan to raise a force of veterans of the Afghan jihad to protect the holy cities of Mecca and Medina against Saddam Hussein.

When I left Assad that day, the view over Damascus from the presidential palace was bleaker than ever. Smoke rose from suburbs held by rebels. In 2015 Assad's forces were at their lowest ebb, but help was coming, from President Vladimir Putin of Russia and his generals. The war was changing. New layers of conflict were being grafted onto each other. I could feel it near the front line, in the heart of Damascus and on the road to Homs or Aleppo.

Islamic State's rampage through Syria was the catalyst. The arrival of the ruthless, predatory jihadists on the edge of another town became the most frightening sight in the Middle East. On 19 May 2015, it was the turn of Palmyra. This was the defeat that convinced the Kremlin to step in. Palmyra was one of the greatest cities of the ancient world, the jewel of a civilization that came before Islam. It developed around an oasis in the heart of the Syrian desert, halfway between the Mediterranean and the settlements along the Euphrates River, where humans discovered they could grow crops and then turned settlements into civilizations.

Palmyra was a superpower two thousand years ago, made rich by the trade that moved through it on the Silk Road between Asia and

Europe. When Palmyra declined and was abandoned to the desert, the architectural legacy of centuries of wealth and power survived. The temples that still stood in the desert reminded the jihadists of an idea they hated: that there was a religious life before the prophet Muhammad revealed the word of God. Capturing Palmyra was about more than taking command of an important and ancient crossroads; it was their chance to smash the idolatrous relics of the past. Baghdadi's more savvy followers were not planning to destroy everything. Collectors who did not ask questions would pay big money for the smaller, portable insults to the God of the caliph of the Islamic State.

The small Syrian town that grew around the ruins of the ancient city is known in Arabic as Tadmur. Before the war, Palmyra entranced tourists, but Tadmur made Syrians shudder. The reason was its jail – a place of 'pure patriotic fear' according to Faraj Bayrakdar, a Syrian poet who was incarcerated for four years in Tadmur's world of nightmares, where prisoners could disappear or emerge broken if they survived.[1] Syria under the Assads has had plenty of prisons designed to crush the human spirit, and Tadmur was the worst. Prisoners were whipped and tortured, sometimes daily, by sadistic guards. Eye contact with other prisoners would be severely punished. When the guards were close, they had to look down; they learned to separate the worst, the killers, from those who were just brutal by the look of their boots. No wonder prisoners expected to die, hoping only that it would be quick. A survivor told investigators from Amnesty International, 'When death is a daily occurrence, lurking in torture, random beatings, eye-gouging, broken limbs and crushed fingers, [when] death stares you in the face and is only avoided by sheer chance ... wouldn't you welcome the merciful release of a bullet?'[2] After a failed attempt by the Muslim Brotherhood to assassinate Hafez al-Assad in 1980, his men went from cell to cell inside Tadmur, shooting the men inside. Their graves have never been excavated or their bodies counted, but between 250 and 1,000 prisoners were killed.

When Islamic State arrived in Palmyra in 2015, a new kind of savagery descended on the town. Beating the Iraqi army in Mosul the year before had left the advancing fighters with a vast amount of military booty. They upgraded from the Toyota pick-ups mounted with heavy machine guns used by insurgents across the world, and surrounded Palmyra with armoured Humvees, heavy artillery and tanks. All were part of the billions of dollars the Americans had pumped into the Iraqi armed forces, who were supposed to fight terrorism and instead collapsed in the face of a few thousand jihadist killers.

The day Palmyra fell to Islamic State, Khalil Hariri and Mohammad al-Asaad could hear them coming. The sounds of bullets, shells and revving tank engines were getting closer. Grunting and sweating, they kept on manhandling wooden crates out of the door of the Palmyra Museum and down to three trucks that were parked outside. Bullets were hitting the museum, like enraged insects hissing over their heads. Hot pieces of shrapnel from exploding mortars fizzed through the air, blowing fragments of wood off the trees and turning them into daggers. The men bundled the last crate into the nearest truck and jumped in after it. As the vehicles careered out of Museum Square, a bullet hit Khalil, the museum director. Shrapnel wounded two of his colleagues. They hurtled down the road to Homs, away from the jihadists they believed would kill them, not even stopping to treat the wounded until they were well clear of Palmyra. Against all the odds and under heavy fire, five middle-aged archaeology experts had rescued Palmyra Museum's priceless collection of artefacts from one of the world's earliest civilizations, and thwarted the new barbarians of Islamic State.

This was not what they had signed up for; they were not commandos, or removers. They reminded me of *The Monuments Men*, a Hollywood film released a year earlier, loosely based on the story of an unlikely squad of antiquarians who joined the invasion of Europe to rescue works of art looted by the Nazis. A line delivered by George Clooney in the film belonged to Khalil Hariri, the man who took the bullet leaving the museum: 'You can wipe out an entire generation, you can burn their homes to the ground and somehow they'll still find their way back. But if you destroy their history, you destroy their achievements and it's as if they never existed.'

Khalil Hariri and his monuments men reached Damascus with their cargo. They are ordinary men who smoke a lot and get scared as well as brave. When I met them in the garden of the Syrian National Museum in Damascus later that summer, Khalil was still recovering from his bullet wound. He told me that Syria's history was such a vital part of their own identities that they were ready to die to save the objects ISIS was going to smash or steal, just as they had done in Iraq.

Khalil lit another cigarette and inhaled the smoke into the base of his lungs. He was struggling not to think too much about the ways a group in love with killing might take their revenge. The Damascus Museum was closed, and its collection was being packed up to be sequestered somewhere secret. In a secure area in the basement, behind heavy steel doors, museum staff and archaeology students were wrapping thousands of artefacts in tissue paper and laying them in Tupperware boxes lined with foam rubber. We sat on stone benches in the garden, surrounded by a few pieces from the collection of sculptures that were disappearing into the dusty grass.

'I'm going to get a harsh sentence if they get hold of me,' Khalil said.

Ten minutes after they escaped Palmyra with the artefacts, Islamic State fighters had entered the building to find the display cases empty. Nothing was left inside except big statues that would have needed a crane to move them. Khalil had decided that it was safer to leave his wife and young son behind; it took a month to get them out. When they were reunited, his wife told him that the jihadists had stormed through their front door, demanding to know what he had done with the collection.

Archaeology in Palmyra was a family affair. Khalil's father-in-law, Khaled al-Asaad, was appointed director of antiquities in 1963. Even in retirement, he was the man whose judgement about Palmyra and its treasures mattered most. Khaled named his daughter Zeinobia, after Palmyra's second-century warrior queen. His Zeinobia married Khalil Hariri, who followed him as museum director.

Mohammad al-Asaad, one of Khaled's two sons, had not been scared when the bullets were flying, because 'we believed that what we were doing was important'. Like all Syrians, they were immensely proud that the some of the earliest civilizations had emerged in their land. The whole family had been brought up by their father to venerate Palmyra, its buildings and its treasures. Khaled refused to leave Palmyra. The men from Islamic State cut off his head and left his body hanging on a traffic light to rot. Khalil's brother and two cousins were also killed.

'My father was eighty-three years old,' Mohammad told me, 'and a true believer in the importance of Palmyra. He was deeply attached to it, and refused to flee.' Mohammad had been his father's right-hand man at the museum for twenty-five years. The only photo he had left of him was on his phone. All the others were lost in Palmyra.

The nihilists of IS were a greater threat to Palmyra than two millennia of earthquakes, sandstorms and wars. Within weeks, they had blown up its two greatest temples, both around two thousand years old. They put twenty-five people in front of a firing squad in the amphitheatre, smashed the big statues left in the museum with sledgehammers, and blew up Tadmur Prison.

It was their last big victory. Forces were gathering that would smash the Islamic State caliphate. Iran, the preeminent Shia state, went into the fight against the violently sectarian Sunni jihadists. In northern Syria, Kurdish-led forces earned American respect by stopping the ISIS advance and were rewarded with equipment, training and air support. Barack Obama still believed America needed to kick its habit of bombing itself deeper into Middle East crises, but the danger from Islamic State threatened to go global if the US did not act. The US started bombing after a request from the Iraqi government to stop a genocide against Yazidis in the north-west. Before long, the US target list included Islamic State in Syria.

Big battles were ahead to recapture Raqaa in Syria and Mosul in Iraq, the two main cities of the caliphate. Islamic State's fighters included an experienced core of veterans of Saddam Hussein's army who had fought the Americans in Iraq and now transferred operations to Syria. Jihadists were formidable enemies because they were happy to die. As they were killed, foreign reinforcements came into Syria along smuggling routes from Turkey, joining young local men who were seduced by the certainty of the IS ideology.

Russia intervened to save the Assad regime as well as to fight ISIS; it changed the course of the war, with serious consequences for the region. When the war started, Russia gave Assad arms shipments and diplomatic cover at the UN. After 2015, President Vladimir Putin and his generals decided that Assad needed more – the regime would fall if Russia did not deploy its own forces. It was decisive for the Assad regime; Putin's move put rocket boosters under the war effort and delivered a blow to American prestige and influence, ending America's position as the only major foreign power in the Middle East. Since the death of the Soviet Union, the US had plenty of enemies in the region, but no rivals.

Now Russia was back. Putin's plan had worked. It fitted in with his long-term goal of rebuilding Russia's position as a world power after the humiliating, chaotic end of the Soviet Union. The foundations were already in place: Russia's relationship with the Syrian military went back to the 1940s. In the fifties, Hafez al-Assad himself had learnt to fly fast jets in the USSR. Syria was Moscow's ally and client throughout the Cold War, and Russia had never given up a small naval base on Syria's Mediterranean coast. The Russian military knew much more about Syria and the Assad regime than NATO. Whenever I visited generals in the Ministry of Defence in Damascus, I would see Russian military textbooks on their bookshelves, and mementoes from the time they had spent as young men at Soviet military academies. Many even spoke Russian.

Two years after the fall of Palmyra, General Valery Gerasimov, chief of the Russian General Staff, told the Russian tabloid *Komsomolskaya Pravda* why they made their move: 'If we had not intervened in Syria, what would have happened? Look, in 2015 just over ten per cent of the territory remained under government control. A month or two more, by the end of 2015, and Syria would have been completely under ISIS.'

Barack Obama did not want Islamic State to gain any more ground either, and ramped up the military campaign to destroy the caliphate. But the US and NATO, unlike Russia, did not want Assad in power. Obama stuck to the script he had been using since 2011: Assad had 'lost legitimacy' and would have to be 'transitioned out'. Obama's critics pointed out that he'd had his chance in August 2013, when he pulled back from his threat to bomb the regime. And he dismayed Americans who believed the US had no choice about being involved in the Middle East, and was gifting the Kremlin a chance to be the war's most influential power.

Russian force imposed a certain calm, but it could never be

called peace. Removing Islamic State from Palmyra was a priority, though it had to be done twice after the jihadists forced their way back in. TASS, the Russian news agency, published photographs of the museum in Palmyra after it was recaptured. Display cases were smashed and it looked as if they had tried to burn the building down; mortars had blasted holes in the roof, and the walls inside were pitted with bullet holes. It looked as if there had been a battle in there, but it was not a fight between armies. Instead the extremists of Islamic State were waging war against the past as well as the present. The statues that were too heavy to be rescued lay on their sides in pieces, slammed to the floor. Sculptures had their faces hacked off to obey the religious injunction not to portray the human form. Palmyra's best-known individual sculpture, the Lion of al-Lat, was in pieces in a blackened heap.

The US decided to make war on Islamic State, not the Assad regime. Had Obama gone ahead with air strikes in 2013, Assad might still have survived; the US wanted to make a point, not unseat the regime. But effective foreign policy is based on credibility, and Obama's change of mind meant that he did not sound credible when he talked about removing Assad from power. Neither did Britain's prime minister, David Cameron, whose government lost a parliamentary vote on intervention that he had assumed they would win. Both leaders never overcame a fundamental dilemma for the West: they wanted Assad out, but feared that Islamic State was ready and waiting as a replacement. The lesson of Iraq after Saddam Hussein and Libya after Muammar al-Gaddafi was that dethroning dictators without having a Plan B was dangerous. The US concentrated on the military campaign against Islamic State, which succeeded, and on trying to build a united political opposition to Assad, which failed.

Putin, on the other hand, could see that war was beating diplomacy. Deep splits crippled the Syrian political opposition. Assad had proved that he would bring down the house to save his regime; trying to persuade him to step down without direct military coercion was a waste of time. By October 2015, the Russian foreign minister Sergei Lavrov was dismissive about the diplomatic process, observing caustically to journalists in Moscow that the Americans and the Saudis could not even agree with him which groups should be called terrorists. It should have been clear by then that Assad had destroyed the country to save his regime, and would not be prepared to hand over its corpse in some negotiation in a hotel ballroom in Vienna or Geneva.

Putin's answer was that Russia would keep the regime in power, and Assad would owe him. He framed it as a fight against terror, gave some credit to the Kurds, and told the UN General Assembly in New York that it was the only way to beat Islamic State and other dangerous extremists: 'the Syrian government and its armed forces', he said, 'are valiantly fighting terrorism face to face.' Islamic State was a contagion of criminals who had 'tasted blood'. They could not be allowed to return home to continue their evil deeds. Putin also had a domestic incentive for action; he wanted to stop any more attacks inside Russia by jihadist extremists who had already killed hundreds. Russia had attempted no serious military expedition outside the former Soviet Union since the Afghan disaster in the 1980s. Now it was intervening to save Assad, to show that Russia was reborn as a power, and to deal a decisive blow to their mutual enemies.

After three days of heavy Russian air raids in support of Assad's forces, with the air of a man who had made up his mind and did not like to see it challenged, Barack Obama warned Putin that it would end badly. He would get 'stuck in a quagmire and it won't work'. Obama was wrong.

20.

Scorched Earth

A dank evening came in through the broken glass of an apartment that by some bomber's miracle had survived mostly untouched. The street in Sha'ar, one of the poorest quarters in eastern Aleppo, was so blocked with smashed masonry that it was impassable in a car. The view from his balcony still made Abu Hussein happy. 'Nothing is better or more beautiful than our home,' he said. 'It's the place to be in good times or in bad.'

Umm Hussein, his wife, was also there, cooking dinner on a charcoal stove. The smoke hung on the wet and heavy night air. They were home as 2015 expired because the Assad regime had just won the battle for Aleppo. The last rebels had surrendered. The price of victory was counted in dead bodies and the almost total destruction of the eastern side of the city, which was taken from the regime in the summer of 2012. In the narrow alleys of Sha'ar, the cramped, shoddily built concrete flats were always freezers in winter and sweatboxes in the summer. Across eastern Aleppo the bombs made some collapse in on themselves. Others had the fronts ripped off, like dolls' houses in a nightmare, exposing beds still made up with sheets and blankets, and sofas. One more shock wave and they would have followed the rubble of the walls and the roofs into the street.

At the peak of their power in Aleppo, rebels almost encircled the regime side. The first time I arrived in wartime in western Aleppo, the sector held by the regime was under its own siege, only accessible along a narrow corridor that bumped through a landscape chewed up by the fighting, past an estate of tower blocks that were still fought over. Screens made of tarpaulins two or three storeys high hung between the towers to make it harder for snipers on the rebel side to pick off passers-by. Hundreds of civilians with nowhere else to go still lived in the parts of the towers that were still intact and faced away from the front line.

I spent days in the pulverized east side of the city after it fell. You could drive for a mile or so in one direction and see nothing but destruction, then drive a mile in another direction and see more rubble, torn buildings and cold, hungry people trudging through the freezing winter days looking for their lost and former lives. Running water and mains power were a fantasy from another world. Children struggled through the muddy, broken streets carrying water for their families, climbing over mountain ranges of concrete and brick from the buildings that were flattened by artillery fire, barrel bombs or air strikes. When the war stopped in late December and early January, thousands of people came back to find their homes, moving in if they were still standing or taking over a neighbour's if they weren't. Eastern Aleppo was an insanitary piece of hell but it was better than where they had been, because at least it was home. In Syria, after five years of war, life stories were translated into an unimaginable new language.

The anti-Assad forces' best moments in Aleppo came early in the war, when they were pushing to surround the regime side but were never strong enough to cut off the last corridor into it. The fall of Aleppo, Syria's biggest city, would have been a fatal blow for Assad. Taking it back made his regime safe. It was the biggest and most decisive victory of the war, and it was only possible because a year earlier Putin's Russia had intervened.

Vladimir Putin was not hampered by the constraints of democracy. Even so, his decisiveness was a sharp contrast to the vacillation of Western leaders, led by Barack Obama, who had declared early in the war that Assad must go and then shied away from the risks of making it happen. Russia saved the Assad regime. The Russian air force multiplied the killing power on the regime side, adding force and firepower that Assad's forces never had. Strategic bombers flew

4,000-mile sorties from Russia and shorter trips from airbases in Iran.[1] The main ground fighting was still done by the Syrian Arab Army, Iran and its militias as well as Hizbullah from Lebanon and mercenaries from Russia. The Russians improved organization, training and firepower. They brought in heavy artillery, which I saw dug in alongside the Syrian army in firebases around the towns and villages held by rebel forces.

One by one, places held by rebels since the beginning of the war were forced into surrender deals. Over the years the Syrian Arab Army and its militias never had enough men to isolate bigger rebel enclaves. Front lines leaked. People could sometimes slip through to buy food and supplies, even to earn some money. Smugglers dug tunnels or bribed soldiers to look the other way. Russian power tipped the balance, and steadily, the enclaves were besieged. It is an ancient tactic. Modern weapons make a siege more direct, but the principles are the same as they were in the age of scaling ladders and boiling oil. First, cut off reinforcements and resupply to fighters. Stop the smugglers so food and medical supplies run out. Hammer defenders with artillery and air strikes. Sooner or later, resistance will collapse.

Enclaves went hungry once they were sealed off, or were under the guns of a powerful military unit. The UN estimated that the regime side was besieging at least seventeen different places in 2016. The regime and its allies worked systematically. Once a target was earmarked, they concentrated forces to seal it off, while the Russians and Syrians smashed it with air strikes and shells. Someone came up with the word 'reconciliation' for the deals that were offered to end the sieges. In the real world it meant surrender or die. On offer was a ride in a green municipal bus to the province of Idlib up against the border with Turkey in the north-west. It was the last big area controlled by rebels. Idlib was the only place left for people on the regime's hit list. It was not for everyone, as it was run by jihadists, bombed frequently by the regime and the Russians, and widely assumed to be the future venue of the war's climactic battle.

Anyone who turned down the transfer to Idlib would have to take their chances as the regime's cruel intelligence agencies moved back in. Men of military age, from their teens to middle years, risked conscription and the front line unless they were rich or influential enough to bribe their way out. At the beginning of 2016 a ceasefire was arranged by the Russians and the Americans. It was a complicated deal for a complicated war, and it did not take long for cracks to appear. Fighting in the countryside around Aleppo never stopped; around Damascus, the ceasefire more or less held. Partial ceasefires suited the Syrian Arab Army, giving them time to redeploy men to active fronts and to apply big new firepower provided by the Russians to the steady dismantling of rebel enclaves.

I watched the fall of Darayya, a suburb of Damascus held by rebels from 2012 to 2016. Scores of people of all ages emerged along a straight road lined with concrete honeycombs that had been buildings before years of shelling. The oldest and weakest were pushed or pulled in improvised carts. Some were on crutches, with missing legs. Darayya was four miles out of the centre of Damascus on the road to the Lebanese border, and by 2016, with the regime's confidence increasing with every enclave that fell, the contrast was extreme. Someone visiting downtown Damascus for the first time might wonder where to find the war. In Darayya, besieged fighters were being starved into surrender. In downtown Damascus, the old city was packed with shoppers. Traffic jams snarled the streets. People with money could eat in restaurants, even sushi, driven up from Beirut in refrigerated vans.

The ceasefire meant that for the first time in five years, the city did not echo with the flat thunderclaps of the regime's heavy artillery. Yarmouk, a Palestinian refugee camp just outside the centre, was a silent, deserted ruin. Empty and broken concrete tenements loomed over streets that used to teem with people and honking cars. For the first time since the war started I could walk into Yarmouk, allowed through checkpoints by regime soldiers who were delighted it had stopped being a front line. At street level, every building was smashed and gutted by bullets and blast, a sign that fighting had gone from house to house. Before the war started, 160,000 Palestinian refugees lived in Yarmouk in barely two square kilometres. Only a few Palestinians held onto a small area, until a final government offensive in 2018.

As Darayya surrendered after five tormented years, it was astonishing to see rebel fighters having warm conversations with Syrian army soldiers, young men standing with arms around each other's shoulders like exhausted footballers at the end of a match. The bad news for all of them was that the match was not over. It wasn't even in extra time. They were too tired for anger. Instead they were locked in a nightmare they could not control, dictated by powerful men who might even decide when they died. They listened quietly as a man who said his name was Danny spoke. I pointed out one of the regime soldiers who had sewn a badge with Bashar al-Assad's portrait onto his uniform.

'I don't hate him,' Danny said, 'but I hate the people who killed us and those who did must be judged . . . he's a person. He's a Syrian man. I am a Syrian man also. I want all the people who killed us, who killed our children, who attacked us with chemicals, to be judged and put in jail.'

I was the first outsider Danny had seen in years, and he spoke to me as if I was a visitor from another planet. 'I don't know how much you know about what happened, about the siege, the crippling siege, about not having anything to eat, about eating cats and dogs and herbs, about not having electricity for like four years, about not having water.' He questioned whether any of it had been worthwhile. 'We had to be fighters,' he said, 'because we didn't find any other job . . . All this war is a lie. We had good lives before the revolution. Anyway this is not a revolution. They lied to us in the name of religion.'

The Syrian war created millions of individual tragedies that added up to one collective catastrophe, from parents whose children were killed to fighters who would rather not fight. Quite a few of the children being evacuated had been dressed up in their best clothes for the next stage in lives, as one of the mothers said, that were like death. Two sisters teamed their best toy jewellery with immaculately tied pink bows, sunhats and white summer outfits. They did not smile for the new, suspicious world. Brothers were dressed for a party, with gelled hair, white shirts and black bow ties.

Rows of buses, lined up for the journey to Idlib, signalled the endgame as enclaves were recaptured. The faces at the windows of the buses heading north were miserable, exhausted and gaunt. It was a not a happy ending. Idlib's future was uncertain. The same week that the children emerged from the ruins in their best clothes, a Syrian general at the Ministry of Defence reminded me that the civil war in Lebanon had lasted sixteen years. This war, he said, was much more complicated, 'so we could have at least another ten years of bloodshed'. One of his underlings, a conscript with the luck or influence to have the safest job in the army, brought in another tray covered with glasses of hot, sweet tea. Neither the general nor the private wanted to be stuck, like the men, on the front line.

The war was moving north that summer, as the regime and the Russians prepared the final battle for Aleppo. The general signed the papers that would get us through the roadblocks to Aleppo. The journey from Damascus was long and meandering. The main highway had been blocked for years, so military engineers paved a back road across empty moors, past the remains of abandoned villages of conical mudbrick houses that looked like beehives. I wanted to know more about the way they had lived in those remote and traditional settlements, but no one was left to ask.

During the final battle in Aleppo, the regime sealed off the rebel-held east of the city, where 275,000 people were trapped. The east side was a microcosm of why rebels were losing the war. It was split into informal sectors controlled by armed groups with serious ideological differences. Those identifying as components of the US-backed Free Syrian Army controlled part of the east, while jihadists from the former al-Nusra Front were just a few streets away. Nusra broke links with al-Qaeda, its old mother ship, rebranding itself as Jabhat Fateh al-Sham, the Front for the Conquest of Syria and the Levant. Its leader Abu Mohammed al-Jawlani was ambitious and intelligent and wanted to broaden his political options. He was a former protégé of Abu Bakr al-Baghdadi, the self-declared caliph of the Islamic State; they fell out after Baghdadi sent him into Syria in 2011 to organize jihadist fighting groups.

Kurds controlled another sector, which had reasonable food supplies because it had an open road into the countryside. People in the rest of besieged eastern Aleppo went hungry, unless they could pay more and more for less and less food. Water came in privately owned tankers; the bombing had smashed water and power systems. Cellars were death traps when the buildings above them collapsed. Moving through the streets carried a considerable risk of death, but it was the only way to get water and food. Hundreds were killed in the first few weeks of bombing alone.

In the west of the city, bombing still boomed across the front line, but families could also stroll around on warm late summer evenings, when the air was heavily scented by perfumed tobacco from shishas. The west was impoverished and isolated, but not nearly as battered as the east. Regime territory in Aleppo was much safer than the other side of the front line, though rebels still fired into it to kill and maim civilians.

Does it matter which side civilians are on if they are killed and wounded? At Aleppo University Hospital, every corridor made me think about all the lives that had been swept up and spat out by the war. The regime and the Russians and their allies killed many more people than the rebels, but many of the wounded in the hospital had been hurt by rebels. An eight-year-old boy called Hani Jadid was lying on a trolley outside the hospital. He had been wounded in a village under government control, about an hour's drive from the centre of Aleppo. The day was hot and all he was wearing was a disposable nappy with a catheter leading to a plastic bag to collect his urine. His right arm was gone, amputated above the elbow. The stump was wrapped in cream-coloured bandages, like both his legs.

Hani was being sent home to start his new life. He had to face it without four cousins who had been killed by the shell that maimed him. The affiliation of whoever fired that shell could not have been on the mind of a boy whose friends were dead, whose arm had gone. He groaned with pain and called for his father, who wasn't there. An uncle and cousin helped an orderly lay him across the back seat of a taxi. His head was squeezed into the door and he faced an agonizing drive back to a home that was still in the firing line.

Inside the hospital, seven-year-old Rawda al-Youssef, small for her age like many Syrian children who were growing in the war with malnutrition, was asleep with a bullet lodged in her spine. Rawda was paralysed and her mother, Turkieh, was worrying about who would look after her other seven children, one of whom was already handicapped. A bullet and a paralysing wound had been the last thing on her mind when they sat down to eat dinner outside their house on a breezy evening, enjoying the fading of the summer heat. Rawda was chatting to her father, a shepherd, when she was shot.

'I thought maybe she'd been hit in the back by a pebble,' Turkieh said. 'She asked her dad to carry her indoors. We took her into the house, took out a torch, and we saw the blood coming out of her back. A bullet had hit her in the back, without any sound.'

Hani and Rawda both had wounds that would change everything about their lives. Neither was killed. In the mincing machine of the war in Syria they were not even a blip in the statistics. Overwhelming numbers of people were dead and wounded. A monitoring group based in the UK called the Syrian Observatory for Human Rights reported that 600,000 people had been killed by June 2021. What do more than 600,000 dead bodies look like? Old Trafford, Manchester United's theatre of dreams, holds 76,100. Syria's theatre of nightmares could fill it nearly eight times over, a corpse on every seat.

Mohammad Marzen Saboni, a middle-aged dentist, lay in a room further down the corridor with what remained of his family. 'Last Friday, we were outside the house, the whole family. Nothing was going on, there was nothing happening in the street. Then a terrorist mortar fell. My wife was badly hurt and died. And then my son passed away. We were just walking in the street. I never thought it would happen.'

Mohammad looked down at his smashed legs. Orthopaedic surgeons had fixed stainless steel rods in them to help the fragments of bone knit together, but the nerves were so badly damaged that he had been told he might never walk again. 'I blame the terrorists. We are innocent, kids and civilians. I just want to walk again. My heart is dead.' Many people in western Aleppo called the rebels terrorists.

Mohammad's nine-year-old daughter Mayah was in the next bed, with both her legs in plaster. Someone had given her a doll. It was propped up next to her pillow, a Barbie in a pink box she had not opened. Mayah looked away from anyone who tried to catch her eye, and scowled when a nurse tried to interest her in the doll. Mayah had seen her mother and her baby brother die, and like Hani Jadid, the boy outside the hospital, she was facing a dark future. Her fourteen-year-old brother Mohammad Amer, who was there when the attack happened but wasn't injured, had grown up so fast that he was as weary as an old man.

'There's no life here,' he said. 'We're very tired. All I want from the future is to see my father and sister walking again.'

Victory in Aleppo at the end of 2015 changed the war for the regime, but it took until the spring of 2018 for it to win the battle for Damascus by breaking resistance in Eastern Ghouta, the arc of towns on the edge of the capital. The years of killing blur into each other, so I try to fix the deadly sequence of events by scrolling through my photos and videos. The boys I saw burning plastic to keep warm on the dystopian streets of Douma in the first winter of the war were old enough to carry guns by 2018.

Everyone there, young or old, was eligible for death. In 2012, I watched hundreds of young men from the area volunteering for Liwa al-Islam, the Brigade of Islam, which as it expanded took the name Jaysh al-Islam, the Army of Islam. Its founder, Zahran Alloush, was a well-known Salafist; the Saudis became their biggest backer. I have the video we shot in 2012 of enthusiastic and naive recruits being put through their paces at a big military base Liwa had just captured, running past burnt-out tanks and unexploded shells still buried in the pathways. The men shouting orders like drill sergeants in any army were dressed like jihadist warriors, with inscriptions from the Quran on bands around their arms and heads and calf-length tunics touching the tops of their combat boots. Many of the volunteers had faces too soft to grow beards. It looked more like football training at school than the assembly of an army, with the athletic guys leading the runs around the parade ground and the tubbier ones panting to keep up. But they fought until 2018, and many of those that survived went to Idlib to wait for another battle.

The man who had taken us to that military base called himself Islam Alloush. He was beefy and friendly, looking in his combat fatigues as if he was still an officer in the Syrian Arab Army, except for his black Quranic headband. Alloush had the usual plan for what should happen to Assad. 'Killed,' he said. 'Definitely killed.' Islam was the brother of Zahran Alloush, Liwa's founder. The next time I saw him, about nine months later, he had acquired an M4, the latest American assault rifle, impressive military bling in a war where most fighters used battered Kalashnikovs.

When we stopped for coffee he put the M4 on the table, the frontline equivalent of showing off the most desirable mobile phones. I photographed the gun on the oilcloth over the table, the coffee and the hands of the fighters stirring sugar into their thick coffee. After the Russian intervention, Islam Alloush offered me an interview with Zahran, his brother. He said we'd have safe passage into Douma through one of the tunnels they had dug to keep their mini state going. It was tempting, but I turned it down in case Syrian intelligence heard about the trip. I reckoned that the Alloush organization must have been penetrated by regime informers. The Russians were hitting Eastern Ghouta hard. They could track me and put a missile through the ceiling once I was in the room with the Alloush brothers. In the end, they hit Zahran Alloush on 25 December 2015. He was killed by a missile strike on the building he was using as a headquarters.

A photo from 2021 shows Islam Alloush in defeat. It was released by French police and captioned with his real name, Majdi Nehme. He was no longer the cheerful young man predicting victory and Assad's death but was in custody in France, under investigation for war crimes. The photo showed he had been badly beaten, with cuts to his bald head, two black eyes and bloodshot, pummelled eyeballs.

By 2018 the Syrian regime and the Russians were ready to make their move against Eastern Ghouta. They could smell victory. Since the Russian intervention, Assad's side had recaptured the territory inhabited by two-thirds of the population. The cost in lives and damage was immense. Every time I left the strangely untouched centre of Damascus, the road wound through miles of ruins, past houses and shops that were empty facades pockmarked by bullets and shrapnel. The people who had lived and worked there, who had taken their children to school from homes that had been made into ruins, were either dead, displaced inside Syria, or refugees abroad. It was a tainted victory, but the regime was delivered from extinction, its greatest fear.

* * *

The defenders of Douma created a vast underground network of tunnels, strengthened with steel and concrete, to protect them against shelling. Some were big enough for cars and lorries. I walked through the tunnels after the people who dug them were defeated. A field hospital was created in one of the caverns. Next to a command centre in another was a jail. In the end it wasn't enough. Eastern Ghouta was overwhelmed by a siege and Russian firepower, the same formula that had worked in Aleppo. Heavily armed Russian combat troops were visible in and around the front line, controlling the battle and bringing in supplies in lines of trucks. In a strongpoint someone had taped up photos of Putin and Assad on the wall next to each other, a shrine on the front line.

A war of attrition creates its own pressures. Douma in its last battle was no longer the place I reached at the beginning of the war, united in the fight against the regime. The years of grinding stalemate that followed made the armed groups inside Eastern Ghouta more dictatorial. They believed harsh discipline was necessary to prolong the fight, and stories emerged that they were shooting people who tried to leave the enclave without permission. When people no longer want to fight for a cause, it begins to collapse.

Videos emerged at the beginning of April that seemed to show another chemical attack, a terrible echo of the one in August 2013 that almost, but not quite, led to American bombing. The Russians said it was a lie fabricated by British intelligence; others said the video was faked inside Douma to get Western help. The US was convinced it was real. President Donald Trump, in one of his first big foreign policy decisions, ordered a limited missile attack. A year later, an investigation by the Organization for the Prohibition of Chemical Weapons confirmed gas had been used. Trump's missiles made the point that he was not Obama. They did not affect the course of the war.

After Douma fell I spent a lot of time walking through its destroyed neighbourhoods that had been turned into another Syrian wasteland. Humanity was inching back through ice cream. Syrians are proud of the way they make it by hand. Cream and sugar are thrown into a churn and pounded with a wooden pole. It is hard physical work, and the ice-cream men of Douma were doing good business.

Civilians displaced from Douma were kept under close watch in a camp. A woman dressed in black told me that six years ago her husband had gone out to buy some nappies for their baby. He was stopped at a checkpoint run by state security and disappeared. She veered between thinking he was dead and dreading what still might be happening to him in some prison cell. The daughter who had needed nappies that day hugged her mother's waist. Both of them were crying. The world they had spent six years rebuilding had just been knocked down again. The authorities had taken an older son to be conscripted into the army. They didn't know where he was either.

Wars are not just huge, noisy engines of destruction and chaos. They also seep into lives like a virus. Bashar al-Assad, back in 2011, said Syria faced conspiracies that spread like germs. Dr Assad's prescription was the wonder drug of his own presidency. The Syrians who did not like his diagnosis went to the streets. The war virus infected everyone in Syria. Once I stopped to bandage a boy who had gashed his leg badly playing with his friends. A pleasant woman in her twenties stopped to help. She told me her husband and their ten-month-old had been caught in the open by a shell. The husband lost his leg, the baby was killed.

Walking through Douma that summer was a reminder of how hard it will be to rebuild Syria. It is not just a matter of clearing rubble and twisted steel, burying the bodies that lie underneath and finding the money to rebuild. When war takes hold, it does not simply break bodies, hearts and minds. It poisons the future.

21.

The Taste of Fire and Smoke

Abed Takkoush was too cool to hang around with the drivers in the arrivals hall at Beirut Airport. He would stand back from the emotional storm of family reunions, catch my eye, appear at my elbow to take control of the trolley and we would saunter out to his Mercedes taxi to drive into the city. Beirut was rebuilding after fifteen years of bloody and destructive civil war. On the way into town, Abed would point out with grim relish the places where hideous events had happened. He had seen it all since he was a young taxi driver hired to work with television reporters when the war started in 1975. His card said 'driver/producer'. More than anything he was a fixer, the kind of person that foreign correspondents need in places like Beirut.

Abed's special subject was Israel's invasion of Lebanon in 1982. He would often point out Sabra and Shatila, the Palestinian refugee camps where the Christian Phalangist militia perpetrated the most notorious massacre of the civil war, between 16 and 18 September 1982. Estimates of the numbers they killed range from 700 to 3,000. Bodies of civilians, from babies to old men and women, were left in the streets. The Israeli army was in control of the area and held the perimeter while their allies in the Phalange went on a murderous rampage through the cramped alleys and buildings. The leader of the Phalange, the president-elect Bashir Gemayel, had just been killed along with dozens of his supporters in a huge bomb explosion at his headquarters in Beirut.

The first excuse offered by the Christian killers and their Israeli allies was that they were going after Palestinian fighters who had stayed behind when, as part of a ceasefire agreement, Yasser Arafat and his men left for Tunis by sea. In fact, the PLO's departure meant that the civilians in the camps had lost their protection, and their enemies saw a chance to kill them.

The Lebanese can chart their modern history through massacres, executions and wars. You can even see it in the street maps. Beirut's central plaza, Martyrs' Square, is named after Lebanese nationalists who were executed by the Ottoman Turks during the First World War. A bronze statue that commemorates their deaths is riddled with bullet holes from fifteen years of civil war after 1975. Close by, past the Maronite Cathedral and the enormous mosque built by the assassinated prime minister Rafik al-Hariri, is a smaller square named after Riad al-Solh, also assassinated, who led the country after independence from France in 1943.

Older people in Lebanon dream about an age they think of as lost and golden, before the civil war turned Beirut from tolerant to rubble. Fairuz, the great Lebanese diva, in one of her best-known songs, mourns the time when Beirut went dark and tasted of fire and smoke. At the airport, and on hoardings around new plate-glass developments, black and white photographs display the way they were; steam engines in snowy mountains, 1960s Mercedes taxis with rounded bonnets queuing in Martyrs' Square, and beautiful women at glittering parties, Lebanese Hepburns and Lorens in jewels and gowns and long gloves.

The glamorous legends about skiing on the Mediterranean in the morning and in the snowy mountains in the afternoon obscured crushing poverty in a population that was just part of the background for an elite whose power and wealth depended on Lebanon's great weakness, sectarianism. The constitution was designed to keep the peace by recognizing eighteen different sects and dividing power between them. The way the system has worked since an agreement to end the civil war in 1989 has allowed Lebanon's array of hereditary leaders, warlords turned politicians, and financiers to direct money and privileges towards their own sects; building a strong and functional state came a distant second. A generation after the end of the civil war, as Lebanon suffered one of the worst economic collapses in history, the problem was still the same. A corrupt and inept elite was more eager to preserve a sectarian system that gave them power and wealth than to stop the country slipping over the edge.

Sectarianism was a way of managing conflicts between Lebanon's communities. It was also a reason why they happened. The state was too weak to stand up for the rights of individuals; they fell back on their sects, which raised militias. A winemaker I know, a Christian, told me that when he was growing up his grandfather showed him the family's guns and told him they were ready for the moment the Druze came for them.

Lebanon has been held hostage by the turbulence around it and the interests of powerful countries that have used it as a battlefield. One way of thinking about the Middle East is to imagine a circuit board of political, geographical and religious connections. Most of them come together in Lebanon, which means it is hard-wired into the turbulence of the region. The irony is that the diversity that makes Lebanon fragile also makes it the most beguiling country in the Middle East. I'd see it all from Abed's taxi. We would drive past the bars and restaurants of downtown Beirut, along the corniche facing the Mediterranean where men and women strolled and even exercised together, an unusual sight in the Middle East. A few miles further on, the road enters the Shia southern suburbs, where most women wear hijab and stern ayatollahs stare down from posters. Some of their neighbours in adjoining Sunni areas regard Shia Islam as heresy. It can get tense.

At the weekends, secular Lebanese can order beers and cocktails at beach clubs as if they were at the other end of the Mediterranean, in Spain. Pious Shias can drive to a picnic area overlooking the border with Israel, decorated with portraits of Iranian clerics and Lebanese martyrs. Families have barbecues in sight of Israeli farmers and soldiers on the other side of the wire, neighbours who live in a different world.

Driving down south with Abed in the 1990s was a tour of Lebanon's mighty and troublesome neighbours. Syria's president, Hafez al-Assad, sent troops into Lebanon during the civil war and had kept them there. Before Western imperial powers carved up the Ottoman Empire during the First World War, Lebanon was part of Greater Syria, a much bigger entity that stretched down into Palestine. The Assads and others in Syria believed Lebanon's natural place was still with them. For many years, the two supposedly fraternal states did not exchange ambassadors. Why bother, the regime must have calculated, when its head of intelligence in Lebanon, Ghazi Kenaan, was the most feared man in the country?

Abed stopped making jokes and put on his stern face as we slowed down for the miserable-looking Syrian conscripts manning checkpoints on the highway south towards Israel, Lebanon's other troublesome neighbour. *Yatik al Afiyah*, he would growl, staring straight ahead: 'God give you health.' Lebanon's relationship with Syria was destructive enough. The one with Israel was much worse. Abed would take the old coastal highway through Sidon and further south to Tyre. After that, it was unwise to get too close to the broad slice of Lebanon occupied by Israel that was a remnant of the 1982 war. Three years after the invasion, Israel downsized its occupation of Lebanon, pulling back to what it intended as a secure buffer zone.

As Israel won its independence in 1948, over 100,000 Palestinians were forced out into Lebanon. Despite that, it was relatively quiet for twenty years, compared to the all-out wars, guerrilla attacks and reprisal raids between Israel and Syria, Egypt and Jordan. Everything changed after the Black September war of 1970, when King Hussein of Jordan ejected Yasser Arafat and the Palestinian militias when they looked set to take over his country. Arafat believed that Palestinians needed to lead the fight to restore their land and freedom, as they would be waiting for ever if they expected the big Arab states to do the job. He needed a base after Jordan. Syria was possible, but the Baathists in Damascus were too controlling. The government in sectarian Lebanon was too weak to stop Arafat moving in and at first his fighters had plenty of support from sympathetic Lebanese. That disappeared after Arafat's determination to conduct his war with Israel from Lebanon helped destabilize the country and push it into civil war.

Arafat found plenty of new recruits among Palestinian refugees:

young people who had grown up angry in camps that became miserable dumping grounds after 1948. Even fifty years later, young refugees in the camps' UN schools knew the names of their families' lost villages. When Yasser Arafat and other leaders of armed Palestinian factions told them that the only way they would win back their land was to fight for it, they were ready to listen.

The presence of armed Palestinians bent on a war of national liberation dragged Lebanon into the mainstream of the Arab–Israeli conflict. Cross-border raids were only part of the problem. The late 1960s and early 1970s were the heyday of Middle East airliner attacks and hijackings. In December 1968, the Popular Front for the Liberation of Palestine killed an Israeli in an attack on an El Al Boeing 707 at Athens Airport. Israel's response was to land commandos at Beirut Airport who blew up most of the fleet of Lebanon's national carrier, Middle East Airlines. At that time, the United States was not yet automatically using its veto to protect Israel at the UN. The Security Council unanimously passed Resolution 262, condemning Israel's action and giving a 'solemn warning' that further steps would be considered if it happened again. More than fifty years on, after wars and countless rounds of attacks and reprisals, the resolution reads like a diplomatic curio from another age.

By 1982 Israel's defence minister Ariel Sharon, a former general, believed that invading Lebanon would remove the Palestinian threat to the north. His prime minister, Menachem Begin, was a believer in military force who had led the attack on the British headquarters at the King David Hotel in Jerusalem that killed ninety-one people in 1946; but Sharon, known as 'the bulldozer', drove the invasion. He made his move after Palestinians from the group led by the notorious killer Abu Nidal tried to assassinate Shlomo Argov, the Israeli ambassador in London, leaving him grievously wounded. The 1982 invasion broke Palestinian power in Lebanon and forced Arafat into another exile, but it did not bring peace. Many of Israel's own citizens believed that the destruction and the massacres shamed their country. Shlomo Argov spent years in hospital, paralysed and blind. Before dying from complications from his wounds in 2003, he condemned Sharon's disastrous war of choice.

'Our soldiers should never go to war unless it is vital for survival,' he dictated to a friend. 'We are tired of wars. The nation wants peace.'[1]

In Tel Aviv, 10 per cent of the population packed the city's main square to protest against the Lebanon war. Sharon was forced to resign after an official enquiry found him indirectly responsible for the massacres in the refugee camps. The damage to his political career was only temporary; when Israelis decided they needed a strongman in the face of an armed Palestinian uprising after 2000, he became prime minister.

Israel inflicted terrible pain, loss and death on Lebanese civilians. Tens of thousands of impoverished Shia were forced out of their homes in the south and settled in Beirut's southern suburbs. The 1982 war revealed once again the deadly nexus at the heart of the conflict between Israel and the Arabs. Israeli generals and politicians claimed they had no choice about using deadly force. The blame for civilian deaths, they said, rested with terrorists who wanted to destroy the Jewish homeland. On the other side of the front lines, Israel was seen as a colonial outpost of the West that used its superior wealth, power and connections to take land and kill anyone who stood in its way.

In 1982, Israel's invasion removed Yasser Arafat from Lebanon and replaced him with a much deadlier enemy. Shia Muslims, the downtrodden of their world for a millennium, were suddenly stronger after the Islamic revolution in Iran. In the aftermath of the invasion the new Shia regime in Tehran saw ways to damage Israel. A determined coalition of Iranian revolutionaries and radicalized Lebanese clerics channelled the rage of Shias into a new armed group called Hizbullah, the Party of God.

In the first years of its fight against Israel, Hizbullah relied more on religious passion than on military prowess. Iranian instructors taught them not to mount suicidal frontal attacks in broad daylight. By the time Abed Takkoush was driving me around South Lebanon (often, as he liked to say, 'under the shelling'), Hizbullah was highly efficient. Its attacks forced thousands in northern Israel into bomb shelters for days on end and inside the occupied 'security zone', Hizbullah fighters were killing Israeli soldiers and destroying their tanks. Most Hizbullah fighters were local men who took Mao's advice to move among the people as fish swim in the sea — a sea that Israel tried and failed to drain.

Some Israeli units drove round the occupation zone in South Lebanon in battered Mercedes taxis that looked like Abed's. The roof racks were piled high with boxes disguised as luggage but which were in fact electronic countermeasures to stop Hizbullah detonating roadside bombs. When I travelled with them, the inside door panels had been stripped out and replaced with racks for assault rifles.

The Israelis formed their own militia, the South Lebanon Army, to do routine and often highly dangerous work in the occupation zone. Most of its fighters were local Christians and so many were killed that some people, disparagingly, called them Israel's sandbags. I crossed over the border from Israel to see how they fought. On the parade square at their headquarters in Marjayoun in South Lebanon, the SLA wore Israeli uniforms and sported the high red combat boots worn by Israel's elite soldiers. Families were allowed into Israel to work, which was good propaganda for Israel but not a good life for the men of the SLA. They were renegades who risked their lives fighting for an occupier.

By 1996, Israel and Hizbullah were deeply entangled in a war. The two sides measured success and failure differently. Lebanese of all sects saw Hizbullah as a legitimate resistance. Its metric of victory was never stopping the fight against the occupation, and inflicting steady pain on Israel by killing its soldiers and rocketing its border towns. From Israel's point of view, any attack was a defeat, because the 'security zone' it occupied in Lebanon was supposed to prevent them happening. I lived in Jerusalem in those years and sometimes visited the grieving families of soldiers who had been killed in Lebanon. They were proud of their dead sons, but more and more of them asked why they had to die for a strategy that was not working.

Generals and politicians choose the names of military offensives carefully. Israel's invasion of Lebanon in 1982 was called Operation Peace for Galilee. When in 1996 the Israelis wanted to change the equation in Lebanon to stop intolerable and politically damaging Hizbullah attacks, they chose a name that seethed with biblical fury:

Operation Grapes of Wrath. Israel had a new prime minister, Shimon Peres, who had taken over when Yitzhak Rabin was assassinated the previous year. Peres decided against a snap election, keen to show he was his own man. But he was facing a strong electoral challenge from Benjamin Netanyahu, the young leader of the right-wing Likud opposition. Peres had always struggled with his military credentials in the eyes of Israel's electorate, especially in comparison with Rabin, a former general and a war hero since independence in 1948. Pictures of Peres always showed him in a suit. Rabin, a lifelong rival, was often portrayed in a dusty, sweaty uniform on some battlefield. Netanyahu had served as an officer in Sayeret Matkal, Israel's elite special forces unit; his older brother Yonatan was killed leading the same unit at the Entebbe raid to free hostages in 1976.

The image problem infuriated Peres, with some justification, as he had done more than most generals to build Israel's military power. In 1948 he was a twentysomething aide to Israel's first prime minister, David Ben-Gurion. Peres sourced weapons that helped Israel win independence from sympathetic governments in France and Czechoslovakia. By the late 1950s, Peres was the prime mover behind Israel's development of nuclear weapons. But when, later on, he stood for office, Israelis did not trust him with security the way that they trusted Rabin or many other generals who went into politics. It wasn't just the suits. It was also his love of political intrigue. When his manoeuvres went wrong, he looked like an opportunist. Peres could never make Israelis feel safe the way Rabin did.

As Israel mounted Operation Grapes of Wrath, Peres sported a leather bomber jacket, the kind Rabin might have worn, as he was filmed riding helicopters to inspect the troops. A new invasion of Lebanon would not have played well with Israeli voters, so the plan was to use artillery and air power to hit Hizbullah. The objective was to force a mass exodus of civilians from the south, putting so much pressure on the Lebanese government that it would disarm Hizbullah and the other Shia militia, Amal. The plan flouted the protection due to civilians under the laws of war. The Israeli government issued an ultimatum, which was replayed in Arabic on the radio station run by its Lebanese militia, the SLA:

> In light of the continued terrorist actions by Hizbullah, the Israeli Army will intensify its activities against the terrorists starting tomorrow, 14 April 1996. Following the warning broadcast by the Voice of the South to the inhabitants of forty-five villages, any presence in these villages will be considered a terrorist one, that is, the terrorists and all those with them will be hit. Any civilian who lags behind in the aforementioned villages and towns will do so on his own responsibility and will put his life in danger.

In just over a fortnight, Israel launched around 600 air strikes and fired 25,000 shells into Lebanon. Around 400,000 Lebanese civilians fled north, but many did not. Vehicles travelling north on the coastal highway were left alone. Anyone driving south could expect to come under fire.

Israel stationed a gunboat where the highway between Sidon and Tyre ran along a beach. The warship was easily visible. So were the flashes from its guns, and the burnt-out cars that it had already hit. Going further south meant running the gauntlet down the beach. We spent about half an hour on a headland watching before risking the kind of challenge that Abed Takkoush enjoyed, even though his Mercedes taxi had long lost all its zip. Our plan was to build up speed downhill from the headland, so the old Mercedes would be close to its maximum velocity as it came into the sights of the gunboat.

Inside the car, the screaming engine of the bouncing, shuddering Mercedes drowned out the noise of the gun. Abed's hands were gripping the steering wheel hard. I was thinking about a shell cutting through the sea breeze towards us. The time between the flash and the explosion was only a few seconds, but every time we drove south along that beach, it seemed longer. Hearing the shell explode on the road and not on us was always a big relief. Abed would yell abuse at the gunboat, give the crew the finger and crow with laughter. We laughed with him. It was a calculated risk. The alternative was turning back to Beirut without a story.

Lebanese civilians in the area that Israel was attacking did not have the same choices. The worst day was 18 April. An Israeli helicopter rocketed a house in Nabatiyeh in the early morning, killing nine civilians including a mother, her newborn baby and six other children under the age of thirteen. Men from the family were still digging through the rubble when I arrived there. But back in Beirut, when I was getting ready to tell their story, news came through of something so bad that the killing of a family in Nabatiyeh never made it to air.

It happened in Qana, a large, mostly Shia village, one of at least four that claimed to be the place where Jesus performed his first miracle, turning water into wine. Qana had a long-established base for UNIFIL, the UN peacekeeping force in Lebanon. Hundreds of civilians crowded into the base, a landmark well known to the Israelis, because they thought that being there would keep them safe. After Hizbullah opened fire from a spot close by, Israeli artillery started a barrage that hit the camp. The civilians did not have a chance. Afterwards, UNIFIL told me that their liaison officers were 'screaming' at the Israelis that they were killing civilians, but the shelling did not stop for twenty minutes. I rushed out of the Commodore Hotel in West Beirut to find Abed Takkoush, who was sitting in the sun with a cigarette after the rigours of a tough morning in Nabatiyeh. We raced south, past the Israeli gunboat into the zone Israel had declared to be a killing ground for terrorists.

Israel claimed the strike was not designed to kill civilians, but a legitimate response to an attack from Hizbullah. The UN disagreed, correctly, given the evidence that was emerging. Earlier that year, Israel's 'Lebanon Coordinator', a veteran diplomat called Uri Lubrani, had told me at the Defence Ministry in Tel Aviv that they knew every village and every house in South Lebanon. I never doubted that they knew exactly what they were doing.

A few hours after the massacre, I watched Fijian soldiers, big men who looked like a rugby team in uniform, delicately picking fragments of flesh and body parts out of the remains of the flimsy, fire-blackened building where the dead had been sheltering. A few miles away, Tyre Hospital was overflowing, the wards filled with wounded and the dead packed into the mortuary. Most of them were women and children. Men often stayed at the family property to protect it or to guard the tobacco crop. Perhaps some of the fathers or husbands were Hizbullah fighters; that was no reason to kill their families. 'Why?' a woman asked, in English, when she saw the camera, 'Why, why? Israel why?'

And she kept saying it. Tragedies were in every room. Across the hall, a man called Mohammed, who told me twenty-two members of his family were dead, looked after his wounded three-year-old nephew.

I asked an Irish UN officer what might have happened had Hizbullah killed 106 civilians in northern Israel. 'President Clinton would be at the funeral, we'd be in our shelters and the Israelis would be in Beirut,' he said grimly.

When Israel goes to war, two clocks start running. One counts the time needed by the military. The other is for the time left until the outside world demands a ceasefire, which Israeli diplomats work hard to slow down. The massacre at Qana made the diplomatic clock run at double speed towards a ceasefire.

Over all the years of its existence, Israel has insisted it respects the laws of war and takes pains to spare civilian lives. But Operation Grapes of Wrath, named after an avenging angel spilling blood, showed a deep-seated disregard for the lives of others. Back in Jerusalem a few weeks later, a local paper quoted an Israeli soldier who had been part of the attack saying 'A few "Arabushim" died, there's no harm in that.' Arabushim is a derogatory Hebrew term for Arab. In 2015 it emerged that the shelling came after an appeal for help from an Israeli special forces unit that was the target for the Hizbullah attack from close to the UNIFIL camp. The young officer who radioed for assistance was Naftali Bennett, who became Israel's prime minister in 2021.[2]

The dead were buried a few days later in a mass grave in the centre of Qana. At the funeral I met a young man called Hassan Balhas. He used a wheelchair; a few years earlier, a stray Israeli bullet had left him paralysed when he was laying a path with his father at their house. Thirty-five members of Hassan's extended family had been killed at the base, and he was wondering how he would get around as the cousins and friends who pushed his wheelchair were dead. Hassan observed the anguish, the noise and the dust of the funeral, and looked into the future. 'They will hate the government of Israel,' he said. 'They will hate those who are responsible for all these crimes as long as they remember their children.'

That morning, I walked in the rolling hills outside Qana. It was spring, the grass was still lush from the winter rain and regiments of wildflowers besieged every olive tree. The landscape was beautiful – perhaps made by God, certainly shaped by Lebanese farmers – and it was a perfect place to contemplate the way that war makes humans revert to their most base instincts. Winning means killing, and both sides did it. Israel killed more because it had so much firepower, but Hizbullah has spent years building up its arsenal of rockets to be ready to kill more Israelis in the next war.

After Grapes of Wrath, Shimon Peres lost the election, narrowly, to Benjamin Netanyahu. Israel's Palestinian citizens, around a fifth of the population, made the difference, refusing to vote for Peres after Qana. Once again the power of connection in the Middle East was at work. Events in Lebanon had a direct bearing on the peace process between Israel and the Palestinians. Netanyahu had sworn to reverse the Oslo accords; Peres, whose role in making the agreement won him the Nobel Peace Prize with Rabin and Arafat, would have tried to salvage the peace process that Rabin's Jewish assassin had set out to destroy. It is impossible to say whether he would have succeeded. But Peres lost his chance to make Oslo work because he needed to show he was a war leader as tough as Rabin, determined enough to take on Hizbullah, and he bungled the mini-war that followed.

In Beirut in 1996, a man in his thirties was watching. He became so skilful at playing the Middle East's game of connections that he was still alive and in his job more than a quarter of a century later. He was Hassan Nasrallah, the secretary general of Hizbullah – and in the years after Grapes of Wrath, Hizbullah developed into the strongest force in Lebanon. Nasrallah became the most powerful man in the country, widely admired across the Arab world for his success against Israel. But as his reach grew, for some Lebanese Nasrallah went from hero of the resistance to a baleful presence, one whose dark alliances with Iran and Syria exposed their country to terrible risks.

Nasrallah became Israel's most effective enemy; he knows that his enemies there would like to see him dead. Since the 1990s, Hizbullah has acquired sophisticated missiles from its patrons in Iran and Syria. Estimates of the size of the arsenal vary but most are well over 100,000. Hizbullah's success is not just about weapons. It became the most powerful group in Lebanon because it was also a political movement, a welfare network and a staunch ally of Iran and Syria.

Although Israel and many of its Western allies classify Hizbullah as a terrorist organization, it runs a clever media operation, offering journalists a polite welcome along with glasses of sweet tea. Foreign female journalists usually cover their hair in the Hizbullah press office. During the 2006 war with Israel the hijab-wearing female staff in the office used to embrace my producer, Maha Barada, a young woman with long hair, tight clothes and high PVC boots. The male cleric in charge smiled from a safe distance. They were all Shias, and all from Beirut.

Nasrallah rarely meets outsiders. His predecessor was killed by a missile fired from an Israeli helicopter. I've only managed to sit down with him once, not long after Grapes of Wrath, when he appeared more regularly in public. Arranging the meeting involved plenty of negotiation, long afternoons in stuffy waiting rooms drinking tea and sludgy Arabic coffee with as much sugar as I could find to try to stay awake.

Nasrallah's people told us to meet at the Hizbullah press office in Haret Hreik, a congested district of concrete blocks of flats in southern Beirut. Outside, a van was waiting, with flattened cardboard boxes taped over the inside of the windows and between the front and the back seats. Flashes of Beirut's streets came in through gaps in the cardboard blackout. The van stopped and started and the driver honked his horn, and I had the sense that we were weaving circles around the same area. Then it went dark as the van drove into an underground car park, where a similar blacked-out vehicle was waiting. Businesslike men with guns and beards made a thorough search of all our gear as it was moved between the vehicles. Another driver took us up the ramp for more circuits of the southern suburbs, until we went down into another underground car park. More armed men showed the way to a lift that led to a modest apartment, and we set up for the interview.

Hassan Nasrallah was somewhere upstairs in the building. Once the camera and lights were ready, he came in: a man about my age, slightly stout, wearing the robes of a Shia cleric and a black turban showing his status as a Sayyed, a descendant of the prophet Muhammad. He was polite and serious, and Israel was not referred to by name but as 'the Zionist entity'. He did not give much away, except his unshakeable determination to keep on fighting.

Nasrallah agreed to let me visit some of his men in South Lebanon. Another cardboard-lined Hizbullah van took us down there from Beirut. I could see why they were getting the measure of the Israelis. The men looked disciplined and well equipped. Instead of the rag-bag of battered Kalashnikovs that armed groups usually have, they were armed with the latest American assault rifles. They had telescopic sights, night vision equipment, uniforms that matched and proper boots. The right kit does not guarantee a successful insurgency, but it shows the organization and discipline that can be the difference between defeat and victory – or survival, which for insurgent fighters is never a defeat.

By 2000, Israel's prime minister was Ehud Barak, not only another retired general but the country's most decorated soldier. Benjamin Netanyahu, whom he had beaten in the 1999 elections, had served under Barak in Sayeret Matkal. Barak's military exploits included leading a special forces raid on the PLO headquarters in Beirut, as part of Israel's revenge for the murder of eleven of its athletes by Palestinian gunmen at the Munich Olympics. Barak was disguised as a woman as they approached the building to start the assault that killed at least twenty members of the PLO. His wife asked him why he was wearing blue eye makeup when he arrived home. As prime minister, Barak had no military points to prove, unlike Shimon Peres. He could see that occupying a 'security zone' in South Lebanon was making Israel less secure. He pulled out Israeli forces and gave the South Lebanon Army and their families asylum.

On the last day of the Israeli occupation, Abed Takkoush cracked jokes and ran through his repertoire of war stories as he drove me and Malek Kanaan, a Lebanese cameraman who worked for the BBC, down south. Abed was desperate to see the end of an occupation that had been a big part of his adult life. We had the radio on in the car, trying to follow what was happening. It looked as if Israeli troops were leaving through a single gate in the wire, like water draining out of a bath, ending a battle with Hizbullah that they could not win, though not the war. We drove through villages that had been off limits for eighteen years, where Hizbullah fighters were being greeted as liberators, with women throwing rice as if it was a wedding.

Then I made a big mistake. I stopped to record a piece to camera at a spot overlooking Israel, not realizing that an Israeli battle tank on the other side of the border wire had us in its sights. When we stopped, Abed stayed in the car to finish a phone call to his son. Malek got out, took the camera gear and walked about a hundred yards away down the hill to film. A big explosion made me spin round and for a split second I couldn't work out where the flames were coming from — then I saw that Abed's Mercedes taxi was on fire. I shouted to Malek that Abed must be dead. The shell had hit the back of the car and he had been in the driver's seat. Then, through the flames and smoke, Abed, with his clothes on fire, was forcing himself out of the driver's window. He fell down onto the road, out of sight. I said to Malek, let's get up there to help him. Malek's face was contorted. 'No, don't do it. Abed is dead. He can't have survived that. And if you go up there, they'll kill you too.'

I couldn't see Abed's body. I tried shouting, but there was no answer. He was dead. Forcing his way through the window was the last thing he could have done. The blast from a tank shell exploding so close to him would have burst his internal organs. I felt terrible hiding behind a building. Abed had never left me in a war zone, and I didn't want to leave him. So, cautiously, I moved a few yards into the open, towards the burning car. As Malek had predicted, the tank crew opened fire. Bullets fizzed over my head and I ducked back into cover.

I had not killed my friend. The Israelis did that. But I decided to stop, and if I hadn't, Abed Takkoush, a fifty-three-year-old man with a wife and three teenage boys, might still be alive. Or perhaps they would have killed all three of us. Not far from the tank, Israeli civilians formed a bizarre tableau of deckchairs and picnics to watch the war. My friend Sam Kiley, the correspondent for *The Times*, was near the Israeli spectators and his driver was listening to the tank's radio traffic. He heard an Israeli soldier saying, 'We've killed one of them, we'll get the other two with the heavy machine gun,' which is what they tried to do. Later, I went to see a general in the Defence Ministry in Tel Aviv. He asked for some understanding.

'Look', he said. 'There were young boys in that tank and they'd been warned they might be attacked by terrorists. They were scared.'

I wasn't sympathetic. They were in a tank and we were civilians, non-combatants. I think they opened fire not because we were foreign journalists but because they thought we were Lebanese, and our lives did not, for them, matter much. Conflicts in the Middle East have deep roots. Fighters in every war, on every side, regard their enemies as something less than living, breathing humans who can feel love and fear and happiness. That way, it's much easier to kill them.

22.

Retreat to the Mountains

Text messages from beyond the grave are hard to receive, to read and hardest to delete, a window into the last few hours of a life. Ferhat Balcal was a young man of nineteen, so when he was killed his life had barely started. He was a Kurd in the town of Cizre in south-eastern Turkey, caught in a war with the Turkish state and trapped in a basement surrounded by its security forces. Shelling and street fighting had smashed the district where he lived, as Turkish soldiers and paramilitary police fought their way through barricades and defences built by militant separatists from the Kurdistan Workers' Party, the PKK. It was 'apocalyptic . . . a picture of the wholesale destruction of neighbourhoods', witnesses told United Nations investigators.[1] Ferhat was one of almost 200 people who were trapped for weeks in basements without access to water or food or doctors to treat their wounds.

The basements were on Bostanci Street – more of a memory than a street, because it was a flattened ruin. People who knew Bostanci stood in the wasteland that was left and told me the street was not rich and its residents' lives were not easy, but mostly they were safe. All of that changed in the summer of 2015.

I sat with Ferhat's parents in the courtyard of a house they rented after their own home was destroyed. His father Mehmet read out his last messages, while his mother Murside clutched two portraits of their dead boy as if her arms could bring him back and sobbed with the grief that knows they cannot. Ferhat's desperation radiates out from all the messages, but so does the energy and optimism of a nineteen-year-old boy who was young enough to believe his parents would find a way to save him. Ferhat wanted them to organize a demonstration, to confront the armed men with people power and a message that they were civilians who should be allowed to live. *Come to the municipality*, he texted. *Wave a flag or we'll dieee :(((.*

His parents did their best, but Murside was arrested, Ferhat was not rescued, and the texts stopped arriving. He was killed, along with between 130 and 180 others. When an assault started, a group of Kurdish politicians were on the phone to someone else in the basement, promising to get help. The call was recorded; you can hear screams and fire from automatic weapons, and then the line cuts out.

The Turkish security forces sealed off 100,000 people in Cizre for seventy-eight days, from mid-December 2015 to early March 2016. They levelled the ruins with bulldozers, pushing rubble to cover up the basements where Ferhat and the others were killed. It was some of the worst fighting since the PKK started its insurgency in the early 1980s, with hundreds of people killed on both sides, though the UN decided the casualty data was not reliable and the basements were never treated as crime scenes.[2] The Turkish government seemed more interested in a cover-up than working out what had happened. When families dug into the burnt-out basements, they found cinders and a few pieces of bone. One man was summoned to the public prosecutor's office to receive the remains of his dead sister. He was given three small pieces of charred flesh.

Firat Duymark, an eighteen-year-old, took me to the basement where his father Mahmud was killed. It was marked by a pile of rubble in the bulldozed flatland of concrete fragments. Firat said his father had been a civilian helping civilians, not a PKK man. 'They are the terrorists; the ones who commit all these atrocities. Even if those people were from the PKK, why does the state have to destroy and burn their lives? Even war has rules. Can you rip the people up when you catch them? You have courts; you have a justice system. In Turkey, we have nothing.'

Back at the family home, Firat's mother, Lutfiye, sat with the youngest of her five children, a boy of three. She was contemptuous about the way soldiers had desecrated people's homes. 'When they come back home, the residents opened their blankets and saw they are all full of shit. How does a person who does that claim to be a human being? My kids will grow up with a grudge. Do you think you can finish Kurds? You cannot.'

In Kurdish villages and towns of south-eastern Turkey – places like Cizre – the PKK is often seen as a protector. Turkey, the European Union and the US, as well as some Kurds, condemn them as terrorists. The laws of war demand that only force proportionate to the threat must be used. Back in Ankara, Ilnur Cevik, chief advisor to President Recep Tayyip Erdoğan and a man with the air of a university professor, told me that the government would never kill its own citizens. Any deaths, he insisted, were caused by the PKK using them as human shields. I could not find many Kurds who agreed with him.[3]

Kurds make up around 18 per cent of Turkey's population; in Cizre, a scruffy town on the border with Iraq, they are the majority. The fighting in 2015 was not the first time it had been in the arc lights of a Middle East crisis. After the 1991 Gulf War, oil smuggled out of the chaos of Iraq came through Cizre. Cheap oil was so popular that the smugglers ran out of tankers. They welded extra tanks onto every flat surface of ordinary lorries, even the underside of trailers that barely cleared the ground when they were fully loaded. On the Iraqi side, a queue well over a mile long of filthy, dripping vehicles waited to cross into Turkey. Cizre was sodden with pools of black, sticky sludge.

A quarter of a century later, in a downpour outside a camp for Turkish Kurds displaced by the fighting, I couldn't work out whether I was hearing thunder or shelling. At least the Turkish state had improved the roads; in 1991, my car had skidded gracefully towards a watery grave in the deep gorge of a raging river before, white-faced, the driver regained control.

Time passes, but heartbreak never goes away; sometimes politics change, but not when it comes to the Turkish state and the Kurds. In Ankara, immaculate, imposing soldiers continued to mount a ceremonial guard at the mighty mausoleum built around the tomb of Mustapha Kemal Ataturk. He was the founder of modern Turkey, given the honorific Ataturk, meaning father of the Turks, by a grateful nation. Ataturk bequeathed his people a powerful state with an unresolved weakness. It was the future of a large Kurdish minority, whose leaders wanted political and cultural freedoms that ranged from using their own language to a state of their own.

As the war with the PKK was restarting in 2015, I noticed some middle-aged men paying their respects at the mausoleum. They were all wearing the blue berets of elite Turkish military units, and retained a touch of parade-ground pride in spite of their thickening bellies. The berets sent my mind racing back to the mountains between Turkey and Iraq after the end of the war against Saddam Hussein, and elite commandos with faces burnt by the winter sun. These men at the mausoleum were the right age to have lined up to stop Kurdish refugees crossing the border from Iraq.

Ataturk believed Turkey's future was in secular Europe, not the religious Middle East. He abolished the title of Caliph, which Ottoman sultans had claimed for 400 years, and replaced the Arabic alphabet with the Roman one. He had no time for Islamic law; all religions, he said, should be at the bottom of the sea. Always immaculately tailored himself, he believed modern people wore Western clothing – he even passed the Hat Law, which banned turbans and the fez, a hat made without a brim so men could touch their forehead to the floor in prayer while wearing it. Women were still allowed to wear headscarves as long as they took them off in state institutions, which included schools and universities.

Religion, Ataturk insisted, was for the home, not the state. After he died in 1938, as well as guarding his tomb, the army considered it a national duty to safeguard his secular legacy. Turkish politics were turbulent and often violent, but no leader tried to match him until, at the start of the twenty-first century, a man emerged who wanted to remake the country that Ataturk had created. He was Recep Tayyip Erdoğan, who has dominated Turkey ever since: first by forming an Islamist party that shares DNA with the Muslim Brotherhood, then as prime minister, and as president since 2014. Erdoğan's campaign song in one of his election victories says he is the 'feared nightmare of the oppressor' and 'the light of hope of millions'. Ataturk's supporters used to say similar things about him. The video that goes with the song shows Erdoğan waving to a vast audience in a sea of red Turkish flags. Ataturk too addressed huge rallies. But that is where the similarities end. A few steps behind Erdoğan is his wife, wearing an Islamic headscarf.

Erdoğan is an Islamist, and he allows women to wear headscarves whenever they want. His message to pious, conservative voters was that Islam should be part of the state. He is not a religious extremist, more a populist who won the votes of Turks who resented the power of the secular elite. He delivered on religion, made his followers feel better off, and won more elections. In 2017, Erdoğan had a narrow victory in a referendum to change the constitution to make him executive president. His critics said it was a giant step towards dictatorship.

Erdoğan's brand of politics split Turkey down the middle. Secular, urban, educated people felt as if they were the losers in Erdoğan's Turkey. He does not like protests, but there have been big ones. In 2013, a plan to build on Gezi Park – one of the few green spaces left in central Istanbul – led to violent clashes between police and demonstrators. For the young protestors who occupied the park for days, it wasn't just about saving grass and trees; they wanted freedom. When I pointed out to them that they had the vote, a typical answer was, 'This isn't democracy. This is fascism.'

Erdoğan wasn't just prepared to fight culture wars. In the 1990s, Turkey's foreign policy was based on its NATO membership and its desire to get into the European Union. Turkey is still in NATO, though it has done arms deals with Russia that the Americans resented. As for Europe, it was clear that however much Turks wanted the EU, important member states did not want Turkey. Erdoğan moved Turkey back into the Middle East that Ataturk had rejected, facing east as well as west to open up new markets and new influence. Then the Arab uprisings changed everything and Turkey intervened in the Syrian civil war, backing militias that fought the regime of Bashar al-Assad.

And this is where Turkey's long saga with the Kurds comes back into focus. Contagion from the Syrian war leaked into Turkey through a border almost 1,000 porous kilometres long. It came in the form of a big opportunity for Syrian Kurds. In 2012, Assad's forces pulled out of the north as they struggled to hold the centre of the country. The Kurds filled the vacuum with their Peoples' Protection Units, known as the YPG. That rang all Erdoğan's alarm bells. The Syrian Kurds drew their strength from a deep political and military relationship with the PKK, the group that had been fighting the Turkish state for forty years.

Erdoğan's anger deepened when the Syrian Kurds joined forces with the Americans to fight the jihadists of Islamic State. The US provided air cover and artillery, and armed and trained Kurdish-led militias who did most of the ground fighting and dying. Erdoğan could not tolerate the prospect of weapons and expertise given to Syrian Kurds by the Americans getting to the PKK, to use against his forces. By the summer of 2015 a peace process with the PKK, which seemed to be working, was dead, as Erdoğan moved on two fronts: deeper into Syria, to force the Kurds back from the border, and inside Turkey against the PKK, which was why the centre of Cizre was flattened.

Many Turks supported Erdoğan's strategy. About the time that the military was wrapping up its Cizre operation, a suicide bomber from a group allied to the PKK killed thirty-seven people in Ankara. I sat in a park in the city with a woman called Pinar Saglam, whose brother Kirim had been killed by the bomber. A man with a portable tin samovar served glasses of sweet tea, but Pinar's hands shook too much at first to hold hers. Instead, she lit another cigarette, and the ash dropped onto a photo she had of a huge poster on the side of a building in a Syrian Kurdish town. It showed the leader of the PKK, Abdullah Ocalan, who is held on a Turkish prison island, next to the woman who had killed her brother and so many others. Pinar was incredulous at the way the bomber was being glorified: 'Like a leader, like an angel. I mean, when I saw this picture I can't believe my eyes . . . She was a murderer, the murderer of my brother. Now her picture is displayed on the streets of Syria.'

Pinar insisted that she wanted peace, not revenge. Plenty of other Kurds and Turks felt the same way, but the tension, repression and killing were about much more than unbearable personal tragedies. Unfinished business from the break-up of the Ottoman Empire is still playing out. Kurds were left without their own state. They argue that their chances of freedom and independence were sacrificed by Britain and France more than a century ago, as they carved up the Ottoman Empire to win a world war and strengthen their imperial power.

In the early 1990s, the best hotel in Diyarbakir, the biggest Kurdish city in south-eastern Turkey, was the Caravanserai, built to serve travellers and their caravans powered by horses and camels on the Silk Road between Europe and China. I had to bend double to get through the tiny doorway of my room, which came off a big open courtyard. Inside, the ceilings were twenty feet high. The restaurant was a frontier saloon: men with guns stuck in their waistbands clapped belly-dancers in an atmosphere heavy with three Turkish staples: pungent tobacco, thick coffee and raki, their version of the spirit distilled from toasted aniseed that is ubiquitous in the Middle East.

Outside, the proudly Kurdish city of Diyarbakir was part of an intricate political and historical story. Kurds are spread across Turkey, Iraq, Syria and Iran, around thirty million people, the biggest ethnic group in the Middle East without a state of their own. Kurdish separatists have demanded independence for more than a century. Like other stateless peoples, they make waves without being strong enough to sweep away the barriers to independence.

The reasons begin with the map. Establishing a Kurdish state would require four countries to give up big chunks of strategically important land, some of it rich with oil. Another barrier comes from within: Kurds are chronically disunited. Together they would be stronger, but rivalries run so deep that they have at times gone to war with each other. The third barrier is that Kurds have to rely on bigger allies. Kurds die in other people's wars, sometimes because they are squashed by them and sometimes because they have joined in to make alliances and seize opportunities. That does not work when they pick the wrong side, get greedy or overconfident, or assume that powerful states they help will return the favour by supporting their independence. World powers have used the Kurds as pawns in bigger games, disposable allies to be discarded when they are no longer useful.

Iran, Iraq, Syria and Turkey have fought their own wars. Something they can all agree on is that Kurdish independence is an unacceptable threat. The last century is studded with attempts by Kurds to get independence that ended badly. For most of 1946, the USSR occupied a slice of Iran. Stalin kept the Kurds happy by allowing them to create a statelet they called the Republic of Mahabad. It collapsed when the Red Army pulled out of Iran and Stalin had no further need for the Kurds. When the shah's men came back, Mahabad's leader, Qazi Muhammad, was hanged for treason.

Iranian Kurds tried again in 1979 when the shah was overthrown, but the Revolutionary Guards crushed the uprising, killing about ten thousand.[4] All that is left of Mahabad is the flag, a red, white and green tricolour with a many-rayed sun. It is used by the Kurdish region of Iraq, which is run by Masoud Barzani, a regional president who is treated more like a king by his supporters.

While Saddam Hussein was president of Iraq, I used to see Masoud with his men in the Iraqi mountains, cutting a fine figure in the uniform of a Kurdish fighter, a *peshmerga*, 'one who faces death'. Barzani would usually wear a turban made from a red and white checked keffiyeh scarf, a combat jacket, and baggy traditional trousers held up with a cartridge belt or knotted cummerbund. The British government invited him to London. I bumped into him as he sat with his advisors, all buttoned uncomfortably into Western business suits, waiting to see a junior Foreign Office minister on a pair of sofas next to a sweeping staircase. An extravagantly wrapped gift for the minister was on the table in front of them, dripping with bows and ribbons. Barzani was a mighty figure on his home soil. Inside the Foreign Office, surrounded by statues and portraits glorifying Britain's imperial past, he couldn't even get a meeting with the foreign secretary. It felt as if the Kurds were being reminded of their place in the world.

Saddam Hussein saw the Kurds as a serious threat to his regime. The Barzanis and their Kurdish Democratic Party supported the Iranians against him in the 1980s. Saddam's response was a series of savage reprisals: eight thousand men and boys were taken from the Barzani clan and killed. Reprisals turned into genocidal attacks in 1987 after Saddam appointed his cousin, General Ali Hasan al-Majid, as governor of the north. He was nicknamed 'Chemical Ali' because of the weapons he used to kill thousands of Kurds. The greatest of his many crimes was Operation Anfal, a series of genocidal offensives that killed at least 100,000 Kurdish civilians. Around five thousand were killed in March 1988 with chemical weapons in a single town, Halabja, near the Iranian border. News teams were able to get in from Iran to film corpses lying where they had choked to death, mothers dead in the street still clinging to the corpses of their children. In Halabja three years after the attack, a blind tailor who worked by feel told me about the day the regime's mustard gas destroyed his sight. Through the windows of his workshop, I could hear children who had survived screeching with laughter as they slid down the collapsed concrete roofs of houses that had never been repaired, as their owners were dead.

Halabja was the most notorious single attack because it killed so many. But by then 'Chemical Ali' had been ordering his men to use mustard gas against the Kurds for a year, as well as the nerve agents VX and Sarin. Villages were cleared and men and boys were taken away and killed. I visited a Kurdish village that in 1991 had no males over the age of twelve. A young woman, a teacher, presided over the children in the local school: girls and a few small boys whose big brothers, fathers and uncles were all dead.

Ali Hasan al-Majid eventually went to the gallows, like his cousin Saddam. At his trial for war crimes, he was unapologetic, even proud of what he had done, claiming he was rooting out Iranian agents. 'I am not apologizing. I did not make a mistake . . . Yes, I gave my instructions to consider these villages as prohibited areas and I gave orders to the troops to catch anyone they found there and execute them after investigating them.'[5]

Operation Anfal and genocide were still on the minds of everyone I met in the early 1990s in the Kurdish regions of northern Iraq. Many people's anger went back to the British, to the promises made and broken as they carved up the Ottoman Empire. Kurds had a detailed knowledge of a treaty that most of the world had forgotten, signed at Sèvres in France by the victorious allies and the beaten Ottoman Empire in August 1920. Kurds remember Sèvres because they believe it was their lost opportunity for self-determination, to get their own state, like the Czechs and the Poles and the other peoples who emerged from fallen empires with their own states. It would have ended differently, they said, had they been European and Christian.

It was no consolation to point out that the British specialized in breaking promises in the Middle East during and after the First World War. The pin-striped and frock-coated diplomats and politicians who stuck pins in maps and drew frontiers with crayons were building careers and their nations' empires. They were not there to help the Kurds. Britain dangled the prospect of Kurdish self-determination, but only to strengthen its imperial position. The Kurds were led by tribal elders, who were better at accepting sweeteners from Britain than they were at agreeing with each other. Loyalty to their own clans mattered much more to them than national unity, which made Britain's familiar tactic of divide and rule much easier.

The Ottomans, in their final decline, had no say in the matter. The dying empire's leaders were effectively prisoners of the British, French and Italians who were occupying Istanbul when they agreed at Sèvres to 'a scheme of local autonomy for the predominantly Kurdish areas'; independence would follow if the new League of Nations agreed. The treaty was never worth the ink dispensed from its signatories' expensive fountain pens. It was rejected by the new force in the land, Mustafa Kemal's Turkish National Movement. Kemal was the handsome and charismatic architect of the defeat of the British and ANZAC forces at Gallipoli, who was fighting to drive off hungry imperialists and create a modern Turkish state. He won a bloody war and packed the last Otttoman sultan off into exile on a British warship.

A world that defines itself through borders will always be a hard place for the stateless to navigate. It happened again after 2011, as the Middle East entered a period of violent upheaval that was still going strong a decade later. The hurricane caught up with the Kurds as Islamic State jihadists rampaged through Iraq and Syria. For a while, the Kurdish strategy of riding the storm seemed to be working. They had to fight, and for a while they looked like winners, with the prize as ever the prospect of independence. But in the end, old weaknesses and misfortunes surfaced. Bigger powers used and abandoned them while their leaders became greedy, overreaching and made mistakes.

After hard days and nights in Mosul during the battle for the city in 2017, I drove back to Erbil, the capital of Iraqi Kurdistan. Signs that independence was on the agenda were obvious, starting with the big Kurdish checkpoint on the edge of their territory that felt like an international border. Less obvious was a series of poison pills that had been planted by the old Middle Eastern diseases of corruption and the failure of governance.

I walked up the hill to the six-thousand-year-old citadel that dominates the city. At first sight, Erbil had the economic energy that Baghdad, Basra and the rest of Iraq had not seen for decades, along with much more freedom. Young men and women sat in the sun, taking selfies and chatting each other up, as they might do in well-off parts of Beirut or Istanbul. One of the women said she did not have to wear a headscarf or dress modestly because she was not religious and, unlike the Arabs in Baghdad, they were free – or anyway 90 per cent free, because a few people still had the old prejudices. A tall young man next to her disagreed, arguing that the property boom was powered by oil money controlled by the big families, and dirty money being washed. 'They're taking all the money this country is making and investing it for themselves to make more money,' he said. 'They are definitely corrupt. One hundred per cent corrupt.'

Independence, he said, would be a disaster, because of corruption and incompetence at the top. I asked what he had learnt at school about the 1991 crisis, when Iraqi Kurds died in the mountains in their thousands.

'The people run away,' he said. 'Everyone was dying, no one was surviving . . . Kurds would never surrender.' But now corruption was killing them instead, from inside, like cancer. 'The Middle East will never change . . . Islamic religion is not what makes this country corrupt – it tries to make it great. But then it's the people who are corrupt. I'm realistic . . . Our country is just looking for money.'

Kurds remember their history. They knew that American support for their independence was not guaranteed. But they believed they had built up enough moral and strategic credit to make it happen. It was another mistake. In September 2017, Masoud Barzani, the president of Iraqi Kurdistan, went ahead with a referendum on independence against the wishes of his Turkish and American allies. The proposition passed by a landslide, which only hardened opposition. Barzani's allies stood aside as the Iraqi government, with the cooperation of Iran and a rival Kurdish faction, sent in troops to recapture the ground Barzani's Kurds had taken when they fought ISIS in 2014, starting with the oil fields around Kirkuk. Barzani's side ignored the inconvenient truth that the Americans had invested the lives of soldiers and billions of dollars to keep Iraq together. The US believed that altering borders would make the Middle East even more dangerous, brittle and unstable and it issued public warnings against the referendum. When the Barzani family brought on disaster by pressing on with it, they watched and let it happen.

In Syria, it was the same old story for the Kurds. They were going to fight Islamic State whatever happened, because the jihadists were bent on killing them as heretics. If ground forces led by Kurds had not been prepared to fight and die to break the resistance of Islamic State fighters in northern Syria, the Americans would have had to use their own troops. Heavy US casualties would have changed the political calculus in Washington beyond recognition. The Kurds were useful allies for the Americans until the battle was won, and then they weren't.

23.

The Last Dance

In a big room overlooking the great gate into the old city of Sanaa, the capital of Yemen, dozens of men were sprawling on long cushions indulging in the national pastime: chewing qat. The room was crowded, and there were no women. It was the Yemeni equivalent of going to the pub. Qat is a mildly narcotic, stimulating leaf. The volume in the room rose the more they chewed. Murmurs turned into laughter and shouts. I decided to try some. It looked like privet, the favourite hedge of the British suburbs, and tasted just as bad. Discreetly, I removed a gobstopper of partly chewed leaves from my mouth. The BBC had a driver and a fixer whose cheeks bulged with qat as the day wore on. When the car narrowly missed a collision, the two men would cackle with pleasure.

Walking through Sanaa's old city feels like stepping back a couple of centuries. Inside a darkened workshop, a blindfolded camel was tethered to a beam, condemned to walk in endless circles to power millstones that were grinding sesame. The skyline is a stately geometric parade of elaborately decorated ochre buildings made a thousand years ago of the rammed earth known as pisé. The UN counted 103 mosques, fourteen hammams and over six thousand houses built before the eleventh century.[1] From around eleven in the morning, the qat rush starts. Men in robes with curved daggers stuck under broad tribal belts and women in black abayas and veils bustle around with bundles of qat under their arms. Rich families have rooms set aside for a qat chew, which is where the real business gets done. Before Sanaa became too dangerous for Western embassies, an American diplomat complained that he was losing out on information because he was not allowed to go to chews; the US classified qat as a drug. He told me he relied on his colleagues from Britain, where qat was not yet illegal, for secrets spilled over a pile of privet.

Yemen was already in desperate trouble as it slid downhill through the first decade of the twenty-first century. The economy was collapsing. Yemen's only real export industry was oil, but the wells were almost exhausted. Hunger was endemic, and in 2010 Sanaa was close to being the first capital city to run out of water. The mains were dry, so water was delivered in tankers and was expensive. Qat farms used water that humans might have drunk; growers would irrigate the thirsty green plantations by illegally drilling into aquifers.

The leaf of choice for the British is tea, infused rather than chewed. Most of the customers at the long and elegant Promenade tea salon in the Dorchester Hotel on Park Lane in London are, in fact, from the Middle East. I sat at the Dorchester over a tray of tea and biscuits with Prince Mohammed bin Nawwaf bin Abdul Aziz, a nephew of King Abdullah and the Saudi ambassador to the United Kingdom. It was March 2015, and Saudi Arabia had just started bombing Yemen. The reason given in official statements was to reinstall the internationally recognized government that had just been forced to flee to Saudi Arabia by Ansar Allah, the supporters of God; they are better known as the Houthis, a clan and religious movement with a long history of rebellion. US Marine guards at their embassy had left in such a hurry that they destroyed their weapons with sledgehammers rather than leave them behind for the Houthis.[2]

Prince Mohammed did not say much about restoring the government. The operation, he told me, was really about Iran, and stopping its dangerous mission to dominate the Middle East. Saudi Arabia was convinced that the Iranians were behind the Houthi offensive. Prince Mohammed took calm sips from his tea, ignoring the biscuits, but he was angry. The Iranians, he told me, were treating them like fools, trying to turn Yemen into a forward base like Lebanon and Syria. Saudi Arabia would put a stop to it once and for all.

The war turned into a catastrophe for Yemen as its northern neighbour led a coalition that escalated the conflict and created the worst humanitarian crisis in the world.[3] Saudi Arabia also imposed a blockade that made humanitarian aid hard to deliver, while armed groups inside Yemen blocked shipments. The killing and destruction broke a country that was already fragile. By 2021, according to the United Nations, nearly twenty million people in Yemen suffered from hunger and malnutrition, and the world's biggest outbreak of cholera was gripping the country even before it was hit by the Covid-19 pandemic. The economy was destroyed and two million people lost their homes.

A few weeks after tea at the Dorchester with the ambassador, I was in the deep south of Saudi Arabia watching Yemen being pounded. To get to the Saudi artillery we drove up steep, narrow roads into the cool, misty mountains that rolled away in peaks and rocky spines into Yemen. The flower men of Jizan had set up observation posts on the side of the mountain road. They were Qahtani tribesmen, warlike men with an unwarlike nickname because they wore elaborate crowns made of woven wildflowers, herbs and grasses, jasmine, marigold, fenugreek and basil. An old man with a crown of muted blooms, a beard dyed ginger and a curved dagger at his waist carried an ancient carbine with a worn wooden stock. Younger men had brighter, brasher flowers in their crowns and carried Kalashnikovs. A few of them wore white Saudi ankle-length thobes, but mostly they had striped or checked izaars wrapped around their waists. Other customs that spanned the border included a liking for qat.

Saudi officers paused the bombardment to entertain us at their mess with a lunch of whole roast sheep arranged on cliffs of rice. The Saudis were expecting an easy victory, as they had the best weapons that a vast defence budget could buy. The talk in the mess was of the new Saudi minister of defence, Prince Mohammed bin Salman, a young son of the new king, the octogenarian Salman bin Abdulaziz Al Saud. The officers did not know much about the young prince, who people had started calling 'MBS'. He was dynamic, determined, inexperienced, and they agreed that he was driving the offensive in Yemen.

For years, the Saudis had spent billions on their armed forces but never trusted themselves to operate on their own. When it really mattered, they would turn to the alliance with the Americans. It began with a meeting on the USS *Quincy* on the Great Bitter Lake in the Suez Canal on Valentine's Day 1945 between President Franklin D. Roosevelt and King Abdulaziz Ibn Saud, the founder of Saudi Arabia. The bargain was cheap oil in return for security. It kicked in when the Iraqis seized Kuwait in 1990 and the Saudis feared that they could be next; King Fahd grabbed the offer of military intervention by the United States and its Western allies.

Going it alone in Yemen was hard evidence that Saudi Arabia was changing. The new King Salman was the twenty-fifth son of Abdulaziz, a direct link to the time when the House of Saud conquered territory with camels. But MBS was born in 1985, a different age. The Saudi royal family was shaken by the popular anger of 2011's Arab uprisings. The king's decision to make MBS his leading advisor, skipping a generation, was an admission that Saudi Arabia's leadership needed new blood, and reform.[4]

Before MBS could get to grips with the frustrations of an overwhelmingly youthful population, he had to respond to the Houthi takeover of Sanaa. The Saudis concluded they were going to have to look after themselves; their faith in the Americans had taken severe knocks. President Barack Obama had abruptly, even casually, dumped Egypt's president, Hosni Mubarak, after a few weeks of demonstrations in Cairo. Mubarak was considered America's closest Arab friend in the Middle East. If President Obama could do that to a Sunni ally of thirty years' standing, he might do the same thing to the House of Saud.

The Saudis were already alarmed by the way that America's response to the 9/11 attacks had empowered their old rival Iran. America had removed two of its enemies, the Taliban in Afghanistan and Saddam Hussein in Iraq. Taking out the Taliban was expected and on its own might have been understandable, but Saddam's connection with 9/11 was non-existent; he was simply in the sights of the White House because President George H. W. Bush had not finished the job in 1991. The Saudis had no particular love for Saddam, but he had provided a Sunni bulwark against Iran during the long and bloody war in the 1980s. To make matters worse, the US imposed a political system on Iraq that delivered a government dominated by Shia leaders, friends of Iran. From the Saudi point of view, the Americans were lashing out, settling scores and in the process saddling them with a serious strategic challenge. It was not, they concluded, the action of a reliable friend.

By early 2015, Saudi suspicion turned to alarm as Iran signed a deal with the world's most powerful countries about its nuclear programme. The agreement was known officially as the Joint Comprehensive Plan of Action, the JCPOA. It was a remarkable achievement, agreed by Iran, the US and the four other permanent members of the UN Security Council, plus Germany and the European Union. The Saudis, like Israel, did not like the deal or the sight of the foreign minister of Iran, Javad Zarif, hobnobbing with John Kerry, the US secretary of state, at the signing ceremony in Vienna. Critics of the deal argued that it postponed an Iranian nuclear bomb when it should have been prohibiting one. In plants blasted deep into mountains, they said, Iran was enriching uranium to create a nuclear arsenal. Iran's claims that the stockpile was for civilian purposes were excuses and lies.

Obama insisted that he would never allow Iran to possess a nuclear weapon, a bottom line that was an essential backstop to the deal. At the heart of the JCPOA was an exchange: if Iran accepted limits on its enrichment programme, sanctions would be lifted. It became a cornerstone of Obama's foreign policy. He believed that it stopped the Islamic Republic going nuclear and halted a slide towards war. All the conversations I had in Israel suggested the Israeli prime minister, Benjamin Netanyahu, was flirting with the idea of a military strike; if that happened, the US would undoubtedly get dragged into the crisis. Obama was right about the risks. One advisor working for the Israeli government after years in Mossad told me that a war with Iran was inevitable, so she was telling her boss that it was better fought sooner rather than later.

A cache of secret US diplomatic cables released by the whistleblowing website WikiLeaks revealed the Saudis' suspicion of Iran. King Abdullah, Salman's predecessor, told the Americans 'to cut off the head of the snake', according to a cable in April 2008 after a meeting in which the Saudi ambassador to the United States, Adel al-Jubeir, 'recalled the king's frequent exhortations to the US to attack Iran and so put an end to its nuclear weapons programme'.[5] In a meeting with General David Petraeus, the top US military commander in the Middle East, in November 2009, the king of Bahrain, Hamad bin Isa al-Khalifa, a close ally of Saudi Arabia, argued 'forcefully for taking action to terminate [Iran's] nuclear program, by whatever means necessary'.

With Iran on their minds, Prince Mohammed bin Salman and his father took Saudi Arabia and its state-of-the-art air force to war in Yemen. Militarily, the war was a fiasco for Saudi Arabia. MBS put together a coalition of nine Sunni countries, of which the most militarily significant was the United Arab Emirates, and called the operation 'Decisive Storm'. It caused a storm of destruction and killing in Yemen, but it was not decisive. The Houthis were not easy to scare or deter, and the Saudis came nowhere close to beating them.

Some homework might have punctured MBS's arrogant assumption that it would be an easy war. Yemen's tribes were heavily armed, with a history of fighting invaders. Britain seized the huge natural harbour of Aden in the south of the country in 1839. It became a vital staging post on the sea route to India, especially after the Suez Canal was opened at the other end of the Red Sea. The British were often attacked during their time in Aden. By the 1960s, as they struggled to retain a world role, they were fighting a losing battle against an insurgency. Brutal reprisals against insurgents also killed civilians and deepened the determination of Yemenis to send them packing. Britain was forced out by the end of 1967, with its last troops leaving under the protection of a naval taskforce led by aircraft carriers.

As Britain tried to hang on in the south in the 1960s, Egypt intervened, disastrously, in a civil war in North Yemen. It became Egypt's Vietnam, with 70,000 troops in the field at its peak and 10,000 dead. The loss of trained soldiers and materiel was so serious that it contributed to the Egyptian army's heavy defeat in the 1967 war with Israel.

From the 1970s until his violent death in 2017, one man, Ali Abdullah Saleh, dominated Yemen. In many ways the model Arab dictator, Saleh was never likely to die in his bed. He was an army officer who became president of North Yemen in 1978 after his two predecessors were assassinated within months of each other. Saleh, then in his mid-thirties, established himself as the man who could impose stability; his most famous saying about governing Yemen was that it was like 'dancing on the heads of snakes'. Saleh unified North and South Yemen and in 1990 became president of a country that never felt united. He was a master of intrigue, playing off tribal leaders and outside powers, and hanging onto the presidency and control of the money at all costs.

By the time I met Saleh, in Sanaa in 2009, he was balding, wearing a business suit that looked too big, a shrivelled man in his early sixties who looked older. Still, age had not mellowed him; more than any other Arab leader, except perhaps Hafez al-Assad of Syria, he had perfected the arts of political manipulation and ruthless betrayal. He brushed aside accusations of massive corruption; a UN report in 2015 said he had raked off between thirty and sixty-two billion dollars, mostly from oil and gas contracts that he had stashed in a financial empire that spread across the world.[6]

Saleh leapt aboard America's response to 9/11, which was having as big an impact at the bottom of the Arabian Peninsula as it had across the rest of the Middle East. A Saudi offensive against al-Qaeda forced the jihadists to move south to regroup in the remote mountains and deserts of Yemen, where the involvement of the central government had never been more than tenuous. Saleh welcomed offers from the US and its allies to beef up his forces. I travelled into the desert outside Sanaa to watch advisors from American and British special forces training Yemeni commandos how to burst into buildings and kill or capture everyone inside. Bulging counterterrorism budgets were always welcome for a man who needed a healthy bottom line to buy and maintain power.

The spread of the fight against al-Qaeda to Yemen made life harder for the sprinkling of Westerners in the country. One night, I had dinner with the British ambassador and some of his colleagues at a market in Sanaa, of fish bought at one stall, grilled at another and eaten spread out over a table covered in newspaper. The ambassador's close protection team, alert to the chances of an al-Qaeda attack, positioned themselves around the fish table, cradling backpacks in their arms with the ends of the barrels of their submachine guns poking out.

Saleh's long dance across Yemen's snakes began to falter in the face of big demonstrations against him as Yemen was swept up in the Arab uprisings of 2011. Tribal leaders can be bought off, but bribes and broken promises did not work with tens of thousands of protestors. In the mountains of the north, the new world that followed 9/11 was also making matters more fluid, and more radical. Hussein al-Houthi, the son of a religious scholar, became a political and religious phenomenon, making dozens of speeches in the northern province of Saada, telling his followers to resist what he identified as a new American tyranny in the Middle East. His audiences, like him, were Zaydi Muslims, followers of a minority sect in Shia Islam. The movement's favourite slogan was plastered on posters all over the areas they controlled: *God is great: Death to America: Death to Israel: God curse the Jews.*

After 9/11 and the American invasions they echoed the mood of millions across the Middle East. They guaranteed a collision with Saleh. It did not matter that he was also a Zaydi; he had positioned himself as America's ally, and he had held onto power by stamping on challengers, which made enemies. Hussein al-Houthi was killed in 2004 in the first of six wars between Saleh and the Houthis.

In June 2011, as Yemen was again descending towards civil war, Saleh was badly hurt as he narrowly survived an assassination attempt. He was forced to go to Saudi Arabia for medical treatment after a bomb attack at the mosque in his presidential compound left him with 40 per cent burns, shrapnel wounds, internal bleeding and lungs damaged by smoke. Saleh blindsided enemies who hoped he was finished by abruptly leaving his sickbed to return home, but that did not stop the demonstrations or fighting between rival clans. At the end of 2011, in the face of big demonstrations for change, he was finally forced to resign, signing an agreement to step down as he sat next to Saudi Arabia's King Abdullah.

Saleh could not accept that his moment had been and gone. He did a deal with the Houthis, splitting the army as units loyal to him followed him into the rebellion, and together they swept into Sanaa. President Abd-Rabbu Mansour Hadi, the man who had taken Saleh's job, fled to Saudi Arabia. I saw him with his cabinet at a luxury hotel in Riyadh, protected by the Saudis and surrounded by marble and mahogany panelling, marooned in a glum five-star exile, so dependent on their hosts that they were almost prisoners.

The consequences of Ali Abdullah Saleh's last dance outlived him. By 2017, he had fallen out with the Houthis. Tensions exploded into a shoot-out at a parade ground on the edge of Sanaa, outside a huge mosque that Saleh had named after himself. Under pressure, Saleh tried to double-cross the Houthis by switching to the Saudi side. The Houthis attacked his compound, killed Saleh, and proved it by publishing a photo of his body lying twisted in the back of a pick-up truck, still recognizable with his skull split open.

The Saudi blockade made it hard for foreigners to get into Sanaa. When I managed to fly in from Jordan, I joined Mohammed Ali al-Houthi, a leading member of the clan, as he went walkabout in one of Sanaa's open markets. Al-Houthi was a prime target for Saudi Arabia; at the time, he was in effect the acting president. He strode past sacks of lentils and spices with a small crew of bodyguards brandishing Kalashnikovs. It was a flamboyant display of strength. A large curved dagger in a silver scabbard stuck out of his embroidered belt. It set off his white thobe and his dark woollen turban. A crowd formed straight away, laughing and lining up for selfies as he peeled banknotes from bundles he was handed by one of his entourage. He kissed the hand of a little girl before pressing a wad of cash into it. When her brother popped up, he was rewarded, too.

Everyone could hear Saudi military aircraft overhead. Mohammed Ali al-Houthi looked up at the sky with an expression that said *Bring it on*. A man at one of the stalls was saying it was like the German blitz on London when an explosion rumbled across the market, close enough to be alarming. He blamed the Saudis. In fact it was a car bomb, detonated by jihadists from Islamic State – one of a series of deadly attacks on mosques. The Houthis, as Zaydi Muslims, were targets for the Sunni extremists of Islamic State and as foreigners, so was our BBC team. All the Yemenis I met were remarkably friendly, but we travelled around with a dozen armed men in case we encountered some who were not. Our hotel had a high wall around it, a big gate and tyre spikes to stop intruders. And on our corridor at night, we had a couple of men with guns, who were usually snoozing gently on their sofas by the morning. Going around with armed men is not the ideal way to report, but the alternatives were not risking the trip or getting into big trouble.

Our problems were tiny compared to those of the Yemenis, who had no escape from war and hunger and could not fly home to somewhere safe. It was bad enough before the Saudis entered the war, but home-grown conflicts were more susceptible to deal-making than an offensive by a big power with a regional strategy. Tribal leaders could put on the brakes. Once Yemen became part of a wider confrontation between Saudi Arabia and Iran, all that changed.

The Houthis were not, as the Saudis insisted, puppets of Iran. They were allies rather than clients, who took money and increasingly sophisticated weapons but not orders. The alliance worked well for Iran, too. It watched as Saudi Arabia became bogged down in a war it could not win; just as useful was the condemnation the Saudis were getting in the West for killing and isolating Yemeni civilians. The Middle East's fatal fault line, between Shia and Sunni Muslims, ran through the conflict. The Zaydis, though a Shia sect, had religious differences with the Shia clerics who ran Iran. Saudi Wahhabis and Yemeni Zaydis were old enemies. As the war stalled, the Saudis tried to muster support in the Sunni world by presenting it as a jihad against infidels.

In Sanaa and the other places on the Saudi-led coalition's target list, the poorest Arabs in the Middle East were being attacked by some of the richest. One sweltering night, I looked out across Sanaa's darkened roofs; mains electricity had disappeared months earlier. Explosions thumped across the city, lighting up the sky. The next morning, I went to the site of a Saudi raid. A relatively well-off district had been flattened. It was just a fence away from a base used by Houthi fighters. Perhaps the Saudis had hit their targets inside the fence; it was impossible to tell. What was clear was that despite the latest Western military technology, some of their bombs had killed civilians.

A young man from the area, who was just back from studying medicine in the United States, told me what he had seen. 'I walked close by and I saw the kid with his head cut open and his brains out, and there's no words to describe what I saw.'

'How many kids died here?'

'Five from this family alone,' he replied. 'His cousin was six years old, and his two sisters, one of them was beheaded.'

'What are people saying around here about the Saudis?'

'They really hate them right now.'

The corridors in Sanaa's main hospital were always scrubbed clean, and every airless room off them contained another small part of the disaster that was gripping Yemen. Badly burnt babies and children lay with their mothers, many of whom were burnt as well. A man down the corridor had burns covering his entire body. He was a migrant worker from Eritrea who had been trying to get to Saudi Arabia to find a job. Not far from the border in northern Yemen, he had been caught in an air strike and his chances of survival were very low. More than pain was in his eyes; it was as if he could see his own death getting closer. Every breath rattled through his damaged lungs and throat. So many patients there had wounds caused by bullets and explosions that I had to keep reminding myself it was not a military hospital.

By every measure of pain and suffering, Yemen was the harshest place in the world to be born, to live and to die by 2021, five years after I sat with the Saudi ambassador in London. Yemen was the world's hungriest country. Two-thirds of the population, more than twenty million people, needed food aid. The UAE was supporting a separatist movement in the south that had set up a rival government. All sides violated the laws of war, recruiting child soldiers, making arbitrary arrests and detaining people illegally. Saudi air strikes went on; a third of them since 2015 had hit civilian targets. And the Houthis fired artillery indiscriminately and used land mines banned by international conventions.

At the end of 2021, the centre of the war was in Marib, a strategic town that controlled most of the Yemeni oil industry. When I took the bumpy five-hour drive across the desert from the Saudi border, Marib was full. Since the Saudis intervened in 2015, something over one million Yemenis had fled there for their lives. In the three months before my visit, another 45,000 displaced inside Yemen by the war were camping on rolling, bone-dry sand and scrub outside the city.

A man called Abdullah wanted to talk. At the tent he had built out of scraps of tarpaulin and cardboard, he told me how he had rescued his wife, Latifah, and their six children as the war reached their village. They had left their possessions and fled.

'All this war, the bombs, explosions and everything it's done make me hopelessly bitter about life, thinking we won't survive.'

Latifah joined in: 'Warplanes and strikes terrify our children ... It is very cold. The situation is tough. There is nothing to keep us warm, no mattresses. Our tents are just made of cardboard. We have nothing.'

The pressure of the war pervaded every part of life in Marib. The doctors at the hunger clinic said that ten out of every hundred children were malnourished. Of that ten, two had severe malnutrition. In one of the beds was Taqua Tarish, who was six months old and weighed 2.5 kilos, less than many newborns.

In the camp, I asked Abdullah who was responsible for their misery. He didn't have food, or much water for his family. 'I cannot blame anyone. This was destined for us and all Yemenis. This has to do with the big guys, not the ordinary people.'

When the Covid-19 pandemic was raging, rich states cut the funds that were needed to keep Yemen going. The UN humanitarian chief Mark Lowcock warned that it made Yemen's future even worse. 'It feels like the end, it feels like a calamity,' he told me over Zoom, a bizarre blend of modern communications and timeless despair. 'They feel as if the world has forgotten them. It's chaotic and anarchic and desperate ... Unless action is taken straight away, we're going to see a tragedy of globally catastrophic proportions.'

24.

Deal of the Century

In a world where most people get their news online and on TV, 14 May 2018 was declared to be the ultimate split-screen moment. Screens across the planet showed two intimately connected events in adjoining boxes. One was the opening ceremony for the new embassy of the United States of America in Jerusalem. The other screen showed Israeli troops shooting at Palestinian demonstrators across the wire that separates Israel from the Gaza Strip, and many dead and wounded being rushed towards ambulances by their friends.

Guests at the embassy, mostly Americans, had been shuttled to the ceremony by bus. It felt like the complacency express, with an atmosphere on board of self-congratulation and long-overdue victory. The people in the seats around me had mostly come from the American Midwest. They did not know much about the Middle East, except for a strong belief that Israel knew best and the Palestinians were making a big mistake if they didn't agree with Donald Trump and Benjamin Netanyahu. As the guests arrived, they were presented with souvenir baseball caps to mark the moment. Some swapped them with the red caps branded with Trump's 'Make America Great Again' slogan that they had worn for the journey.

On the opposite side of the screen, around sixty miles away in real life, thousands of Palestinians were taking part in a protest Hamas called 'the Great March of Return'. The crowds were big. Some

Palestinians, mostly young men, were getting close to the wire; a few tried to breach it. Israeli soldiers were shooting at them. About a kilometre back, out of range of gunfire, were thousands of peaceful demonstrators. Women had brought picnics. Families, including many children, screamed and scattered when Israeli drones buzzed overhead bombing the crowds with tear gas.

Between fifty and sixty Palestinians were killed that day, and many more suffered gruesome bullet wounds. In the months that followed the embassy's inauguration, the Friday demonstrations continued. Palestinians flew incendiary balloons across the border that would crash-land and become firebombs, burning crops in the fields. The Israeli army used live bullets to control crowds close to the wire. Gaza's surgeons are experts in dealing with the impact of high-velocity bullets on human bodies, but dozens of catastrophically damaged limbs were amputated, many from teenage boys who had been shot as they demonstrated or threw stones. Every Friday the sun laced through dust, gas and gunfire, and there was the sight and sound of casualties being rushed to hospital. At the end of March 2019, the UN humanitarian agency OCHA said that the pressure of almost 29,000 wounded, 7,000 of them hit by live bullets, had driven the healthcare system in Gaza close to collapse. By then, Israeli security forces had killed 195 Palestinians at the border demonstrations, including forty-one children.[1]

On a screen within a screen, President Donald Trump was piped in to the embassy from Washington to claim that he was putting right an old wrong. 'For many years we failed to acknowledge the obvious,' he said. 'The plain reality that Israel's capital is Jerusalem.'[2] To make up for his absence, Trump sent over his administration's most photogenic power couple: his daughter Ivanka, who had converted to Judaism when she married, and her husband Jared Kushner, who was slim, wealthy, and the president's senior advisor.

Hamas, the Palestinian faction that took control of Gaza by force in 2007, organized the demonstrations to channel the anger brewed by years of isolation and pressure away from itself and towards Israel. Gaza had been squeezed for more than ten years by a blockade imposed by Israel and supported by its allies, who agreed that Hamas was a terrorist organization. The tough life imposed on Gaza was so familiar that it took a lot to get it on the news. To try to change the game, Hamas linked its strategy to the fundamental pillars of the conflict. For Palestinians none were more important than Jerusalem's future and the loss of homes and land in 1948, when more than three-quarters of a million of them were expelled or fled Israel's war of independence, never to be allowed back.

When the casualty figures came in, Donald Trump's officials blamed Hamas for inciting Palestinians to break into Israel and use murderous violence to attack soldiers. At the embassy, Ivanka Trump's blonde hair shone in the sun as she unveiled a commemorative plaque on the new embassy. She was rebadging the former consulate as an embassy until a new one could be built, so that her father could keep a campaign promise to move the US ambassador from Tel Aviv. Until then, America, like almost all foreign countries, had kept its embassy out of Jerusalem because Israelis and Palestinians were bitterly divided about its future, and legally its precise status was undefined. Both sides wanted it as their capital; most countries said embassies should wait until a peace deal answered the question. But Donald Trump had strong political reasons to offer Prime Minister Netanyahu's government everything it wanted.

Trump dropped any pretence of even-handedness to keep his electoral base happy. The core of support for Israel in the US Republican Party comes from evangelical Christians; traditionally, most of the Jewish vote goes to the Democrats. Coach parties of pilgrims from American evangelical churches are fixtures at Israel's biblical sites. Megiddo, the biblical Armageddon, is one of their favourites. Amiable, deeply religious Christians, often in safari or hiking outfits, stroll around excavated ruins, stopping for prayer sessions and blood-curdling Bible readings describing the prophecy that the kings of the earth would gather at Armageddon to battle God, who would destroy them. Politely, they excused themselves from my questions to bow their heads to pray as they listened to Matthew's account of how 'the Lord cometh, cruel both with wrath and fierce anger, to lay the land desolate: and he shall destroy the sinners'. A round of passionate amens went round each group before they dusted off their trousers and headed for the next stop.

Donald Trump believed in winners and losers, friends and enemies.

His friend Benjamin Netanyahu was a winner, so he could have all he wanted. Sometimes it was even more than he had asked for, like encouragement from the White House to annex occupied territory in the West Bank, a move the Israeli security establishment advised would be a needless provocation. If Israel was the winner in Trump-world, Palestinians were the losers. He stopped American taxpayers' money going to help Palestinians, even for medical care, and closed the Palestinian mission in Washington, DC. Diplomats with families were not allowed to stay long enough to get their children through the school year.

Trump believed he was the best dealmaker ever to inhabit the White House, and what bigger deal was there to be done than bringing peace to the Middle East? Jared Kushner was put to work on Trump's 'deal of the century'. Just over a year after the bloody day when the US embassy in Jerusalem was opened, I met Kushner with some other journalists at Winfield House, the palatial London residence of the US ambassador. 'Call me Jared,' the polite and friendly Kushner told a deferential reporter. Trump, he said, believed that the conflict needed a solution, even though it was only the fourth most serious problem in the Middle East, after 'Iran, ISIS and radicalization'.

Kushner said that he had told his father-in-law that short-term problems after they opened the embassy were inevitable, but 'people in the Middle East respect strength'. The last twelve months had proved it: 'When we moved, people said the world would end. But the sun came up the next day and it didn't happen. We did Jerusalem and the Golan for Israel. [Trump also recognized Israel's annexation of occupied Syrian land.] We did it so no one could say that we would compromise Israel's security.'[3]

Jared was going to forget traditional diplomacy in the Middle East. It had failed, so he would use the skills that had made his family real-estate moguls in New York. His lawyer had an 'issues list': talk of history or process was out, because 'these guys are professionals in not making a deal'. So was old language like 'two-state solution', because it meant different things to different people. Instead, Kushner had drawn up a business plan for the Palestinians that he said came with 'world-class' grants, loans and private capital. Kushner presented it in Bahrain a few weeks later; the politics would come second. He talked very fast, like an exceptionally articulate salesman. The problem was the product he was selling, which was a crude attempt to buy off the Palestinians with unreliable promises of 50 billion dollars of investment. The Trump message was that their dreams of independence were dead, but they would lose twice over if they turned down such a great deal. Trump loyalists, the Israeli government and its friends applauded loudly. Most other observers saw a one-sided plan designed for the requirements of the Israeli government and responded with everything from scepticism to derision and outright rejection.[4]

They unveiled the Deal of the Century in the packed East Room of the White House six months later, in January 2020. I joined the crush in the media pen, uncomfortably aware of news reports about a deadly virus that was on its way from China. It may have been the deal of the century for Trump and Netanyahu, but it was no kind of peace plan for the Palestinians, who had not been consulted and were not in the room. The East Room was sweaty and euphoric, more like a wedding reception than a state occasion. Israeli and American VIPs and staffers whooped and hollered. The biggest cheers were for President Trump's reminders of what he had done for Israel. Prime Minister Netanyahu said it was one of the most important moments of his life – as important for Israel as independence in 1948.

They were celebrating a surrender document that said, in effect, that Israel had won and would decide the future along with its American friends. If Palestinians refused to sign up, even though they had no part in its drafting, Israel would still get what it wanted and they would be even worse off. The Palestinians were extremely weak, but they refused to sign. Kushner's work broke records for the fastest time from delivery to a place in the dustbin of history.

The party in the East Room was the high point of a fantasy that Trump and Netanyahu had created for themselves. Together, preening with power, they would deliver the fatal blow to Palestinian nationalism and declare victory after a century of conflict. It was a fantasy with deep roots. Unlike Trump, Netanyahu was an expert in Zionist thought. He knew the most famous line from *Altneuland* (*Old New Land*), Theodor Herzl's utopian novel about a Jewish state: 'If you will it, it is no dream.' Netanyahu's father, Benzion, was an early disciple of Ze'ev Jabotinsky, the founder of right-wing Jewish nationalism. Jabotinsky's 1923 essay 'The Iron Wall' contains a political prophecy that is still an article of faith on the Israeli right: 'It is utterly impossible to obtain the voluntary consent of the Palestine Arabs for converting "Palestine" from an Arab country into a country with a Jewish majority.' Zionists, Jabotinsky wrote, would have to protect themselves by force of arms; they would build an iron wall around their state. The Arabs would dash themselves against it time and again, until they realized that Zionism was unbeatable.

> As long as the Arabs feel that there is the least hope of getting rid of us, they will refuse to give up this hope in return for either kind words or for bread and butter, because they are not a rabble, but a living people. And when a living people yields in matters of such a vital character it is only when there is no longer any hope of getting rid of us, because they can make no breach in the iron wall.[5]

Only then would Palestinians reject radical leaders and agree to coexist with the Jews. The two sides could then negotiate the future. Jabotinsky was a dissident; he challenged mainstream Zionist thinking, but his views defined Israel's position towards the Palestinians long after his death in 1940. As the Oxford historian Avi Shlaim argues, successive Israeli prime ministers absorbed the first part of Jabotinsky's theory of the iron wall, about unassailable military power. But only Yitzhak Rabin at the time of the Oslo agreements in the 1990s tried to activate the second part, by negotiating a coexistence deal.

Netanyahu and Trump deluded themselves that Israel and American power had made the iron wall so strong that it was safe to bypass the negotiations Jabotinsky believed were vital. They decided that the Palestinians were so badly beaten that they would accept surrender, leaving America and Israel free to deal with Iran, the real threat. If Kushner had read Jabotinsky, he had ignored the stricture that Palestinians could never be 'bribed to abandon to us their claim to priority in Palestine, in return for cultural and economic advantages'.

I left the celebrations at the White House and went back to the BBC office in Washington, DC. The whooping at the party in the East Room felt divorced from the reality I had seen in Israel and the Palestinian territories; the danger of ignoring Palestinian anger and denying they had rights to the land was obvious. In the lift at the office, a video screen played new headlines about the virus in Wuhan. The pandemic in the spring of 2020 meant that much of the world was distracted while the old conflict between Israelis and Palestinians was reigniting, and was surprised when in the early spring of 2021 it exploded again.

It happened after a tangible step by the Trump administration to impose its vision of a new Middle East. Just before the presidential election in 2020, Jared Kushner delivered agreements that normalized relations between Israel and four Arab countries: the United Arab Emirates, Bahrain, Morocco and Sudan. From the balcony of the White House, Trump proclaimed that they would 'change the course of history . . . we mark the dawn of a new Middle East'. A comprehensive peace was on the way. The deals were named the Abraham Accords, acknowledging that the signatories traced their religious roots to the same Old Testament prophet.

These were not peace deals, because none of the countries were at war with Israel. The accords cut across a peace initiative the Saudis had put on the table in 2002, offering Israel full recognition in return for leaving the territory captured in 1967, agreeing to Palestinian independence with a capital in East Jerusalem along with a just solution for Palestinian refugees. It was a framework that fitted most international interpretations of the two-state solution, but it required concessions that Israel would not make.[6] The Abraham Accords offered Israel normal diplomatic relations without concessions.

The Arab side was given sweeteners for signing up. The Emiratis were allowed to buy the F-35, the latest American warplane, though when Trump left office that part of the arrangement fell apart. The US recognized Morocco's claim to sovereignty over the disputed Western Sahara. Sudan was removed from America's list of terrorist nations. The side deals helped, but the main reason why the rulers of the UAE and Bahrain signed was that they were more worried about Iran and building their economies than resolving Palestinian grievances, and they believed slavish loyalty to the Palestinian cause was holding them back. Netanyahu called the accords a 'pivot of history'. It was conventional wisdom in Israel that the Palestinians were just another issue to manage. Palestinians knew they could not win and it was time for everyone to move on. Jabotinsky's iron wall had done its job. The problem was that, while Gulf Arabs were tired of the conflict and happy to certify a relationship with Israel that had been quietly strengthening for decades, they were a long way from Palestinians, who were as far from surrender as ever.

The folly and hubris of ignoring the power of religious and national passion was exposed during the spring of 2021. A long-running court case to evict Palestinians from their homes in Sheikh Jarrah, a leafy, well-to-do neighbourhood in occupied and annexed East Jerusalem, escalated into weeks of violence. Israeli police fired stun grenades and CS gas into al-Aqsa Mosque on Laylat al-Qadr, the holiest night of Ramadan. It was more than just a dispute over a handful of homes. Both sides saw it as the latest instalment in the long campaign by successive Israeli governments to make Jerusalem more Jewish.

It is easy to see why Israelis believed so strongly that they were winning. Since 1967, when the Palestinian territories were captured, they had built a ring of settlements for Jews on occupied land around Jerusalem in defiance of international law. When it was almost complete, the priority switched to moving Jews into areas that were solidly Palestinian in and around the walled Old City. Between 1967 and 2021 they had settled more than 620,000 Jews on occupied land, including more than 210,000 in occupied Jerusalem. I had watched as the first Palestinian house was turned over to Jewish control in Sheikh Jarrah back in the 1990s. It made international news for a few days, before fading back into a landscape where the settlers lived in a world of security cameras and armed guards.

But in Jerusalem, quiet does not mean acceptance. Anger and frustration built up among Palestinians as they saw land being taken. The Palestinian writer Raja Shehadeh tramped around the West Bank seeing the familiar sights of his life disappearing. 'The worst thing', he wrote, 'is the sense of being a stranger in your own land and feeling that not a single part of it is yours.'[7] Small moments like the first house being taken by settlers in Sheikh Jarrah faded from the international consciousness quite quickly. But each extension of Israeli control fed Palestinian nationalism.

It always takes a spark to set off deep-seated anger. In the spring of 2021 it came with Israel's dangerous attempt to make political points about who was boss during Ramadan in Jerusalem. For believers, one of the pleasures of the holy month is sitting out on a warm evening with friends and family after the meal that breaks the daily fast, and the steps outside Damascus Gate, the entrance into the Old City most used by Palestinians, were a favourite place to hang out. When a new police chief decided to rope off the area and issue orders to move on anyone who tried to sit there, it turned into a predictable and unnecessary nightly riot. Water cannons fired stinking 'skunk water'; young Palestinians took on the police; activists confronted Israeli nationalist politicians who jumped on the bandwagon with their thuggish followers.

Palestinians were used to getting little or no leadership from the president of the Palestinian Authority, Mahmoud Abbas. He was elderly and presided over an administration that many Palestinians saw as inept, corrupt and compromised by cooperating with Israel over security. Just before Ramadan, Abbas cancelled elections, which would have been the first for Palestinians since 2006. He said it was because Israel would not let Palestinians in Jerusalem vote. His critics said it was because it looked as if he was going to lose. Netanyahu's hubris and the passivity of Abbas gave Hamas an opportunity to take the lead in Jerusalem. Hamas issued an ultimatum to Israel to remove its forces from the al-Aqsa compound and from Sheikh Jarrah. Like most people, I assumed this was empty talk – until they fired rockets at Jerusalem when their ultimatum was ignored. Almost immediately, Israel hit back with air strikes in Gaza.

At the end of eleven dangerous days, both sides accepted a ceasefire while also claiming victory. Israeli leaders listed the buildings they had destroyed, the Hamas commanders and fighters they had killed, and the way that their Iron Dome anti-missile system knocked out most of the salvos coming from Gaza. Most, but not all; there was evidence, worrying for Israel, that Iron Dome struggled to deal with big bombardments. This would matter much more against Lebanon and Hizbullah, which has a bigger, more powerful arsenal than Hamas.

A new war between Hizbullah and Israel would be a nightmare for both sides. Wars with Hamas are less alarming for Israelis. The Palestinians in Gaza have a fraction of the missiles available to Hizbullah, and everyone knows that once honour is satisfied on both sides, mediators will deliver a ceasefire. Much more alarming in Israel was the unexpected way that the conflict spread to cities with a mixed population of Arabs and Jews. Around 80 per cent of Israelis are Jews, and almost all the rest are descendants of Palestinians whose families did not leave during the Nakba of 1948. In 2021, they came out on the streets to support their cousins in Gaza and the West Bank. The result was days of ugly violence between Palestinian and Jewish youths, all of whom carried Israeli identity cards. There had been occasional violence ever since the Israeli government lifted military rule over its Palestinian population in 1966, but this was different. It showed a solidarity between the Palestinians of Gaza, Israel and the West Bank, including Jerusalem, that heartened them and alarmed Israel's Jews.

It was another reason why the leader of Hamas in Gaza, Yahya Sinwar, emerged triumphantly from hiding the day after the ceasefire. Huge banners of Hamas leaders were draped from the Dome of the Rock in Jerusalem, sixty miles from Gaza, and their slogans were chanted outside the al-Aqsa Mosque after prayers. The simple message from Hamas – that it would fight to the death for Jerusalem – resonated with Palestinians who despaired at the inability of President Mahmoud Abbas to slow down, let alone stop, the steady progress of Israel's colonization of the land they wanted for a state.

Once the ceasefire came into force, Israel unlocked the gates of the Gaza Strip and let in journalists. Entire streets in Gaza City were blocked with concrete and masonry from buildings that had been destroyed by air strikes. I drove south along the beach to Khan Younis, a town dominated by a big refugee camp. The town had stopped for the funeral of nine fighters from Islamic Jihad, whose bodies had been dug out of the tunnels where they were killed by Israeli air strikes. The dead were brought in on stretchers, wrapped in Palestinian flags. In the heat I could smell the rot wafting across the football stadium, where several thousand men had gathered for a mass funeral. Fighters from Islamic Jihad lined up with their weapons, their faces covered in black balaclavas or wrapped in black and white checked keffiyehs. When the scarves slipped, I could see that they were little more than boys still trying hard to grow beards.

Masked and armed young men are a common sight in Gaza. What surprised me was the support they had in the town, considering they had brought Israel's wrath down on the heads of the people. The streets were packed, with men and boys marching behind the bodies to the cemetery, and women and girls crowding onto doorsteps and balconies to ululate and clap as they went by. Part of it was relief. The ceasefire meant that the latest round in the long war was over.

In the twenty-first century, everyone with a smartphone can be a war cameraman. I wanted to find the location of a video that had appeared online in May 2021 during the latest Hamas–Israel war. In it, a man filming with his phone runs towards a place that had just been hit, getting more and more agitated as he realizes what he's about to see. I could hear it in his breathing. Women, heard but not seen, are screaming louder and louder as he gets closer. The man's voice is thick with shock as he calls out to God. After that, he can only manage single words. Children. Martyr. Massacre, a new massacre.

All the pain and pity of war are in those few seconds. The man recognizes one of the bodies – *They're Youssef's kids*, he mutters. He goes from body to body. It's hard to tell how many are dead from the video; at first I think six, but in fact there are eight. Someone finds a teenage boy alive. He's unconscious and they bundle him into a car to take him to the hospital. The dead bodies are shredded. Delicate human tissue has no chance against high explosive and shrapnel. They have been working – a cart, with an empty harness for a horse or a donkey, is half loaded with white sacks and others are stacked up, waiting to be taken away. A man in his thirties, a father holding the body of a small boy, throws back his head and roars with grief to God as he lays the body down next to another dead boy.

I went looking for the sandy lane that the man had run along in the video and found it just north of Beit Hanoun, a town close to Israel's border fortifications. The road led to a village that was too small for a proper name. Local people called it 'the end of Masrideen Street'. It is around 800 metres from the boundary wire with Israel. And in the early evening of 10 May, the first day of the war, it turned into a small corner of hell.

Near the place I recognized from the video, where bodies had lain broken in the sand, I saw men sitting to mourn their dead. Small boys ran around, offering cups of bitter coffee and sweet dates to visitors who had arrived to offer their condolences. At the centre of it was the man I recognized from the video. His name was Youssef al-Masri.

The dead boys I had seen Youssef laying down next to each other on the blood-soaked sand were his sons, seven-year-old Marwan and eleven-year-old Ibrahim. Three of the other dead came from the family of Youssef's brother, Mohammed Attallah, who was still badly wounded in hospital. They were his son Ahmad, who was twenty-one, his daughter Rahaf, eight, and his fourteen-month-old grandson, Yazan. Two other children from neighbouring families were killed, sixteen-year-old Ibrahim Abdullah Hassanein and ten-year-old Hussein Munir Hamad. Another neighbour, twenty-three-year-old Mohammed Ali Nusseir, was also killed. He had a small business with Ibrahim Hassanein, selling the animal feed that the older children were bagging up.

The Masri family were not Hamas supporters. When families in Gaza gather to mourn their dead, they tend to display their political or military affiliations. The Masri family flew the flags and insignia of Fatah, who took no part in the war, on the memorial tent, next to photographs of the victims. Youssef al-Masri told me with some pride that he was a member of the Palestinian police force, loyal to the president Mahmoud Abbas in Ramallah. An official from Fatah was there with his entourage to offer sympathy. And sitting quietly next to Youssef was his surviving son, nine-year-old Mohammed.

The boys who had been running around with coffee and dates were sent to get the debris left by the Israeli projectile. They laid it out while Youssef talked about the memory that replayed endlessly in his head of picking up his sons' bodies: 'Until now, I can't get those images out of my head, when you see your kids torn apart and shredded in front of your eyes. I can't describe it any more. This is the most heinous and criminal thing I have ever seen committed against our children. Every year or two, they wage war on us and our children and our homes. Our life in Gaza is indescribable. There's no life, drinking water, food, electricity or hospitals like other humans have.'

Israel insisted that Youssef was blaming the wrong side. Lieutenant-Colonel Jonathan Conricus, the army spokesman, told me when I was back in Jerusalem that he could not be 100 per cent forensically certain, as it was a chaotic time, but their best assessment was that the deaths had been caused by an Islamic Jihad missile falling short of its target in Israel. Israeli forces, he said, were not active in the area at the time of the strike.

Like every Palestinian I have ever met, Youssef al-Masri believes that Israel tells lies to cover up the brutal requirements of its project to strengthen its state. I asked him about his wife, who in a traditional society I was not able to visit. She was coping, he said; sitting with the women in their home, away from the eyes of strangers. Sometimes in Britain, we tell ourselves that it is better not to intrude into other people's grief. In Gaza and across the Middle East, it is the other way round, and the bereaved have constant, unannounced visits. Men sit in lines of chairs outside the family home, surrounded by photos of the dead. The women do the same, in private. No one is left alone to grieve.

Youssef al-Masri spoke with great intensity, staring at me from under his black baseball cap. 'I will face my future with boldness and with full force. I will get babies. Instead of Marwan and Ibrahim, I will get another Marwan, Ibrahim and Khalil, Mohammed and Mahmoud.' His dead boys, he said, were martyrs for Jerusalem. If necessary, the children yet to be born could be, too.

I looked at nine-year-old Mohammed, the survivor, sitting next to his father, listening, saying nothing and absorbing every word. I wondered about the colossal impact that seeing his brothers die so violently would have on his life. I remembered how, during the second Palestinian intifada in the first years of the century, I used to sit with the late Palestinian psychiatrist Dr Eyad el-Sarraj in his garden, discussing the pain that the conflict was implanting in children.

The children we talked about are now adults. They are the generation that lined up with guns and masks at the funeral of Islamic

Jihad fighters in Khan Younis on the day that I got back into Gaza into 2021. Twenty years earlier, Sarraj told me, 'Twenty-four per cent of our children up to the age of twelve think that the best thing in life when you are eighteen is to die as a martyr. There is a second life out of the misery of this life of deprivation, of hardship, of humiliation . . . People want to cling to that hope, and some are ready to take the test by challenging death through killing and killing themselves.'

Youssef al-Masri did not look like the kind of man who would bring up his children to waste their lives. I feared for the future of his son Mohammed if the crushing weight on the shoulders of everyone in Gaza could not somehow be lifted. Most people in Gaza struggle to provide a decent life for their children. In 1998, Ehud Barak, one of Israel's most illustrious soldiers, had a candid moment during his successful campaign to become prime minister. He told an Israeli journalist, 'If I were a Palestinian of the right age, I would join, at some point, one of the terrorist groups and fight from there, and later try to influence from within the political system.' He added the caveat that 'From our standpoint, their methods are very abominable, villainous, inhumane and inappropriate.' The point was that young men who are brought up to fight see no alternative. When the British were in Palestine in the 1940s, they condemned the Jewish nationalists who had picked up guns against them as terrorists. Two of them, Menachem Begin and Yitzhak Shamir, became prime ministers of Israel. Begin made peace with Egypt. In his memoir, *The Revolt*, he wrote that the British establishment regarded him as 'Terrorist Number One'. He said he hated British rule, but not the British people. Palestinian nationalists often say the same thing about Israelis.

A few dozen steps away from the Masris, another family was mourning a son. Ibrahim Hassanein was the sixteen-year-old who had been killed while loading the feed sacks. His family had none of Youssef's defiance and simply looked broken. Like all the other families in the village, they had left their homes after the raid. When they came home they found their house destroyed by Israeli shelling. Ibrahim's older brother Mohammed showed me the damage. He was a medical student, and his brother's death had unmoored him, leaving him stuck in the horror of the first day of the war and full of questions to which he knew the answers.

'What did they do wrong?' he asked. 'Were they launching missiles? Were they firing anything at all? Innocent children. They just want to play and to eat. That's all they do. I can't study. My brother's martyrdom was sudden and shocking. It's just so strange and it has shattered my dreams.'

Outside the ruined house his mother, Amena, was sitting in the garden, surrounded by women from her family. They would not leave her alone with her grief and the memories of the last time she saw her son alive.

'Ibrahim, may God have mercy on his soul, he was happy, he took a shower and put on aftershave, and he was laughing and walking around the house. It was a very special laugh.

'I'd call to him, where are you, and he'd say, I'm here Mum! He was going round and round the house like a bird. He was very happy that day. He left then, and he never came back.

'I ask God to bring justice [to the Israelis]. I pray for that, night and day. The children were innocent. They did nothing wrong.'

They sat in the garden next to the ruins of their home, serenaded by songbirds in cages that somehow they had saved. Ibrahim's father, Abdullah, was a poor man who borrowed money to buy his son the cart that was still standing, half loaded, next to where the children had been killed. Talking about his son seemed to give him a moment of peace. 'You start to imagine him alive in front of you. You look at his picture to calm yourself down. You want your son to breathe, you want to carry him and sleep next to him.'

Ibrahim was the family dynamo, who had given up school to support his family and pay the university fees for his quieter, studious brother. The cart his father took on debt to buy was going to be the start of a better life, and they were lost without his dreams and plans.

Abdullah spoke directly to the Israelis: 'He's a boy like your boys. I have a son and you have a son, so why kill him? We are trying to make a living, not to fight wars. We don't have artillery to hit you. The distance between us is just eight hundred metres. We used to sleep well, because there's no fear here. But when you decide to break our hearts and set them on fire by killing him, we get to hate life and only hatred will exist between us.'

Like Youssef al-Masri, Abdullah Hassenein did not believe Israel when it insisted it tried hard not to kill civilians. Sometimes, Israel does warn civilians to leave buildings that are about to be bombed. Human Rights Watch reported after the ceasefire that both Israel and Hamas, and other armed groups in Gaza, violated the laws of war during the eleven-day conflict. Its report said that Israel had not provided any information to justify the attack on the people at the end of Masrideen Street.

Gaza is a unique and terrible experiment. Palestinians who live there often say it is the world's biggest open-air prison. The rich world felt hemmed in when it missed foreign holidays during the Covid-19 pandemic; in Gaza, more than two million Palestinians spend their lives stuck on a narrow stretch of coast around twenty-five miles long and no more than seven miles wide. One of my Palestinian colleagues there in May 2021 was forty-one years old, the father of three children, and had never left.

Palestinians in Gaza survive, and even enjoy life, because the human spirit is remarkably bright and strong there. Most people I've met in Gaza are warm and open, even to the citizens of Western allies of Israel whose countries have given them a lot about which to complain. On the first evening after the ceasefire came into force, the streets of Rimal, the best-off part of Gaza City, were crowded. Less than twenty-four hours earlier, they had been empty as civilians stayed inside, hoping their homes were strong enough to protect them against another air strike. At the most popular falafel restaurant, the arms of the man who shapes and cooks the little chickpea balls in hot oil were a blur as he tried to keep up with demand. Children bounced on trampolines in play areas of open-air cafes as their parents sat drinking tea and smoking shisha. Even the sound of Israeli drones, endlessly circling and watching, did not spoil their good mood. Like the previous rounds of fighting between Israel and Hamas, the ceasefire was just a pause. The conflict was not just unresolved; it was not even frozen.

Without question, Israelis also suffer when wars start in and around Gaza. During the eleven-day war in May 2021, a five-year-old boy called Ido Avigdal was killed in Sderot, a small border town, when a Hamas rocket hit his home. I was in Ashqelon, just north of the Gaza Strip, as it suffered repeated red alerts while missiles that had not been stopped by the Iron Dome system came in from Gaza. When the sirens sound and a phone app blinks a message to take cover, it is frightening. The app tells you how long you've got. In Ashqelon, you have around ten seconds; in Sderot, it is less than that. We were in a restaurant run by Russian Israelis which had a refuge with a reinforced concrete roof and walls. Some of the kitchen staff took cover in a walk-in fridge.

But the two experiences, in Gaza and Israel, were not the same. In 2021, Israel showed once again that for all its power, it could not beat enemies who count survival as victory. It also showed how deluded it is to think that a mutually acceptable peace is not necessary because the Palestinians are beaten. Far from being over, the conflict festers and looks to be intensifying. Without remedial action, the next war is always inevitable.

25.

Pawns on the Global Chessboard

One summer evening in 2006, I was sitting in a hotel bar in the centre of Beirut watching the fruits of our labours on BBC *World News*. A terrible and destructive war between Israel and Hizbullah was going on outside the hotel, with more bloodshed a certainty. We could hear the Israelis bombing Hizbullah's power base in the city's southern suburbs.

My BBC colleague Simon Wilson mused, darkly, over his glass of beer. I wonder, he said, whether this is how it felt to be in Europe sometime in the 1930s. I knew what he meant: foreboding, a profound and debilitating malaise, the knowledge that a deeper crisis was on its way. Our Beirut bar was picking up echoes of W. H. Auden's uncertainty and fear in a bar in New York in his poem 'September 1, 1939': 'As the clever hopes expire/Of a low dishonest decade'.[1] They were just echoes. It wasn't a world crisis. But the Middle East was divided, angry, slipping into the hands of extremists, resentful and unsure of its place and oppressed by the weight of its history. On that hot night, with more bombs shaking the city and more beers chilled by the roaring hotel generator, it was bleak. Not Europe 1939 bleak, but the Middle East was in the middle of the worst decade most people could recall.[2] The war in Lebanon was more evidence of how fast things could catch fire.

On 12 July 2006, Hizbullah and Lebanon went from uneasy peace to all-out war in less than a day. Around dawn, Hizbullah fired anti-tank missiles at an Israeli armoured Humvee that was patrolling the border, killing three soldiers. A Hizbullah raiding party followed the missiles in, captured two more Israelis, and killed five of the Israeli squad that chased them back into Lebanon.

After the initial skirmish, the war escalated quickly. Up to 1,300 Lebanese and 165 Israelis were killed in the next thirty-four days. When it ended, Hizbullah had fought Israel to a standstill and claimed victory; at the very least it was a draw. Well-prepared Hizbullah fighters mauled Israeli infantry in battles in small villages in South Lebanon. A local man who worked for UNIFIL, the United Nations peacekeeping force, told me that Hizbullah had built a network of bunkers near where he worked, a mile or so from the Israeli border, with such tight security that he had no idea it was happening. 'I didn't know they had brought in even a spoonful of concrete,' he told me with some wonderment. Israel had declared that the war was to stop Hizbullah rocket fire across the border. On the day before the fighting ended, it fired more rockets than on the first.

After the war, Hizbullah's leader, Hassan Nasrallah, made the rare admission on Lebanese television that authorizing the kidnap operation might have been a mistake: 'We did not think, even one per cent, that the capture would lead to a war at this time and of this magnitude . . . You ask me, if I had known on 11 July . . . that the operation would lead to such a war, would I do it? I say no, absolutely not.'[3]

Nasrallah claimed that his decision only sped up the timetable; Israel, he insisted, was planning an attack later in the year. The two kidnapped Israelis died, making them less valuable than Nasrallah had hoped, though Hizbullah still used their remains in an exchange of prisoners and bodies two years later. Both sides build up reserves in the bank of bodies; Israel has a cemetery in the Jordan Valley where the bodies of its enemies' fighters are stored until they are required to buy back their own.

Two overlapping streams of events defined and reinforced each other in the Middle East in the first two decades of the twenty-first century. As outside powers moved in with their own agendas, they created new opportunities for the region's authoritarian rulers that were already exploiting the people. Without Russia, Assad might have fallen. Further east, without America, the government in Kabul collapsed. The first stream, the international dimension, flowed from al-Qaeda's attacks on the US on 11 September 2001 and the consequences of America's response – its war on terror. The other was a home-grown, chronic crisis of governance. Leaders repeatedly failed their people, with the social contract imposed by the military strongmen who seized power in the 1950s and 1960s left in tatters. The deal was that regimes would provide for their people, if the people stayed out of politics. They didn't promise riches, or a European-style welfare state, but there would be jobs, and food, and a new ideology of Arabism that would return a people who had been crippled by foreign interference to the glories of their golden age.

For a while, millions were bewitched in the middle of the twentieth century by the rhetoric of an Arab renaissance, but Israel's crushing defeat of all its Arab front-line enemies during six days in June 1967 proved that it meant nothing. On the first morning of the war, Egypt's President Gamal Abdel Nasser's radio station, Voice of the Arabs, pumped out hours of lies about shooting down dozens of Israeli warplanes; the truth was that the Egyptian air force had been destroyed on the ground by a surprise attack. After the humiliation of defeat, people looked for new answers, and some found them in the comforting certainties of the mosques. Arabism was tarnished, but Islam was on the march. That feeling was reinforced by the sight of millions of Iranians overthrowing the shah of Iran in 1979, the same year that the Afghan mujahedeen went to war to drive out Soviet invaders.

By the end of the twentieth century, the social contracts imposed by authoritarian Arab regimes were as hollow as their boasts about destroying Israel before 1967. Only the oil-producing states had the money to keep their side of the bargain to provide a minimum standard of living for their people. The ageing leaders who did not have oil and gas revenue to buy off discontent embezzled billions from the people to make sure that their families and their charmed circles of cronies did not suffer. Regimes stayed in power not by consent, but by building ruthless police states, often with competing intelligence agencies that spied on each other as well as on the people. Plans were made to transfer power to the next generation. It worked in Syria, where Hafez al-Assad was able to bequeath the presidency to his son Bashar when he died in 2000. Hosni Mubarak in Egypt and Muammar al-Gaddafi in Libya planned to do the same for their sons.

For anyone who believed that the Middle East, not to mention the rest of the world, would be happier and healthier without corrupt governments repressing their people, it was a bleak time. A short walk from the hotel where Simon Wilson and I compared the Middle East at the start of the new century with Europe in the 1930s was the gleaming headquarters of Lebanon's leading newspaper, *An Nahar*. The building had a trendy rooftop bar that looked down on the lights of Beirut's port and embodied the desperate hedonism of some middle-class Lebanese who are proud that they can party at the worst of times. On 4 August 2020, the bar and a big part of Beirut took the full force of the devastating explosion caused by a cache of ammonium nitrate in an abandoned and overlooked warehouse.

Even at the height of the 2006 war, a few restaurants stayed open in Beirut. I used to fumble my way along the pitch-black streets on moonless nights until I saw dim lights in dark windows. The biggest danger was stepping into an uncovered manhole. The Israelis were bombing Beirut, but they were concentrating on Hizbullah areas a few miles away. In all the wars I've seen in Lebanon, sun-worship has not stopped at Sporting, the beach and pool club on the Beirut Corniche. In 2006, people with skin like varnished mahogany only checked out the NATO naval flotilla that was evacuating foreigners when they looked up to order a drink or apply more oil.

A sign of the bad times hung down the front of the *An Nahar* building. It was a big poster of Gebran Tueni, the paper's editor and son of its founder, who was assassinated just before Christmas in 2005. His killing on 12 December came at the end of a year of assassinations in Lebanon. On 14 February, a huge bomb had blown up the motorcade of the former prime minister, the billionaire tycoon Rafik Hariri, whose company rebuilt Beirut after the civil war. Twenty-one others were killed alongside him. Hariri had argued with Syria's still relatively new president, Bashar al-Assad, who was promptly accused of ordering the hit. Big demonstrations and international outrage forced Syria to end a military occupation of Lebanon that had started in the 1980s. A long investigation authorized by the UN Security Council failed to link the Assad regime to Hariri's assassination; years later, operatives from Syria's ally, Hizbullah, were convicted in absentia. Hizbullah will not give them up.

Gebran Tueni's assassination was part of the same wave of killings of people who dared to question Syria's rights over Lebanon. One more of 2005's car bombs killed another critic of the Assad regime, the historian and journalist Samir Kassir. He was deeply pessimistic about the stagnation and failure that had devastated so many Arab lives. The year before he was killed, he wrote that: 'The Arab people are haunted by a sense of powerlessness; permanently inflamed, it is the badge of their malaise.' Foreigners were not to blame for all their troubles, but Arabs were 'powerless to suppress the feeling that you are no more than a lowly pawn on the global chessboard even as the game is being played in your backyard.'[4]

The biggest game in the Middle East in the first quarter of the twenty-first century involved the unfolding consequences of the 9/11 attacks on the United States. The Arabs that Kassir saw being stripped of autonomy by their country's leaders had received another deadly reminder of the power of others when the United States invaded Iraq in 2003. Not only, Kassir wrote, could Arabs do nothing to stop the deployment of thousands of foreign troops. Just as bad was the realization that the US took only a few weeks to 'put paid to a state that was much feared, at least by its own citizens and neighbours'. Even more mortifying, international pressure had the best chance of stopping the invasion, not the 'Arab masses'.

It was a surprise when, at the end of that dreadful first decade of the century, the sun came out for a while in the Middle East. At last, it felt as if the people who had been crushed for so long by their own leaders and foreign powers were taking matters into their own hands. That pessimistic conversation in Beirut with Simon in the summer of 2006 felt like the result of too much work and too much beer in a city at war.

In 2011, millions of people across the Middle East rose up against their leaders in a season of revolutions. The comparison with Europe that counted seemed to be with the hopes of 1848 and 1989, not with the despair of the 1930s. The Egyptian novelist Alaa Al Aswany wrote that the eighteen days he spent in Tahrir Square in Cairo during the uprising against President Hosni Mubarak were 'without doubt, the most wonderful days of my life'.[5] His new comrades in Tahrir, and all the others who emulated them in squares across the Middle East, were much younger than Aswany. The revolutions were driven by anger and frustration in a region where at least 60 per cent of the people were under thirty. For a while, they lost their fear of the regimes they believed were stealing their futures.

Demonstrating made people feel like citizens, with common purpose, dignity, and pride. Tawakkol Karman, a Yemeni human rights activist in her early thirties, shared the Nobel Peace Prize. In Cairo, thousands brought brushes and buckets to clean up Tahrir Square the morning after Mubarak was forced out. In 2011, authoritarian presidents who started out as military officers fell in Tunisia, Yemen and Egypt, as well as in Libya, where Colonel Gaddafi claimed until the end to be just another citizen.

Time magazine's person of the year, illustrated on the cover by a masked woman, was 'The Protestor'. The magazine said that 'In 2011, protesters didn't just voice their complaints; they changed the world.' Change was not only marked by wild scenes on the streets; in May 2011, American naval commandos killed Osama bin Laden inside a ramshackle mansion in Pakistan, and in December, the Americans pulled their forces out of Iraq.

It did not turn out the way that the protestors or their supporters wanted. The men who had the power were not just corrupt and authoritarian; they were tenacious. For a while, it looked as if the future belonged to political Islam. The Muslim Brotherhood was rooted in its communities and had won credibility after years of opposition to dictators. Senior British diplomats told me they were giving the Brotherhood the benefit of the doubt. The conservative, neatly barbered, middle-aged and middle-class engineers, doctors and other professionals who led the Brotherhood were a world away from the bloodthirsty, shaggy-bearded jihadist extremists of al-Qaeda and

Islamic State. The Brotherhood was cohesive and organized, unlike dozens of disorganized, brand new secular parties. But in Egypt, the template, things went wrong fast. The Muslim Brotherhood was good at running clinics and schools, but it was greedy for power and appallingly bad at governing the country. It turned out that Islamists could be as bad at governance as monarchs or generals.

Dreams, and people, died as dictators struck back and ISIS, the poisonous new jihadist variant, emerged from al-Qaeda in Iraq and Syria. Counterrevolution prevailed, and Iraq, Yemen and Libya sank into all-out war. Syria suffered the greatest disaster as Bashar al-Assad and his regime broke the country to preserve their power. No one knew exactly how many died in the first ten years of Syria's war. Half a million was a common estimate.

In Egypt, Abdul Fattah al-Sisi overthrew the elected Muslim Brotherhood government and became the latest general to become president after Neguib, Nasser, Sadat and Mubarak. The Egyptian military was never going to allow democracy to break its hold on power, politics and the economy. The Brotherhood's Mohamed Morsi, the only Egyptian president not to have been a professional soldier, died in prison. Sisi became a tyrant more ruthless than Mubarak had ever been.

The second decade of the twenty-first century was kick-started by the optimism of the Arab uprisings of 2011; it turned out to be even worse than the first ten years. So what about the third decade? A lot that should go right is already going wrong. Just because the conflict between the Palestinians and Israel does not always make news headlines does not mean it is any less dangerous. It continues to leach poison into the region. In 2015 the Iran nuclear deal, the JCPOA, stopped a slide to war. Since the US withdrew from the treaty in 2018, the old dangers are back.

The bad news for authoritarian governments in the Middle East is that the grievances that drove millions onto the streets in 2011 still exist. If leaders cannot satisfy the needs of the people, they will be challenged again. Bashar al-Assad destroyed his country to save his regime, then faced renewed unrest in 2021 in areas that supposedly had been pacified, like Deraa near the border with Jordan. The Syrian economy collapsed after a decade of war. It cannot improve without a political settlement that induces rich countries to start paying the huge cost of reconstruction; that would need stability and a leader who is not called Assad. Both are unlikely. Across the border in 2021, Lebanon was plummeting quickly towards becoming a failed state. Hyperinflation impoverished millions. A corrupt sectarian system desperately needed comprehensive reform. It was impossible while Hizbullah and an elite of superannuated warlords refused to let go, even as the country sank.

The Middle East still cannot find a comfortable place in the modern world. Saudi Arabia and Iran are two major countries that are struggling to rise to the challenge. Both rely on oil and gas. Saudi industry is well financed and efficient; Iran's isn't, because of years of isolation and sanctions. And by the middle of the century, if the industrialized world keeps its promises on climate change, hydrocarbons will no longer be a licence to print money.

Saudi Arabia is approaching the mid-century with Crown Prince Mohammed bin Salman waiting to succeed his father. The rise of MBS began after the late King Abdullah feared the Arab uprisings of 2011 would spread to Saudi Arabia; to stave off unrest he threw billions of dollars at welfare, housing, jobs and education. Longer-term, Abdullah believed the kingdom needed a young and energetic leader instead of another octogenarian. MBS has removed and imprisoned rivals and, even with his father still alive, has become the power in the land. According to the British Saudi social anthropologist Madawi al-Rasheed, Abdullah's original plan was enough modernization to satisfy impatient young people, without conceding fundamental political change. MBS has tried to encourage a Saudi national identity rather than one built on Islam and the holy cities of Mecca and Medina. Social life is more relaxed; he allowed women to drive, and cinemas to open. At the same time, his regime continued to lock up its critics, including women who had been part of the driving campaign. He has a plan called Vision 2030, to try to diversify the Saudi economy and reduce its dependence on oil. Donald Trump encouraged MBS to join the Abraham Accords between Israel and some Arab states. If the Crown Prince was tempted, it was too much for King Salman.

Assuming Mohammed bin Salman follows his father — and the

enemies he has made during his rise might not be strong enough to stop him – Saudi Arabia will be led by a man who has shown himself to be ruthless, impulsive and ready to crush any opposition. He took Saudi Arabia into a war in Yemen that it could not win, with disastrous results. Any dissidents who criticize the ruling family and the Saudi system can end up exiled, imprisoned or dead.

The Saudi journalist Jamal Khashoggi, a leading critic of the regime who wrote for the *Washington Post*, walked into the Saudi consulate in Istanbul on 2 October 2018 to sort out some legal documents. A hit squad was waiting. Minutes later, he had been murdered and dismembered. Turkish intelligence had the building bugged. They recorded Khashoggi's attempts to fight for his life as he was suffocated, and the sounds of a bone saw cutting up his corpse. The Crown Prince denied ordering a murder he called 'a heinous crime'.[6]

No one who had seen how closely he controlled the Saudi intelligence and security agencies believed him, including the US government. In February 2021, one of Joe Biden's first acts after he was inaugurated as US president was to release a report by the Office of the Director of National Intelligence declaring that MBS was responsible for what happened. It concluded that the Crown Prince 'approved an operation to capture or kill Saudi journalist Jamal Khashoggi . . . we base this assessment on the Crown Prince's control of decision-making in the Kingdom, the direct involvement of a key adviser and members of Muhammad bin Salman's protective detail in the operation, and the Crown Prince's support for using violent measures to silence dissidents abroad, including Khashoggi'.[7]

For a while, MBS became an international pariah. Lucrative Saudi contracts persuaded international business to return. The Americans took no further action against the Crown Prince. Saudi Arabia was too important to them, for arms sales, intelligence, its growing relationship with Israel, the fear China was waiting to fill any gaps, and because of its influence on world oil prices. Most of all, America needed the Saudis on side because of Iran. Saudi Arabia, Israel and the United States are all united by a deep mistrust of Iranian intentions. In 2022, as a world economic crisis bit harder after Russia invaded Ukraine, Joe Biden underlined America's need for the Saudis by visiting King Salman and the Crown Prince in Riyadh.

In 2021, Iran's Supreme Leader Ayatollah Ali Khamenei managed the presidential election to guarantee victory for his protégé, the hard-line judge Ebrahim Rantisi. The new president is believed to be manoeuvring to succeed Khamenei, who was born in 1939. In the third decade of the new century, in the Middle East the confrontation between Team America and Team Iran looks to be the most potentially destabilizing contest of them all.

It was pushed back into acute crisis after Donald Trump pulled the United States out of the JCPOA, the Iran nuclear agreement. He claimed, incorrectly, that it was a bad and dangerous deal. Once the US was out, Iran started once again to enrich uranium. By the start of 2022, hopes that the Biden administration could revive the deal were waning. With negotiations stalled, the UN's International Atomic Energy Agency reported that Iran had almost enough enriched uranium to make a nuclear bomb. New enrichment plants buried deep within mountains were coming on stream. The slide towards war arrested by the JCPOA in 2015 was tipping again.

The Middle East is a region of the world where instability is infectious because everything important is connected. Islam's troubles run along the fault line between Shia and Sunnis. Unscrupulous leaders with more interest in power than religion have exploited it to whip up support. It amplifies the regional rivalry between Sunni Saudi Arabia and Shia Iran, which has fuelled wars in Yemen and Syria. Saudi Arabia and Israel both see Iran as their worst enemy, so they have formed an unlikely alliance. This, in turn, could heat up the old conflict between Israel and Lebanese Hizbullah, which gets most of its weapons from Iran. Hizbullah's leader Hassan Nasrallah was a guest of honour at President Rantisi's inauguration in Tehran, and so it goes on: Iran and Hizbullah are key military players in Syria, as are the US, Russia and Turkey. And after Turkey intervened in Libya to support the Tripoli government recognized by the UN, the United Arab Emirates and Russia increased their support for a rival government based in Benghazi. It is geopolitical Jenga. Miscalculations and misperceptions could bring it crashing down.

Iraq is another connected country; Iraqis have fought each other, while outside powers have both helped them and used the country as their boxing ring. In January 2020, I drove out of Baghdad Airport, past the burnt and twisted remains of the car that an American drone strike had destroyed a few days earlier. The attack killed General Qassem Suleimani, the mastermind of Tehran's regional strategy and the head of the Iranian Quds Force that helps enforce it. A leading Iraqi Shia commander, Abu Mahdi al-Muhandis, who was there to greet Suleimani, was also killed. Muhandis was a senior player on Team Iran, a key leader of the Popular Mobilization forces, the Shia militias that were raised to fight ISIS in 2014. Killing Muhandis, who the Americans might not have realized was in the car, weakened the US position in Iraq. Its parliament voted to expel US forces, and the militias increased attacks.

The greater Middle East is a huge circuit board of connections, never ending, feeding into the balance of forces in a region of great strategic importance. The Americans want it to be different. Since President Obama's time, the US has been trying, unsuccessfully, to 'pivot' away from the Middle East towards the Asia–Pacific side of the world, to counter China as it surges to global power in the way that the US did in the mid-twentieth century. At the same time, China is executing its own pivot towards the Middle East. It made a deal with Iran that could give it a toehold in the Gulf. At the end of 2021, the UAE suspended negotiations with the US about buying advanced F-35 warplanes, after the talks stalled over the UAE's links with China and its reliance on Chinese technology. On the other side of Arabia, China's People's Liberation Army opened its first overseas base in 2017 in Djibouti on the Red Sea – just a few miles from Camp Lemonnier, the only permanent US military hub on the African continent.

Superpowers have such outsize influence that their exits can be as destructive as their entries. The Americans demonstrated how not to disengage in Afghanistan in the summer of 2021, with a withdrawal so badly handled that it precipitated the fall of Kabul to the Taliban. After he took office, Joe Biden announced that he would honour a deal that his predecessor Donald Trump made with the Taliban, dismissing criticism that it gave the Taliban too much, and betrayed US allies in the Kabul government. Biden plunged forward, announcing that all American troops would be out by the twentieth anniversary of al-Qaeda attacks on 9/11, which had brought them to Afghanistan in the first place. It was a neat target, with obvious political appeal, but it ended in a debacle with chastening echoes of 9/11 for the Americans. The sight of Afghans desperately clinging to the wheels of departing military aircraft and falling to their deaths was a terrible reminder of people jumping from the burning towers in New York before the flames could reach them.

Jihadists attacked the American cordon at Kabul Airport. Almost 200 people were killed, mostly Afghan civilians but including thirteen members of the American military. Khorasan Province, an affiliate of Islamic State, said it carried out the attack. Twenty years after America invaded Afghanistan in response to attacks by al-Qaeda, bin Laden's heirs were still spilling blood. The rhetoric coming from the White House was remarkably consistent. In 2001, President George W. Bush responded to the Taliban's refusal to give up Osama bin Laden with words every American understood: 'I want him . . . Dead or alive.'[8] President Joe Biden's speech after the bloodbath in Kabul could have been made twenty years earlier: 'To those who carried out this attack, as well as anyone who wishes America harm, know this – we will not forgive. We will not forget. We will hunt you down and make you pay.'[9]

Invading Afghanistan in 2001 and removing the Taliban, the group that harboured Bin Laden and al-Qaeda, was legitimate; America's mistake was to stay for twenty years to try to impose a remade, Westernized country on the Afghans. A better idea would have been to allow Afghans to find a negotiated way ahead. It might have neutered the Taliban, would have cost a fraction of the money spent in twenty years of war, and it could not have left Afghanistan in a worse state than it reached in 2021.

I reached Kabul again a few days after the last Americans left, with my mind rewinding more than thirty years to the same airport in February 1989, when the Soviet Union had pulled out its last troops. America was not on its last legs when it left Afghanistan, as the USSR had been; it had the world's most powerful economy and military. But it was still defeated, and this was final evidence that the freedom of action the US had enjoyed in the Middle East and beyond in the years after the Cold War was as much of a memory as the Soviet Union. Echoes kept coming as America counted down its last days in Kabul. Helicopters evacuating their embassy brought back Saigon in 1975 and the Vietnam disaster. A better comparison was the scramble to get out of Lebanon in 1983, three months after a truck bomb killed 241 Americans at the US Marine barracks in Beirut. That withdrawal gave Osama bin Laden ideas: he believed it showed that Americans were weak.[10]

Unlike the chaos of America's last days, Kabul Airport was orderly when the Soviets went. No crowds rushed onto the tarmac, even though mujahedeen fighters were so close that we could hear their artillery and rumours were everywhere that they were about to enter Kabul. On my way to Afghanistan in 1989, I heard colleagues reporting that trees were being cut down on Kabul's avenues to improvise landing strips for last-minute escapes. I arrived expecting something like hysteria, but the city was remarkably calm and did not fall for another eighteen months.

On a reporting trip through Helmand Province, the Taliban heartland, in the weeks after their takeover in 2021 I could see that the country had changed, in the way that the world has since the 1990s. The Taliban insisted that one of their fighters, a man with a large American assault rifle, travel with us as 'security'. Every hour he watched the latest news from BBC Pashtun on his smartphone. In the town of Lashkar Gar, where the British fought the Taliban, we were surrounded by young Talib fighters who responded to our cameras by filming us with their phones and taking selfies. In the 1990s their fathers were told that photography was banned. I met the Taliban on the road to Kandahar when they were on the rise in the early 1990s, when they were mainly young men who knew very little more than the grindingly traditional culture of Pashtun society in southern Afghanistan. Now cheap data meant they could tour the world on their phones.

In 2021 the new governor of Helmand sat in his office in front of a large Taliban flag, a white banner printed with the Shahada, the Muslim declaration of faith. His men, heavily bearded and dressed like the governor in turbans and traditional shalwar khameez outfits, listened and nodded as he gave us a history lesson. Their Kalashnikov assault rifles were never far away. The young Talibs on the streets taking selfies might have changed, but the governor and his lieutenants had not. Women, he lectured, needed to respect the teachings of Islam and their duties to the men who were their guardians. Western invaders needed to learn their lesson.

'We fought the British and the other foreigners for twenty years. They were defeated. They destroyed our country and they saw how their rented Afghan army collapsed in a few days. We were not paid salaries in twenty years but you didn't see us running away.

'We have a simple message for the British and the foreigners . . . you should help the Afghan people. You've made them suffer enough.'

The uncomfortable truth for the Americans was that the Taliban won, and the real gains in education and equality, mostly in Kabul, were based on a corrupt state that collapsed when its foreign backers left.

The manner of the Americans' withdrawal left doubts about how much they would support allies in moments of crisis. Defeat in Afghanistan was not the only reason why less than two years later the USSR collapsed under the weight of its own contradictions, but it marked the end of the Soviet Union as a global power. Afghans did almost all the fighting, though Arab jihadists like Bin Laden claimed it as their victory too and went home with their ideology and ambition on fire. Without the Soviets to worry about, the US saw itself as the world's hyperpower. Overwhelming military strength did not, however, remove the consequences of its actions. The hubris of power without apparent constraint drove the illegal invasion of Iraq, a catastrophe for all concerned – except Iran, which was strengthened and presented with a menu of new possibilities by the profound alteration of the geostrategic order in the Middle East.

One circle closed with the Taliban's reconquest of Kabul, twenty years after the Americans removed their regime. Only a tiny proportion of Muslims are attracted to the ideology of al-Qaeda and the other jihadist groups that emerged later, but 9/11 still inflicts deep cuts on the Americans, and Kabul showed it. Bin Laden and his men, mostly dead or in prison, and a tiny minority of Muslims, left a poison pill that still works. Every time the consequences of the wars that came out of 9/11 damage the United States and its Western allies, it gives jihadists who revere Bin Laden's memory something to cheer.

In 2010, the year before war started to destroy Syria, I travelled around the country with my mother and my nine-year-old daughter. We knew how vicious the regime was towards anyone who opposed the Assads, but the paradox of police states is that if you're a visitor, they can feel safe. Everyone knows that the security agencies are always watching.

In Aleppo we stayed in the walled old city, which was dominated by the largest covered market in the world: thirteen kilometres of winding lanes. Trade was the reason why Aleppo grew. The narrow street where our hotel stood had a butcher, a baker and a candlestick maker, as well as a small workshop where they blended olives and bay leaves to make Aleppo's legendary soap, the only one in the world which is left to mature like wine.

I found the street again just after the Assad regime recaptured all of Aleppo in 2017. It was difficult to get there because the old city was badly damaged and hard to recognize. In our street, the shops were looted, the hotel was closed and the soap factory was empty, with the moulds they used to shape the square green bars scattered all over the pavement. One of the great *khans*, grand covered squares where traders once sold their goods in warrens of shops, was banked high with sandbags, and the minaret of the eleventh-century Umayyad Mosque was a pile of rubble. Soldiers had built positions in the prayer halls, protecting themselves with oil drums full of stony earth and more sandbag walls. The narrow, covered streets were empty. Outside the hotel where we had stayed in 2010, an unexploded artillery shell stuck out of the road. I was glad that I'd known the place when it was packed with people.

I retraced the route we had taken during our holiday to the great citadel of Aleppo. Mattie, my daughter, had been a subject of great interest to a group of Syrian girls who were a few years older, wearing headscarves when of course she wasn't. The girls grouped round her and took photos, not quite able to believe they were seeing a little girl from London. I wondered what had happened to them. Were they dead or alive? Were they refugees, or did they stick it out in Aleppo? A whole generation of children across the Middle East had grown up without education, stability or safety. By the time Aleppo fell, Mattie was doing GCSEs and planning to go to university.

In 2015, a German photographer called Jörg Brüggemann took a picture of a tourist on the Greek island of Kos on a sunbed, reading a German newspaper. A woman luxuriates behind him in the warm Mediterranean Sea. The photograph on the front of his newspaper shows a woman in a lifejacket hugging a small child – one mother and one son among hundreds of thousands of refugees, mostly from the Middle East, Afghanistan and south Asia, who were trying to find safety in Europe. The land border between Greece and Turkey was closed to them; Kos was only three miles from Bodrum on the Turkish coast, across a stretch of the Aegean that was easy enough to cross for anyone who could handle a boat on a calm summer day. But when smugglers crammed refugees into inflatable plastic dinghies, the narrow strait could be deadly, whatever the weather.

In the summer of 2015, millions of Europeans were being reminded of what life could be like beyond the horizon of their summer beaches. Jörg Brüggemann took other photographs of the collision between the affluence and safety of Europe and the tumult on the other side of the Mediterranean. In one, two dark-skinned young men ponder their next move now they have reached Europe, while a pale-skinned man walks past with a selfie stick, wearing a holiday T-shirt and sunglasses. In another image, two European women in bikinis hold their flip-flops as they pick their way past piles of lifejackets, discarded by refugees who had crossed the sea from Turkey.

The photograph that made front pages all over the world that summer showed the dead body of a small boy wearing blue shorts and a red T-shirt, lying face down in gentle waves. The toddler's name was Alan Kurdi; his family's attempt to cross the sea to Kos had failed, and the current washed his body back to the Bodrum coast. Alan drowned along with his mother Rihanna, his older brother Ghalib and perhaps ten others. Their boat had capsized in one of the Mediterranean storms that blow up quickly as summer turns to autumn.

Only Alan's father, Abdullah, survived to take the bodies of his family home to their village in Syria for burial. Abdullah's sister Tima, who had left Syria for Canada in 1992 and was trying to get permission for them to settle there, too, remains wracked with regret over the $5,000 she paid the smugglers. The appalling fate of the Kurdi family became headline news because of the symbolic power of Alan's dead body, but many more children were killed and families destroyed trying to cross the Mediterranean to get out of the Middle East and into Europe without bothering the headline writers.[11]

Since the late 1980s, most of my time as a journalist, in the Middle East, Afghanistan and beyond, has been spent trying to report on and understand the way the world was changing as it emerged from the Cold War. By 2022, global power was already being reshuffled; Russia's renewed invasion of Ukraine on 24 February was the definitive end of the post-Cold War era. President Putin's move into Syria in 2015 paid off for Russia. It enhanced his project of restoring his country's prestige, position and power, and left America and the West looking flat-footed. Invading Ukraine was different. Within days, the US and its NATO allies were nose-to-nose with Russia in a way that had not been seen since the height of the Cold War. That mattered, because between them they had most of the world's nuclear weapons. President Putin did not hesitate to remind his enemies that Russia might use them.

The immediate fallout from Russia's invasion was in Europe. Buried, bad memories of the years of the Iron Curtain came back. The war did not have the same resonance in the global South. Western rhetoric about the need to oppose Russia to uphold a 'rules-based' international order went down badly with audiences that believed it was code for the powerful and rich countries of the West making rules that were in their own interests, which they could break when they chose. Invading Iraq in 2003, or tolerating Israel's illegal settlement of Jews in the occupied Palestinian territories, seemed to be particularly egregious examples of Western countries choosing when to enforce the rules.

Israel, the biggest beneficiary of Western support in the Middle

East, did not rush to support its NATO allies' confrontation with Russia. It needed to protect the arrangement it had with the Kremlin that allowed the Israeli air force to bomb its enemies in Syria without interference from Russian forces based there.

Arabs, once again, became pawns on the global chessboard, as identified by the Lebanese writer Samir Kassir. They were the poorest, because of the fundamental human need to eat. Middle Eastern countries had become dependent on imports of food, especially wheat, from Ukraine and Russia. Before the February invasion, more than a quarter of global wheat exports came from Russia and Ukraine, and the Middle East was dependent on them as a relatively affordable source of food. Then sanctions hit Russian exports. War stopped most of Ukraine's. Egypt, the world's biggest importer of wheat, had been sourcing 70 per cent of its needs from the Black Sea. Overnight, it became a theatre of war, not a safe sea route for ships carrying food and fertilizer. Prices rose steeply. Lebanon, already in one of the worst economic depressions since the nineteenth century, had been buying three quarters of its wheat from Ukraine and Russia. Hunger in Yemen became even worse as prices rose. Relief organizations like the UN World Food Programme found that budgets that had already been cut did not buy as much as they had. Other countries in the region that bought at least a third of their wheat from Ukraine and Russian included Libya, Oman, Saudi Arabia, Yemen, Tunisia, Iran, Jordan and Morocco.[12]

People often talk, during bad times in the Middle East, about subsisting on bread and tea. When the wheat to make the bread comes from Ukraine or Russia, that makes difficult lives even harder.

One dank afternoon during the war to destroy the jihadists of Islamic State, I was in Mosul in Iraq, the city where Abu Bakr al-Baghdadi conjured their caliphate into existence following a lightning advance across Syria and Iraq. The winter light was fading fast when our team climbed into an armoured Humvee belonging to a special forces unit of the Iraqi police. The door was heavy, and I grunted as I pulled it shut. The catch was faulty – I didn't want to have to open it in a hurry. We kept the microphones recording, and they picked up bits of chat between our team as we skirted a front line. Every minute or so, a rocket with a fiery tail streaked out from the ISIS positions, followed by lines of tracer bullets. I wasn't sure the danger was worth it.

My phone pinged with a message from London. A British man, radicalized in jail as a Muslim convert, had killed five people, including an unarmed policeman, and wounded around fifty others in Westminster before being shot dead by the bodyguard of a government minister. I could see the irony of a would-be jihadist killing innocent people in London while we were a few hundred metres from ISIS jihadists fighting for their bloodstained caliphate. More connections. My musings were stopped by gunfire and explosions. It was not a good place to park.

That evening, the Humvee drove through a broken town. Apart from its headlights the only light came from campfires lit by soldiers, who were burning bits of wood dragged out of wrecked buildings. The lumps taken out of the windows in the Humvee's armoured glass by ISIS snipers diffused some of the light. I tried to think of a way to describe the chunks dug out by the bullets. What were they? Spider holes, maybe. Nasty contusions, love bites gone mad. It didn't matter much in the ruins of Mosul.

Iraq was one of the most advanced countries in the region, in everything except freedom, the first time I visited in 1990. I sat in the back of the Humvee and thought about everything that I had witnessed in the intervening years, all the trouble, violence and pain. In the 1990s, the Middle East was stagnant, waiting for a generation of authoritarian rulers to die; discontent and pressure for change was smouldering but mostly failed to catch fire. After 9/11, everything was different. Afghanistan, Iraq, Lebanon, Gaza, Hamas and Israel, the Arab uprisings, overthrown and exiled presidents, Gaddafi's brutal death, al-Qaeda, ISIS and Iran's nuclear programme. From the back seat of the Humvee it felt like a long transition, hopes for change that turned violent. That evening in Mosul, I couldn't see where it would end, and it was the kind of place where getting through each day was more important than reflecting on the future that the war was going to create. We were not nearly through to other side, and we still aren't. It will go on for a while yet – another generation, perhaps.

Foreigners – the meddling West – carry heavy responsibility for everything that has happened over many years in the Middle

East, through unwanted interference, invasions, arms sales and the encouragement of dictators who did their bidding. Being a bulwark against the Soviets forgave many sins. So did Israel's close relationship with the United States. Building strong alliances without asking too many questions helped authoritarian regimes prosper and prevented proper opposition. Donald Trump didn't even bother to cover it up. 'Where's my favourite dictator?' he quipped as he waited for a meeting with Egypt's president Abdul Fattah al-Sisi at the G7 summit in France in 2017. In the end, much of it came down to a crisis of governance. If corrupt rulers repress their people, rob them blind and steal their freedom, extremists will always find recruits.

Millions of people wanted change when they rose up to protest in 2011, and when their hopes were smashed they did not want it any less. Repression, war and a lack of champions to follow made it harder for people who wanted to try to make their lives better, but that wasn't simply the fault of the West. Their countrymen who had taken the top jobs used their power to enrich themselves, their families or their tribes, and they didn't care if fellow citizens they made into their subjects were crushed, killed, imprisoned, swindled or defrauded. All that is much easier in a country that has plenty of guns and poor men prepared to pull the triggers, and an absence of laws and courts to enforce justice.

The Humvee stopped suddenly on a dark Mosul street. I watched as the young gunner on the fifty-calibre in the turret threw away his cigarette and looked around, a bit too keenly. Shooting was always in the background, but I hadn't noticed anything louder, or closer. Our safety advisor Baz Kenny, an ex-para with jump wings tattooed on his forearm, told us to stay inside the vehicle. It was nothing, in the end, just a checkpoint, and more Iraqis trying to stay warm next to fires. Most of my career as a journalist in the Middle East, Afghanistan and beyond has been spent trying to report and understand the world that emerged at the end of the Cold War.

The Middle East is relatively small, but it matters because it is right in the centre of the world. The new forces unleashed by the war in Ukraine do not change that. The shockwaves of everything I saw in

Mosul that month — and in many other places, over more than thirty years — were transmitted all over the world. We feel them in Europe, see the refugees, the political killing and terrorism that links back to events in the region. So Iraq and Iran, Israel and Palestine, Libya and Egypt, Yemen and the rest are everybody's problems, and they should not be ignored. Powerful states looking in from outside need to stop making it worse. Do no more harm. Then try to make things better.

ACKNOWLEDGEMENTS

I owe a huge debt to all those people who've agreed to talk to me about the lives they were living in tumultuous times. Quite often, meeting a Western reporter – with or without a microphone and a camera – was a considerable act of courage.

The idea for this book came from a series I wrote and presented for BBC Radio 4, called *Our Man in the Middle East*. It was commissioned by Gwyneth Williams, the then controller of the network, who pushed me to come up with a series, aided and abetted by Mohit Bakaya, her successor. Cara Swift and Mark Savage did the hard work of producing twenty-five programmes and forcing me to boil down my thoughts. Cara excavated from the archives and transcribed vast amounts of my reporting in the Middle East since 1990, which was also invaluable when it came to writing this book. Cara and her predecessor, Jane Logan, have been my producers, friends and the driving forces of dozens of trips to the region since the BBC appointed me as Middle East Editor in 2005. Jane introduced me to Jerusalem as my first producer there when I moved to the city in 1995. Cara was with me throughout most of the turmoil that followed the Arab uprisings of 2011. So was Nik Millard, a great cameraman, editor, journalist and friend since the first story we did together, in Libya, in 1991.

The reporting that provides the core of this book was made possible by dozens of BBC colleagues and friends. It's impossible to name everyone, but special thanks to some remarkable people. In Egypt: Angy Ghannam and Amr Aboulfath. In Syria: Lana Antaki and Lina Sinjab. In Lebanon: Tima Khalil, Malek Kanaan and the much-missed

Abed Takkoush. I've relied on Jimmy Michael's great and empathetic pictures and wise counsel in the West Bank since 1995. Thanks also in Jerusalem to Jeannie Assad, Gidi Kleiman, Oren Rosenfeld and Youssef Shomali. In Gaza: Rushdi Abu Alouf and Hamada Abuqammar. In Iraq: Laith Ali, Dylan Kareem and Bader Katy. The late Abu Ali, once Saddam Hussein's chef, used to feed us at the BBC house in Baghdad and regale us with stories of his former employer's visits to the palace kitchen to see what was for dinner. Thanks also to Juliette Touma and Matt Hollingworth of the United Nations. In Kabul, in 2021, I had the pleasure of working with Mahfouz Zubaide.

My agent Julian Alexander at the Soho Agency gently prodded me to write the book and to finish it. I tried the patience of George Morley and her team at Picador repeatedly and grievously. Writing a book is a full-time job but, unfortunately, I had one already.

Many thanks to Eugene Rogan of St Antony's College Oxford and Sanam Vakil of Chatham House for making invaluable comments and corrections. I own any remaining errors. James Arroyo and Sir John Holmes invited me to seminars at Ditchley Park that helped distil my thoughts. Much of this book was written in the London Library, a haven for anyone trying to turn thoughts and experiences into words.

I took many of the photographs, which wouldn't have happened without the encouragement of my mother Jennifer Bowen, a much better photographer than I will ever be, who let me use her darkroom and cameras when I was still at primary school. I might not have gone into the news business without the example of my late father Gareth, also a BBC journalist, who died in 2016. He was in Lebanon when Israel invaded in 1982. My father's non-stop support included recording all my reports from Baghdad during the 1991 Gulf War on a stack of VHS tapes. Now that my own children are venturing out into the world, I realize how alarming it must have been for my parents to track my movements across the Middle East at times of crisis.

Over many years my partner Julia Williams and my children Mattie and Jack have put up with months of absences while I've been working in the Middle East or staring at a screen writing about it. This book is dedicated to them.

BIBLIOGRAPHY

Haidar al-Abadi, *Impossible Victory: How Iraq Defeated ISIS* (London: Biteback Publishing, 2022)

Abbas Amanat, *Iran: A Modern History* (New Haven & London: Yale University Press, 2017)

George Antonius, *The Arab Awakening* (Beirut: Libraire du Liban, 1969)

Thomas Asbridge, *The Crusades: The War for the Holy Land* (London: Simon and Schuster UK, 2010)

Hanan Ashrawi, *This Side of Peace: A Personal Account* (New York: Simon and Schuster, 1995)

Alaa Al Aswany, *Democracy is the Answer: Egypt's Years of Revolution* (London: Gingko Library, 2014)

Peter Baker and Susan Glasser, *The Man Who Ran Washington: The Life and Times of James A. Baker III* (New York: Doubleday, 2020)

James Barr, *A Line in the Sand: Britain, France and the Struggle that Shaped the Middle East* (London: Simon and Schuster UK, 2011)

Menachem Begin, *The Revolt: Story of the Irgun* (Jerusalem, Tel Aviv, Haifa: Steimatzky's Agency Ltd, 1972)

Meron Benvenisti, *City of Stone: The Hidden History of Jerusalem* (Berkeley, CA: University of California Press, 1996)

Peter L. Bergen, *The Osama Bin Laden I Know: An Oral History of al Qaeda's Leader* (New York: Free Press, 2006)

Jeremy Bowen, *Six Days: How the 1967 War Shaped the Middle East* (London: Simon and Schuster, 2003)

Jason Burke, *Al-Qaeda: The True Story of Radical Islam* (London: Penguin, 2004)

Ross Burns, *Monuments of Syria: An Historical Guide* (London & New York: I.B. Tauris, 1994)

George Bush and Brent Scowcroft, *A World Transformed* (New York: Vintage Books, 1998)

Andrew Cockburn and Patrick Cockburn, *Out of the Ashes: The Resurrection of Saddam Hussein* (New York: HarperCollins, 1999)

Sam Dagher, *Assad Or We Burn the Country: How One Family's Lust For Power Destroyed Syria* (New York: Little, Brown, 2019)

Malik R. Dahlan, *The Hijaz: The First Islamic State* (Oxford: Oxford University Press, 2018)

Nikolaos van Dam, *Destroying a Nation: The Civil War in Syria* (London & New York: I.B. Tauris, 2017)

Toby Dodge, *Iraq: From War to a New Authoritarianism* (London: Routledge/International Institute of Strategic Studies, 2012)

Tyler Drumheller with Elaine Monaghan, *On the Brink: A Former CIA Chief Exposes How Intelligence Was Distorted in the Build-up to the War in Iraq* (London: Politico's, 2007)

Abba Eban, *Personal Witness* (New York: Putnam, 1992)

Amos Elon, *Jerusalem, City of Mirrors* (London: Flamingo, 1996)

Marion Farouk-Sluglett and Peter Sluglett, *Iraq Since 1958: From Revolution to Dictatorship* (London: I.B. Tauris, 2001)

Lawrence Freedman, *The Evolution of Nuclear Strategy* (New York: St Martin's Press, 1981)

Sandy Gall, *Don't Worry About the Money Now* (London: New English Library, 1985)

David Gardner, *Last Chance: The Middle East in the Balance* (London & New York: I.B. Tauris, 2009)

Shlomo Gazit, *The Carrot and the Stick: Israel's Policy in Judea and Samaria, 1967–68* (Washington, DC: B'nai B'rith Books, 1995)

Fawaz A. Gerges, *The Far Enemy: Why Jihad Went Global* (Cambridge: Cambridge University Press, 2009)

—, *Making the Arab World: Nasser, Qutb, and the Clash that Shaped the Middle East* (Princeton and Oxford: Princeton University Press, 2018)

Kim Ghattas, *Black Wave: Saudi Arabia, Iran and the Rivalry that Unravelled the Middle East* (London: Wildfire, 2020)

Mikhail Gorbachev, *Perestroika* (London: Collins, 1987)

Gershom Gorenberg, *The End of Days: Fundamentalism and the Struggle for the Temple Mount* (New York: Oxford University Press, 2002)

David Hannay, *Britain's Quest For A Role: A Diplomatic Memoir from Europe to the UN* (London: I.B. Tauris, 2013)

David Hirst, *Beware of Small States: Lebanon, Battleground of the Middle East* (London: Faber & Faber, 2010)

David Horovitz (ed.), *Yitzhak Rabin: Soldier of Peace* (London: Peter Halban, 1996)

Ben Hubbard, *MBS: The Rise to Power of Mohammed Bin Salman* (London: William Collins, 2020)

Brian Jones, *Failing Intelligence: The True Story of How We Were Fooled into Going to War in Iraq* (London: Biteback, 2010)

Samir Kassir, *Being Arab* (London and New York: Verso, 2013)

Malcolm H. Kerr, *The Arab Cold War: Gamal 'Abd Al-Nasir And His Rivals, 1958–1970* (Oxford: Oxford University Press, 1971)

Rashid Khalidi, *The Hundred Years' War on Palestine: A History of Settler Colonial Conquest and Resistance* (London: Profile Books, 2020)

Henry Kissinger, *Years of Upheaval* (Boston: Little, Brown, 1982)

Tima Kurdî, *The Boy on the Beach* (New York, London and Toronto: Simon & Schuster Canada, 2018)

Robert Lacey, *The Kingdom* (London: Hutchinson, 1981)

Wolfram Lacher, *Libya's Fragmentation: Structure and Process in Violent Conflict* (London: I.B. Tauris, 2020)

Ulf Laessing, *Understanding Libya Since Gaddafi* (London: Hurst, 2020)

Quil Lawrence, *Invisible Nation: How the Kurds' Quest for Statehood is shaping Iraq and the Middle East* (New York: Walker, 2008)

David Lloyd George, *War Memoirs of David Lloyd George* (London: Odhams, 1936)

David McDowall, *A Modern History of the Kurds* (London: I.B. Tauris, 1996)

Sean McMeekin, *The Ottoman Endgame: War, Revolution and the Making of the Modern Middle East, 1908–1923* (London: Allen Lane, 2015)

Margaret MacMillan, *Paris 1919: Six Months That Changed The World* (London: John Murray, 2019)

Michael J. Mazarr et al., *What Deters and Why: Exploring Requirements for Effective Deterrence of Interstate Aggression* (Santa Monica, CA: Rand Corporation, 2018)

Aaron David Miller, *The Much Too Promised Land: America's Elusive Search for Arab–Israeli Peace* (New York: Bantam Books, 2008)

Fitzroy Morrissey, *A Short History of Islamic Thought* (London: Head of Zeus, 2021)

Jerome Murphy-O'Connor, *The Holy Land: An Archaeological Guide from Earliest Times to 1700* (Oxford, Oxford University Press, 1992)

Vali Nasr, *The Shia Revival: How Conflicts within Islam Will Shape the Future* (New York: W.W. Norton, 2006)

Ramita Navai, *City of Lies: Love, Sex, Death and the Search for Truth in Tehran* (London: Weidenfeld & Nicolson, 2014)

John Nixon, *Debriefing the President: The Interrogation of Saddam Hussein* (London: Bantam Press, 2016)

Amos Oz, *My Michael* (London: Vintage Books, 1991)

—, *Under This Blazing Light* (Cambridge: Cambridge University Press, 1996)

—, *A Tale of Love and Darkness* (London: Vintage Books, 2005)

Trita Parsi, *Losing An Enemy: Obama, Iran and the Triumph of Diplomacy* (New Haven, CT and London: Yale University Press, 2017)

Derek Penslar, *Theodor Herzl: The Charismatic Leader* (New Haven, CT and London: Yale University Press, 2020)

Christopher Phillips, *The Battle for Syria: International Rivalry in the New Middle East* (New Haven, CT and London: Yale University Press, 2016)

Patrick Porter, *Blunder: Britain's War in Iraq* (Oxford: Oxford University Press, 2018)

Sayyid Qutb, *Milestones* (New Delhi: Islamic Book Service, 2020)

Madawi al-Rasheed, *A History of Saudi Arabia* (Cambridge: Cambridge University Press, 2014)

—, *The Son King: Reform and Repression in Saudi Arabia* (London: Hurst, 2020)

Eugene Rogan, *The Arabs: A History* (London: Allen Lane, 2009)

—, *The Fall of the Ottomans: The Great War in the Middle East, 1914–1920* (London: Allen Lane, 2015)

Dennis Ross, *The Missing Peace: The Inside Story of the Fight for Middle East Peace* (New York: Farrar, Straus and Giroux, 2004)

Jonathan Rugman, *The Killing in the Consulate: Investigating the Life and Death of Jamal Khashoggi* (London: Simon and Schuster, 2019)

David Rundell, *Vision or Mirage: Saudi Arabia at the Crossroads* (London: I.B. Tauris, 2021)

Thomas Ruttig, *Crossing the Bridge: the 25th Anniversary of the Soviet Withdrawal from Afghanistan* (Afghan Analysts Network February 2014 https://www.afghanistan-analysts.org/en/reports/context-culture/crossing-the-bridge-the-25th-anniversary-of-the-soviet-withdrawal-from-afghanistan/)

Marwa al-Sabouni, *The Battle for Home: The Memoir of a Syrian Architect* (London: Thames and Hudson, 2016)

Ziauddin Sardar, *Mecca: The Sacred City* (London: Bloomsbury, 2014)

Yezid Sayigh, *Armed Struggle and the Search for a State: The Palestinian National Movement, 1949–1993* (Oxford: Oxford University Press, 1999)

Jonathan Schneer, *The Balfour Declaration: The Origins of the Arab–Israeli Conflict* (London: Bloomsbury, 2011)

H. Norman Schwarzkopf (with Peter Petre), *It Doesn't Take A Hero* (New York: Bantam Books, 1992)

Patrick Seale, *Asad of Syria: The Struggle for the Middle East* (Berkeley, CA and Los Angeles: University of California Press, 1988)

Tom Segev, *A State at Any Cost: The Life of David Ben-Gurion* (London: Apollo, 2019)

Vincent Sheean, *Personal Story (In Search of History)* (London: Hamish Hamilton, 1935)

Raja Shehadeh, *Palestinian Walks: Notes on a Vanishing Landscape* (London: Profile Books, 2007)

Avi Shlaim, *The Iron Wall: Israel and the Arab World* (New York and London: W.W. Norton, 2000)

Hans C. von Sponeck, *A Different Kind of War: The UN Sanctions Regime in Iraq* (New York and Oxford: Berghahn Books, 2006)

Anthony Swofford, *Jarhead: A Marine's Chronicle of the Gulf War and Other Battles* (New York: Scribner, 2003)

Ronald Storrs, *Orientations* (London: Nicholson & Watson, 1945)

Ray Takeyh, *The Last Shah: America, Iran and the Fall of the Pahlavi Dynasty* (New Haven, CT and London: Yale University Press, 2021)

Wilfred Thesiger, *Arabian Sands* (London: Penguin, 1964)

Yaroslav Trofimov, *The Siege of Mecca: The Forgotten Uprising in Islam's Holiest Shrine* (London: Penguin, 2008)

Mark Twain, *The Innocents Abroad, or The New Pilgrim's Progress* ([1869] London: Wordsworth Classics, 2010)

Lawrence Wright, *The Looming Tower: Al Qaeda and The Road to 9/11* (New York: Vintage Books, 2006)

NOTES

PROLOGUE

1 Thomas Ruttig, 'Crossing the Bridge: The 25th Anniversary of the Soviet Withdrawal from Afghanistan', Afghan Analysts Network, February 2014. https://www.afghanistan-analysts.org/en/reports/context-culture/crossing-the-bridge-the-25th-anniversary-of-the-soviet-withdrawal-from-afghanistan/
2 Steve Rosenberg, 'Mikhail Gorbachev: The man who lost an empire', *BBC News*, 13 December 2016. https://www.bbc.co.uk/news/world-europe-38289333

1. WATCH AND LEARN

1 Remarks and an exchange with reporters on the Iraqi invasion of Kuwait, 5 August 1990. https://www.margaretthatcher.org/document/110704
2 H. Norman Schwarzkopf (with Peter Petre), *It Doesn't Take a Hero* (New York: Bantam Books, 1992), p. 92.
3 George Lardner Jr. and R. Jeffrey Smith, 'CIA shared data with Iraq until Kuwait was invaded', *The Washington Post*, 28 April 1992. https://www.washingtonpost.com/archive/politics/1992/04/28/cia-shared-data-with-iraq-until-kuwait-invasion/2d4684e5-0a62-4697-933a-d3bf9107701e/
4 'National Security Directive 26: US Policy Toward the Persian Gulf', 2 October 1989. https://fas.org/irp/offdocs/nsd/nsd26.pdf
5 Schwarzkopf, *It Doesn't Take a Hero*, p. 295.
6 John Nixon, *Debriefing the President: The Interrogation of Saddam Hussein* (London: Bantam Press, 2016), p. 113.
7 David Hannay, *Britain's Quest for a Role: A Diplomatic Memoir from Europe to the UN* (London: I.B. Tauris, 2013), p. 177. The day after President Bush told

the world to watch and learn, Resolution 661 imposed sanctions on Iraq under Chapter VII. By the end of August the Security Council had demanded Iraq's withdrawal, declared that its annexation of Kuwait was illegal and imposed a naval blockade. In November, the UN Security Council authorized the use of force to reverse Saddam's invasion of Kuwait.

8 Mikhail Gorbachev, *Perestroika* (London: Collins, 1987), p. 140.
9 Adel Darwish, 'Obituary: Sheikh Abdul Aziz bin Baz', *Independent*, 14 May 1999. https://www.independent.co.uk/arts-entertainment/obituary-sheikh-abdul-aziz-bin-baz-1093400.html
10 Peter L. Bergen, *The Osama Bin Laden I Know: An Oral History of al Qaeda's leader* (New York: Free Press, 2006), pp. 111–12. The friend was Khaled Batarfi, speaking to Bergen.
11 Excellent accounts of the eighteenth-century Wahhabi religious revival are in Ziauddin Sardar, *Mecca: The Sacred City* (London: Bloomsbury, 2014), pp. 214–43, and Robert Lacey, *The Kingdom* (London: Hutchinson, 1981), pp. 10–11.
12 Anthony Swofford, *Jarhead* (New York: Scribner, 2003), p. 7.

2. MISSION IMPASSABLE

1 Extract of a letter from Commodore Napier of HMS *Powerful* to Admiral Sir Robert Stopford, 16 September 1840, published in the *London Gazette* on Friday 9 October 1840, p. 2227.
2 See Eugene Rogan, *The Fall of the Ottomans: The Great War in the Middle East, 1914–1920* (London: Allen Lane, 2015).
3 One of many examples. https://www.amnesty.org/en/latest/news/2019/09/israel-opt-legally-sanctioned-torture-of-palestinian-detainee-left-him-in-critical-condition/
4 Rogan, *The Fall of the Ottomans*, pp. 285–7.
5 See 'Biography: David Lloyd George', *Balfour Project*. https://balfourproject.org/lloyd-george/#13
6 Jonathan Schneer, *The Balfour Declaration: The Origins of the Arab–Israeli Conflict* (London: Bloomsbury, 2011), p. 344.
7 David Lloyd George, *War Memoirs of David Lloyd George* (London: Odhams, 1936), pp. 349–50.
8 Ronald Storrs, *Orientations* (London: Nicholson & Watson, 1945), p. 344.
9 See Rogan, *The Fall of the Ottomans*, pp. 281–5.
10 Quoted in Schneer, *Balfour Declaration*, p. 80.
11 George Antonius, *The Arab Awakening* (Beirut: Libraire du Liban, 1969), p. 248.
12 Quoted in Avi Shlaim, 'The Balfour Declaration and its Consequences', 2003, at *Balfour Project*. https://balfourproject.org/the-balfour-declaration-and-its-consequences-avi-shlaim/

13 Imperial War Museum, 'General Allenby's Entry into Jerusalem', https://www.iwm.org.uk/collections/item/object/1060008299 It's an extraordinary glimpse of Jerusalem as it was in the winter of 1917 as the British Empire marched in.
14 Lloyd George, *War Memoirs*, p. 1455.
15 Vincent Sheean, *Personal History [In Search of History]* (London: Hamish Hamilton, 1935), p 391.
16 Sheean, *Personal History*, pp. 376–7.
17 Sheean, *Personal History*, p. 423.

3. ALL FLESH IS GRASS

1 The speech is compulsive viewing. https://www.youtube.com/watch?v=U9HgdVN9C_k
2 Nixon, *Debriefing the President*, pp. 99–100.
3 '22 Sentenced to Die in Iraqi Conspiracy', *The New York Times*, 8 August 1979.
4 Marion Farouk-Sluglett and Peter Sluglett, *Iraq since 1958: From Revolution to Dictatorship* (London: I.B. Tauris, 2001), p. 41.
5 Farouk-Sluglett and Sluglett, *Iraq since 1958*, p. 85.
6 Schwarzkopf, *It Doesn't Take a Hero*, pp. 488–9.
7 George H. W. Bush Presidential Library and Museum, Public Papers, Remarks to Raytheon Missile Systems Plant Employees in Andover, Massachusetts, 15 February 1991. https://bush41library.tamu.edu/archives/public-papers/2711

4. JERUSALEM: GOD, POWER, POSSESSION AND LOSS

1 Amos Oz, *My Michael* (London: Vintage, 1991), p. 13.
2 Amos Oz, *A Tale of Love and Darkness* (London: Vintage, 2005), p. 27.
3 Herzog's words are quoted in Shlomo Gazit, *The Carrot and the Stick: Israel's Policy in Judea and Samaria, 1967–68* (Washington, DC: B'nai B'rith Books, 1995). The story of the 1967 war is in my book *Six Days: How the 1967 War Shaped the Middle East* (London: Simon & Schuster UK, 2003).
4 David Rubinger (1924–2017) spoke to me in 2002 for my book *Six Days*.
5 Mahmoud Darwish, 'In Jerusalem', trans. Fady Joudah. https://www.poetryfoundation.org/poems/52551/in-jerusalem

5. GUNS AND OLIVES

1 Arafat's body was exhumed in 2012. Although traces of radioactive polonium were found, the results were not conclusive.

2   'Guns and Olive Branches', part 14 of BBC radio series *Our Man in the Middle East*, 15 June 2017.
3   Derek Penslar, *Theodor Herzl: The Charismatic Leader* (New Haven, CT and London: Yale University Press, 2020), p. 68.
4   Avi Shlaim, *The Iron Wall: Israel and the Arab World* (New York: Norton, 2000), p. 3. I have quoted this before, but it is so apposite it is worth repeating.
5   Quotes from the correspondence between Herzl and al-Khalidi are from Rashid Khalidi, *The Hundred Years' War On Palestine* (London: Profile Books, 2020), pp. 5–7.
6   Britain's chief rabbi, Jonathan Sacks, quoted in Johnny Solomon, 'Jewish Prayer at Home and in the Synagogue', British Library, *Discovering Sacred Texts*, 23 September 2019. https://www.bl.uk/sacred-texts/articles/jewish-prayer-at-home-and-in-the-synagogue#
7   Quoted in Tom Segev, *A State at Any Cost: The Life of David Ben-Gurion* (London: Apollo, 2019), p. 268.
8   Movietone News, 'Last British Troops Leave Palestine'. https://www.youtube.com/watch?v=4FyLX_mV3UI
9   The Oxford historian Avi Shlaim writes: 'There was no love lost between Abdullah and the other Arab rulers, who resented his expansionist ambitions and suspected him of being in cahoots with the enemy'. Shlaim, *The Iron Wall*, pp. 35–6.
10 Investigations include one by *Haaretz* newspaper and the Akevot Institute for Israeli-Palestinian Conflict Research. The cabinet minister quoted was Haim-Moshe Shapira, minister of health, speaking on 7 November 1948. See Adam Raz, 'Classified Docs Reveal Massacres of Palestinians in '48 – and What Israeli Leaders Knew', *Haaretz*, 9 December 2021.
11 Quoted in David Horovitz (ed.), *Yitzhak Rabin: Soldier of Peace* (London: Peter Halban, 1996), p. 26.
12 Quoted in Segev, *A State at Any Cost*, p. 452.
13 The reference to 'madman' is in Yezid Sayigh, *Armed Struggle and the Search for a State: The Palestinian National Movement 1949–1993* (Oxford: Oxford University Press, 1999).
14 *Time*, 'The Guerrilla Threat in the Middle East', 13 December 1968. http://content.time.com/time/subscriber/article/0,33009,839649,00.html
15 Quoted in Bowen, *Six Days*.
16 For his own account see Henry Kissinger, *Years of Upheaval* (Boston, MA: Little, Brown, 1982), pp. 575–91.

6. TELL THEM HE'S DEAD

1   President Bush's speech to the Joint Session of Congress after the Gulf War took place on 6 March 1991. https://millercenter.org/the-presidency/

presidential-speeches/march-6-1991-address-joint-session-congress-end-gulf-war
2 Abba Eban, *Personal Witness* (New York: Putnam, 1992), p. 451.
3 'The Intent of Resolution 242: A Discussion with Lord Hugh Caradon', *Arab Studies Quarterly* 7, no. 2/3 (1985): 167–74. http://www.jstor.org/stable/41857778
4 *Norwegian Arts*, 'Meet Ambassador Mona Juul as surprise hit OSLO opens in London', 2017. https://norwegianarts.org.uk/event/meet-mona-juul-oslo/
5 Eban, *Personal Witness*, p. 470.
6 *Jerusalem Post*, 'Yigal Amir after his arrest: I don't regret killing Rabin', 22 November 2007. https://www.jpost.com/israel/yigal-amir-after-his-arrest-i-dont-regret-killing-rabin

7. DEATH ON THE NILE

1 Quoted in Bergen, *The Osama Bin Laden I Know*, p. 134.
2 Sardar, *Mecca*, pp. 325–34.
3 A very good account of the siege can be found in Lacey, *The Kingdom*, pp. 24–36. See also Yaroslav Trofimov, *The Siege of Mecca: The Forgotten Uprising in Islam's Holiest Shrine* (London: Penguin, 2008).
4 In conversation with Jason Burke; quoted in Burke, *Al-Qaeda: The True Story of Radical Islam* (London: Penguin, 2004), p. 57.
5 Jamal Khashoggi, 'By blaming 1979 for Saudi Arabia's problems, the crown prince is peddling revisionist history', *Washington Post*, 3 April 2018. https://www.washingtonpost.com/news/global-opinions/wp/2018/04/03/by-blaming-1979-for-saudi-arabias-problems-the-crown-prince-is-peddling-revisionist-history/
6 A good place to start is Bergen, *The Osama Bin Laden I Know*, chapter 1.
7 Details of 'humiliation, disappointment and hurt, sublimated into violent hatred' in Burke, *Al-Qaeda*, p. 140.
8 Digital file from the Court Reporters Office, Southern District of New York, 6 February 2001. https://cryptome.org/usa-v-ubl-02.htm
9 Quote from Chris Hedges, 'Egyptian Leader Survives Attack', *The New York Times*, 27 June 1995. https://www.nytimes.com/1995/06/27/world/egyptian-leader-survives-attack.html
10 Among accounts of this: Bergen, *The Osama Bin Laden I Know*, pp. 124–5, and for Sadat's assassination and Zawahiri see: Lawrence Wright, *The Looming Tower: Al Qaeda and The Road to 9/11* (New York: Vintage Books, 2006), pp. 59–67. See also Hedges, 'Egyptian Leader Survives Attack'.

8. GAZA

1. Translation of 'A non-linguistic dispute with Imru al-Qays', taken from S. Antoon, 'Mahmud Darwish's Allegorical Critique of Oslo', *Journal of Palestine Studies* 31, no. 2 (2002): 66–77. DOI: 10.1525/jps.2002.31.2.66
2. Edward Said, 'The Morning After', *London Review of Books*, 21 October 1993. https://www.lrb.co.uk/the-paper/v15/n20
3. Haydar 'Abd al-Shafi, S. Elmusa and L. Butler, 'Moving beyond Oslo: An Interview with Haydar 'Abd Al-Shafi', *Journal of Palestine Studies* 25, no. 1 (1995): 76–85. DOI: 10.2307/2538106
4. US Department of State Archive, Remarks at the American University in Cairo Secretary Condoleezza Rice Cairo, Egypt, 20 June 2005. https://2001-2009.state.gov/secretary/rm/2005/48328.htm
5. Conversation with Dr Eyad el-Sarraj in Gaza, January 2009.

9. THE FINAL FRONTIER

1. Denis Halliday quoted in Mark Siegel, 'Former UN official says sanctions against Iraq amount to "genocide"', *Cornell Chronicle*, 30 September 1999. https://news.cornell.edu/stories/1999/09/former-un-official-says-sanctions-against-iraq-amount-genocide
2. H. C. von Sponeck, *A Different Kind of War* (New York: Berghahn Books, 2006), p. 10.
3. Von Sponeck, *A Different Kind of War*, p. 8.
4. Von Sponeck, *A Different Kind of War*, p. 4.
5. James P. Rubin, State Department spokesman. Excerpt from the Daily Press Briefing Department of State Press Briefing Room, Washington, DC, 14 February 2000. https://1997-2001.state.gov/regions/nea/000214_rubin_excerpt.html
6. As shown on Iraqi state TV, 19 December 1998.
7. Francis X. Clines and Steven Lee Myers, 'Attack on Iraq: The Overview', *The New York Times*, 17 December 1998. https://www.nytimes.com/1998/12/17/world/attack-iraq-overview-impeachment-vote-house-delayed-clinton-launches-iraq-air.html
8. Dennis Ross, *The Missing Peace: The Inside Story of the Fight for Middle East Peace* (New York: Farrar, Straus and Giroux, 2004), p. 370.

10. IN THE NAME OF GOD

1. 'Who We Are', BP website. https://www.bp.com/en/global/corporate/who-we-are/our-history/first-oil.html, and 'William Knox D'Arcy, https://www.stanmoretouristboard.org.uk/william_knox_darcy.html

2 Abbas Amanat, *Iran: A Modern History* (New Haven, CT and London: Yale University Press, 2017), p. 392.
3 Figures and descriptions from Kaveh Ehsani, 'Social Engineering and the Contradictions of Modernization in Khuzestan's Company Towns: A Look at Abadan and Masjed-Soleyman', *International Review of Social History* 48 (2003): 361–99. DOI: 10.1017/S0020859003001123
4 Description quoted in Amanat, *Iran*, p. 520.
5 Quote from the *New York Times* report in Ray Takeyh, *The Last Shah: American, Iran and the Fall of the Pahlavi Dynasty* (New Haven, CT and London: Yale University Press, 2021), p. 64.
6 'Man of the Year: Challenge of the East', *Time*, 7 January 1952. http://content.time.com/time/subscriber/article/0,33009,815775,00.html
7 Quoted in David D. Kirkpatrick, 'How a Chase Bank Chairman Helped the Deposed Shah of Iran Enter the U.S.', *The New York Times*, 29 December 2019. https://www.nytimes.com/2019/12/29/world/middleeast/shah-iran-chase-papers.html
8 Amanat, *Iran*, gives a highly readable account of the shah's downfall. The description of a photo of the shah stooping to stop the guard's show of respect just before he boarded the flight from Tehran is on p. 731.
9 *The New York Times*, obituary of John J. McCloy, 12 March 1989. https://www.nytimes.com/1989/03/12/obituaries/john-j-mccloy-lawyer-and-diplomat-is-dead-at-93.html
10 Kirkpatrick, 'How a Chase Bank Chairman Helped'.
11 See 'Beginnings', *Washington Post*, 28 August 1988. https://www.washingtonpost.com/archive/entertainment/books/1988/08/28/beginnings/839da65c-e469-4a13-b202-6a20fb3c23e4/
12 Quotes from Jonathan C. Randal, 'Women, Blacks Ordered Freed in Iran', *Washington Post*, 18 November 1979.

11. GROUND ZERO

1 Sayyid Qutb, 'The America I have Seen: In the Scale of Human Values' (Kashf ul Shubart Publications, 1951). https://www.cia.gov/library/abbottabad-compound/3F/3F56ACA473044436B4C1740F65D5C3B6_Sayyid_Qutb_-_The_America_I_Have_Seen.pdf
2 Movietone News, 'Results of Cairo's Black Day'. https://www.youtube.com/watch?v=CsjmQq1nNU4
3 Eugene Rogan, *The Arabs: A History* (London: Allen Lane, 2009), pp. 281–5.
4 Sandy Gall, *Don't Worry About the Money Now* (London: New English Library, 1985), p. 276.
5 Pathé News, 'Farouk in Capri'. https://www.youtube.com/watch?v=uBAywZ96CI8

6. For a definitive account of the feud, see: Fawaz A. Gerges, *Making the Arab World: Nasser, Qutb, and the Clash that Shaped the Middle East* (Princeton & Oxford: Princeton University Press, 2018).
7. Fitzroy Morrissey, *A Short History of Islamic Thought* (London: Head of Zeus, 2021), pp. 196–202. See also Fawaz A. Gerges, *The Far Enemy: Why Jihad Went Global* (Cambridge: Cambridge University Press, 2009), p. 4.
8. Naji Sabri al-Hadithi speaking in New York, 19 September 2001. From my BBC radio series *Our Man in the Middle East*, Part 11, 'A Strike to the Heart'. https://www.bbc.co.uk/programmes/b08tby76
9. Ariel Sharon speaking in Jerusalem, 11 September 2001. https://www.c-span.org/video/?179286-1/terrorist-attacks-us
10. Gideon Sa'ar quoted in *Haaretz*, 'How 9/11 Changed US Policy Toward Israel', 9 September 2011. https://www.haaretz.com/us-news/how-9-11-changed-u-s-policy-toward-israel-1.5168556
11. Nabil Sha'ath, 'September 11 One Year On'. http://news.bbc.co.uk/2/hi/in_depth/world/2002/september_11_one_year_on/2205433.stm
12. 'A Strike to the Heart', part 11 of BBC series *Our Man in the Middle East*, 12 June 2017.
13. Ambassador James Dobbins to National Security and Foreign Affairs Committee of US House of Representatives, 'Iran: Reality, Options and Consequences, Part 2 – Negotiating with the Iranians: Missed Opportunities and Paths Forward', 7 November 2007. https://www.govinfo.gov/content/pkg/CHRG-110hhrg50111/html/CHRG-110hhrg50111.htm
14. Trita Parsi, *Losing an Enemy: Obama, Iran and the Triumph of Diplomacy* (New Haven, CT and London, Yale University Press, 2017), p. 43.
15. *The New York Times*, 'After the Attacks: The White House: Bush Warns of a Wrathful, Shadowy and Inventive War', 17 September 2001. https://www.nytimes.com/2001/09/17/us/after-attacks-white-house-bush-warns-wrathful-shadowy-inventive-war.html

12. MISSION UNACCOMPLISHED

1. George A. Lopez and David Cortright, 'Containing Iraq: Sanctions Worked', *Foreign Affairs* 83, no. 4 (2004): 90–103. DOI: 10.2307/20034049
2. Sir Stephen Wall, Blair's former advisor, interviewed by Michael Cockerell in the BBC series 'Blair: The Inside Story', programme 2, *A Man with a Mission*, first broadcast 27 February 2007.
3. 'US Congress opts for "freedom fries"', *BBC News*, 12 March 2003. http://news.bbc.co.uk/1/hi/world/americas/2842493.stm
4. Kofi Annan was interviewed by Owen Bennett-Jones on the BBC World Service, September 2004. http://news.bbc.co.uk/1/hi/world/middle_east/3661640.stm

5 Greenstock was speaking in 'Blair: The Inside Story'.
6 Tony Blair speaking in the House of Commons, 18 March 2003. https://www.theguardian.com/politics/2003/mar/18/foreignpolicy.iraq1
7 For the full account by the interrogator see Nixon, *Debriefing the President*.
8 See Cheney's speech to Veterans of Foreign Wars, 26 August 2002, as reported in *The New York Times*. https://www.nytimes.com/2002/08/27/world/eyes-iraq-cheney-s-words-administration-case-for-removing-saddam-hussein.html
9 'Iraq: US Should Investigate al-Falluja', Human Rights Watch, 16 June 2003. https://www.hrw.org/news/2003/06/16/iraq-us-should-investigate-al-falluja
10 Ken Adelman, '"Cakewalk" Revisited', *Washington Post*, 10 April 2003. https://www.washingtonpost.com/archive/opinions/2003/04/10/cakewalk-revisited/9fc29e36-9230-4ccb-8f2f-7602f1df560f/

13. ONE THOUSAND SADDAMS

1 Yaseen Raad, 'A Spatial History of a Main Baghdadi Street', Jadaliyya, 27 October 2015. https://www.jadaliyya.com/Details/32628
2 Fatwas reported in *The Times* by Richard Beeston, 27 June 2007.
3 CNN, Rumsfeld on looting in Iraq: 'Stuff happens', 12 April 2003. https://edition.cnn.com/2003/US/04/11/sprj.irq.pentagon/
4 L. Paul Bremer III, *My Year in Iraq: The Struggle to Build a Future of Hope* (New York: Simon & Schuster, 2006), p. 57.
5 International Crisis Group, 'Baghdad: A Race Against the Clock', 11 June 2003. https://www.crisisgroup.org/middle-east-north-africa/gulf-and-arabian-peninsula/iraq/baghdad-race-against-clock
6 Quote from Andrew Cockburn and Patrick Cockburn, *Out of the Ashes: The Resurrection of Saddam Hussein* (New York: HarperCollins, 1999), p. 198. Chapter 8 of the book, 'Deaths in the Family', is a gripping account of the Kemal defection and subsequent execution.
7 Toby Dodge, *Iraq: From War to a New Authoritarianism* (Abingdon: Routledge, 2013), p. 53.
8 Quoted in Dodge, *Iraq*, p. 64.

14. THE PEOPLE WANT THE FALL OF THE REGIME

1 Conversation with activist Zyad Elelaiwy. First reported by me in 'Analysis: Egypt's Unfinished Revolution', 8 February 2011. https://www.bbc.co.uk/news/mobile/world-middle-east-12396728

2 They are collected in Alaa Al Aswany, *Democracy Is the Answer: Egypt's Years of Revolution* (London: Gingko Library, 2014).
3 Murad Batal al-Shishani and Dalia Elsheikh, 'How "Thugs" Became Part of the Arab Spring Lexicon', *BBC News*, 5 September 2012. https://www.bbc.co.uk/news/world-middle-east-19467017
4 Al Aswany, *Democracy Is the Answer*, p. 9.
5 Report of the Bahrain Independent Commission of Inquiry, https://www.bici.org.bh/BICIreportEN.pdf, p. 416.
6 Amnesty International, 11 February 2021. https://www.amnesty.org/en/latest/news/2021/02/bahrain-dreams-of-reform-crushed-10-years-after-uprising/

15. THE ROAD TO DAMASCUS

1 *Wall Street Journal*, 'Interview with Syrian President Bashar al-Assad', 31 January 2011. https://www.wsj.com/articles/SB10001424052748703833204576114712441122894
2 Zoom interview with Karam Shaar, non-resident scholar at the Middle East Institute, Washington, DC, 14 March 2021.
3 Conversation with Jihad Makdissi in London, 15 July 2011.
4 Quote from Sam Dagher, *Assad or We Burn the Country: How One Family's Lust for Power Destroyed Syria* (New York: Little, Brown and Company, 2019), p. 163.
5 Yara Bayoumy, 'Dead Syrian boy emerges as symbol for protesters', Reuters, 1 June 2011. https://www.reuters.com/article/oukwd-uk-syria-boy-idAFTRE75039120110601
6 By far the best book on the life of Hafez is Patrick Seale, *Asad of Syria: The Struggle for the Middle East* (Berkeley and Los Angeles: University of California Press, 1988).
7 Seale, *Asad of Syria*, p. 39.
8 Seale, *Asad of Syria*, p. 164.
9 Peter Baker and Susan Glasser, *The Man Who Ran Washington: The Life and Times of James A. Baker III* (New York: Doubleday, 2020), p. 444.
10 Interview with Ribaal al-Assad, 8 June 2020.

16. THE MOSQUE ON MAKRAM EBEID STREET

1 'All According to Plan: The Rab'a Massacre and Mass Killings of Protestors in Egypt', Human Rights Watch, 12 August 2014. https://www.hrw.org/report/2014/08/12/all-according-plan/raba-massacre-and-mass-killings-protesters-egypt
2 Interview with Essam el-Erian, Cairo, 26 November 2011.

17. THE PIVOT OF WAR

1. Interview with Frank Gardner, BBC Security Correspondent, quoted in 'Syria conflict: Central Damascus hit by clashes', *BBC News*, 17 July 2012. https://www.bbc.co.uk/news/world-middle-east-18866265
2. Joshua Landis, 'Regime's Top Sunni Defects', Syria Comment blog, 5 July 2012. https://www.joshualandis.com/blog/regimes-top-sunni-defects-general-manaf-mustafa-tlass-flees-to-turkey/
3. Sam Dagher, *Assad or We Burn the Country: How One Family's Lust for Power Destroyed Syria* (New York: Little, Brown, 2019), pp. 311–13. Dagher had exclusive interviews with Tlass and his account is authoritative, convincing and riveting.
4. Interview with Faisal Miqdad, Foreign Ministry, Damascus, 11 December 2012.
5. Matt Hollingworth told me about his journey in Damascus when he returned from Aleppo.
6. Figures quoted in Christopher Phillips, *The Battle for Syria: International Rivalry in the New Middle East* (New Haven, CT and London: Yale University Press, 2016), p. 127.
7. 'Government Assessment of the Syrian Government's Use of Chemical Weapons on August 21, 2013', White House archives. https://obamawhitehouse.archives.gov/the-press-office/2013/08/30/government-assessment-syrian-government-s-use-chemical-weapons-august-21
8. Remarks by the president to the White House press corps, 20 August 2012. https://obamawhitehouse.archives.gov/the-press-office/2012/08/20/remarks-president-white-house-press-corps
9. Quoted in analysis by Matt Spetalnick, 'How Kerry's off-hand remark put a deal on Syria in play', Reuters, 10 September 2013. https://www.reuters.com/article/us-syria-crisis-analysis-idUSBRE98902D20130910
10. Martin Pengelly et al., 'John McCain and Lindsey Graham criticise US–Russia deal on Syria', *Guardian*, 14 September 2013. https://www.theguardian.com/world/2013/sep/14/john-mccain-lindsey-graham-syria-statement
11. Jeffrey Goldberg, 'The Obama Doctrine', *The Atlantic*, April 2016. https://www.theatlantic.com/magazine/archive/2016/04/the-obama-doctrine/471525/

18. THE ROAD TO HELL

1. 'Iraq: Parliament Report Alleges Officials Ordered Raid', Human Rights Watch, 4 May 2013. https://www.hrw.org/news/2013/05/04/iraq-parliament-report-alleges-officials-ordered-raid

2 Aki Peritz, 'The Great Iraqi Jail Break', *Foreign Policy*, 26 June 2014. https://foreignpolicy.com/2014/06/26/the-great-iraqi-jail-break/
3 Suadad al-Salhy, 'Al Qaeda says it freed 500 inmates in Iraq jail-break', Reuters, 23 July 2013. https://www.reuters.com/article/us-iraq-violence-alqaeda-idUSBRE96M0C720130723
4 David Remnick, 'Going the Distance: On and Off the Road with Barack Obama', *The New Yorker*, 19 January 2014. https://www.newyorker.com/magazine/2014/01/27/going-the-distance-david-remnick
5 Paul Wood, 'Iraq's hardest fight: The US battle for Falluja 2004', *BBC News*, 10 November 2014. https://www.bbc.co.uk/news/world-middle-east-29984665
6 Susannah George et al., 'Mosul is a graveyard: Final IS battle kills 9,000 civilians', Associated Press, 21 December 2017. https://apnews.com/article/only-on-ap-islamic-state-group-archive-iraq-bbea7094fb954838a2fdc11278d65460
7 'Falluja: Iraqi Shia militia "killed and seized civilians"', *BBC News*, 5 July 2016. https://www.bbc.co.uk/news/world-middle-east-36716494

19. THE RUSSIANS ARE COMING

1 'Inside Tadmur: the worst prison in the world?' *BBC News*, 20 August 2015. https://www.bbc.co.uk/news/magazine-33197612
2 Amnesty International report, 'Syria: Torture, Despair and Dehumanization in Tadmur Military Prison', 18 September 2001. https://www.amnesty.org/en/documents/MDE24/014/2001/en/

20. SCORCHED EARTH

1 Sebastien Roblin, 'How Russia's Bombers Helped Assad Devastate Syria's Cities', National Interest blog, 8 May 2020. https://nationalinterest.org/blog/buzz/how-russias-bombers-helped-assad-devastate-syrias-cities-152141

21. THE TASTE OF FIRE AND SMOKE

1 *The Daily Telegraph*, obituary of Shlomo Argov, 24 February 2003. https://www.telegraph.co.uk
2 *Jerusalem Post*, 'Was Naftali Bennett responsible for a massacre of Lebanese civilians?', 6 January 2015.

22. RETREAT TO THE MOUNTAINS

1 Office of the United Nations High Commissioner for Human Rights, 'Report on the human rights situation in South-East Turkey July 2015 to December 2016', February 2017 https://www.ohchr.org/Documents/Countries/TR/OHCHR_South-East_TurkeyReport_10March2017.pdf, p. 8. See also: Mazlumder Conflict Investigation and Resolution Group, 'Curfew Imposed on Cizre Town of Sirnak Province Investigation and Monitoring Report covering December 14, 2015 – March 2, 2016', March 2016. https://www.mazlumder.org/fotograf/yayinresimleri/dokuman/MAZLUMDER_CIZRE_REPORT_20162.pdf
2 The UN estimated that in the eighteen months after the ceasefire broke down around 800 members of the security forces were killed in south-eastern Turkey, and around 1,200 local people. See Office of the United Nations High Commissioner for Human Rights, 'Report on the Human Rights Situation in South-East Turkey', p. 7.
3 Interview with Ilnur Cevik, the chief advisor to President Recep Tayyip Erdoğan. I reported the Cizre curfew and killings for the BBC: 'Inside Cizre: Where Turkish forces stand accused of Kurdish killings', *BBC News*, 23 May 2016. https://www.bbc.co.uk/news/world-europe-36354742
4 Figure of 10,000 cited in United States Institute of Peace, Iran Primer, February 2021.
5 *The New York Times*, 'Hussein Aide "Chemical" Ali Executed in Iraq', 25 January 2007, https://www.nytimes.com/2010/01/26/world/middleeast/26execute.html, and Al Jazeera news, "Chemical Ali" Defiant in Court', 24 January 2007, https://www.aljazeera.com/news/2007/1/24/chemical-ali-defiant-in-court

23. THE LAST DANCE

1 See 'Old City of Sana'a', UNESCO website. https://whc.unesco.org/en/list/385/
2 Reuters, 'US Marines say they destroyed weapons before leaving Yemen', 12 February 2015. https://www.reuters.com/article/uk-yemen-security-pentagon-idUKKBN0LF2D220150212.
3 World Food Programme, 'Yemen: The World's Worst Humanitarian Crisis', 2022. https://www.wfp.org.yemen-crisis
4 Discussion with Dr Madawi al-Rasheed.
5 Reuters, '"Cut off head of snake" Saudis told U.S. on Iran', 29 October 2010. https://www.reuters.com/article/us-wikileaks-iran-saudis-idUSTRE6AS02B20101129

6 Panel of experts on Yemen, report to the UN Security Council, 20 February 2015. https://digitallibrary.un.org/record/788246

24. DEAL OF THE CENTURY

1 UNRWA, 'Gaza's "great march of return"; one year on', 2019. https://www.unrwa.org/sites/default/files/content/resources/gaza_gmr_one_year_on_report_eng_final.pdf
2 Text of Donald Trump's speech, 14 May 2018, https://www.politico.com/story/2018/05/14/text-trump-on-opening-of-us-embassy-in-jerusalem-transcript-584452
3 Meeting with Jared Kushner at Winfield House, London, on 2 June 2019.
4 Audrey Wilson, 'Kushner launches Middle East Peace Plan', *Foreign Policy*, 25 June 2019. https://foreignpolicy.com/2019/06/25/kushner-launches-middle-east-peace-plan/
5 Zeev Jabotinsky, 'The Iron Wall'. http://en.jabotinsky.org/media/9747/the-iron-wall.pdf. See also Avi Shlaim, 'The Iron Wall Revisited', *Journal of Palestinian Studies* 41(2), 2012, pp. 80–98.
6 Full text of Arab peace initiative, 28 March 2002, https://www.theguardian.com/world/2002/mar/28/israel7.
7 Raja Shehadeh, *Palestinian Walks: Notes on a Vanishing Landscape* (London: Profile Books, 2007).

25. PAWNS ON THE GLOBAL CHESSBOARD

1 W. H. Auden, 'September 1, 1939', from *Another Time* (London: Faber and Faber, 1940), p. 103.
2 A point made by the incomparable historian Eugene Rogan of St Antony's College Oxford. I'm most grateful for invitations to some of his seminars, which helped shape some thoughts in this chapter.
3 *The Guardian*, 'Hizbullah leader: we regret the two kidnappings that led to war with Israel', 28 August 2006. https://www.theguardian.com/world/2006/aug/28/syria.israel
4 Samir Kassir, *Being Arab* (London: Verso, 2013), pp. 4–5.
5 Al Aswany, *Democracy Is the Answer*, p. ix.
6 *BBC News*, 'Jamal Khashoggi: All you need to know about Saudi journalist's death', 24 February 2001. https://www.bbc.co.uk/news/world-europe-45812399
7 ODNI, 'Assessing the Saudi Government's Role in the Killing of Jamal Khashoggi'. https://www.nytimes.com/interactive/2021/02/06/us/report-jamal-khashoggi-killing.html

8 *The New York Times*, 18 September 2001. https://www.nytimes.com/2001/09/18/us/nation-challenged-president-bin-laden-wanted-attacks-dead-alive-president-says.html
9 Remarks by President Biden, 26 August 2021. https://www.whitehouse.gov/briefing-room/speeches-remarks/2021/08/26/remarks-by-president-biden-on-the-terror-attack-at-hamid-karzai-international-airport/
10 The White House, 'In Their Own Words: What the Terrorists Believe, What They Hope to Accomplish, and How They Intend to Accomplish It, 5 September 2006. https://georgewbush-whitehouse.archives.gov/news/releases/2006/09/text/20060905-7.html
11 The family's tragic story is told by Tima Kurdî in her book *The Boy on the Beach* (New York, London and Toronto: Simon & Schuster Canada, 2018).
12 'The importance of Ukraine and the Russian Federation for global agricultural markets and the risks associated with the war in Ukraine', Food and Agriculture Organization of the United Nations, 10 June 2022. https://www.fao.org/3/cb9013en/cb9013en.pdf